The Afterlife of Empire

→ typologies of decolonization
like typologies of colonialism
→ End to post-coloniality?

THE BERKELEY SERIES IN BRITISH STUDIES

Mark Bevir and James Vernon, University of California, Berkeley, editors

The Afterlife of Empire

JORDANNA BAILKIN

Global, Area, and International Archive
University of California Press

BERKELEY   LOS ANGELES   LONDON

The Global, Area, and International Archive (GAIA) is an initiative of the Institute of International Studies, University of California, Berkeley, in partnership with the University of California Press, the California Digital Library, and international research programs across the University of California system.

University of California Press, one of the most distinguished university presses in the United States, enriches lives around the world by advancing scholarship in the humanities, social sciences, and natural sciences. Its activities are supported by the UC Press Foundation and by philanthropic contributions from individuals and institutions. For more information, visit www.ucpress.edu.

University of California Press
Berkeley and Los Angeles, California

University of California Press, Ltd.
London, England

Library of Congress Cataloging-in-Publication Data

A catalog record for this book is available from the Library of Congress

Manufactured in the United States of America

21 20 19 18 17 16 15 14 13 12
10 9 8 7 6 5 4 3 2 1

The paper used in this publication meets the minimum requirements of ANSI/NISO z39.48–1992 (R 1997) (*Permanence of Paper*).

Contents

Illustrations

Acknowledgments

Five years ago, my father asked me over dinner one evening what my new book was all about. I told him that I wasn't sure yet, but I thought it would have something to do with how certain fields of knowledge—anthropology, development studies, law, psychology, sociology, and social work—were reshaped according to the powerful demands of decolonization and the new world order after 1945. My dad beamed. "Hey, it's all about me!" he cheerfully declared.

He had a point, although I scoffed at the time. As an American, he'd gotten hold of the wrong empire and, trained at the University of Chicago, mostly the wrong group of experts. But as the book shifted and grew from its original conception, my father's complex relationship to the 1950s and 1960s was much on my mind. A former Peace Corps volunteer, lawyer, and urban planner, my father had told me his version of the American story of these decades many times. His study of these disciplines, and the activism they seemed to entail, had been the defining experiences of his life, rescuing him from a troubled youth in ways that he could not always fully articulate.

As a recovering Victorianist, I had thought of the postwar years as my father's very American domain. Now I found myself grappling with the insights that British narratives of this same era might yield, and the ways in which they converged with or diverged from what I thought I already knew. It was daunting, but also exciting to move into new terrain. I am glad to have this chance to thank the many individuals and institutions who helped me to make this shift and to think about its implications.

First of all, the librarians and archivists: I thank Grant Buttars, Irene Ferguson, and Sally Pagan at the Edinburgh University Library for providing access to their materials while the library was closed for renovations. Mary Bone at Chatham House, Chris Ledgard at BBC Bristol, Katie Mooney at the Institute of Education, and Kathleen Dickson, Katrina Stokes, and Steve Tollervey at the British Film Institute were also extraordinarily helpful. Closer to home, I thank Theresa Mudrock and the Interlibrary Loan Office at the University of Washington for working heroically on a shrinking budget to meet the needs of demanding faculty members such as myself.

I began working on this project in the idyllic, richly interdisciplinary environment of the National Humanities Center. I thank the staff and fellows for helping me conclude one book and start another. I also thank Kathy Woodward, the perennially optimistic director of the Simpson Center for the Humanities, for inviting me to join the Society of Scholars, and my fellow fellows, especially Ted Mack, Stephanie Smallwood, and Adam Warren for their outstanding insights. The Giovanni and Amne Costigan Endowed Professorship, along with the Keller Fund, the South Asia Center, the Hanauer Fund, and the Simpson Center, provided time and money to complete this project, and I thank Kent Guy and John Findlay, my most recent chairs, for their support. Ali Bilow, Morgan Schoenecker, and Sarah Young provided research assistance with West African newspapers.

One of the pleasures of this project has been that it has expanded the group of supportive and generous scholars with whom I am in conversation. I thank Hakim Adi, Frank Biess, Deborah Cohen, David Feldman, Grahame Foreman, Michael Hassett, Lisa Cobbs Hoffman, Kali Israel, Seth Koven, Nicola Lacey, David Lieberman, Julie Livingston, Werner Menski, David Mills, Radhika Natarajan, Margaret O'Mara, Susan Pedersen, Steven Pierce, Gautam Premnath, Alice Ritscherle, Carrie Ritter, Bill Schwarz, Ileana Rodriguez-Silva, Tehila Sasson, Priya Satia, Prakash Shah, Carol Summers, Yinka Sunmonu, Kathleen Wilson, and Chris Waters for offering their valuable thoughts on this project.

Even as dialogues with new colleagues emerged, longtime readers and friends remained vital. Lynn Thomas cheerfully read multiple drafts of multiple chapters with her characteristic enthusiasm, saving me from many errors of fact and thinking. She is also the only person in the world with whom I would even consider taking a meditation class, and even though it never happened, I did think about it really hard. Sarah Stein's judgment regarding this project (and many other things) has been unerring. We all miss her terribly since she went to sunny Santa Monica, but she is still a stalwart pal, even if I can no longer zip down Denny Way to see her. George Behlmer, Philippa Levine, Lou Roberts, and Peter

Stansky all continued to be important mentors, and Philippa's insights into earlier versions of this project proved both bracing and encouraging. Kate Washington offered her sharp editorial eye, but more importantly, her ongoing friendship, as did Stephanie Camp, Rebekah Gross, Lara Kriegel, Viviane Silvera, and Molly Watson. In Seattle, Abbie Raikes remains one of my very favorite social scientists, and Paulene Quigley is the world's best camping and spa companion (I will leave it to her to guess which one I prefer).

I feel extremely fortunate that this project brought me into the orbit of the Center for British Studies at UC Berkeley, an institution that has played a major role in shaping this book at several crucial junctures. I thank James Vernon and Ethan Shagan, the center's successive directors, for inviting me to present my work in such a stimulating environment. This would not be the same book (nor a book at all) without James's astute questions and provocations. He suffered through many unconscionably long drafts, for which I owe him an apology! I cannot thank him enough for the energy he has brought to this project. I am honored to participate in the University of California's new series in British Studies, and it has been a pleasure to work with James, and with his insightful partners in this venture, Mark Bevir and Nathan MacBrien. The anonymous readers for the press also provided enormously valuable feedback and suggestions for revision.

Sections of chapter 5 appeared previously as "The Postcolonial Family? West African Children, Private Fostering, and the British State," *Journal of Modern History* 81.1 (2009): 87–121; and a shorter version of chapter 6 appeared as "Leaving Home: The Politics of Deportation in Postwar Britain," *Journal of British Studies* 47.3 (2008): 852–82. I thank the editors of both journals for permitting me to reproduce this material.

Although I did not conduct my interviews for this project in a particularly systematic way, I very much appreciate the people who spoke with me about their experiences of the afterlife of empire. I especially thank Aggrey Burke, who was the first to tolerate my awkward forays into oral history. Michael Banton gave me access to his unpublished papers, and fielded many questions about his work in Edinburgh and Sierra Leone. For other interviews, I thank Dick Bird, Suzanne McGregor, Anne Murcott, Anthony Richmond, Sandy Robertson, Chris Tipple, and Ailsa (Tommy) Zainu'ddin. At Edinburgh's Department of Social Anthropology, Alan Barnard and Francesca Bray helped me track down former students, and located Kenneth Little's teaching materials. If some of these individuals were unnerved by having "become history," as one put it, then they were still unfailingly gracious about looking back at their lives and work, with all its promises and limitations.

My unruly gang of guys—Christopher, Tobias, and Finn—is the whole point of everything. Nothing would be any fun, nor make any sense, without them. As my husband, Christopher, knows, two adults with two young children writing two books in one apartment did not always make for simple math, but it had its thrilling moments. I think we should definitely do it again in the next ten, or perhaps twenty years. We would have been lost without the phenomenal babysitting services of Mom-Mom June, who flew in from New York to rescue us on multiple occasions, and whose faith in me and my family is one of the joys of my life. Christopher's unparalleled ability to make our daily life extraordinary is another such joy, and yet one more reason, along with Tobias's startling observations and Finn's merry mayhem, that I feel so lucky.

To return to my father, who started me thinking about the ongoing high stakes of this era, I am glad to have participated in at least a few of his utopian adventures, which have taken him from a chicken farm in India to a kibbutz in Israel to vineyards in Schenectady. Those winter days of farming in upstate New York went particularly unloved by this city girl, and I am not sure that they actually built my character as intended, but they have provided much entertainment in recollection over the years. And so you were right, Dad. This one was (almost) all about you.

Introduction

This book is about cycles of lives and afterlives, not only of individual people but also of the ideas and institutions that were forged in imperial days and outlived the regimes under which they were born. Most of all, it is about the afterlife of empire itself. By this I mean the ways in which decolonization changed British society in the 1950s and 1960s, and how imperial missions were sustained or revamped by new actors in new forms. I am not offering an explanation of why or how Britain lost its empire. Rather, I am charting the impact of these events upon metropolitan life, and the ways in which the empire continued to be lived in Britain after it appeared to come to an end elsewhere.

The history of decolonization has been charted primarily through its diplomatic details, its triumphant or violent moments of formal political independence. But decolonization could also be deeply personal, taking place through daily routines, social interactions, and individual experience. This is not a story of elegy and loss, at least not exclusively. The process of dismantling the empire was not only characterized by narratives of anxiety and decline, but also functioned as a creative and recuperative project.[1] Here, I seek to capture not only how decolonization was *thought* in Britain, but also how it was *lived*.

WHERE (AND WHEN) WAS THE POSTWAR? RETHINKING THE 1950S AND 1960S

This book argues that decolonization aided in the transformation of that other behemoth of post-1945 history: the welfare state. The distinctive forms of welfare that took shape in the 1950s and 1960s—most notably in the domains of mental health, education, child welfare, and criminal law—were shaped by decolonization and its perceived demands. In this way, decolonization transformed the social relationships in Britain that have constituted our image of what is conventionally known as the "postwar," and played a significant role in the reconstruction of community in 1950s and 1960s Britain. Thus, I seek to make visible the intersection of what have typically been taken as divergent historical themes by bringing the postwar and the postimperial (two fields that have long been juxtaposed, but rarely integrated) into closer conversation.

Not every experience of decolonization bore equally on every form of welfare in Britain. My claim is more specific: that *certain paths* of decolonization transformed *specific domains* of welfare. I explore the mutual influence of welfare and the end of empire as they arose in particular sites. More broadly, I aim to disrupt monocausal accounts of both decolonization and welfare by illustrating that there are multiple histories of each, and that some of these histories are intertwined.

Welfare has often stood in an uneasy relationship to empire. In some sense, welfare was the empire's most powerful justification, its reason for being. The claim that empire improved the moral and material lives of its subjects pervades imperial history, with widely varying accounts of the costs and benefits of these schemes. The proponents of metropolitan welfare had a long history of thinking imperially. The recruitment campaigns for the Anglo-Boer War, for example, exposed the weak physical condition of working-class Britons and galvanized state-sponsored programs for infant and children's medical care.[2] Similarly, the state's response to poverty in Britain could be shaped by imperial migrations. Maintenance and family liability laws in the late nineteenth and early twentieth centuries encompassed the overseas territories, creating an imperial "welfare zone" that entangled poor relief with imperial discourses of humanitarianism and citizenship.[3] In the 1920s and 1930s, welfare depended on the denial of local difference, mingling imperial and metropolitan sites in order to promote universal categories of "the child" or "motherhood."[4]

Yet these studies have all been temporally bounded by the age of empire. The history of welfare in Britain after 1945 has often appeared to be a pristinely metropolitan story. The assumption seems to have been that after the Second World War, welfare was severed from the world. Except, that is, when it recurred in the former colonies, where it was handily reclassified as "development" or when highly politicized debates about welfare focused on migrants of color.[5] The final chapter of this story of the imbrication of welfare and empire has not yet been told.

Here I argue that the transnational and the local continued to be intertwined in welfare's history after 1945, as the decline of formal imperialism provoked new demands for the governance and care of Britain's diverse populations. The welfare state was caught up in the worldwide transformations that accompanied independence. It was not a "pure" domestic creation, but rather an entity shaped by global forces ranging from the experiences and expectations that individual migrants brought with them from their countries of origin to the construction of new legal regimes in Africa and Asia. The ambitions and fragilities of the welfare state were increasingly inflected by global concerns, which in turn contributed to this state's unevenness.[6]

Decolonization reshaped the social norms and relationships that welfare sought to govern. At the same time, welfare was energized—if also complicated—by the cataclysmic transformations of independence, when welfare in Britain and abroad underwent a period of intense public scrutiny.[7] Welfare often functioned as a means of racial differentiation, as fears that migrants would abuse Britain's welfare system were deployed to justify immigration restrictions. But the consequences of these modes of knowledge extended beyond any single population. Welfare regimes dealt not only with newly diverse populations, but also with Britain's place in the shifting world order, in which the failed promises of colonial development were all too apparent. Debates about welfare's boundaries— which aspects of social life welfare would encompass, and which elements would be truly universal—intensified.[8] Just as postwar development schemes were supposed to contribute to welfare in Britain by creating wealth (indeed, the empire's final gasp could be said to take place in the domain of welfare), so too did these schemes' missteps, and their inability to abolish poverty and create equality, signal new doubts about welfare's promises.[9] At the same time, new African and Asian states were evaluated by the measure of welfare they offered their citizens. Within the context of independence, the provision of welfare was one crucial means of legitimation.[10] In this sense, welfare was a key nexus between colonial and postcolonial regimes.

This book is concerned with where and when the "postwar" took shape, as well as investigating the utility of this convenient shorthand. Recently, scholars have critiqued the excessive isolation of the post-1945 period, asking how this era can be reintegrated into broader narratives of modern British history.[11] The 1950s, it has been said, suffer from both an image problem and an identity crisis.[12] Overshadowed by the austerity of the 1940s and the rebelliousness of the 1960s, the 1950s in Britain have often either been glossed over as a less than compelling moment in the progressive march toward a more liberal society or held up as a bland, golden age of family values.[13] In terms of Britain's global relationships, the 1950s can seem a mere punctuation mark between the end of imperial rule in India in 1947 and the rush to dispose of the tropical empire in the 1960s, although this is surely not how it felt at the time.[14]

As Frederick Cooper has noted, what is striking about these years was how vital the empire still seemed. Through the apparatus of development, the British state generated new modes of intervention, seeking not to escape or reject empire but to transform it.[15] The imperial mission was revitalized with interventions in British Guiana, counterinsurgency campaigns in Cyprus, Malaya, and Kenya, and a dedication to Commonwealth relations.[16] This was the era of the activist colonial state at its most intrusively ambitious, eager to obtain knowledge about all dimensions of life, from labor to public health.[17] The colonialism that collapsed in Africa and Asia in the 1950s and 1960s was interventionist, reformist, and accordingly open to challenge.[18] Indeed, it was precisely as Britain's power to control the course of colonial events became more precarious that the search for solutions to colonial problems stimulated greater and more controversial metropolitan activity.[19] Even in places where independence was secured, the processes of decolonization could intensify the enmeshments between Britain and its former colonies rather than lessening them. New engagements were sought, not only with areas of former colonial control, but also with unforeseen allies and enemies, from the United States to the Soviet Union.

In this book, I follow multiple, intersecting timelines, not only of the transformation of welfare and a new phase of racialized migration policy in Britain, but also of independence movements abroad.[20] Therefore, the chapters also move freely across geographical borders, tracking the transnational flow of people and ideas from Britain to Africa, South Asia, and the Caribbean, as well as the United States, Europe, and the Soviet Union. I am concerned generally with the two decades following the Second World War, but the core of this book is in the pivotal period of 1958–1962. These parameters represent a particular moment in the histories of welfare and decolonization. In India, where the process of independence had begun even before the Second World War, political independence had been achieved, but the violence of partition was highly visible. So too were the aftereffects of the Suez debacle, a psychological watershed moment that exposed the Commonwealth's frailties.[21] During these years, bracketed by the Notting Hill and Nottingham riots—which focused new attention on migrant welfare, as well as critiques of welfare's aims and achievements regarding white youths—and the restrictions on the rights of entry for individuals from South Asia, Africa, and the Caribbean that accompanied the Commonwealth Immigrants Act 1962, as well as the turmoil of independence in Ghana and Nigeria, the intertwining of decolonization and metropolitan life was especially intense.[22]

Welfare after 1945 was shaped partly by British hopes and goals about specific parts of the declining empire and the Commonwealth, which ranged from the intensification of interest in the colonial endgame and development in Africa, especially West Africa, to relative disengagement in India. It is for this reason that West Africa figures so prominently in this project. Independence in South Asia and federation in the West Indies cast their own shadows over life in Britain, but it was the fraught and urgent trajectory of African independence (especially Ghanaian independence in 1958 and Nigerian independence in 1960) that drew the most avid governmental attention. Africans were never as numerous in the metropole as West Indians or South Asians, but British investment in African development and Africa's perceived significance in the Cold War meant that their impact was disproportionate. Unlike South Asians and West Indians in Britain, West Africans were largely assumed to be temporary sojourners who would return from the metropole to newly independent countries. They were highly prized (and under intense surveillance) during their time in Britain—less as migrants than as bearers of new nationhood, who represented all the promises and perils of independence. Metropolitan experts who sought to guide the trajectory of independence saw the creation of welfare for Africans in Britain as one means to achieve this end.

It is no revelation to say that welfare was discriminatory, or that its achievements fell short of its universal claims. My aim here is to understand the particular ways in which welfare was configured in relation to decolonization, how this alchemy bore on British life in the 1950s and 1960s, and how the postimperial played its part in the making of the postwar. During these years, Britain's global role was rearticulated rather than abandoned. Instead of focusing on the cozy domesticity of the 1950s, I wish to stress how Britons looked out rather than inward, and how decolonization shaped their daily lives and personal relationships.[23]

I am not arguing that Britons were especially knowledgeable about the end of empire. Rather, the consequences of imperial collapse were built into the structures of their world. Decolonization changed how people in Britain lived whether they knew it or not. It altered the perception of the problems to be resolved by welfare and the solutions that welfare proposed, which created new family forms, laws, and social relationships. Like welfare, decolonization was experienced in the metropole not only through diplomatic shifts at Whitehall and Westminster, but also through the conceptualization of social problems that entailed the participation of multiple departments of state.

The process of decolonization did not end with political independence in the colonies. It was what came after—a world of new states fractured by new conflicts—that most concerned Britain's leaders.[24] Thus, I seek to configure decolonization as more than the end of something.[25] Decolonization could prompt a reanimation or reconfiguration of imperial forms of power, giving the impetus to new personal and political relationships as well as bringing others to abrupt or protracted conclusions. Even for Britain, it was a starting point rather than a conclusion: an inauguration of new investments in Britain's global identity. Although the popular view is that Empire came clattering down in 1960s, the withdrawal of all forces east of Suez was not completed until 1971, and Rhodesia was not resolved until 1980.[26] The waning of the formal empire was as much the beginning of a story about the recalibration of British interests as it was an ending of a narrative of domination. Indeed, it was not always clear in the 1950s that the empire *was* ending, at least not everywhere. One reason I speak in the spectral terms of an afterlife is precisely because the timeline of the empire's death is so hazy, and geographically uneven. The indeterminacy of empire's end is one reason that its intersection with other themes of postwar history has been so difficult to discern.

Just as the 1950s and 1960s were shaped by wartime agendas, so we continue to live with the unpredictable outcomes of postwar allegiances and disaffections. Although specific laws and policies have evolved, our methods of identifying and resolving social problems still emanate from postwar modes of thinking. This is perhaps especially true for those of us who inhabit the disciplinary divisions that grew out of this period. In very real ways, we are still living in the world that was made by the people in this book and are carrying out many of their agendas. The postwar is thus still happening now. Some of our most enduring images of the postwar years—for example, of a sharp divide between the static, golden 1950s and the troubled, rebellious 1960s—were in fact created during these decades, to be enshrined in archives as well as in popular memory. We have been telling ourselves stories about the postwar years ever since, and even while, they occurred. These stories have had powerful ramifications for the ways in which states and selves have been experienced or perceived. It is time, I think, to examine these narratives with a more critical eye.

DECOLONIZATION AND ITS WAYS OF KNOWING: EXPERTS AND THEIR CRITICS

How, then, might we begin to integrate the histories of the postwar and the postimperial? One powerful possibility for revaluating this period lies in an investigation of its competing modes of knowledge. Thus, I seek to capture the often chaotic intellectual energies that were devoted to making sense of Britain's imperial past and its uncertain global future, as well as the very real social and political consequences of these pursuits. How did Britons imagine their place in a postwar/Cold War world? What new ways of knowing did this world demand?[27]

During the 1950s and 1960s, British scholars in a variety of fields—anthropology, development studies, legal theory, psychology and psychiatry, social work, and sociology—sought both to shape the new world order and to define their role within it.[28] These scholars offered competing visions of how Britain might best negotiate the transformations of independence, cataloging an array of new syndromes and pathologies that they believed would accompany decolonization. Each discipline bore a different relationship to imperial history, some having sustained (or challenged) its structures of inequity, and others conjured partly to manage the consequences of its decline. I ask how shifts in, and critiques of, these disciplines can illuminate British efforts to grapple with the distinctive demands of a multiethnic empire and its aftermath. They serve as a useful point of entry into the more tumultuous view of the 1950s and 1960s that I offer here, constituting an important mode of making selves—and relationships between them—in postwar Britain.[29]

These fields all experienced stunning rates of growth in the postwar years. Between 1959 and 1969, social science graduates in Britain increased by 206 percent. The London School of Economics, the Fabian institution established in 1895 by Beatrice and Sidney Webb, quickly evolved into the principal center of social science education in postwar Britain. The Oxford sociologist A. H. Halsey vividly described the LSE's energetic buzz in the early 1950s, when "demob suits and battle jackets, incongruously adorned by the college scarf, thronged the streets." Here, the prominent American sociologist Edward Shils tutored an uneasy amalgam of "awkward foreigners and restive lower-class boys and girls":

not only British-born graduates but also young African and Asian nationalists who had their own stake in imagining the consequences of empire's end. At Edinburgh, Kenneth Little, formerly a physical anthropologist who had measured the heads of black migrants at Tiger Bay, mobilized a small army of prolific, young, and racially mixed researchers to explore how anthropological research on African indigenes might forge a new sociology of migration.

Decolonization and welfare both catalyzed new forms of knowledge production, bringing some projects to an end while galvanizing others.[30] The welfare state required a constant flow of information in order to monitor the success of its redistributive projects, and it relied on an army of experts to provide this knowledge.[31] Although expertise was never monopolized by a single political party, Labour advocated strong funding for the social sciences, positing that the scientific method could be usefully applied to social and political issues and eliminate Britain's problems in a planned society.[32] Several leading sociologists served as Labour parliamentary candidates or advisers.[33] Clement Attlee, the Labour Party leader and prime minister from 1945 to 1951, had also held a post in Social Science at the LSE, and William Beveridge, one of the key architects of social security and other modern welfare reforms, had been the director of the LSE between the wars.[34] Indeed, the French sociologist Raymond Aron damningly described the whole field of British sociology as an attempt to make intellectual sense of the political problems of the Labour Party.[35] Other disciplines, such as demography, enabled the creation of national insurance schemes; Harold Wilson, the Labour prime minister from 1964 to 1970 (and 1974 to 1976), was a statistician trained by Beveridge, who promoted the new professionalism of socialist planning.[36] These scholars possessed great faith in the transformative power of their fields as an instrument for achieving the Attlee brand of democratic socialism that had proved so seductive during the war.[37]

But the politics of expertise in Britain were never simple. Its practitioners' agendas were far more multifaceted than simply striving after the New Jerusalem. Here I follow the sociologist Nikolas Rose, who defines "expertise" as the capacity of a discipline to provide a trained and credentialed corps of persons who claim special competence in the administration of interpersonal relations, as well as a body of techniques claiming to make possible the rational and humane management of various aspects of life.[38]

Expertise was forged in many sites, but the colonial laboratory was key. From the perspective of the colonizing state, the violent realities of conquest made the pretense of political neutrality and altruism offered by lay experts—from botanists to excise men, political economists, and engineers—both difficult to achieve and highly desirable.[39] If the modern category of expertise emerged partly to sustain the fraudulent charisma of imperialism, then so too was it deployed in the service of empire's end.[40] The collapse of the formal empire constituted an intellectual opportunity as much as a practical crisis.[41] Funding for anthropological research increased under the guise of development, even as specific fieldwork pursuits became less plausible.[42] British scholars delved into new domains of research, examining forms of association that cut across ethnic lines, such as occupational groupings and mutual aid societies.[43] It was in the minds of experts—particularly in the fraught realm of development—that empire lived on most vitally after its formal conclusion. Expertise could function as a growth export aimed at the recuperation of British prestige. Yet it was also in the context of decolonization that experts risked losing their sanctity, as they clashed over how to interpret its consequences. Expertise offered new ways to mediate relations between individuals and states, as well as competing visions of Britain's changing role in the world.

This story is about experts, at least in part. But experts never reigned alone, nor did they exist in a vacuum. Their sway was extensive but not absolute. Different players held conflicting interpretations of what constituted expertise, and its desirability in metropolitan and overseas milieus. Expertise had to be negotiated, not simply imposed. Furthermore, experts themselves were not a monolith; many of the clashes depicted here were actually between rival forms of expertise. What has been aptly termed the "protean nature of the relations between the researcher and the researched" meant that the power of experts was rarely assured.[44]

In the 1950s and 1960s, many individuals defined their status in explicit opposition to a culture of expertise. They included migrant men and women who publicly denounced social scientific interpretations of their experiences, but also prominent journalists and leaders of voluntary organizations, who rejected the wisdom of experts in specific domains. Their critiques of expertise were conducted in different, often contradictory registers. But they were drawn together by their emphatic insistence that they were *not* experts, that they had other, more personal forms of knowledge to offer—grounded in authenticity and experience—that were deeply relevant to contemporary society. Often, they demonstrated vividly what the experts got wrong, which in turn captured the attentions of the decolonizing state.

Why, and when, did certain forms of knowledge prevail? When was expertise revered or devalued, and by whom? It is tempting to think in terms of a shift from the unity of experts in the early 1950s to their fracturing in the wake of independence by the end of the 1960s. Indeed, it was partly the challenges posed by decolonization that undermined the coherence of expertise. Yet struggles over expertise were also highly localized, varying not only by geographical site but also by branch of state. Expertise and its critiques were always intertwined.[45] Their intimate proximity was as striking as their opposition.

The entity we think of as postwar Britain emerged not only out of the ether of expertise but also from highly tactical attacks upon it. These conflicts had consequences for *all* Britons, structuring the social forms within which they lived. It is both experts and their critics, then, who together form the cast of characters for this book. Their dynamic was not one between winners and losers. Rather, it reflected the complexities of defining this era's competing voices of authority, and how the distribution of power—and the nature of governance in post-1945 Britain—can only be fully understood through these global dimensions. The dialectic between experts and their critics gave distinctive shape to the postwar state as concerns about the empire's demise were woven into the making of the New Jerusalem. Decolonization and welfare were fields of expertise that were subject to powerful critiques, and were also often in conflict with each other. The major postwar narratives—of which welfare and decolonization were only two—were not merely static historical phenomena, but fields of inquiry upon which experts and their critics meditated and to which they contributed their own inventions.

The shadows cast by postwar experts have been long, and it has been difficult to move away from seeing these individuals as teachers, mentors, and conveyors of truths.[46] For those of us who work on the postwar years, the writings of experts constitute our source base as well as the objects of our critiques.[47]

Our ability to know about the afterlife of empire remains circumscribed by the archival structures put into place in the 1950s and 1960s, which spoke as much to the fantasies of their creators as anything else. What were these fantasies? One, at least, was that the effects of decolonization could be circumscribed by the sphere of diplomacy. This fantasy has proved sufficiently powerful to shape the historiography of decolonization itself, and to delimit the places that scholars look to understand its processes and outcomes. Experts were especially effective in the archive, where they were largely successful in getting audiences to adopt their point of view. Overwhelmingly, they sought to create an image of Britain that muted the impact of decolonization, asserting the isolation of the postwar and the postimperial. It is this view that I seek to challenge here.

WHERE DID THE EMPIRE GO? ARCHIVES AND DECOLONIZATION

Scholars have painstakingly detailed the vagaries of colonial archives, but sources pertaining to decolonization have rarely received the same attention.[48] This oversight has reinforced other key divisions: for example, between the colonial and the postcolonial, but also between the postimperial and the postwar. I argue that the spheres in which we can chart the afterlife of empire are far more diffuse than has previously been acknowledged. My claims, however, are not only about the extent of decolonization's impact on the metropole, but also about the question of how we evaluate this impact. The evidence for the afterlife of empire depends, after all, on where we look.

This project speaks to decolonization's multiple archives. I draw on the unprecedented availability of National Archives files from the departments conventionally associated with welfare, such as the Children's Department, and National Insurance. Many files from the 1950s and 1960s dealing with "private" information—for example, on individuals' mental health—have only recently been declassified. I set these newly released documents against the writings of prominent social scientists and other experts, who explicitly guided state policy on decolonization. Taken together with oral histories, newspaper reports, and court records, these sources reveal the multitude of ways in which decolonization constantly marked social and political life in Britain.

At stake here is the question of what we mean by the term "decolonization." Scholarship on decolonization has divided into two camps.[49] Political historians have insisted that the end of empire was largely ignored in Britain. This thesis was forged in the 1980s, in the days of the Falklands War and the twilight of the Cold War, when the topic of imperial decay seemed especially absorbing.[50] John Darwin, for example, has argued that the disappearance of Britain's world role left scarcely any visible traces in Britain itself. Most Britons were distracted from the pangs of imperial loss by the special relationship with the United States and the popularization of the Commonwealth: "It was like a man in the dentist's chair, soothed by smiling nurses and laced with painkillers, while a dentist with a manic grin probed his jaw. Only later does he find that all his teeth have gone."[51] On this view, decolonization is driven by states, but the state is constrained to a limited set of players: Cabinet, the Colonial Office, perhaps the Foreign Office.

Cultural historians, on the other hand, have been more prepared to take the end of empire seriously. They have explored how decolonization infused British novels, popular films, and the mass media in the 1950s and 1960s, and they have tried to assess the impact of this process on more recent imaginings of British identity.[52] Bill Schwarz has argued that memories of empire did not magically disappear with political independence. Rather, these memories seeped into the wider cultural dramatizations of ethnicity stirred by the onset of black migration. Migrants of color lived on the front lines of decolonization, and became agents for imagining Britain's postcolonial future.[53]

In contrast to both of these views, this book seeks to excavate the competing definitions of decolonization that emerged in the 1950s and 1960s. When decolonization took place in Britain, it was not only a diplomatic or military process but also a social one, one which contributed to the reconstruction of personal relations. Looking at decolonization as a social phenomenon reveals its impact to be far wider and deeper than has previously been acknowledged. Still, my aim is not simply to press for a social definition of decolonization over a political or cultural one. Rather, it is to explore the cacophony about how the end of empire was understood, and to register its scale. Decolonization shaped postwar Britain—and shaped the category of the "postwar" itself—in ways that we are only beginning to understand. It saturated a wide range of metropolitan debates about youth, education, marriage, child rearing, and crime. It was not confined to a minority of policymakers at Whitehall and Westminster, but drew in a thicket of departments—not only those engaged with foreign policy—but those responsible for child welfare, policing, and health. Debates about decolonization emerged in previously unexplored realms, such as family and criminal law. In these unexpected sites, we find the ongoing entanglement of global and local concerns.[54] Thus, I delve into some of the catchwords of the postwar era—such as "youth" and "migration" and "welfare"—by investigating the truly global conditions under which they emerged.

Why has the afterlife of empire been so spectral, so difficult to see? Thinking about the full scope of decolonization is at least partly an archival problem. It was during the era of decolonization that the British state became most explicit about its role as an object and a creator of archives.[55] Prior to 1958, there was no standard preservation policy for records in Whitehall.[56] The Public Records Act 1958 mandated the transfer of state documents (albeit with numerous exceptions) to the public domain within fifty years; this rule was amended to thirty years in 1968.[57] The narrative of the state's increasing transparency regarding its own secrets was thus itself an artifact of the postwar years, gaining strength from the Freedom of Information (FOI) campaigns of the 1960s. Decolonization accelerated these campaigns, as the Suez crisis increased public demand for the dismantling of secrecy around imperial wrongs.[58]

The secrets of empire and its often violent collapse have remained vital to debates about FOI. In this regard, archives can appear to have become more forthcoming, more quickly, about state secrets than personal ones.[59] The Freedom of Information Act 2000, which came into force in 2005, granted the right to appeal decisions to withhold information, and it exposed the security services that had been shielded by the previous legislation; the thirty-year rule may now be further reduced.[60] Scholars have protested that these shifts do not ensure the transparency of the state's actions, as national security exemptions can still prompt the retention of documents for up to 100 years.[61] Meanwhile, the privacy of information about individuals, enshrined both in Freedom of Information and in the Data Protection Act 1998, has received very little critical attention.

What this has produced is a blinkered asymmetry about where we look to find the decolonizing state. In hundreds of National Archives files, the violent wrongdoings of the British state can often be brutally visible (and are becoming more so all the time), from the framing of Irish migrants for terrorism charges to the forcible repatriation of West Indians who were labeled mentally ill.[62] Only twice was I denied access to files because of section 27 of the Freedom of Information Act: that is, the information might damage relations between Britain and another state.[63] But denials under section 38 (the file could damage an individual's mental or physical health or safety), and section 40 (the file contains sensitive personal information that an individual would not expect to become public) were far more common.

My point is not that exemptions for personal information should be withdrawn. Rather, I wish to illuminate how archives determine which documents pertain to individuals and which pertain to states. The state is still making its own call about where we can locate its presence, and "personal" documents may hide ways of seeing the state as well.[64] Documents that pertain to marriages, child welfare, or certain crimes often remain classified beyond the thirty-year rule because of the presumed sensitivity of personal information. For this reason, many files from the 1950s and 1960s are just becoming publicly available now, typically when the individuals involved have no living descendants: an uneven and random process of declassification that emphasizes how we are still living with the world described here. Those files that remain closed speak, in their own way, to the afterlife of empire—to relations of states and individuals that are not yet concluded.

Files on the 1950s and 1960s have been released in perplexing fits and starts, which demand their own analysis. But we should be wary, I think, of reading our present moment of declassification as revelation. As new types of sources become publicly, if still unevenly, accessible, what kinds of questions do we want to ask about them?

For British researchers, personal relationships offered a key to interpreting the end of empire. Thus, experts devoted themselves to charting the changing nature of these relationships as well as creating a wider public investment in them. Precisely because the economic and political ties of the Commonwealth were so fragile, policies around its development were heavily imbued with the language of sentiment. Contemporary policymakers anticipated that social relationships would be key to sustaining the Commonwealth as other forms of entanglement came apart. My interest in humanizing the histories of decolonization and welfare reflects not only a dissatisfaction or unease with the existing historiographies, but also guidance from key actors in the 1950s and 1960s, who believed that politics depended on interpersonal relations and that international relations were based on individual and collective experience rather than geopolitical abstractions.

It is precisely in these personal files that the complexities of decolonization reside. For example, in suits by polygamous wives to obtain widows' benefits from insurance tribunals, we can see the diversity of the state's efforts to govern the process of decolonization far beyond the diplomatic sphere and into the realm of social and affective relationships. Such documents offer new possibilities for investigating the multiple meanings of decolonization. First, they begin to illuminate how the major themes of twentieth-century history were not only conceived from above, but also lived from below.[65] More specifically, they can reveal how individual lives in Britain were shaped by the perceived demands of decolonization, even as the nature of these demands was under debate. Finally, these sources can help us in locating the welfare state in a more global lens. They render visible what has previously been obscured: the extent to which seemingly "domestic" policies were structured by the needs of decolonization itself. We can use these sources to think more expansively about the multiple locations of the welfare state's construction, mapping these locations onto the diversity of the former empire itself, and the new world order that emerged in its place. The impact of the end of empire has been cloaked in these individual files from the departments conventionally associated with welfare, masking the globality of the conditions that helped to forge the postwar state. Here, I aim to recast the genealogy and geography of welfare by charting its proximity to, but also its unseen dependence on, the end of empire.

Where, then, did the empire go? In archival terms, it reemerged not only in the postcolony, but also in the metropole, cloaked in the avalanche of paper that accompanied welfare, and hidden in welfare's own, contentiously evolving systems of classification. The afterlife of empire is imprinted in the archive of welfare, often in ways that have been protected or hidden long beyond the expected life span of confidentiality. The longstanding divide between decolonization and welfare is all the more striking, and all the more necessary to overcome, when we recognize their archival intimacy.

ON STRUCTURES AND FUNCTIONS: THE LIVES OF EMPIRES

In thinking about the afterlife of empire, I found myself critically engaged with the idea of the life cycle. The life cycle concept—that given units (individuals, families, nations, empires) pass through irreversible stages of development in which progression is made with age—is by no means new. It is an ancient trope, with antecedents in classical philosophy. But its significance peaked at particular historical moments. Both decolonization and welfare depended on the idea of citizens progressing through distinct stages, during which the state's intervention was warranted or withdrawn. For this reason, the life cycle captured the imaginations of British researchers in the 1950s and 1960s, structuring their policies and polemics and becoming one of their dominant and enduring, if also highly contested, motifs. Here, I adopt and adapt what we might call the life cycle fetish, in order to rethink the historical conditions of its emergence.

This idea had a specific grounding in colonial history, where the interplay between notions of personal and national development was especially entrenched. Colonial authorities routinely depicted colonized societies as childlike and deployed age imagery in order to naturalize situations of conquest and rule.[66] Colonialism generally cast subject peoples not as radically different but as underdeveloped or youthful versions of their rulers, who were not quite ready for self-government—what Dipesh Chakrabarty terms the endless "not yet" of imperial history.[67] The basic political and economic fact of imperial time was that the colonies could not be permitted to come of age under the rule of empire. At the same time, if collective development was to be delayed, then the development of colonized individuals was a focal point of academic and governmental interest. Colonial stability seemed to require detailed knowledge of the indigenous life cycle.[68] The belief that age grades were central to African society was a hallmark of colonial anthropology. As Christian missionaries attacked African rites of passage, the idea of age groups functioned as a site of political contestation.[69] Ethnographers intensified their study of the African life cycle in the 1950s, as British administrators linked their problems of governance to indigenous rites of passage—lamenting, for example, how Northern Kenyans marked the transition to adulthood by undertaking violence against their enemies.[70]

During decolonization, the life cycle concept was not abandoned, but galvanized. All of the life stages under investigation here were areas of vigorous regulation under colonialism; how these interventions should be altered for a postcolonial age was widely debated. The progressive rhetoric of the life cycle held a particular appeal during the empire's final days, as it worked to naturalize the struggles of independence and to make sense of the new generation that was moving into power with alarming speed. The notion that divergent systems of age consciousness marked "developing" and "civilized" societies was endemic in postwar social science, a key method of differentiating the First and Third Worlds.[71]

There are many points of origin for the life cycle concept, but one of its first uses emerged in British welfare. The sociologist Seebohm Rowntree's pioneering studies of poverty in York posited a cycle of needs in which the life of the average laborer was marked by five phases of want and plenty: childhood, young working adulthood, parenthood, parenthood with young earners living at home, and the end of work life.[72] Rowntree thus considered not only *who* was poor, but also *when* they were poor, pinpointing the ages at which poverty was most likely to strike. Influentially, his model imbued age with social, as distinct from biological, meaning.[73] Furthermore, Rowntree situated poverty in a progressive frame, in which periods of privation were normal and predictable features of the life cycle; individuals moved out of phases of economic stress just as naturally as they fell into them.[74] After the Second World War, Rowntree's links between poverty and the life cycle were explored by a new generation of British sociologists and linked to specific welfare provisions. The life cycle model in Britain thus came out of an optimistic effort to identify problem populations more precisely and to determine which aspects of poverty could be meliorated.

British researchers posited that disruptions in the life cycle heralded both the benefits and ills of modern life. War, affluence, migration, and modernization—along with decolonization and welfare—could all shape the ways that individuals and groups progressed (or failed to progress) through developmental stages. Modern welfarism was widely perceived to have restructured the life cycle, creating new "slots" of identity such as adolescence and retirement, as it offered benefits from cradle to grave.[75] Indeed, the welfare state was structured around the notion of the life cycle, as the state sought to define moments of dependence for its citizens. Thinking in terms of life phases—childhood, parenthood, retirement—constituted a valuable mode of political discourse in the 1950s and 1960s. Even welfare's most ardent proponents were unnerved by how it altered life cycle patterns, mostly by lengthening periods of "natural" dependency. If social benefits fell out of harmony with the cycle of actual needs, then individual and collective psychic stresses might result.[76]

The life cycle concept was ecumenical, uniting different branches of expertise.[77] In anthropology, the life cycle concept grew out of research into kinship systems and intergenerational tensions.[78] The early-twentieth-century anthropologist Arnold van Gennep argued in his work on rites of passage that life cycles were not dictated by biological age.[79] His ideas were subsequently elaborated by Victor and Edith Turner, Meyer Fortes, and Audrey Richards, who viewed age groups as crucial to cultural continuity.[80] Generations were structurally opposed parts of kinship systems, which persisted in their function even as the people within them lived and died.[81] Anthropologists initially dominated this area of research, most notably in Margaret Mead's landmark study *Coming of Age in Samoa* (1928). After the Second World War, sociologists and psychologists led the field. In *From Generation to Generation* (1956), the Warsaw-born scholar Shmuel Eisenstadt argued that human beings attained different capacities at each stage of life. Every phase constituted an irreversible step in the unfolding of life from its beginning to its end.[82] Relentlessly progressive, the life cycle model was also deeply relational, as the characteristics of one phase could only be understood with respect to those of another.

Fundamentally, the life cycle was an analytic for thinking about change. It offered a rich vocabulary for describing the processes of indi-

individual and national transformation that were taking place on a worldwide scale, and a way to interpret how these processes were intertwined. The life cycle also served as a powerful rubric of social and political control—governing high-stakes issues such as when people could leave or enter countries, and under what circumstances their families might be divided or remain intact.

The life cycle is a powerful if deeply flawed rubric, a souvenir of a not-quite-bygone way of thought. Much like modernization theory, which also relies on the idea of staged development, it has been criticized as ahistorical, universalistic, and deterministic.[83] And yet it seems an apt way to narrate the intertwined histories of welfare and decolonization, which both sought to alter people's development and sense of social time. The life cycle concept is itself a product of the history I seek to trace, a category invented partly to grapple with the rapidly changing relationships between metropolitan and postcolonial lives. It was a remnant of the colonial era, which was transformed in the postcolonial metropole. But it is a delicate problem to try to recapture this framework without simply embracing it.

Clearly, there are hazards in deploying the image of the life cycle to unearth the afterlife of empire when it was itself linked to colonialist principles. For some, decolonization constituted a traumatic disruption in the imperial life cycle. For others, it was a natural or overdue death. Had colonialism finally achieved its ends, enabling colonized subjects to "grow up" to independence? Was this the moment when the colonized moved out of the waiting room of history, into adolescence and adulthood? Was the empire truly coming to an end? Or had it simply entered a new phase—an afterlife?

The life cycle concept was deployed in an era of decolonization to evaluate the empire's successes and failures. Thinking critically about the evolution of the life cycle concept can help to denaturalize the history of decolonization and remove it from a narrative of inevitability.[84] My aim is not to take the life cycle literally but to elaborate its historically specific significance, to push against it (as it was challenged in its own heyday), and to consider its political freight.

Chapter 1 addresses the "birth" of the migrant in social science. I highlight how the state derived its conception of migration from scholars in anthropology, psychology, psychiatry, and sociology, who were zealously debating how to interpret the different forms of population transfer that characterized the postwar world. The conjuring of the migrant, with its byzantine systems of classification, was inflected by the localized demands of decolonization and Cold War imperatives as experts created a mythology of postwar migration.[85] I analyze the racial politics of pathologizing migration, from studies of schizophrenia among Caribbean and Irish individuals in London to research on mental breakdowns among white Britons in Australia.

Chapters 2 and 3 focus on youth, a stage of life that served as a crucial axis of debate about postimperial governance. In the 1950s and 1960s, youths in Britain and its former empire came under intensive expert investigation, even as the category of "youth" was constantly redefined. Of the life phases under investigation here, this was the one that was most vitally "new"—a powerful symbol of the stresses and promises of change. The final days of empire saw a reconceptualization of colonized peoples as openly rebellious adolescents, set on the path to independent adulthood. These chapters place two seemingly disparate groups of young travelers in conversation with one another to show the variety of ways that individuals enacted the dramas of decolonization.

Chapter 2 addresses the history of Voluntary Service Overseas (VSO), founded in 1958 as a response to the phase-out of National Service and the desire to create an outlet for the energies of elite school-leavers. VSOs were celebrated for their youth and amateurism, qualities that the program's leaders defended against American technical expertise. These distinctively British "coming of age" stories illuminate the ideological tensions within the broader culture of development, which operated in tandem with—not in isolation from—metropolitan welfare, and which imagined the transformation of the agents (as well as the recipients) of aid.

Chapter 3 analyzes another "young" population: students from the former colonies. Widely perceived as the future leaders of new nations, these individuals were considered essential to peaceful decolonization. As the United States and Soviet Union competed to attract African and Asian scholars, Britain played a distinctive role as the mother country to tens of thousands of overseas students. Higher education was supposed to commit these youths firmly to the path of development. But this trajectory did not always go as planned. Psychologists and sociologists described new syndromes, such as "brain fag" among West African students, and "overintegration" among West Indians. The stories of these students' glittering successes and tragic failures point to the high stakes and dilemmas of education in the new world order.

Scholars of colonialism have led us to see certain domains of intimacy as highly charged arenas of governance for both rulers and ruled.[86]

Chapters 4 and 5 ask how decolonization prompted family dramas of its own. Colonial interventions in marriage and child rearing were typically mobilized around the reconstruction of indigenous domesticity and racial segregation. But decolonization invoked new conceptual frameworks for such interventions, shifting definitions of the "normal" family for migrants and Britons alike. It is difficult to characterize the relationships that were engendered by decolonization, which both evoked and reworked the colonial. Doctrines of nonintervention and withdrawal could affect individuals and families just as powerfully as colonial intrusions. The consequences of empire's end were unpredictable, highlighting the impossibility of a simple reversal for colonialism's own social and affective relations. These chapters illustrate how domains that typically have been segregated in histories of postwar Britain—such as changing notions of marriage or parenthood and decolonization—are deeply interconnected. Furthermore, they demonstrate how the history of decolonization need not be bounded by questions of foreign policy, but might also incorporate an examination of how the state sought to renegotiate private life in Britain and elsewhere as the empire drew to an official close.

Chapter 4 examines the British response to a key problem in postwar metropolitan law: that is, the problem of how to honor (or criminalize) polygamous marriages in Britain. I analyze how legal scholars, sociologists, and social workers conceived of polygamy cases in relation to independence movements in South Asia, Africa, and the Caribbean. As African and Asian states legalized their own new affective regimes, decolonization haunted the case law on polygamy in Britain. Experts in African and Asian law were called upon to validate particular forms of union, while individuals from purportedly "polygamous" countries rejected expert opinion and asserted their own definitions of marriage.

Chapter 5 treats another aspect of decolonization's influence on the family in Britain. During the 1950s and 1960s, tens of thousands of African children—mostly the children of West Africans who were studying in Britain—were placed in temporary private foster care arrangements with working-class whites while their biological parents completed their degrees. Social workers, psychologists, and sociologists sharply criticized these arrangements as detrimental to the children's well being. The fate of African children in Britain was historically intertwined with a specific set of metropolitan concerns about decolonization in West Africa, in which British authorities both detailed the "failure" of African families in the metropole and pronounced their reluctance to intervene. At the same time, expert anxiety about other parents—West Indian mothers and

South Asian fathers—intensified, illuminating the diversity of responses to the family structures created by independence and the shifting status of the child in an era of decolonization.

This book begins with the birth of the migrant. It concludes in chapter 6 with the migrant's legal death through deportation. I analyze British efforts to expel Commonwealth citizens who were convicted of crimes after the Notting Hill and Nottingham riots of 1958, exploring both the criminological fantasy of West Indian deportation and the striking reality that the vast majority of deportees were Irish. Here, we see an overt disconnect between expertise and the state, as criminologists' findings were superseded by the perceived demands of national security. This final chapter illuminates the origins of the security state in the age of decolonization, and highlights the ongoing and truly global reverberations of this era's regimes of knowledge.

One of the most salient characteristics of the life cycle concept was its unfailing, unrelenting optimism. Although individuals might be briefly derailed by the upheavals of independence, the model always implied the certitude of progress. More broadly, the prevailing view of postwar social science has stressed its faith in the power of its own findings to create positive changes in the political and social realm. The generation of experts who emerged from the Second World War, so the story goes, were preoccupied by the meliorative study of prosperity and social cohesion, only later turning to the bleaker realms of poverty and racial strife. These scholars have been depicted as resolutely cheerful even in their treatment of black marketeering, juvenile delinquency, and illegitimacy. They perceived these unfortunate trends as having been induced by the war, and thus easily reversible by sensible public policies. This was, after all, the age of the "happiness survey," in which Britons described themselves as "very happy" or "fairly happy" more than in any other country.[87]

One might ask, then, whether in taking on the life cycle motif as the structure for this book, I have adopted all of its energetic optimism as well. Regrettably, perhaps, the answer is no. In looking back at the creation of this world, it must be said that its limitations have, for me, often eclipsed its promises. But one reason that I have found it especially powerful to revisit this period is precisely because it allows for a more careful examination of the interdependence of optimism and pessimism, and the ways in which they so often went hand in hand.

It may be that the histories of the postwar and the postimperial have been kept separate precisely because they appeared to have been conducted in such discordant emotional registers. If the welfare state represented a triumph of optimism about Britain's future, then decolonization would seem to signify the exact opposite. But one aim of this book is to show how very deeply optimism and pessimism—along with the global and the local—were intertwined in the 1950s and 1960s: simultaneous, rather than successive phenomena. This is crucial not only for the experts of the past, but for their counterparts in the present as well—to whose ranks the present author continues to aspire, for better or worse.

1.   The Birth of the Migrant

Pathology and Postwar Mobility

In the wake of the Second World War, migration was one of the largest growth areas of expertise. Migrants, of course, were not new, nor was public interest in their experience. What was distinctive to the 1950s and 1960s was the *insistence* that the migrations of these years were unique, that they represented a break with the population movements of the past. Postwar experts articulated key mythologies: for example, that a relatively benign trickle of migrants of color was being replaced by a "flood" that threatened Britain's historic tolerance, that these migrations were qualitatively and quantitatively unprecedented, and that their impact on British identity was more important than that of any other movement of peoples in the 1950s and 1960s.

The precise nature of the connection between migration and decolonization has not been fully explored, although they are often mentioned in the same breath. Stuart Hall describes the timing of large-scale migration as a cruel dilemma for the British, who "had just got rid of these people, thinking that they could now cut the umbilical cord, give them independence, and not have to do with them in Wolverhampton, Bradford, and Oxford."[1] If decolonization represented a strategy of containment—isolating the troublesome parts of the world so that they would not roil domestic politics—then the simultaneity of independence and migration to Britain from these same territories undermined this effort in spatialized thinking. According to this view, migration was both an inevitable final stage and an unhappy byproduct of decolonization. Indeed, some scholars believed that racism arose from white Britons perceiving migrants of color as awkward reminders of their own imperial humiliations.[2] Critics of the welfare state often evoked parallels between whites in Rhodesia, who had been "abandoned" by Westminster, and English whites, whose interests were "sacrificed" for those of migrants.[3]

But the imbrication of migration and decolonization was more complex than can be expressed by treating migrants as the lone survivors of colonial history, a thesis that was itself a product of postwar expertise.[4] In truth, the connections between these phenomena went far beyond the temporal. Migrants were bearers not only of the colonial past, but also of the decolonizing present. Postwar thought on migration was influenced by the imperatives of decolonization and the desire not to derail its "natural" course. Thus, although migrants figure prominently in this book, their import extends beyond the history of migration. Treating migration—yet another of the "big stories" of the postwar—within the same analytic frame as decolonization can allow us to confront populations that have been largely overlooked in histories of Britain. Furthermore, it demonstrates how welfare itself could be resolutely global, entrenched in the transformations of independence.

Migration was one of the first issues that postwar experts were called upon to manage and define. It is this process of definition that has become invisible, a testimony to their power of their efforts. The vast social history of migration has assumed "the migrant" as a transparent category, an easily designated classification for people who move across various types of borders.[5] Here, I highlight how the decolonizing state derived its conception of migrants from experts, who themselves vigorously debated how to interpret the population transfers taking place around the globe. Many highly mobile populations –for example, returned colonial servants—were left out of this scholarship entirely.[6] As the groups entering and leaving Britain diversified, researchers contributed to a larger framework of visibility and invisibility, in which only some of the era's population transfers warranted the state's attention.

This field was relentlessly comparative. Within the pantheon of migrant health and pathology, subjects from the former colonies had a special status. But they were joined by the Irish, European refugees, and white Britons themselves. Decolonization influenced the state's response to different populations and structured the relationships between them. Experts created elaborate classificatory systems to understand the populations that were moving to and from the metropole, and to evaluate their perceived successes and failures. Their obsessively hierarchical thinking was shaped not only by numbers but also by the shifting terrain of colonial and postcolonial geographies and the trajectories of independence abroad. The process of making migrants was influenced not just by the economic and social processes that led citizens of Africa, Asia, and the Caribbean to Britain, but also by Britain's interventions in the Cold War and by the taxonomies that emanated from decolonization and its often subterranean demands. Decolonization shaped migration—not only as a social phenomenon, but also as a way of thinking that in turn structured migration's own laws.

The birth of the migrant was linked to the genealogy (and competition) of disciplines. The 1950s and 1960s offered a new variety of registers in which debates about migration were conducted. Each represented the migrant differently. As the state engaged these competing definitions, there were often profound consequences—in terms of rights and resources, interventions, and surveillance—that flowed from whether the state viewed individuals and groups through the lens of anthropology, psychology, or sociology. These disciplinary frameworks also took different views on the adaptability of migrants. Anthropology provided the most optimistic lens; psychology and sociology took a far dimmer view.

The study of the migrant led British experts into their own global sojourns, although they rarely theorized these movements as "migrations." Indeed, the concept of migration did not adequately encapsulate the flows of entry and return that characterized most of the population movements of the era, but postwar researchers were generally untroubled by the limitations of this category. Metropolitan experts were themselves exceptionally mobile, crisscrossing the borders of empire and its aftermath.[7] From London to Sierra Leone, from Poland to Australia, they sought to classify the flow of people and ideas that they believed structured Britain's changing place in the world.

ANTHROPOLOGISTS INTO SOCIOLOGISTS, AFRICANS INTO WEST INDIANS

The study of migration was forged through Britain's ongoing engagements with its former colonies, but also through its relationships with the United States, the Soviet Union, and Europe. North American migration studies, dominated by sociology, were powerfully influential, illuminating how population movements were conceived in relation to building—or losing—empires.[8] But in order to create the migrant, British scholars also drew on their own distinctive anthropological past. Studies of migration in Britain were conceived not only in terms of adjustment and assimilation, which were drawn from American sociology, but also from a more anthropologically-derived interest in how African communities were able to change. Fieldwork about adaptation in Africa was as important as contact with the Chicago School of urban sociology and its emphasis on assimilation.

This anthropological strand of scholarship on migration has been largely forgotten. It is important to recall, because it is the thread of the story that most closely connects the history of migration to that of decolonization. Given its long service to colonial endeavors, anthropology might have seemed an outdated rubric for understanding migration in the postcolonial world. But many of Britain's experts on migration were trained as anthropologists of Africa, and their fieldwork was intimately engaged with the trajectory of its independence. They saw the topic of migration as a way to sustain their relevance. Their disciplinary background haunted their thinking on migrants and indigenes in unpredictable ways. Here, I chart how one group of scholars crafted links between the African subject of the anthropological past and the black migrant of the sociological future. Forging connections—and disjunctions—between indigenes and migrants was one crucial task of postwar anthropological scholarship.

This exploration focuses on the Department of Social Anthropology at Edinburgh, one of the institutional focal points of race relations research in Britain, which has received rather less attention than the traditional sites of social anthropology at the LSE, University College London, Oxford, Cambridge, and Manchester. Ultimately, the Edinburgh department was vital to the trajectory of British sociology,[9] and to its investment in the idea of multicultural Britain. Here, I aim to recapture the intellectual universe of the 1950s in which the migrant was formed, and to understand how scholars deployed this topic in order to effect their own disciplinary transformations.

Kenneth Little was a pioneering figure in the creation of the migrant. Born in 1908, Little had been a mature student at Cambridge with a background in repertory theater. When the Second World War began, he was deemed medically unfit for active duty but began delivering lectures when his own physical anthropology teacher, Jack Trevor, was called up to serve.[10] Little's research on the "Anglo-Negroid cross" was published in the *Eugenics Review* in 1942, but he quickly moved away from physical anthropology. He trained with Raymond Firth at the LSE and completed his doctorate in 1944. His thesis on the black population at Tiger Bay, Cardiff, was published as *Negroes in Britain* in 1948. Little claimed that the book was welcomed by African and West Indian nationalists such as George Padmore.[11] But, he pleaded, "please rule me out as a 'reformer' of any sort! I have a hard enough task . . . steering a precarious course between the Scylla of the reactionary 'White' and the Charybdis of the ultra-'Coloured'"![12] Little was inspired by the Chicago School of urban sociology to approach Cardiff's docklands as an ecological phenomenon, in which one could witness the interaction of groups in a single locality over time.[13] He avidly read scholarship on race in the United States, such as John Dollard's *Caste and Class in a Southern Town* (1937), and spent a term at the historically black Fisk University in Tennessee in the 1940s.

Little was appointed to a readership in race relations at the LSE in 1950, and he moved to Edinburgh that same year.[14] There, he participated in the Department of Social Anthropology's ascension as a driving force in the study of race relations. The topic was included in the applied anthropology course, which explored the impact of European institutions in colonial territories, problems arising from culture contact (such as "detribalization"), and community development.[15] Edinburgh scholars were pioneering in their use of interdisciplinary sources.[16] Little, for example, showed great verve in discussing how Chinua Achebe's fiction illuminated African identity. Most faculty conducted research in Britain and in developing countries, making few distinctions between the locations of their work.[17] As Little argued, it was not only African pastoralists who were confronting massive cultural changes. Britons, too, faced the transformation of their social organization, whether through advertising campaigns to alter their spending habits, or taxation plans to restructure the class system.[18]

The "race relations" scholars worked in a cozy Georgian house, stationed in an attic above the mathematics department. In these close quarters, personal and professional rivalries flared. Little behaved erratically, with mood swings that were variously attributed to alcoholism, depression, and undiagnosed cerebral malaria.[19] He had a rakish reputation in Sierra Leone, where he was distinctly unpopular with the local intelligentsia. He married three times, once to a Jamaican woman (although Little's students speculated that she was actually Mende).[20] African drummers often performed at gatherings at Little's house in Edinburgh, which was built on the form of a Mende compound. One student recalled that these parties were frequently raided by the police, once four times in a single night.[21]

Little employed a team of energetic young researchers to explore different aspects of the migrant experience. Michael Banton studied the "coloured quarter" of Stepney. Sydney Collins interviewed Muslim Arabs in North and South Shields, and Eyo Bassey N'dem examined migrants' organizations in Manchester. Alex Carey, Philip Garigue, Violaine Junod, and Sheila Webster investigated the formation of black elites.[22] Little argued that these studies would advance the cause of social anthropology more generally: the Nuffield Foundation was sufficiently convinced to fund all of these projects.[23] Little insisted that anthropologists were limited in studying "primitive" peoples because they could not be fully accepted in the groups they observed. Their techniques, however, could be redeployed to study "enclaves of coloured people in this country, who provide a special kind of problem in the impact, culturally and socially, between colonial peoples and our western society."[24] Migrants thus offered unique methodological possibilities, allowing the anthropologist to know the indigene more intimately. Migrants also challenged existing definitions of acculturation, which were conceived for the mutual exchange of traits between widely different cultures: a rubric that did not seem to describe adequately, for example, the complexities of West Africans' lives in Britain.[25] Little argued that because West Africans were increasingly entering European educational and social systems, they must be conceptualized in relation to Europe.[26] Although he was interested in the quotidian realities of housing, employment, and family structures, for Little migrants were best understood as a social category, an ideal type.[27]

Starting in the 1930s, anthropologists were using concepts like "social situation," "social field," and "social network" to emphasize that Africans did not live within a bounded universe, but created new patterns of relations as they moved into different places.[28] Little was engaged with this work and became vitally interested in urban change in West Africa. Thus, he took part in a much broader movement dedicated to understanding African adaptation, which emphasized how quickly Africans adjusted to new environments.[29] Accordingly, Little and his students researched voluntary associations in West Africa: incredibly popular groups based on economic interest, religious sympathies, or common origin.[30] Voluntary associations had complex, transnational roots. For example, the Egbe Omo Oduduwa (Society of the Descendants of Omo Oduduwa, the mythical founder of the Yoruba people) originated in London, but then reappeared in Nigeria in 1948 to propagate a Yoruba state.[31] The Edinburgh school perceived voluntary associations for migrants in Britain as highly adaptive, mediating the transition to independence.[32] Its participants theorized that by educating migrants from the African hinterlands in thrift, punctuality and sexual respectability, the associations staved off political upheaval and anomie.[33] These ideas had been rehearsed elsewhere, most notably at the Rhodes-Livingstone Institute and the Manchester School of anthropology.[34] But, crucially, Edinburgh scholars used this research as the basis for the study of migrants in Britain.[35]

Little never synthesized the evidence that the Edinburgh team gathered; they only met together once for two days in 1952.[36] The most influential member of the group was Michael Banton, who was born in Birmingham in 1926. Banton served in the Royal Navy at the end of the war and went to the LSE.[37] Here, Edward Shils encouraged him to read social anthropology, which Banton had avoided, fearing that it might doom him to a career in colonial service. But Shils told him that he would actually learn more about the discipline of sociology from anthropologists. Banton took this advice, studying with Edmund Leach, Maurice Freedman, and Raymond Firth.

In 1950, Little hired Banton as a postdoctoral fellow to conduct anthropological research on colonial stowaways to Britain.[38] This project was inspired by Little's recent voyage from Sierra Leone to Liverpool, during which West African stowaways had been found on board; among their number was the future Ghanaian nationalist leader Nana Joseph Emmanuel "Joe" Appiah. Little perceived the stowaways as a crucial link between indigenes and migrants. He asked Banton to interview the stowaways in prison, but Banton thought it would compromise him to be identified with the state authorities in this way. Struck by a gift from Shils—William Whyte's participation observation study, *Street Corner Society* (1943)—Banton proposed a broader study of migrants of color in the East End.[39]

His Stepney research was published as *The Coloured Quarter* in 1954, just after he completed a stint of fieldwork on internal migration in Sierra Leone. Banton now recalls that his work in Stepney and Sierra Leone was driven by the central notion of "community studies," and the desire to examine communities in transition. But he was unsure whether blacks in Stepney truly constituted a community at all. He sought to create an associational life for blacks in Britain that was compatible with what he had seen in Africa. Working with other whites in the 1950s, Banton established the Stepney Coloured People's Association, which quickly foundered.[40]

The indigene in Africa haunted the creation of the migrant in Britain, much as anthropology haunted the emergent discipline of sociology.[41] When I interviewed him in 2008, Banton insisted that his work in Sierra Leone and London occupied separate intellectual spheres, and that there was little, if any connection between them.[42] But he and his colleagues ranked migrant groups not only by how thoroughly they "assimilated" (a framework influenced by American sociology), but also by their associational life (a concept drawn from the anthropology of Africa). Understanding how migrants in Britain organized themselves was thought to yield insight into their collective health.[43] Judged by these criteria, urbanized Africans in Africa were performing better than migrants in Britain. Just as Little highlighted the value of voluntary associations in West Africa, so too did Banton emphasize that Kru organizations in London aided the fight for social equality and facilitated assimilation with white Britons. He also believed that such organizations provided an effective means of social control over blacks in Britain, although many of the functions served by African associations were usurped in Britain by the Unemployment Exchanges, the National Assistance Board, and other agencies of the welfare state.[44] The anthropology of the African indigene thus crucially shaped expectations of how migrants should act in Britain, and promoted certain stereotypes—for example, that South Asians were more "organized" than West Indians.[45]

It might seem that in their analysis of migrant communities, British experts had found a new population of "primitives" to explore, or that they chose to view migrants solely through the lenses they had created for indigenes. But that would be oversimplified. Little's investigation of African urbanity was inspired in part by work with West Africans in East London.[46] He traced migrations to Britain back to what he saw as an "original" migration in Africa: that is, the movement from the country-side into the cities. Like many anthropologists who worked on "circular" migration, Little's work on the African indigene was itself also about migrants—the African who interested him was the one who moved.[47] The road led not only from Africa to Britain, but also the other way around, and the "dark strangers" that Banton and Little studied in Britain were not really strangers to them at all. Moreover, the interplay of scholarship on indigenes and migrants had high stakes in terms of creating taxonomies regarding which migrants might receive different kinds of welfare in the metropole, and in shaping expert opinion about what kinds of institutions could aid migrants in their transition to Britishness.

Anthropology was one of the key disciplines deployed in making sense of migration. But it was also the first to be written out.[48] The key terms of the field were increasingly sociological.[49] As sociological analyses gained ground, influenced by North American studies, its subjects were recast as West Indians: a population of greater interest to American scholars, as Caribbean migrants rapidly entered the United States. The optimistic emphasis on adaptation fell away, as new studies focused on how migrants violated British norms. The journalist Elspeth Huxley, who rejected what she called the "sociological cant" on race and migration, pointed to the omnipotence of Britain's powers of transformation. She described how the first "trickle" of blacks in Britain had "vanished as completely as a conjurer's rabbit—biologically absorbed into the mainstream of Anglo-Saxon pallor." The postwar "flood" might pose new challenges, but conformity to English norms would triumph in the end. English life, she wrote, was a "massive, suety, close-grained thing with great powers of absorption— like a jellyfish that enfolds in its grey, soft, caressing tentacles any rashly venturing organism and then slowly, undramatically, ingests its prey."[50]

Academic sociologists, however, were less confident about the powers of the jellyfish.[51] In Liverpool, Anthony Richmond evaluated levels of assimilation among West Indian technicians.[52] He studied ten men who represented different stages of adjustment, meaning the degree to which they accepted the duties that were expected in their role as industrial employees.[53] Richmond detailed the case of S.T., a West Indian who came to Britain in 1942, but failed to acquire proper skills. Richmond described S.T. as poorly adjusted, because he refused any physical labor, "but insists that he wants a job as a 'welfare officer' . . . He assiduously reads on subjects such as law, politics, economics, and theology and frequently poses as a *bona fide* student, while actually being dependent upon National Assistance." This pretense, Richmond suggested, reflected his "complete failure" to adjust to the reality of his situation.[54] Another technician, A.B., was criticized for his strong dislike of the term "'nigger,' even in such phrases as 'to work like a nigger.'"[55] Richmond described A.B.—who was married to a white English girl—as psychologically maladjusted, with excessive color consciousness. But, "in sociological terms, A.B. has proved himself one of the more outstanding members of the scheme." The study thus distinguished between psychological and sociological forms of adjustment.

Like Little, Richmond was influenced by the Chicago School. But if British scholars readily acknowledged their debts to American sociologists of race and migration, they were also often self-congratulatory about the absence of a legal color bar in Britain.[56] Because the position of people of color in Britain was "not legally, but sociologically inferior," they believed that social science could more easily provide a cure for racial inequities in Britain than in the United States.[57]

The view from across the Atlantic was less salutary. Ruth Landes, an American anthropologist who came to Britain on a Fulbright scholarship in 1951–52, took a team of Little's students to London, Cardiff, Liverpool, Manchester, and Newcastle. With wonder, she described the unions between "immigrant Negroes [who] were establishing families with native white women and rearing their children in the host community." These interracial families were *sui generis* in having a recognized male head to a mixed family, with the dominant race in a subordinate position within the marriage. Landes argued that the racially mixed family in Britain must be understood through the filter of contemporary global events. The facts of decolonization meant that the "Negro elite," who might have mediated the experience of black disillusionment in Britain, were only trained for leadership in their own new nations, and not for transforming relations between blacks and whites in the metropole.

Landes became convinced of the absolute disconnect between race relations in Britain and the United States. As one British psychologist informed her, "there are no 'Negroes' in Britain, no 'coloured'—we just don't think that way. We think of men from Jamaica, and from the Gold Coast and from Barbados—no so-called Negroes.'" In the United States, according to Landes, neither race could do without the other; the races were locked in a deadly but intimate struggle. No such intimacy, she found, existed in Britain. The sight of the "Negro" served only as a reminder of empire, situated not within domestic history, but only "in some removed limbo of colonial grace." For this reason, "To me, Negro subjects in Britain appear as a weakly equipped agglomeration of individuals bruising themselves as they insistently attempt entry into this society operating entirely apart from them. Everything conspires to keep them unmistakably separate." Landes was skeptical that the canonical sociological terms of prejudice, tolerance, and acceptance could be applied in Britain. The particular constellation of decolonization and racialized migrations in Britain seemed to demand new categories of analysis.[58] Radical black activists in Britain described themselves not as migrants, but as "failed refugees" from nationalist independence movements, which had failed to bring about the desired degree of transformation. They viewed police harassment in Britain as an extension of the colonial policing they had experienced overseas, and explicitly equated racial prejudice against migrants with neocolonialism. Such interpretations raised important questions about how the successes and failures of decolonization were playing out on metropolitan terrain, and how people of color in Britain might view the discourse of "migration" through the lens of decolonization.[59]

These relentless comparisons across the Atlantic were not new. The sociologist Talcott Parsons had long described Britain as an important site for American scholars of race because he believed it was transitioning from a homogenous to a multiracial society.[60] Migration attracted renewed interest from postwar American social scientists under the rubric of modernization theory. Migrants were portrayed as progressive types who transmitted innovations to their home communities. The key terms of migration studies—adaptation, adjustment, and assimilation—reflected modernization theory's dichotomization of the world into "traditional" and "modern" zones, which corresponded to places that "pushed" versus those that "pulled."[61] In the afterlife of empire, American interest in migration extended beyond the borders of the United States to consider how to manage what the collapsing European empires left behind.

The tensions between anthropological and sociological interpretations reflected that the study of migration was always a multidisciplinary affair, as well as a disciplinary competition. Next, I consider the distinctive contribution of British "psy"—the cluster of practices and ideals associated with psychology, psychiatry, and psychoanalysis—to the creation of the migrant, and how the experience of decolonization shaped the study of psychopathology and population movement. Researchers in the field of psy diagnosed a host of ills associated with new global migration regimes. In turn, government agencies redeployed these studies to shape the laws of migration.

Nikolas Rose has argued that the Second World War forged the expectation that good government must take account of the mental health of the governed.[62] One might add that the flip side of this expectation was also true; that is, "mental illness" could be used to assess the parameters of citizenship. What was at stake in designating certain migrants as mentally ill? How did studies of different groups—for example, of the West Indian in Britain, or the Briton in Australia—influence one another?

For psychologists and psychiatrists in the 1950s and 1960s, the migrant served as a trope that emblematized the fragilities of the postwar self. These frailties appeared to be accelerating in multiple locales, each with its own distinctive relationship to Britain. As these researchers charted migrant pathologies, they created elaborate apparatuses for evaluating which groups demanded different forms of intervention. They also intertwined global and local concerns, highlighting how academic and governmental conceptions of mental health were structured by both decolonization and the Cold War. Here, I show how psychology and psychiatry offered a valuable set of mechanisms for regulating migration and sought to impose a new logic on the often chaotic realm of population movement.

British psy was deeply bound up with the Cold War. This invocation of the Cold War may strike some readers as counterintuitive, given that Britain has not always been acknowledged as a key player in Cold War struggles for global dominance. Yet decolonization and the Cold War are entangled in this book, as indeed they were historically.[63] The British desire to counter Soviet influence was inseparable from the need to retain a presence overseas.[64] In this sense, the Cold War represented an opportunity for new kinds of imperial resurgence. The power struggles of the Cold War constantly shaped Britain's own portfolio of imperial interests.[65] Furthermore, British colonialism had its own afterlife in Cold War America, as the torsions of the British empire played a significant role in the articulation of American neoimperial power, whether as an instructive guide or as a cautionary tale.[66]

It is not my intention to recast the Cold War as a people's war, nor to depict Britain as a major player in it. I am not asking what Britain did for the Cold War, but rather what the Cold War did to Britain, and how structures of knowledge in Britain were shaped by its concerns. The Cold War in Britain was often difficult to see.[67] But it played a crucial role in shaping the trajectory of psychology and psychiatry in Britain. Furthermore, it shaped a wide range of seemingly disconnected fields of metropolitan life, including welfare and decolonization. In the task of creating new cadres of specialists, Britain's Cold War had a diverse cast of characters. In this sense, it was an energizing force, creating modes of thought that survived its own battles.

Long before the Cold War began, however, debates about the madness of migrants were well developed in British social science. In particular, the role of the Irish within the pantheon of migrant ills was widely debated. Although the "whiteness" of the Irish seemed progressively more assured within the laws of migration, their relationship to welfare in England and what they revealed about the uneasiness with which populations of color could be comfortably categorized was more complicated.

THE MADNESS OF MIGRATION: BRITISH PSY AND THE COLD WAR

The Irish were the original "mad migrants." Victorian researchers investigated how migration affected Irish mental health, framing the questions that would dominate future investigations. Were mentally unstable individuals prone to migrate (the selection hypothesis), or did the hardships of migration engender new instabilities (the stress hypothesis)?[68] Thomas

Drapes, the superintendent of the Enniscorthy asylum, suggested in 1894 that Ireland's high rates of emigration, along with agricultural depression and evictions, had eased the path to madness:

> Rent abolished, his land and homestead for himself, and a Parliament in College Green, these make up the dream which fills his fancy. Disappointed often, but still not despairing, betrayed as he has often been, he still clings with wonderful tenacity to the picture of an ideal Ireland which his imagination, aided by the eloquence of his political teachers, has fabricated. But the hopes, fears, and anxieties, the stirring up of emotions, some evil, some generous, engendered by this almost chronic condition of political unrest, can hardly fail to have a more or less injurious effect on a not over-stable brain.[69]

Drapes and others were keenly aware of how colonial history bore on Irish mental health, a recurrent theme in later studies of migration and madness.

The field was in abeyance until O. Odegaard's 1932 pioneering study of psychosis among the Norwegian born in Minnesota (50 percent higher than in Norway), which claimed that schizoid personalities were predisposed toward migration. Inspired by Odegaard, Isaac Frost, a medical officer at the Friern Hospital, described acute psychological disturbances among Austrian and German domestic servants in London. Frost believed that these episodes resulted from "the energy of pent-up longing for home," which were converted into full-blown "immigrant psychosis."[70] Over 60 percent of his subjects threatened suicide, and many asked to be returned to their own countries. Frost argued that repatriation served as a "great incentive towards the exercise of self-control and patience" for the mentally ill. But he also advocated increased institutional support for foreign workers and suggested official measures to reduce servants' anxiety about the renewal of work permits. The study of migrant mental health was thus tied from its inception to the state's power of population movement.

These studies were galvanized by the wartime experiences of evacuation and population transfer. Postwar experts saw Britain as a psychological danger zone for refugees. Jacques Vernant, a French expert on refugees at the United Nations, argued that although refugees in Britain were relatively well-off in material terms, "psychologically England . . . is probably the most difficult of all countries."[71] Britain lacked any official program of education for displaced persons, and psychologists warned that the British insistence on getting "back to normal" could damage refugees' mental health.

In the 1950s, several major studies explored mental illness among European Volunteer Workers (EVWs) in order to assess the Cold War's impact on mental health. This research indicated that EVWs in Britain had high rates of psychiatric hospitalization, and were "suffering from persecution mania which may give place later to delusions of grandeur."[72] Psychologists believed that these disorders were caused by the insecurity of hostel life, anxiety about families left behind the Iron Curtain, and the suspicion that communist agents had infiltrated Britain.

Much of this research focused on Poles, who drew special sympathy as anti-Soviet sentiments escalated.[73] In 1943, a psychiatric division was formed for Polish troops who were recuperating in Scotland, and in 1947, a new unit was created in Kent specifically for mentally ill Polish servicemen.[74] Starting in the 1950s, Poles had a special department at the Ministry of Health, and their own sections in British hospitals and rehabilitation centers.[75] In 1950, the rate of first admissions for male Polish refugees was 4.42 per thousand, compared to a British rate of 0.86 per thousand.[76] The majority of Polish migrants were described as highly politicized exiles, who wished to return to their country of origin. As the Polish-born sociologist Jerzy Zubrzycki wrote, their interests were not with Britain.[77] Indeed, psychiatrists linked suicides among Poles in Britain to an obsessive focus on homeland politics, citing a woman who drowned herself in a Bradford canal on Poland's Independence Day.[78] Zubrzycki argued that if the balance of world politics could be restored, it would indefinitely delay the realization of the aims of Polish refugees to return home. Thus, their acceptance of complete assimilation—as yet forestalled—would become inevitable. Within this rubric of Cold War social science, the true barriers to integration were political, not psychological.

Other "Cold War migrants" received intense psychiatric attention. After the Hungarian uprising of 1956, A. G. Mezey studied the 20,000 Hungarian refugees who subsequently arrived in Britain. He interviewed patients at Maudsley Hospital's clinic for Hungarians, established by the British Council for Aid to Refugees.[79] Mezey concluded that although the refugees' social and linguistic isolation favored the onset of paranoia, it was unlikely to create a true paranoid delusion. In Mezey's view, this population of patients had been maladapted in Hungary as well. Despite the timing of their migration, they had moved primarily for nonpolitical reasons. Significantly, Mezey categorized political migrations as less pathological than their nonpolitical counterparts.[80]

By the late 1950s, debates about migrant mental health were increas-

Zionist migration is healthy
If you don't you may have the psychological problem of being a self-hating Jew !!

ingly intertwined with those about demographic control. Research on migrants intersected with the formulation of stricter repatriation policies for mental illness and, later, new entry controls for migrants of color under the Commonwealth Immigrants Act 1962. The ease or difficulty of migration was more finely graded in an age of controlled entry, and social scientists assessed the resilience of migrants from different parts of the Commonwealth accordingly. Debates about migrant mental health were intimately bound up with the logistics of decolonization and the vexed question of who bore responsibility for "failed" migrants from newly independent nations. As I suggest, British researchers established—but could not sustain—a consensus on the racialization of migration's ills.

THE DECOLONIZATION OF PSY? REPATRIATION, PSYCHIATRY, AND THE STATE

One striking feature of the vast literature on black psychoses in Britain is the remarkable durability of postwar research. Scholarship from the 1950s is still routinely cited in discussions of Caribbean-born patients, and is deployed to provide a genealogy of that stock figure in British psychiatry: the schizophrenic Afro-Caribbean.[81] Here, I consider why this stereotype of the mad West Indian migrant has had such remarkable staying power, while the image of the psychologically disturbed white migrant has largely disappeared. One reason for the striking longevity of postwar research is the strength of the link on this issue between expertise and governmental policy. Studies of West Indian mental illness offered scientific rationales for new policies of repatriation, underscoring how psychology and psychiatry could provide a basis for governance during the end of empire. This research had an important afterlife in migration policy, even after it outlived its utility in the domain of mental health.

The intense focus on West Indian migrants' mental health represented the culmination of a long history of treating the black psyche as the site of political struggle.[82] Indeed, migrants of color forged a link between colonial and postcolonial spheres of psychiatric expertise. Colonial frameworks of diagnosis were often transferred to the postcolonial metropole, and applied to migrants through transcultural practice.[83] The value of psychology and psychiatry in making sense of nationalist movements increased in the postwar years, as scholars posited "deculturation" as the cause of African mental illness.[84] J. C. Carothers's influential work, *The*

African Mind in Health and in Disease (1953), which was based on his clinical research on the Kikuyu during the Mau Mau rebellion, linked African schizophrenia to education and urbanization.[85] For Carothers, anticolonial rebellions were motivated not by legitimate socioeconomic or political demands, but simply by the African's inability to adapt to change. The only remedy was strong external leadership, imposed by force if necessary.[86] Carothers also argued that the black psyche was always damaged in the process of migration, whether the movement was within Africa, or from Africa to Europe. Alien codes of behavior left the African "cold or utterly perplexed . . . quite lost or rudderless."[87]

Independence seemed to entail its own psychic complexities. Postwar ethnopsychiatric research was not merely a colonial hangover but also a technology that could be deployed to manage decolonization itself. Most British researchers expected that decolonization would be harmful to mental health.[88] With Ghanaian independence, some scholars predicted an outbreak of psychosis due to the stresses "attendant on a growing nation striving for a respectable place in the sun."[89] C. V. D. Hadley described personality patterns in the West Indies to illuminate the trajectory of self-government, and explain why West Indians struggled to adapt to competitive society.[90] If the West Indies became part of the community of nations, Hadley suggested, then it was bound to suffer a recrudescence of aggression, since the black proletariat would have to accept a new degree of identification with the dominant culture. Any British welfare efforts must provide outlets for the aggression that welfare inspired.

The prognosis for West Indian migrants in the "mother country" of Britain seemed even bleaker. Early studies claimed that West Indians had higher psychiatric morbidity rates than EVWs, with a marked rise in attempted suicide after migration.[91] Scholars were puzzled by the curious timing of breakdowns among West Indians; 47 percent of the patients showed no sign of illness until they had been in Britain for two or more years.[92] For West Indians, the immediate stress of arrival was apparently eclipsed by the extended traumas of acculturation. How might researchers compare the stresses that had faced EVWs—such as linguistic isolation—with those confronted by West Indians, such as racial discrimination? Was it possible that the voluntary migrations of the late 1950s and 1960s might prompt more pathologies than the trauma of war itself?

Researchers in Britain developed an extensive lexicon to describe the unique psychopathologies of migrants of color. Farrukh Hashmi, the senior registrar in psychological medicine at All Saints' Hospital in

Birmingham, outlined what he called a "displaced persons syndrome," prompted by paranoia about racial and ethnic discrimination. Hashmi claimed that many migrants felt guilty about being unable to defend their rudimentary religious beliefs against English logic: "conscience, when injured, is like a wound, which does heal eventually but leaves a permanent scar."[93] H. P. Burrowes, the principal medical officer of Bradford, claimed that the move to Britain prompted either "servile obsequious behavior" or "aggressive behavior" for migrants of color. He argued that migrant delusions typically involved white women, thus pathologizing the effects of interracial relationships on the fragile migrant psyche.[94]

British researchers explored links between disease patterns and migration policies. One psychologist theorized that because West Indians were actively recruited during the London Transport campaigns, mentally unstable migrants had relocated more easily.[95] But scholars emphasized that after the establishment of entry controls in 1962, "schizoid" individuals were unlikely to be able to undertake the accumulation of capital and skills required for emigration. Whereas the labor recruitment campaigns might have allowed dysfunctional individuals into Britain, this pattern should have shifted after the Commonwealth Immigrants Act 1962, when the stresses of restricted migration demanded stellar mental health. The politics of the Caribbean diaspora thus challenged the theory of negative selection in migration.

Christopher Bagley, a social worker and sociologist, argued that for white migrants from Australia and New Zealand, Canada, and South Africa, mental illness was a mark of prior deviance.[96] These groups did not suffer from the stresses of migration, because their migration was not that stressful. For West Indians and Africans, however, psychiatric illness in Britain was related to the challenges of adaptation. Mental illness in white migrants was biological; for migrants of color, it was environmental.[97] Bagley detailed the case of a thirty-nine-year-old Caribbean man who came to Britain in 1958. He worked as an omnibus conductor and then obtained a clerical post in government. He applied for promotion, but his supervisor discouraged him from taking the necessary exams. He purchased a dilapidated house with a mortgage well above market rate, and took evening work as a cleaner. He suspected that his workmates were trying to poison him. In charting this descent into paranoia, Bagley highlighted the man's occupational aspirations and his faith in the possibility of advancement. Influenced by North American studies, Bagley concluded that status striving in a climate of limited opportunity produced pathology.[98] Working-class English whites were insulated by social norms that encouraged them to recognize the difficulty of changing their position. West Indians, conversely, misinterpreted English society as "open." They were compelled to strive, but doomed to fail.[99]

Such studies carried high stakes in the debate about West Indian mental health, which had concrete ramifications for repatriation policy. The Colonial Office had long held the power to fund the return journeys of impoverished colonial seamen, a scheme that gained momentum during the Second World War.[100] But no provisions existed for repatriating other incapacitated individuals to the colonies. In 1949, the National Assistance Board agreed to review applications for sponsored repatriation from colonial subjects who were mentally unfit (or "social misfits").[101] Under this scheme, the Colonial Office alerted the National Assistance Board of any "coloured British colonials" who were mentally ill or unable to adapt to life in Britain. If the board found that the individual would have to be supported in Britain by public funds, then it would pay for repatriation. The specter of repatriation thus haunted the field of migrant mental health, as researchers debated new forms of expulsion.

This system of supported repatriation expanded in the 1950s. Area officers began to ask colonial applicants who seemed "unsettled" if they had ever considered going home.[102] Many migrants who accepted repatriation grants changed their minds at the last moment; others who took up the grants later returned to Britain. Initially, the board considered it essential that the idea of repatriation should be brought up by the individual migrant. By the 1960s, the board's officials were encouraged to suggest repatriation to likely individuals, although migrants were still allowed to make the final decision.[103] The National Assistance Board met the costs of return for about 1,200 families between 1948 and 1969.[104] The board was keen to avoid the appearance that it was deporting people on the grounds of poverty. Instead, it emphasized psychiatric criteria for repatriation.[105] This process required an extensive investigation into the individual's employment, family networks, and housing prospects in the country of origin. The board traditionally denied support in cases where repatriation would break up a family unit in Britain.

The National Assistance Board and the Ministry of Health were much less zealous about supporting repatriations than the Home Office, and less interested in adopting powers for compulsory repatriation.[106] After 1962, Conservative Home Secretary Henry Brooke pressured the board to fund more repatriations.[107] But the Ministry of Health was never certain whether mental disorders constituted grounds for repatriation, and the National Assistance Board was concerned about violating international law. The European Convention of Social and Medical Assistance (1953), which was ratified by Britain, discouraged repatriation solely on the grounds of financial circumstances. The board was reluctant to take statutory powers to repatriate mentally ill individuals, fearing that the distinction between voluntary and involuntary return could easily be lost.[108] The board insisted that migrants express a clear wish to be repatriated, but mental patients were not always able to make their wishes known clearly.

Throughout the repatriation debates of the 1950s and 1960s, the majority of individuals affected were West Indian psychiatric patients.[109] The issue became increasingly complicated after West Indian federation. In theory, Britain's responsibility for repatriated West Indians ceased at the moment of independence. But the Colonial Office was concerned that the West Indies would be unwilling or unable to support these costs, especially as mentally ill repatriates were likely to become "a debit" on their home communities. The Jamaican authorities initially refused to accept any patients who still needed hospital care; by 1965, they had agreed to take these returnees back but still would not assist with the fares. As one minister said, "some of the poorer West Indian Islands, with population and unemployment problems of their own, will take the view that these people have emigrated here and that this is now the country of their adoption. The question as I see it is therefore 'Can we get the West Indies to take over this job effectively or should [Britain] continue to do it in self-interest?'"[110]

Several officials noted that as West Indian authorities were already "hysterical" about the new entry controls of 1962, the issue of repatriation was simply too sensitive.[111] The United Kingdom decided to keep the responsibility for repatriating West Indians itself.[112] Whereas state assistance had been confined to people from dependent territories, aid was now offered to "less developed" independent countries as well.[113] In 1963, the National Assistance Board extended repatriation aid to citizens of all independent African and Asian Commonwealth countries, illustrating the afterlife of empire in the domain of public health and the extent to which even its disengagements were only partial.[114]

As these cases demonstrated, migration was not a single event, but a process. It could be reversed, and it could fail. Joseph Armatrading, who was repatriated to St. Kitts in 1966 by the Ministry of Health, had drifted in and out of mental hospitals in Nottingham since 1960. His wife and children remained in the United Kingdom, and he feared that his wife might have started living with another man. As was normal practice,

Armatrading had surrendered his passport after the Ministry of Health had paid his passage home. In 1966 he petitioned to have his passport returned, so that he could come back to Britain and increase his earnings: "my passport is my life I got five children to maintain with out my passport I cannot maintain these children."[115] In one case, the medical officer argued that a Jamaican schizophrenic would benefit from repatriation because his poor English compounded his difficulty relating to other people.[116] Perhaps the most frequent diagnosis, if one can call it that, was "unable to adjust to life in this country."[117] This vagueness gave British authorities tremendous latitude.

These returnees were seriously overrepresented among West Indian mental patients. In the late 1960s, Aggrey Burke, a Jamaican psychiatrist trained at the University of Birmingham, undertook a study of repatriates at the Bellevue Hospital in Jamaica.[118] Most of these patients suffered from paranoia, but he noted that they harbored no delusions regarding color prejudice, and had not wanted to leave Britain. British therapists had initiated most of these repatriations, either because they believed their patients were unable to settle or because the patients had behaved aggressively in hospital. Notably, 20 percent of the male cases were repatriated from Broadmoor Hospital, a high-security psychiatric facility for the criminally insane.[119]

Repatriation, Burke argued, was a distinctive psychological event, associated with feelings of persecution and negative behaviors. He diagnosed what he termed "repatriate syndrome," a complex of reactions resulting from the combination of mental illness and the stigma of failed migration within the context of independence. The syndrome involved ambivalence regarding the return "home," as well as a high degree of social isolation. The mortality rate for repatriates was high, and Burke predicted that 25 percent would meet a tragic fate. He concluded that the "gross social insult" of repatriation was therapeutically useless and did vast psychiatric harm.[120]

The treatment of migrants was distinctly at odds with broader trends in the field of mental health in Britain. The Mental Health Act 1959 promoted mental health as both a personal responsibility and a national resource, increasing the role of local health authorities in caring for the mentally ill.[121] At the same time, critiques of psychiatric expertise aided the cause of deinstitutionalization.[122] The widespread use of tranquilizers and antidepressants prompted a new emphasis on allowing the mentally ill to rejoin society. But not everyone benefited equally. The Mental Health Act 1959 provided for the repatriation of mentally ill aliens, but the status of colonial and Commonwealth subjects was less secure. As the British population's relationship to mental health was revaluated, migrants constituted an exceptional group.

Ultimately, by the late 1960s, the repatriation schemes for mentally ill migrants provided a rationale for a greatly expanded discussion of mass repatriation. Conservative MP Enoch Powell proposed grants of £2,000 to "unfit" or "unsettled" migrants who wished to leave Britain.[123] Cyril Alexander Braham, a sixty-year-old Jamaican on National Assistance, personally visited the Conservative Party offices at Wolverhampton after hearing one of Powell's speeches, requesting funding for his passage home and a £1,000 resettlement loan.[124] Although Home Secretary James Callaghan publicly dismissed Powell's program as "a fantasy," Home Office files reflect just how seriously Powell's vision was considered.[125] The Home Office estimated that repatriating half a million individuals would cost between £79 million and £116 million: not so far off from Powell's plan to repatriate 600,000–700,000 people for £260 million.[126] Given the previous two decades of expansionist repatriation policy, did the Home Office really find Powell's project so shocking? In 1968, Callaghan was lambasted after he announced on a BBC *Panorama* television program that the government would fund repatriation for any migrant who wanted to go home and could not afford the fare.[127]

Repatriation schemes for mental illness could provide implicit justifications for larger, compulsory repatriation projects, both of which primarily targeted West Indians. But the racial politics of migration studies were complex. Research on migrants and mental health changed in important ways in the early 1960s. The 1961 census made it possible for the first time to compare the numbers of psychiatric patients from a given population to that population's total numbers.[128] It remained difficult to obtain comparable statistics for the migrants' countries of origin. The major exception was Ireland, where researchers had been collecting this data since the nineteenth century. Elsewhere, researchers generally could not compare disease rates among migrants and indigenes. The absence of these morbidity statistics enabled contradictory propositions: for example, that migrants were either the healthiest or the most pathological individuals in their home cultures.

The stereotype of the "mad" West Indian migrant has survived in a way that other groups—even those that experienced high rates of mental illness—did not. Partly, this was because the entry controls of 1962 rendered other populations, such as the Irish, less detectable in the domain of public health. In the wake of the Commonwealth Immigrants Act, the lack of controls on Ireland potentially allowed greater numbers of mentally ill Irish individuals—who would have been excluded if they had been traveling from the Caribbean or South Asia—into the United Kingdom.[129] The Commonwealth Immigrants Act rendered migrants of color highly visible for the purposes of psychiatric research. Simultaneously, Irish migrants became less visible, but social scientists were not necessarily convinced that they were any "healthier." In 1963, John Archer Jackson described a range of psychological traits contributing to the Irish migrant's maladjustment: sexual dysfunction, rebellion against authority, and the tendency of Irish women to cease social contact upon their marriage.[130]

It is difficult to assess the costs and benefits of visibility. Studies from the 1990s indicate Irish migrants had the highest rates of hospital admission for every psychiatric diagnosis except schizophrenia.[131] Even for schizophrenia, Irish rates were second only to those for African Caribbean migrants, and their overall hospitalization rates are higher.[132] The suicide rate for Irish migrants consistently outpaced that for the Irish in Ireland.[133] Irish-born men had the highest death rates of any migrant group and were the only migrants whose health was worse in Britain than in their homeland. This pattern of excess mortality recurred in the second generation, for every social class.[134] For the Irish, migration to Britain would seem to be singularly unhealthy.[135] This pattern became increasingly difficult to see after 1962, as the state controlled not only the movement of—but also data about—various populations. Thus, researchers were confounded by a hyperaccumulation of information about West Indians, and a rapidly declining data set for the Irish.

Yet the Irish were not the only white migrants who prompted anxious investigation. Public opinion polls conducted between 1948 and 1957 revealed that a stunningly large proportion of Britons were "emigration minded." As many as 42 percent of persons polled said they would be happy to settle in another country. Prospective migrants cited economic and social stagnation in Britain, as well as their concerns about rising racial tensions in the metropole. Waves of interest in emigration peaked during the Berlin airlift, the Korean War, and the Suez crisis of 1956.[136] These migrants from Britain drew their own distinctive forms of attention throughout the 1950s and 1960s.

In the United States, researchers began to diagnose white British migrants with distinctive pathologies. Benjamin Malzberg, who was best known for his research on Puerto Rican migrants at the New York State Department of Hygiene, found that English-born migrants in New York had high rates of alcoholic psychoses compared to American-born whites. Furthermore, the English departed from the trend Malzberg had identified for Puerto Ricans, in which mental illness declined for the second generation. For English individuals, this trend was reversed; the younger generation's risk of disease increased.[137]

One of the most intensively investigated migrant populations was that of white Britons in Australia and New Zealand. If the Irish migrant in England was frequently taken as an artifact of colonial history, then the white Briton in the antipodes was an emblem of an increasingly pathological modernity. Compared to white British migrants in other sites (such as South Africa or Rhodesia), this group drew extensive social scientific attention. Partly, this attention was due to the fact that Australia also attracted numerous psychologists and psychiatrists who had fled wartime Europe, and who focused their energies in the 1950s and 1960s on understanding the migrant experience in Australia more generally. Thus, an extensive apparatus for testing migrants from a variety of backgrounds was already in place.

This attentiveness to white Britons in Australia and New Zealand, however, also stemmed from governmental anxieties about how this particular group highlighted the shortcomings or frailties of Britons as migrants more generally. The British were both the most sought after and the most resented of populations in Australia and New Zealand, the "pampered products of the Welfare State."[138] In certain respects, they too were "invisible" migrants, whose problems were ranked below those of displaced persons (DPs) from Southern and Eastern Europe. But if we look carefully, we can see that researchers never characterized Britons as being immune to the ills of migration. Rather, Britons occupied an important place within the compendium of migrant pathologies. During the 1950s and 1960s, British scholars wrote their compatriots into a global narrative about migration and mental illness. One of their key revelations was that white Britons were not faring well in the highly mobile new world order.

ANTIPODEAN PATHOLOGIES: WHITE BRITONS AND THE TRIUMPH OF PSY

Perhaps one of the most noteworthy features of postwar British migration to Australia and New Zealand was its scale. The Free and Assisted Passage Schemes, which began in 1947, brought more than a quarter million Britons into Australia in their first decade.[139] Despite the influx of refugees to from Eastern, Southern and Central Europe, Britons were never less than one-third of all arrivals in Australia and New Zealand in the 1950s and 1960s.[140] All told, more than 1.5 million Britons left for Australia in the twenty-five years after World War Two.[141]

These assisted passage schemes transformed migration studies. Sponsored migrants, who were perceived as the bottom strata of English society, drew more professional curiosity than those who migrated independently.[142] Those who paid their own fares largely escaped expert scrutiny. These schemes were important for social scientists in that they allowed for investigations of individuals who were *planning* to migrate rather than focusing on those who had already moved.[143] Because interviewers could study migrants both before and after they left Britain, they highlighted psychological factors, such as personality differences, rather than the demographic traits that dominated North American migration studies. The psychologist Alan Richardson argued that sociologists and demographers had viewed assimilation only through indexes such as occupational status and fertility rates. They ignored the subjective aspects of psychological change that were also crucial to assimilation.[144] Psychologists could discern a range of other subtle maladjustments in this group that eluded other researchers.[145]

Psychologists targeted Britons in Australia in order to aid their understanding of the personality adjustments that occurred in migration, without the confusing elements of linguistic or racial difference. The experience of British migrants could also illuminate many other aspects of resocialization beyond the realm of migration itself, such as the social adjustments that were demanded when people transitioned from secondary school to university, from military to civilian communities, from residential neighborhoods to new satellite towns, and from prison to regular society. Thus, researchers hoped that their studies of British migrants in the antipodes might shed light on many of the other transformations that were demanded by modern life in the postwar metropole.[146] Whereas sociologists focused on the merging of groups of migrants into the host society, psychologists acknowledged that many individuals could adjust to a new society without assimilating completely. Psychology, in other words, recognized gradations of assimilation, which its practitioners saw as essential in capturing the British experience in Australia.[147]

Ruth Johnston, a Polish psychologist who had taught in London before moving to the University of Western Australia, argued that many migrants in Australia who were considered to be assimilated by the government were in fact only superficially changed; they had not undergone any inner transformation.[148] Psychiatrists also objected to the Commonwealth Immigration Advisory Council's "arbitrary" definition of a migrant as someone who had spent less than five years in Australia, arguing that the period of transition could last up to ten years.[149] Such studies noted the disjunction between governmental measures of assimilation, such as adoption of Australian nationality, and internal adjustments. Unlike psychologists, the state assumed that naturalization and other forms of assimilation were intertwined, and never adopted the more nuanced interpretation of assimilation that psychologists advocated.

The Australian government assumed that Britons would settle easily because of their cultural and linguistic similarities.[150] Individuals from the United Kingdom were also assumed to be relatively unscarred by the war compared to those from Iron Curtain countries.[151] In contrast to the "paranoid" DP, the Briton initially appeared to be the epitome of the modern migrant, who arrived in the antipodes fiercely loyal to the Commonwealth.[152] Yet the British migrant too had distinctive pathologies. Alan Stoller, the chief clinical officer of the Mental Health Authority, Victoria, identified specific "types" of problem migrants: in addition to the Eastern European with war trauma, and the lonely wife from Southern Europe, his study included the young British male with alcohol and marital problems.[153] Several researchers feared an influx of chronic alcoholics from Britain to Australia.[154] Even the most optimistic studies proposed Rorschach testing to identify neurotic British migrants.[155] Researchers claimed that British migrants to New Zealand who applied for assisted passage had higher rates of anxiety than natives, and were more likely to say that they would be unable to marry a doctor's daughter at home: a litmus test for measuring social isolation and resentment.[156] Richardson theorized that these individuals had been dislodged by wartime service from their place in Britain's social fabric, and were now experiencing personality disorganization.[157]

Jerzy Zubrzycki's 1964 analysis of migrants in the brown coal industry offered the case of Mr. B., a forty-three-year-old Englishman who came to Australia in 1948 under the Royal Australian Navy Scheme. Mr. B. left his wife and child behind in England when he emigrated, and then cohabited with another woman in Melbourne. His wife became suspicious when his letters home stopped, and she applied for Assisted Passage for herself and her son. Mrs. B. arrived in Melbourne in 1950, and Mr. B. reluctantly returned to his wife. They lived together at the time of the study, but Mr. B. had become moody, abusive, ambivalent toward his English-born son, and a heavy drinker.[158] Zubrzycki saw such cases as emblematic of the unanticipated strains on the British family in migration.

British responses to Australia were shaped by different memories of the imperial and wartime past. Satisfied migrants mentioned their desire to strengthen Commonwealth ties and promote its collective security. Conversely, unhappy migrants spoke of their frustration with the after-effects of rationing in Britain, and their fears that their children would suffer bombing if there were another war.[159] Those who were described as adjusting poorly to life in Australia were strongly identified with the social hierarchy in Britain, and found Australia's "classless" society psychologically difficult.[160] Migrants cited the White Australia policy, which restricted nonwhite immigration to Australia, to explain their interest in moving there, and complained about malaise and lethargy—as well as racial tensions and violence—in Britain.[161] Many Britons had considered moving to South Africa or Rhodesia, but said they had chosen Australia because they believed it offered less racial strife.[162]

Britons could make surprisingly difficult subjects—even more reluctant than Eastern European refugees to share details of their incomes and spending habits. They resented being classed as "New Australians" and were prone to halt interviews if they were referred to as migrants or foreigners.[163] Although the Australian government employed medical officers in Britain to examine potential migrants, the mental health test was widely considered unsatisfactory.[164] Many Britons were classified after arriving in Australia as "schizoids," who had a "restless search for solitude which leads [them] to forsake family and friends." A brief exam was not useful in identifying such persons before they emigrated.[165] One public health official suggested deportation provisions for individuals who had intentionally concealed mental illness and for schizophrenics who were diagnosed within five years of arriving in Australia.[166]

White Britons in Australia, it seemed, were ultimately no more adaptable than their West Indian or Asian counterparts in London.[167] Researchers argued that the expectation that Australia would be a "Britain in the South Seas" created its own adjustment problems.[168] Migrants from Southern and Eastern Europe were perceived to be affected purely by the stresses of migration, and thus were more easily cured. British migrants appeared to have more intractable mental disorders.[169] Psychologists described how Southern and Eastern Europeans initially faced dramatic problems of acculturation, and then rapidly improved.[170] Conversely, they argued, Britons enjoyed their first few weeks in Australia, but became more negative after six or seven months.

Thus, British migrants could deceive the state apparatuses designed to screen them; their pathologies were slow to emerge but disturbingly durable. Furthermore, their migrations were not always successful. As F. A. Emery at the Tavistock Institute of Human Relations suggested, tens of thousands of Britons had found migration an "inappropriate and costly answer to their problems."[171] Of the 29,000 people who left Australia in 1956, 19,000 went back to Britain.[172] These "boomerang" migrants represented a poor return on a significant investment, and tales of "Pommy ingratitude" were rampant in the Australian press.[173] Returned migrants seemed to reveal much about how Britons were adjusting (or failing to adjust) to the postwar world.[174]

White Britons in the antipodes played a crucial role within the broader study of migration. First, they highlighted the centrality of psychology—rather than sociology or demography—in understanding the nuances of adjustment. Researchers on Britons in Australia and New Zealand sought to cement psy's status by claiming that no other discipline could fully capture the complexities of this group's inner life and social behavior. Cultural kinship could exacerbate—rather than mitigate—the difficulties of assimilation, and this disheartening process was only adequately understood through the powerful capabilities of psy. Furthermore, white Britons prompted researchers to rethink the status of race within the global dynamics of migration. If these migrants had left Britain to escape the tensions that followed from the war and the empire's collapse, then their goal of a future that was truly postwar and postimperial seemed elusive.

Was migration itself inherently pathological? British psychologists and psychiatrists were strikingly pessimistic on this point. Their findings contrasted sharply with a growing body of scholarship in Israel and the United States, which pointed to migration's *positive* impact on mental health even as it documented migration's accompanying social ills.[175] Such optimism was largely absent in Britain. The trajectory of migration in terms of mental health appeared to be uniformly downward, even for Britons themselves.

MAKING MIGRANTS BLACK: THE FAILURE OF INTERDISCIPLINARITY

In 1958, Kenneth Little declared that the race problem in Britain was unimportant: a startling statement from a pioneering scholar of race relations in the year of the Notting Hill and Nottingham riots. But Little insisted that the significance of race relations in Britain was circumscribed. Namely, he argued, the topic gained its significance from its relationship to decolonization. Independence demanded that the government arouse sympathy for colonial peoples among the British public, less for the purpose of racial harmony in Britain than as a way of cementing diplomatic alliances between Britain and its former colonies.[176] He predicted that as independence swept through Africa and the West Indies, racism would be unable to withstand the winds of change. The status of individuals from those new nations would be elevated in Britain. Race, then, was not a metropolitan affair, except insofar as it affected international relations. Banton concurred that decolonization had raised the stakes for understanding race relations, in that the discontent of people of color could no longer be ignored. Migrants of color in Britain were recast as representatives of rising nations, whose friendships must be regained.[177]

This fundamental question of whether race was a "domestic" issue depended on how one viewed the migrant in Britain. By the time that proposals to create the Institute of Race Relations (IRR) emerged in the 1950s, American scholars—and dollars—had begun to play a significant role in shaping research on migration, and emphasizing American sociological categories that had previously been downplayed. In turn, British experts profited from the American view of Britain both as historically white, and as undergoing a fundamental change through a racialized process of migration. Yet although the IRR was an important conduit of American ideas about race and migration in Britain, it was also compelled to make sense of the colonial past and the distinctive circumstances of decolonization. As the anthropological study of the indigene morphed into the sociological study of the migrant, British researchers took an idiosyncratic approach to migration studies. Overwhelmingly, they isolated race relations from international affairs, which entailed seeing race relations as a domestic, rather than a global enterprise.

Today, the IRR is generally thought of as a 1960s affair, as is the study of migration more generally. Its failings and limitations are recollected through this prism, which juxtaposes scholars' efforts to bolster a crumbling liberalism with the racialized entry controls of 1962.[178] Here, I seek to excavate the early Cold War origins of the study of race and migration in the 1950s, and to highlight the durability of this era. This longer history helps us to see race relations in Britain through a global lens and understand how experts sought to isolate the domains of migration and decolonization.

The Institute of Race Relations began its life as part of the Royal

Institute of International Affairs (RIIA) at Chatham House. The RIIA, which received its royal charter in 1926, aimed to give the British public more information about international affairs, as public opinion was expected to play a greater diplomatic role in an age of mass democracy.[179] In 1950, the prominent Conservative editor of the *Sunday Times*, H.V. Hodson, delivered a talk at Chatham House on "Race Relations in the Commonwealth." He warned that racial tensions in South Africa would result in the rapid and disastrous spread of communism, which "appeals irresistibly to those who see their path blocked on the lines of Western democracy." In battling the Soviets for the African soul, Hodson argued that Britain was disadvantaged by its "deep and vast" ignorance about race relations. Yet all was not lost. The Commonwealth offered a "unique laboratory for life-size political experiment, while imperial authority still enables the experiment to be controlled."[180]

The Institute of Race Relations was forged in the crucible of the Cold War, against the backdrop of the war in Korea. But not everyone was persuaded that the global study of race was a Cold War imperative. Sir Hilary Blood, the governor of Mauritius, warned that such an institute "would merely serve to draw attention to differences, the cure for which was to forget them."[181] Hodson scaled back to a more modest proposal for an institute at Chatham House, funded by more than a dozen South African mining companies that were troubled by anticolonial activity in the Copperbelt.

In 1952, the RIIA appointed a Board of Studies on Race Relations. The board was directed by Philip Mason, a longtime member of the Indian Civil Service. He was not a social scientist. Indeed, he portrayed himself as the consummate critic of expertise. He believed it was precisely the absence of expertise that had allowed some 1,200 Britons to rule successfully over millions of Indians: "we were amateurs—all-rounders, none of us specialists. We were taught never to say no to responsibility nor to any kind of job. We might know nothing about it but we could find out and apply common sense."[182] In 1958, under Mason's direction, the Institute of Race Relations broke with the RIIA and became autonomous. Its corporate sponsorship increased, as Mason successfully convinced British business owners that good race relations were essential to the export economy.[183]

At this point, "race relations" was still described simply as a vital aspect of international affairs. Migration had no place in the discussion.[184] The board assumed that it was concerned only with "the causes of the strange things that happened in South Africa and Alabama." The British, presumably, were tolerant and easygoing.[185] Mason faced objections at Chatham House when he tried to connect his research on Rhodesia and Kenya to the troubles of West Indians or Asians in Britain. Early IRR publications addressed racial problems in Soviet Muslim Asia, the Algerian War, and Indians in Fiji.[186] Research on migrations that did not overtly involve race—for example, a study of the German minority in Alsace—were often rejected. Mason stressed that universities should have separate units on domestic and international race relations.[187] Again, American funding proved crucial. The Ford Foundation gave £350,000 for an international unit on race relations and £50,000 for a domestic one.

The formalized study of race in Britain was not initially driven by the presence of migrants of color, but rather by the global transformations that accompanied decolonization. Originally, it was not "about" migration at all, nor indeed about race in Britain, but about how race relations shaped the trajectory of communism in a collapsing empire. Indeed, the IRR newsletter focused exclusively on global events until 1961, when it began to address racism in Britain. At this stage, race within Britain was invisible to the IRR's practitioners. As the reach of the IRR extended to Britain itself, race relations were hived off from international relations. At the same time, the migrant was racialized in new ways, as the IRR crafted a framework that understood people of color in Britain as migrants.

At the heart of the IRR was the notion of interdisciplinarity. But disciplinary synthesis was no simple task. The institute's scholars disagreed about whether the key to race relations lay in individual human personality or social forces that could be understood through statistics. Mason invited biologists, economists, lawyers, and trade unionists to participate, but this breadth was never achieved. Social anthropologists, psychologists, and sociologists led the enterprise. Along the way were numerous missteps and failed projects. The director of Shell Oil offered £1 million to produce an anthropologically informed guide for its regional managers who now had to negotiate with African politicians. The guide would explain "what made Africans tick," and would be based on a massive investigation of thirty African regions, each with its own team of anthropologists (two white and one black) to research the history, ethnic and linguistic background, and present needs of the area. Mason rejected the project, claiming that there were not enough black anthropologists to staff the study.[188]

The culminating moment of the IRR's work, when race and migration were most closely elided, came with the publication of E. J. B. Rose's *Colour and Citizenship* in 1969. Rose, who had served as the literary editor of the *Observer,* had no obvious credentials for this massive survey; he had a classical education, although he did work with Edward Shils at Cambridge and was influenced by Gunnar Myrdal's famed study of race in the United States, *An American Dilemma: The Negro Problem and Modern Democracy* (1944). For his own undertaking, conceived as "a Myrdal for Britain," Rose commissioned forty-one separate research projects: the largest program of planned social research conducted since the Second World War.[189] His researchers visited villages in the Punjab from which Sikhs in Britain had come, and toured five countries in the Caribbean, aided by West Indian graduates of the LSE. The publication of *Colour and Citizenship* was a major media event. The *Observer* published a cartoon of Enoch Powell sprawling downstairs, hit on the back of the head with the book, and lamenting "Lies. Damn lies and statistics." Here, expertise was conceived as an effective rejoinder to racism. With this publication of Rose's volume, race and migration had become inseparable.

The invention of the migrant offered a way for different disciplines to articulate their missions and methods, to capture state resources, and to offer their own distinctive interventions. Each disciplinary framework pictured the migrant in its own terms. Social anthropology dealt with migrants as abstractions, or ideal types. Psychology and psychiatry focused on the individual as the dominant unit of analysis, and sociology emphasized the role of place and community. The Institute of Race Relations tried—and failed—to combine all of these approaches.

In an age of decolonization, the migrant was the ultimate expert creation. Each discipline, however, pictured the migrant in its own terms. Anthropology emphasized the positive ability of migrants to adapt to rapidly shifting cultures, but psychology and psychiatry were more pessimistic about migration, trafficking primarily in images of pathology for hosts and migrants alike. Yet these sciences were also more ecumenical in the populations they encompassed, extending their reach to the Irish, EVWs, and white Britons in the antipodes. Psy was also most effective in translating its theories into state policy, particularly in the realm of repatriation. These competing forms of expertise were simultaneous, not successive, although anthropology—which had taken the most optimistic stance about migrants' adaptability—had largely disappeared as a way of making sense of migration by the 1960s.

All of these experts insisted on key myths of the migrations of their era: notably, that these migrations were unprecedented, and that they were automatically galvanized by (but otherwise unrelated to) the transformations of independence. Such myths allowed, among other things, the persistent, if misleading notion that the decolonizing state was unified, and that decolonization itself could be understood as a single process, in which all roads led to Britain. Looking beneath these myths, to the hierarchies and unevenness of migrations that experts sought both to establish and to obscure, can reveal more fully the precise nature of the link between migration and decolonization.

In the next chapter, I turn from birth to youth, a phase of life that postwar experts described as both uniquely troubling and potentially redemptive. Like migrants, youths in the post-imperial world were perceived to possess their own distinctive promises and pathologies. As the anthropologists John and Jean Comaroff have suggested, youth are complex signifiers, the stuff of mythic extremes, simultaneously idealizations and monstrosities, problems and panaceas. They stand for many things at once: the terrors of the present, the errors of the past, the prospect of a future.[190] The Comaroffs propose that we need to dig deeper into the archaeology of the category of youth, which bespeaks a submerged history of the imperial underbelly of modernity itself. These next two chapters aim to do just that.

2. Young Britons

International Aid and "Development" in the Age of the Adolescent

In the summer of 1958, Christopher Tipple, a Yorkshire grammar-school boy of nineteen whose parents had never left England, boarded an airplane for Kwame Nkrumah's Ghana. Tipple had already won a place to read history at Oxford, but returned servicemen had priority and he faced a two-year delay before he could take up his spot. In his Sunday paper, he spied a letter from the Bishop of Portsmouth calling for British boys to participate in a new international aid scheme, the Voluntary Service Overseas (VSO). After an interview, Tipple was selected to teach English at a Ghanaian secondary school for £1 a week. As one of the first VSOs (figure 1), Tipple bore witness both to the final days of British rule in Ghana and to the initial "confident flush" of African independence: "Nkrumah was everywhere . . . Streets had been renamed, and his picture stared at you from every hoarding. Yet there was no antagonism to the British or a white face. On the contrary, there was universal friendliness mingled with some incredulity at these young men who had simply come to help and not to rule or to trade."[1]

The earliest VSOs were widely celebrated in Britain as the new heroes of a postimperial age. Eager reporters tracked their journeys, and they were feted with interviews on the BBC, luxurious luncheons with the colonial secretary, and tea with the queen. They were lionized specifically for their youth, enthusiasm, and absence of expertise, qualities that would soon contrast sharply with the technocratic juggernaut of the American Peace Corps. The first eighteen volunteers who went out in 1958 to Ghana, Nigeria, and Sarawak were succeeded by sixty more the following year, aided by a £9,000 grant from the Colonial Development and Welfare Fund and free passages from the Royal Air Force.[2] Industrial

Figure 1. Chris Tipple teaching in Akropong, Ghana. Note the poster in the background, "Britain's Age of Atomic Achievement." (Reproduced by permission of Chris Tipple)

firms, such as Esso and Shell, also supported the volunteers, who cost around £550 each.[3]

VSO's founders, Alec and Mora Dickson (figure 2), conceived of it as an outlet for the energies of elite British youths after National Service began its phase-out in 1957.[4] Under National Service, implemented in 1949, every healthy male between the ages of seventeen and twenty-one was required to serve in the armed forces for eighteen months, and to remain in the reserves for four years. This peacetime conscription absorbed some 2.5 million young men, a transformative social experience for this age group.[5] National Servicemen were deployed in the military operations that signaled the empire's final days in Cyprus, Malaya, and Kenya. Before its demise, National Service had been criticized for breaking up family loyalties, unsettling the young, and raising the juvenile crime rate. But in its absence, these problems did not disappear, and calls for a new form of overseas service set in quickly.[6]

VSO diverged from National Service in important ways. National Servicemen frequently oversaw the violence of decolonization. By con-

Figure 2.   Alec and Mora Dickson. (Reproduced by permission of Dick Bird)

trast, VSOs were supposed to preserve the spirit of imperial adventure, while also forging new types of postimperial relationships. Furthermore, one of the key elements of National Service was its universality. But VSO was never intended to encompass all young people, and its leadership constantly debated the question of *which* youths should be drawn into its orbit. The premise of VSO was that British teenagers lacked the chance to develop their characters fully, because they were sheltered from the demands of service by affluence and the provisions of the welfare state. At the same time, the Dicksons argued, young elites in the newly (or soon-to-be) independent nations of Africa and Asia had ample opportunities for service but little desire to give it. The aim of VSO was not simply to improve young British elites by exposing them to the poverty of the Third World, but also to bond them with other elite populations that happened to be located in Africa and Asia.[7] In this new global culture of youth, elite young Britons—along with their equally elite counterparts in the former colonies—would be reoriented toward serving others. This proposed symmetry of interest between First and Third World youths proved difficult to maintain.

With the possible exception of its violence, the history of decolonization—in striking contrast to its predecessors—has been strangely devoid of inner life, stripped of its emotional content by its chroniclers. This chapter considers how key players in the 1950s and 1960s understood decolonization in affective terms, and also how decolonization might be read generationally.[8] Colonial regimes had imposed a wide range of interventions in the affective lives of those they ruled. How did Britons anticipate that independence might change these interventions, render them unnecessary or out of date, or warrant new forms of intrusion? Would decolonization conjure new feelings, along with new leaders and states, and what role was feeling expected to play in the making of the new world order? How could emotional connections between populations be forged when the decolonizing state was increasingly committed to policies of non-intervention and withdrawal?

In exploring the status of sentiment in the context of imperial collapses and reconfigurations, this chapter analyzes the postwar discourse and critique of development. The existence of groups that aimed to engage young people with international affairs was not unique to Britain. Between 1958 and 1965, nearly every industrialized nation started volunteer programs to spread the message of economic development and goodwill. By far the largest of these was the American Peace Corps, created in 1961. Overseas development programs were linked by their efforts to inculcate the martial virtues of self-sacrifice and self-discipline, while also promoting international amity during the Cold War.[9]

To some extent, VSO simply reflected this broader culture of international aid. But it also spoke to a distinctively British set of anxieties and aspirations, a short-lived but intense valorization of the politics of youth, and the particular constellation of class, race, and generation that took shape in 1950s and 1960s Britain. If the Peace Corps sought to reassure critics that America's power could be matched by its humanitarianism, then VSO championed a very different impulse: one that was shaped by the loss of global supremacy rather than its acquisition.

Recently scholars have described development as an intellectual embarrassment, a philosophically moribund instrument of imperial control.[10] But reports of the death of development are perhaps exaggerated, partly because they are based on an overly simplistic account of development in the first place. My aim is neither to justify nor to condemn development, but to explore its multifaceted nature. Indeed, the enduring power of development has stemmed partly from its conceptual flexibility. In VSO, we can see both an ongoing British ambivalence toward development, and the richly contradictory and changeable nature of development itself. These contradictions were engendered not only because of Britain's economic limitations, but also because of a host of ideological divisions regarding development's aims: whether it should be directed toward elites or the masses, and whether metropolitan citizens could be reformed in the same ways as their counterparts abroad. This chapter thus seeks to understand more fully the complexity of development discourse, which was never as crude or univocal as it has typically been portrayed.

At first glance, VSO would seem to have been resolutely out of step with its time. Under the Colonial Development and Welfare Act of 1940, the British government committed itself to provide direct subventions of aid in order to improve colonial living standards. This pledge opened up a new space for British technocratic experts in Africa and Asia, which sustained the imperial mission during the postwar years.[11] The model colonial official of the 1920s, who knew his natives, was supplanted in the 1950s by the technical expert who knew his field.[12] Expertise was crucial to the culture of development, articulating the notion of social life as a technical problem that could be entrusted to a group of impartial credentialed individuals with specialized knowledge.[13] In Britain, the expert had come to represent the meritocracy's ideal citizen.[14]

Given this wider culture of hypervaluing the expert, VSO's insistence on a cadre of young amateurs seems counterintuitive, even mystifying. How did this vision of youth gain traction in the age of expertise? Or, to put the question another way, what was the function of the anti-expert in the age of Cold War? Although the Cold War has typically been associated with the dominance of expertise, the story of VSO illustrates the diversity of the Cold War's energies and the multiplicity of ways in which it was waged. The implied rejection of the expert espoused in the early years of VSO can be read not only in global terms—that is, as a disavowal of American technical expertise (and, ultimately, the launching of the Peace Corps)—but also as part of more localized critique of the planned society at home, which was perceived to have created a dissolute and unresponsive generation.[15]

The Dicksons' emphasis on reforming elites was not unique. American modernization theorists had long recommended focusing the energies of the technocratic state on the best and brightest individuals in the developing world, who might bend the masses to their will. In Britain, the meritocratic ideal, or the view that prosperous society required elites whose power was based on earned superiorities rather than inherited privileges, was a key assumption of postwar politics.[16] But the Dicksons' vision was distinguished by its explicit rejection of technocracy. Their elites were never supposed to be highly trained specialists. Rather, they were to be anti-experts, the virtues of which could be difficult to parse. In this context, critiques of expertise became a high-stakes affair, closely allied with the decolonizing state.

Given that development studies emerged out of analyses of class, it is compelling to see how schemes such as VSO were themselves structured by class divisions. In forging bonds between elite Britons and Africans, VSO sustained class distinctions among young Britons. VSO's short-lived efforts to incorporate working-class Britons as industrial apprentices engendered a host of contradictions. One of the prevailing sociological truisms of the postwar years—that generation was replacing class as the most significant division in British society—was countered by ongoing socioeconomic tensions in the realm of overseas aid. The reformulation of class was enacted on a global stage in ways that both resonated with and diverged from its metropolitan history.

This chapter explores Britain's youth politics as part of the reanimation of global policy in the 1950s and 1960s. According to its proponents, VSO could resolve the ills of postwar society, from the instability engendered by decolonization and communism to the aimlessness of affluent youths around the globe. Most important, it promised to restore both First and Third World youths to their appropriate place in the life cycle, in which they could function as vital members of society. Such claims rested on the invention of "youth" as an analytic category, which could be used to narrate the twinned politics of Britain's Cold War and the afterlife of empire.

WHO WAS "YOUNG"? AGE GROUPS IN POSTWAR BRITAIN AND AFRICA

The postwar baby boom focused unprecedented levels of attention on young people in Britain. By 1963, there were 800,000 more teenagers in the British population than there had been the decade before.[17] The number of university students also skyrocketed; there were 60 percent more students in British universities in 1964 than there had been in 1950. The notion that a "generation gap" had largely replaced socioeconomic divisions, although not universally accepted, became an important conceptual framework for both major political parties. Labour and Conservative leaders shared a firm belief in the uniqueness of postwar youth, and concern about its impact on electoral politics.[18] Within postwar social science, the young figured as "strangers," a distinctive political and sociological group.[19]

At the same time, young people were widely perceived as possessing a particularly privileged form of social capital.[20] Especially with regard to the Cold War, youth was seen as having a positive and irreplaceable value. One of Alec Dickson's persistent beliefs was that the generation gap mirrored the unequal relationship between First and Third Worlds. For him, as for many others, youth was the central problem of the era and yet also the remedy—both the pathology and the cure of the postwar years.

Ever since the 1950s, British sociologists and historians have interpreted the "teenager" as an internal product of the affluent society, whose relevance is limited to a stock set of themes: consumerism, delinquency, sexual permissiveness. The history of youth in Britain has been circumscribed as a metropolitan, or perhaps transatlantic story. What was distinctive about Alec Dickson, and what helps to explain the currency of his ideas in British officialdom, was his conceptualization of "youth" as an issue of international relations that was inextricably bound up with the trajectory of empire. He interwove the conventional postwar themes (youth, adolescence, welfare) with a powerful argument about the opportunities engendered by decolonization. Compellingly, he convinced young Britons that their own lives were affected by decolonization, and that they should reshape their lives to meet its distinctive demands. Through his schemes, the politics of youth in Britain were situated in a global frame.

In examining the Dicksons' plans to unite the young elites of the First and Third Worlds, and the reasons why these projects captured the state's imagination at a specific historical moment, we can revaluate the discourse of "youth" as one that was intimately engaged with the broader question of Britain's changing role in the world. The idea that young Britons required reform affected the particular types of aid that Britain offered abroad. The concept of youth was no less fraught for young Britons than for the African and Asian elites they were supposed to befriend. This framework helps to explain the intensity of the anxieties and hopes that were invested in young Britons during the 1950s and 1960s, which were both global and highly localized.

Alec Dickson viewed youth politics as an essential component in the war of ideas between East and West. He sought to resolve the problem of disaffected youth on a global scale, and in multiple locales. Without the active engagement of Western youth with anticommunism, he warned, "not all the millions of a Ford Foundation, backed by a vague benevolence, can avail us."[21] The relevance of youth to the Cold War was underscored by demographic research. One set of statistics, which became a veritable obsession for British policymakers, claimed that over 50 percent of the Southeast Asian population was under the age of 20.[22] The 1951 elections in Nigeria had revealed that adult males no longer elected "illiterate greybeards," but chose instead the young school teachers whose power extended beyond their own age group.[23] Authority in the Third World appeared to belong to the young. The Colonial Office saw these new leaders as subversive and difficult to control, with little allegiance to the Commonwealth.[24] Decolonization had prompted its own revolutions in the political life cycle.

But what exactly *was* "youth"? There was no consensus on this question, nor was there a government department directly responsible for "Youth" per se. A Cabinet list of "Things to Do" regarding Commonwealth youth included the hazy instruction, "establish what is meant by 'young people.'"[25] As one official wrote, "like the elephant, [youth] is easier to recognize than define, and even when identified it is far from clear how it concerns the Government."[26] Colonial rule inherited indigenous frameworks of age groups, but offered alternative visions of what constituted responsible behavior at each stage.[27] In colonial Africa, adolescence was an elite category of identity, which was applied only to advanced students and young people with semipermanent urban residency.[28] In the 1950s and 1960s, British officials in Africa deployed the label of "youth" as a euphemism for rebelliousness rather than as a strict descriptor of biological age. Youth carried a special charge in the late colonial era, in which it seemed to promise economic and social vitalization, but also told a more troubling story about imperial time. Were colonized subjects "frozen" in adolescence, or could they progress to adulthood? Debates about the role of youth in colonial society registered the temporal and political contradictions of colonialism as a discourse of progress.[29]

For Dickson, "youth" meant anyone from the age of fourteen to twenty-five, but then again some of the African participants in his leadership programs were as old as thirty-nine—and difficult to describe as "young," especially given life expectancies in Africa. Dickson adopted what he saw as a canonical sociological definition of youth: that is, a group that had completed compulsory schooling but had not fully entered into adult responsibilities. He was also interested in psychological conceptions of youth as a period of preparation, of waiting, of enthusiasm, impatience, and idealism.[30] Dickson did not frequently cite psychologists in his own writing, and VSO was much less closely engaged with psychological testing than was the Peace Corps. But he did read widely about individual development. In some sense, developmental psychology provided a means and a language for him to intervene in the technocratic approach to economic development that he feared might otherwise dominate British endeavors abroad. He was critical of what he saw as a neglect of the domain of feeling within particular realms of expertise, such as the rising field of development studies. His critiques of these forms of expertise found their own audience with the decolonizing state. The success of VSO highlights the breadth of the state's own understanding of "development," and the wide range of players it called upon in order to promote it.

As Dickson recognized, "youth" carried a considerable charge, both in terms of attracting resources and as a way to understand new forms of power in Africa. Dickson borrowed this politically freighted category to describe those who were "young" only in the sense of being new to the prospect of political leadership. For Dickson, "youth" was overwhelmingly the province of the elite, both for Britons and for Africans.[31]

Dickson believed that decolonization and the welfare state had jointly disrupted the natural progression of the life cycle in metropole and former colony alike. Because young people in the First and Third Worlds were growing up either too quickly or too slowly, personal development and national development had gotten out of joint. One aim of VSO was to encourage young people in both sites to restore each other to their appropriate phases of development through carefully scripted (though seemingly "natural") interactions.

The next section of this chapter focuses on the prehistory of VSO: specifically, the Dicksons' work during and after the Second World War in Africa. It was here that they feared the effects of development the most. If Africa proved to be a compelling, if frustrating site for development projects, then so here too did the Dicksons' critiques of large-scale development find their most elaborate expression. By tracing the Dicksons' literal and symbolic journeys between Africa and Britain (and their conceptualization of the changing relationship between the First and Third Worlds), we can see the multiple diagnoses they made, and the cures they proposed, for the pathologies of their era.

BEFORE VSO: THE DICKSONS GO TO AFRICA

Alec and Mora Dickson often recounted how VSO was inspired by their work with young people in Hungary in 1956. They had witnessed the ingenuity of student volunteers, who procured an inflatable boat to ferry

Hungarian refugees to safety. According to this narrative, VSO was rooted firmly in the Cold War—namely, in the sight of brave teenagers tackling the Soviet threat. Such a tale gave a moral urgency to VSO, although the details may have been apocryphal.[32] There was, however, a different point of origin for VSO, one with a genealogy that was perhaps less heroic but was more intimately connected with the trajectory of decolonization: the Dicksons' youth work in Africa, especially Nigeria. Before they turned their attention to young Britons, the Dicksons struggled to engage African youths with an ethos of service that was closely linked to the demands of independence.

During the Second World War, Alec Dickson, formerly a journalist, organized a mobile propaganda unit designed to convince African audiences to support Britain's war effort.[33] The unit traveled through Tanganyika, Uganda, Nyasaland, Northern Rhodesia, and Kenya, and its theatrical performances were witnessed by almost three-quarters of a million people:

> The Union Jack tied to a Masai spear was planted proudly in the centre of the showground. As a dramatic opening a runner would appear over the horizon, and an Askari, naked except for a loin cloth, carried a cut stick with a message in it. Panting he flung himself at the knees of the senior Chief. Meanwhile, far away out of sight, the sound of a motorcycle revving at speed was heard. In seconds the runner was replaced before the Chief by machine and crash helmeted rider saluting and handing over his message. The old and the new.[34]

The performance included displays of physical training, which Dickson favored over technological bravura. Wireless receiving sets and Bren guns could astound local audiences but might make Africans despair at the inadequacy of their own contributions to the war. Physical hardiness and dexterity, however, could be attained by all.

Colonial officials admired Dickson's work and hoped to deploy this kind of propaganda in peacetime for mass education. Dickson went to work with displaced persons in Berlin, but his interest in African youth persisted. Under the supervision of a community development leader, E. R. Chadwick, Alec created a leadership training program for young Nigerians. The Man O'War Bay Centre was inaugurated in 1952, just as the drafting of a new constitution took Nigeria closer to self-government. The program was inspired by Alec's experience on an Ibo bridge-building project, at which illiterates had carried out the manual labor while students stood idly by. Unlike many of his colleagues, Dickson believed that it was the students—not the workers—who needed to be retrained: "the village still had much to teach even those who felt themselves to have developed beyond it."[35]

Dickson argued that Britain had routinely misunderstood the kind of aid that would create political stability in Africa. The question was not how to build a bridge, but how to create the kind of person who wanted to build a bridge for others. In his view, technical aid was not only ineffective, it was plebian. The ubiquitous Oxfam posters of hungry children did not capture the true nature of modern Africa's distress. The real portrait of the needy, Dickson suggested, was to be found in "a school-leaver staring at a 'No Vacancies' notice outside some office." The most vital goal was to "break down the pathetic conceit of many young educated Africans." Without such psychological retraining, schoolboys could become the "Spoilt Aristocrats" of a new Africa.[36]

Rather than encouraging learning in greater numbers, Dickson aimed to strengthen the character of the educated few. In his view, it was dangerous to offer schooling to young men who had been emasculated by colonialism without demanding anything from them in return. Furthermore, education disrupted the African life cycle by artificially accelerating a young man's rise over his elders rather than ushering him through carefully ordered stages of advancement.[37] For these reasons, Alec denounced lavish expenditures on the new African universities. Formal education, he argued, was incompatible with true leadership: "Will it be here that the African equivalent of the Oxford and Bermondsey Boys' Clubs . . . will rise amid the tin-roofed shacks of Ibadan, Makerere and Accra? Or will these neon-lit conditions—so fantastically insulated against the surrounding bush of Africa—lead to the emergence of a class of smug and self-satisfied young men, regarding the privilege of education as the right to expect service from others rather than the chance to render it?"[38] The Dicksons established the Man O'War Bay program in order to respond to the perceived challenges posed by and to educated youths in an era of impending self-government. Located on a derelict banana plantation, four miles from Victoria, the site had once had sheltered vessels ("men o' war") that worked to suppress the slave trade. Stunning vistas of Mount Cameroon were intended to convey a sense of the daunting physical and mental tasks that would accompany independence. Alec later regretted the location, which was ideal for adventure training, but poorly situated for community development work. The Bakweri villagers, whom Alec criticized for their "social anemia," and declared "dead to any form of self-help," proved remarkably unimpressed by the program.[39]

At Man O'War Bay, educated young men joined in a series of physical and mental tests for one month in order to prepare them for leadership roles in their communities.[40] Recruitment circulars were sent to district officers, missions, schools, and commercial firms, encouraging them to nominate anyone who demonstrated a special "spark" of responsibility.[41] Participants were typically between the ages of eighteen and thirty. Dickson had considered targeting younger, more malleable boys. But he decided that Africa's greatest need was to train the trainers: that is, to inspire those who were already manifesting the qualities of leadership. His definition of who counted as "young," therefore, was shaped by his perception of decolonization's immediate demands.

Alec required all participants to speak English, which demanded a certain uniformity of educational background. As he said, "we cannot make fine swords out of scrap metal: but if well-tempered blades are sent, we can, we feel, put a keen edge on them."[42] But the program was regionally diverse, and Alec stressed that his program was one of the few places where people from all over Nigeria worked together. One official praised Man O'War Bay for breaking down the students' "tribal" jealousies and helping to "strip off the corsets of self-deception which most Yoruba and Ibo seem to wear."[43]

In its first two years, Man O'War Bay trained 400 men. The program was based on the notion that abstract virtues of citizenship were best forged from a period of physical discomfort and mental terror. Students learned how to make incinerators, work with picks and shovels, swim, build dams, and fight fire. Each man kept a diary on questions such as, "Will the day ever come when Africans climb mountains for fun?" or "Could slavery return?" Mora, a Scottish-born painter and poet, also had the students weave on looms they had built themselves, urging elites to preserve manual crafts. The students then decamped to the bush to aid villagers with road or bridge construction for another two weeks. The community development schemes were widely criticized, and projects were often left unfinished. The Dicksons acknowledged that the participants could not acquire extensive technical skills in such a short period, but sought only to inspire elites to feel kinship with laborers. Ultimately, the community development aspect of the program was sacrificed in favor of individual character training.

In designing the Man O'War Bay curriculum, Alec drew on his wartime experience as a propaganda specialist to lend an air of drama. One exercise called "Civil Crisis" involved a staged surprise interruption—a report of a typhoid fever outbreak, a man running amok, an airplane crash. Prepared in deep secrecy, these exercises were designed to create panic.

Alec believed that theatrical devices were essential to break the students' reliance on white administrators, paving the way for Africanization.[44] The culminating task was the ascent of Mount Cameroon, a treacherous volcanic peak of 13,350 feet. In 1952, two Man O'War Bay students died on the climb. The medical examiner reported that the boys had perished of fright.[45] Mora was shocked by the behavior of the other students, who refused to give artificial respiration and held an "indignation meeting" thereafter. She concluded, "how can you guard against this very African 'will to die?'"[46] The Nigerian press was outraged, and the program nearly came to an end.[47]

Students often vigorously resisted the physical training at Man O'War Bay; several men would not learn to swim.[48] One group appeared for a boating race not in the center's regulation shorts and singlets, but defiantly garbed in their own stylish clothes, with dark glasses and natty Panama hats.[49] The center's focus on manual labor was also highly contentious.[50] The Dicksons saw the denigration of manual labor in West Africa as a terrible legacy of colonial rule, and hoped that students would be stirred by the sight of white Britons wielding shovels with them. But even these edifying images often failed to inspire. There was an ongoing struggle between students who sought to preserve their status as elites and the program leadership, which valued the humblest tasks of nation building. Mora was intensely disappointed when her students refused to participate in building of a footbridge in Zaria. She consoled herself that "at least we left our students with uneasy consciences about the things they left undone and this was always a first step. The grit of this small shame embedded among the splendid dreams of self-government might, someday, produce a pearl."[51]

In 1954, the Man O'War Bay Centre began a course for schoolboys. The curriculum included "Smuggler's Evenings," at which Alec disguised himself as a villain in black greasepaint and surprised the boys while they were dining. The "attack" was followed by group sing-alongs, with American slave songs as part of the entertainment. Students and teachers dressed up as pirates, a venture that Mora acknowledged most Britons would find incomprehensible and childish. She zealously defended the technique of "shared fun," which "makes men forget what colour or race they are and returns them to an innocence which takes no account of these things."[52] The Dicksons saw these racialized masquerades distinguishing their own ventures from the more formalized realm of economic development and technical aid. In their view, postimperial relationships were best forged not only *by* the young, but also by acting as children.[53]

The Dicksons traveled widely for their youth work. Around the globe, they encountered resistance among educated youths to service based in manual labor. In Iraq, Alec was appalled by what he saw as the selfishness of young, urban Baghdadis. He vowed to wean educated youths from the abstractions of nationalism, showing that "the blistered hand, no less than the academic diploma, has its part to play in the formation of a genuine elite."[54] In Pakistan, Alec admitted that "I could have gladly smitten some of our young people here over the head with a shovel."[55] The concern with revitalizing elite youths and bonding them to one another—rather than, for example, succoring the poor—continued to differentiate the Dicksons' projects from contemporary economic development schemes.

One of the key influences on VSO was the Dicksons' visit to Sarawak (Borneo) in the South Pacific, where Alec's brother was the director of education.[56] The colonial history of Sarawak was very recent, as it had become a Crown colony in 1946. It was, as Mora pointed out, a multiracial society, but not an equiracial one; the Dayaks were economically and socially disadvantaged in relation to the Chinese and Malay, and 98 percent of the Sea Dayaks were illiterate. The Dicksons found the battles of Cold War education more overtly pitched in Sarawak than they had been in Nigeria; Mora wrote of Chinese schoolboys refusing to attend "picnics," because to them, this meant a communist indoctrination party. Alec feared that communism could easily fill the "spiritual vacuum" left by decolonization: "if we make no challenge and no call for service, others will: how greatly we err in considering Communism only as an economic phenomenon to be countered by measures for rising standards of living is shown in territories like Sarawak, where it is the student sons of rich Chinese merchants with everything to lose materially, who take to a guerilla existence in the jungle."[57]

Despite these political foibles, Alec and Mora were deeply impressed by the integration of young people in Sarawak into the communal life.[58] Indeed, it was this aspect of Sarawak's culture that provided crucial inspiration for VSO. In Mora's view, Sarawak boys benefited from living "within a recognized framework which gave them a definite position and status." One of social scientists' principal concerns about British youth was their segregation from the adult world.[59] Expected to undergo increasingly lengthy periods of formal education, they waited in limbo to become productive members of society. Sarawak offered an alternative vision. In a riff on the promise of the welfare state, Mora noted that life in a Sarawak longhouse was "an integrated whole from the cradle to the grave . . . there was no time when an age group was not aware of its responsibility to the entire house."[60] In Sarawak, the Dicksons saw how untrained youth played a communally significant role. Through VSO, they would seek to replicate that experience for young Britons.

BETWEEN TECHNICIANS AND TEDDY BOYS: AGE AND CLASS IN VSO'S EARLY YEARS

Despite his frustrations, Alec always believed that the challenges facing young Third Worlders were surmountable, partly because he thought that indigenous traditions of communitarianism would be easily revived. The moral plight of young Britons was another matter. It is easy to forget that idleness—along with want, disease, ignorance, and squalor—was one of the five giants that Sir William Beveridge's welfare programs sought to slay, and idleness could of course affect the privileged as much as the poor.[61] According to the Dicksons, the luxuries of affluence and the highly industrialized welfare state had deprived young people in Britain of the energizing wartime experience of responding to emergencies. British teenagers had few outlets for the heroic impulses that could catapult them to adulthood.[62] The challenge of exhorting British youths to ethical action would, they feared, be even greater than inspiring the young men of Man O'War Bay. Through VSO, the Dicksons sought to extend to British youths some of the transformative experiences they had already proffered to young people abroad, while also taking note of young Britons' distinctive needs. If overseas aid could resolve the generation gap, then youth could redress the pains engendered by independence.

For the Dicksons, both welfare and decolonization required new forms of social relationships, which had to be enacted on a global stage. On this point, they were in line with many contemporaries, who believed that welfare's true potency—as well as its pitfalls—were psychological and social, rather than fiscal or material. Economic redistributions had been anticipated in earlier eras, but the promise of truly universal citizenship in a social democracy that institutionalized the principle of mutual care was a more compelling change.[63] Under the regime of the welfare state, all Britons were to be transformed into both givers and receivers of aid. For Richard Titmuss, one of welfare's chief theorists, the epitome of welfare was not a financial benefit but the blood donor service, in which one citizen voluntarily gave a lifesaving resource to another.[64] Many of the welfare state's architects viewed it as empowering people to manifest concern for each other, which would be manifested in people's daily interactions. The reduction of economic inequality was important primarily

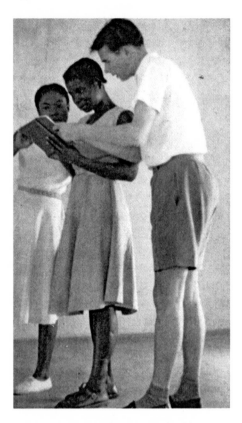

Figure 3.   VSOs rehearsing a Chekhov
production in Ghana. (Reproduced by
permission of the National Archives)

to ensure the basis for a qualitative advance in human relations.[65] For the
Dicksons, the demands of decolonization provided an ideal opportunity
for Britons to correct the lassitude that welfare had engendered in themselves, and for Third Worlders to transform the lofty promises of political
independence into socially useful action.

In their first year, VSOs confronted the dizzying array of tasks that
accompanied decolonization, from emergency midwifery to soil conser-
vation, census taking and police work.[66] In this sense, decolonization provided an outlet and an opportunity to counter the idleness of elite youths
in a variety of locales. Most VSOs worked in education, but volunteers
also built boats in Papua, conducted the State Orchestra of Bolivia,
started college zoos and arranged libraries on the Dewey Decimal system
in Ghana, and supervised elections in Bechuanaland (figures 3 and 4).[67]

Figure 4. VSOs helping to build a community center in Jamaica. (Reproduced by permission of the National Archives)

The largest group of volunteers worked in Nigeria, but the sites of service quickly diversified even beyond the confines of the former empire, thus striving to ensure that Britain's role in the new world order would not be delimited by the imperial past.

Volunteers had to be medically fit and were supposed to be at least eighteen years old, although one member of the first group was actually seventeen. They served for twelve months and were provided with pocket money but no other pay. Typically, volunteers applied to VSO when they were in their final term at school and landed overseas in September. Alec preserved the spirit of adventure by keeping the assignments secret until the final moments of departure.[68] Training was minimal; one volunteer recalled being instructed only on how to build trench latrines.[69] Methods for teaching English, or any other subject, were not discussed, the assumption being that the volunteers' own educational background had prepared them to teach others.[70] In some sense, the sites of service were irrelevant; VSOs were not to become experts in particular fields and thus did not require knowledge tailored to specific regions. For this reason, although the Dicksons were concerned generally with the new social relations that they believed were demanded by independence, their vision of decolonization was largely undifferentiated; the political specificities of how decolonization worked in different parts of the empire did not weigh heavily upon them.

Alec urged that VSOs should be rigorously overworked rather than underemployed.[71] He believed that the true perils of service lay not in remote jungles but on African and Asian university campuses, where VSOs were "exposed to the hypercritical questioning of a sophisticated intelligentsia."[72] Precisely because of the frustrations that Alec had experienced in trying to interest elite Africans in physical labor, he stressed the significance of VSOs engaging in this type of work. One report on a VSO, William Crawley, at a boys' school in Nigeria, stressed his "welcome preparedness to engage in taxing manual activities," which was said to be slowly overcoming the resistance to such labor among the indigenous youths. William's readiness to cut grass, repair bicycles, and perform carpentry, along with his "engaging boyishness" and "artless lack of any form of Superiority," were all cited as inspiration for educated Africans. These tasks were important less for the material benefits they offered to others than for the humility and spirit of service they might inspire in those who undertook them.[73]

In 1959, VSO accepted its first female volunteers, who attracted considerable media attention. Althea Corden taught English, math, and first aid in Sarawak, and Bronwyn Quint taught domestic science in Kenya.[74] The experience of volunteering was intended to be transformative for girls as well, although these transformations were unpredictable. One VSO supervisor was shocked to see a teacher whom Alec Dickson had described as a "church mouse" turn up in Malaya in decidedly new spirits; she was now wearing green eye shadow and declared that she intended to go on the stage.[75] Although these young women figured prominently in both the positive and negative press about VSO, Alec Dickson's own cult of youth emphasized masculine traits, distancing VSO from earlier, female forms of philanthropy.[76] VSO's brand of philanthropy was more closely, if critically, entwined with welfarism, rejecting prior models of female voluntarism.

One of the first public figures to champion VSO was Robert Birley, the headmaster at Eton. Born in Midnapore at a time of fierce anti-British sentiment, Birley was raised in Bournemouth by his grandparents while his father toiled in the administration of West Bengal. As a history teacher at Eton, Birley also undertook social work in Slough. The Birleys acquired a left-wing reputation at Eton, although their political philosophy was rather mild. Critics described their "Soviet living room," which was actually one end of their drawing room, as they tried not to entertain too lavishly.[77] Originally, Birley had wanted more Eton boys to be ordained, and when this proved unsuccessful, he sought other ways to encourage a spirit of service at the school.

From 1958 to 1962, Eton boys represented the largest number of volunteers to VSO.[78] Most of the early VSOs were from public school backgrounds. More than half had been head prefects, and nearly all had places to take up at Oxford or Cambridge within a year.[79] At a 1962 training session, one public school volunteer amiably remarked that this was the first time he had ever met a grammar school boy. The motives for service were diverse; Michael Talibard, an eighteen-year-old from Jersey, looked forward to facing greater physical challenges overseas: a welcome change from the affluent society, "'where all you can die of is lung cancer or thrombosis.'"[80]

Part of VSO's appeal was that it proposed to restore adolescence to its appropriate moment in the life cycle, which had been artificially warped by British affluence. If "Third World" adolescents had no real childhood as it was understood in Europe, then their British counterparts seemed to suffer the opposite problem of prolonged juvenility. Until they acquired professional training, they were set apart from the real business of living except for their disproportionate consumer power.[81] Indeed, one reason that the Dicksons chose teenagers as the first group of VSOs was precisely because this group seemed to be in such desperate need of redemption.[82] As Mora wrote of the first VSOs, "they were boys who had thought of themselves as young men before they left England: now, when they were in truth young men, this new world brought out in them the humble recognition that they were still boys."[83]

It is important to emphasize the specificity of this promise. The VSO was not pledging to turn boys into men, but rather to capitalize upon their boyishness. The volunteer's distinctive contribution was his precarious balance between immaturity and adulthood, which was thought to mimic the psyche of developing countries. The Dicksons believed that adolescents were peculiarly suited to the task of bridging the gap between First and Third Worlds, in that they were nearest to the "emotional turbulence, yearnings, and perplexities" that characterized the collective psyche in newly independent nations.[84] British teenagers and independent Africans (of any age) could revel in and temper each other's enthusiasms.[85] Such interpretations both naturalized the political tensions of decolonization and repackaged these tensions as a generation gap.

This valorization of the adolescent marked a divergence from the paternalistic tropes of imperial days, in which indigenes were routinely infantilized. Adolescence was replacing childhood as the dominant rubric for conceptualizing political action in the former empire. Essential to the new world order was the notion that individuals and nations must move appropriately through developmental stages. In this sense, "development" was personal as well as economic and political. Youth, as the Dicksons saw it, offered a corrective to the imperial past, which had been grounded in unequal relations between colonial authorities and indigenes. Mora admitted that many of the tasks undertaken by VSOs might have been done more effectively by trained adults. Indeed, the receiving territories often derided the quality of VSO's material aid.[86] But teenagers possessed the priceless qualification of love that ran freely outside set channels, when the springs of affection were still unblocked.[87]

What kinds of new people would decolonization and welfare create? How would newly (or nearly) independent Africans and Asians interact with Britons who themselves were engaged with new levels of mutual dependency at home and abroad? The Dicksons were less concerned about feelings of aggression or dislocation that independence might engender than with how they might create a new spirit of communitarian service that colonialism had weakened.[88]

The crux of the VSO idea was not technical aid but international friendship. Technical aid was secondary to affective intimacy. Feelings of humility, followed by mutual amity, might produce material results, but these concrete gains were largely epiphenomenal. Recalling Man O'War Bay, the Dicksons emphasized games and play. VSOs were counseled to take an interest in boxing, especially in West Africa, "the cradle of British Empire featherweight champions."[89] A musical instrument could also be invaluable to "unlock" people in the West Indies. Mora suggested that the music need not be of the "Olde English" folk-tune sort; "even the songs from 'My Fair Lady' can be a hit," and she fondly recalled hearing "Que Sera Sera" sung by the local boys as they cut grass in Sarawak.[90] Scottish country dancing was also highly recommended, although Mora remarked disapprovingly that young people abroad were often more interested in English ballroom dancing. There could be significant tensions between what African and Asian elites wanted to learn about British culture and what VSO was willing to teach.

In rejecting the mantra of technical aid, Alec wrote, "No amount of foreign capital or gigantic dams can create a sense of nationhood, unless or until the educated youth of the country feel themselves to be involved, physically and emotionally: yet the young elite is not going to be prised away from its Baghdad-Bloomsbury axis through exhortations by middle-aged, expatriate experts."[91] Because large-scale development schemes relied on adult experts, they overlooked the emotionally transformative power of youth, and ignored the individual character of both the giver and the receiver of aid.

Crucially, the Dicksons believed that *what* volunteers did was less important than *how* they did it.[92] The high commissioner of Lagos argued that an enthusiastic young volunteer "is a more effective evangelist for his country than the average technical aid man who comes out here to show Nigerians how to spray for capsid beetles or how to file secret documents." Middle-aged civil servants, no matter how knowledgeable, held no sway over the hearts and minds of young nationalists coming to power.[93] Volunteers often asserted that the gains of independence were incomplete, because they left the social prejudices of the colonizers untouched. Thus, they sought to conduct a "wholly original experiment in human relations," transcending the psychological limits of political independence and forging new social bonds in the wake of decolonization.[94] "'You incredible British,'" an Indian education officer reportedly said to Alec in Madras, "'You left as rulers—and return as friends.'"[95]

Friends, perhaps, but of what kind? And how was this anticipated conversation—from ruler and ruled to friend—to take place? Leela Gandhi has fruitfully parsed the politics of the often secret and unacknowledged friendships and collaborations that united anticolonial thinkers in the metropole and colony. In some sense, the Dicksons sought to bring the rubric of colonial friendship into the light, and to instigate it in new forms.

In the colonial era, the term "friend" could serve as a metaphor for dissident cross-cultural collaboration. But the trope of friendship could carry new meanings in an age of decolonization. The friendships undertaken through VSO sought to replace a paternalistic regime with an (ultimately failed) regime of shared adolescence. In earlier eras, anticolonial activists had conceived of friendship as a powerful rejoinder to political structures of inequality.[96] Now, amity and sympathy were reframed as responses to new and increasingly equalizing political conditions, which might synchronize the psyches of former colonizers and former colonial subjects. Such friendships were not simply critiques of a bygone imperial state but were themselves linked to the rapidly evolving aims of the decolonizing state, with its own ambivalence toward the burdens of economic development.

VSO warned receiving territories that volunteers must not be used as status symbols. But some of its own projects belied these claims. In 1965, there was a public outcry in Britain over VSO's role in India's Sainik Schools, wealthy institutions created on the British pattern to produce an elite cadre of civil servants. VSO's participation in these schools seemed to counter the democratic tide that had accompanied independence. The VSO leadership claimed that these prestigious educational enterprises could actually make India more egalitarian by helping to create a stable middle class. That same year, the writer and broadcaster Ludovic Kennedy unflatteringly reported for the *Daily Telegraph* on his visit with two VSO girls in Nigeria, who kept ringing a bell for their servant (because, they said, it was too unladylike to yell for him), and enjoyed a four-course luncheon with soufflé for dessert.[97]

According to VSO field reports, some of the sharpest tensions that arose in aid work were between volunteers and their older white compatriots, who were reluctant to accept dramatic changes in relations between the races. Due to housing shortages, volunteers in Zambia were frequently obliged to lodge with these expatriates, who ridiculed their idealism and placed them under "severe psychological strain."[98] Several VSOs were urged by white settlers to sign lucrative contracts and "forget all that volunteer stuff."[99] Many British expatriates objected to the fact that VSOs turned up at formal gatherings disheveled and unwashed, often in indigenous dress. In Sarawak, VSOs gravely offended the white settler community by dining out in shorts. As Mora saw it, they had "let the side down because they were not on anybody's side . . . they were a transition kind of Briton, no longer a master, not quite a partner."[100]

For Alec, these concerns about racial prestige were an outdated distraction from the more urgent demands of the Cold War. Although he dutifully cautioned volunteers to be careful about their dress and hygiene, he mused, "I cannot help feeling that what clothes are worn at night is not much of an answer to Mao Tse Tung in South-East Asia." He quoted one VSO in Northern Rhodesia, who said, "'It is not Communism that threatens Central Africa so much as pessimism.'"[101] Alec believed that VSO could offer a corrective to pessimism, which would in turn deter communism.

Although VSO was aimed primarily at the revitalization of indigenous elites, the psychological rehabilitation of local white communities was also of interest. Volunteers in Rhodesia and Kenya were explicitly instructed to engage with white settler youths, and to encourage them to join in work on African reserves. James Young, a Cambridge undergraduate who served in Northern Rhodesia, exhorted a group of school leavers that their task was not to campaign for the rights of black Africans alone, but to bring blacks and whites together.[102] The VSO's work with white youths in Africa addressed the organization's most persistent questions. Who was authorized to act as the agent of development? Who, exactly, was perceived to be at moral risk in a postimperial age? In 1960, VSO instituted a program for British industrial apprentices to serve overseas. The industrial apprentice program generated new tensions at VSO, as the drive to democratize overseas service and include working-class Britons was ultimately incompatible with Dickson's vision of young elites engaged in mutual revitalization around the world.

The apprentice program, sponsored by firms such as Rolls Royce and Shell, promised to strengthen Britain's overseas trade connections, and "to make it possible for the ordinary young man in industry to feel that he, personally, could have a stake in this kind of assistance to the underdeveloped countries." The hope was to ensure that faith in internationalism would not be limited to elites, but would spread to anyone who worked with "our Stan in Sarawak" or "our Jim in Jamaica."[103] Dickson was confident that working-class youths had voluntarist impulses, and that existing stereotypes of this group required revaluation. "Between the technician and the teddy-boy," Alec exhorted, "there is a gigantic middle stratum, which must be more significant than either."[104] The question was how to turn individuals who were seen as fiercely local in their sympathies toward the broader world: to pledge young industrial workers to an internationalism that was untainted by radical politics. If the problem with educated Africans was that they were too apt to forget their villages, then the young British worker was seen as too apt to remember his. Again, VSO aimed to correct both tendencies at once.

Dickson conceived of the industrial volunteer program as a rebirth of the *Wanderjahr*, the continental concept of apprenticeship enriched by experience in an unfamiliar setting.[105] Ideally, apprentices would return to Britain with "an added sense of responsibility, and an understanding of the fundamentals of life—poverty, hunger, sickness, etc. from which they are shielded to-day in our Welfare State."[106]

The first industrial volunteers were deployed to Kenya, designing artificial limbs for leper colonies.[107] James Hill, a sheet-metal worker, maintained the electrical equipment at a community development project in Ghana, and helped to breed disease-resistant poultry.[108] Colin Stevens served at the Nigerian Ministry of Works and Transport, where he rewired government buildings and aided in the fireworks displays for the independence celebrations.[109]

The Times reported that industrial apprentices proved "just as good in their own idiom" as public school volunteers.[110] But these apprentices did not always fare well in VSO's selection process, which weighted voluntary service (such as scouting) over technical skills. The VSO leadership believed that overseas service was more difficult for industrial apprentices than for public school boys, especially the experience of reentry to British life. The elite school leaver came back to the new experience of university that helped him over the difficult transition "home." But for the apprentice, Mora warned, life in Britain could suddenly feel routine or flat. He returned to the work bench, often having lost seniority, and felt that his peers did not value the service he had undertaken. Mora cited a high rate of "defections" among industrial volunteers, who turned to the church rather than continuing at their firm.[111] If VSO converted elite public school boys into virtuous leaders, then it seemed to ruin industrial apprentices for their work in Britain.

The idea that apprentices did not settle back into home life as easily as their public school counterparts was echoed at the Colonial Office and in the press.[112] Industrial volunteers were accustomed to a "firmly stratified" working environment, in which the young were seldom encouraged to exercise initiative and where the rules of unions and management tended to frustrate any independent thinking. When such young men found themselves in positions of considerable authority in VSO, they were unlikely to take kindly to returning to "being a kid on the shop floor, working for set hours at a limited pace for modest material rewards."[113]

From its inception, the apprentice program struggled. Although the idea of the philanthropic teddy boy captivated the British press, the alliance of elite school leavers and industrial workers was always uneasy. By 1967, despite numerous publicity campaigns, the number of apprentices had dropped sharply, and VSO's relations with trade unions had deteriorated.[114] Focusing on the socially elite background of VSO boys and girls was one way to distinguish British aid organizations from the Peace Corps. On the virtues of elite youths, Alec wrote: "Available for immediate service now is a boy from Eton with four 'S' levels in science and an Open Scholarship at Cambridge College: a superb musician and plucky games player—the grandson of [a well-known postwar cabinet minister]. To suppose that he is not good enough to teach at some secondary school in East Africa for a year—whereas some youth who has taken a heavens-knows-what degree at some university in the States is regarded as superior—seems madness."[115] Clearly, the young industrial worker had much to offer in terms of technical skills. But Alec was wary of stressing this point, which did not mesh well with his vision of international amity between young elites. The goal was not to teach the recipients of aid how to perform specific tasks, as in traditional development schemes, but to create the impulse in them to serve others. Here, Alec feared that industrial apprentices were less than inspirational. After all, technical aid was designed for the masses. Aimed at creating an orderly and prosperous peasantry, this form of aid belonged to precisely the same culture of development that Alec sought to reject or revamp.[116]

At Man O'War Bay, the Dicksons had proved remarkably naïve in trying to convince educated elites to act as laborers, a deeply resented aspect of the program. The industrial apprentice program proposed to reverse this equation. Although Dickson perceived manual labor as an important way to rehabilitate British and African elites, he was less sure about how to utilize those who had actual skills in this field. He was never confident that industrial apprentices had any kinship with the sophisticated young Africans and Asians they were supposed to reform. The centrality of sympathy in his schemes was supposed to be rooted in a sameness of privilege and status, even if "privilege" might mean different things in London and Lagos. Industrial apprentices, lacking this socioeconomic status in their communities of origin, would be unable to deliver on the promise of parity.

Nor did apprentices fit easily into Dickson's conception of youth as a state of potential and malleability. Despite their biological age, the apprentices did not conform to Dickson's view of the "young." Again, the problem was not with what the apprentices *did*, but with how they *felt*, or failed to feel. The element of kinship between elites was absent, Dickson feared, and without it, material contributions were rendered less meaningful. Essential to the VSO project was the notion that the young participants on both sides were natural companions because of their equivalent social rank. Industrial apprentices threatened to disrupt the affective ideals of the program.

One can see here the resurfacing of socioeconomic tensions in what was supposed to be the universalizing category of youth. Imagining the agents of development proved as fractious as determining its recipients.

For Dickson, the bonds of youth traveled far more easily across cultures and oceans than class. Undertaken precisely at the moment of social democracy's ostensible triumph, his schemes point to the reassertion of class hierarchies within the postcolony and the contestedness of the social democratic moment. Next, I examine a broader range of organizations that sought to deploy young people to further Britain's Cold War objectives, and consider the reasons why various schemes to galvanize youths for this purpose survived or collapsed.

COLD WAR ALTERNATIVES TO VSO: BRITISH PROPOSALS, GLOBAL REACTIONS

The early years of VSO coincided with a thicket of other proposals for engaging British youths in global affairs, all of which explored the nexus of youth politics, anticommunism, and postcolonial discontent.[117] Different players deployed the category of "youth" in order to capture Cold War energies and resources. But unlike VSO, most of these other movements quickly foundered. This section explores the distinctive appeal of the Dicksons' vision by considering why alternative movements appeared to be doomed.

Originally, all of these proposals conceived of overseas service for British youths and programs to encourage Commonwealth youths to come to Britain as complementary enterprises. In government circles, the flow of young people in both directions was understood as a key Cold War objective, which would defeat communism by increasing the sentimental attachments between First and Third World youths. In all of these movements, we can see the uneasy coexistence of anxiety and optimism that the British state displayed toward young people during the Cold War, and the persistent goal of using First and Third World youths to cure each other's pathologies.

The World Assembly of Youth (WAY) was established in 1948, largely on the initiative of the Labour foreign secretary and staunch anticommunist Ernest Bevin. It aimed to counter the considerable attractions of the Soviet World Federation of Democratic Youth, which claimed a membership of more than 100 million young people in 112 countries. According to the WAY Charter, the assembly was a democratic organization, which existed for the "true satisfaction of youth's needs and for the fulfillment of youth's responsibilities."[118] WAY articulated interracial respect as a crucial part of its mission. One of its first members was Peggy Cripps (later Mrs. Joseph Appiah and the mother of the philosopher Kwame Anthony

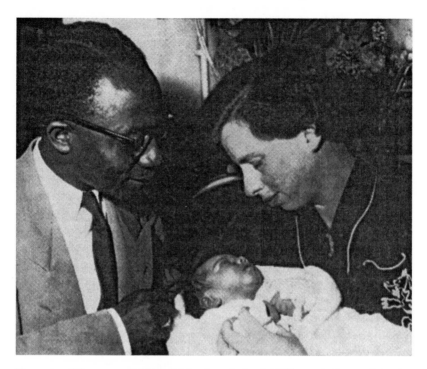

Figure 5. "Kwame, and Mr. and Mrs. Joseph Appiah" (formerly Peggy Cripps). This photograph, the first of many pictures of Kwame Appiah to be circulated in the British and African media, was taken at the hospital of St. John and St. Elizabeth in London. (*West African Review* 25 [June 1954]: 503)

Appiah), the daughter of the Labour politician Sir Stafford Cripps (figure 5). Peggy Cripps was one of the British delegates to the WAY conference in 1948 and was an energetic worker for racial unity in London.[119]

Despite Bevin's early leadership and the fact that one of its first presidents (1952–54) was a British citizen, Guthrie Moir, the British government's investment in WAY was never strong. The British National Committee (BNC) of WAY was continually plagued by financial woes, which severely limited its activities. Originally, the BNC was funded by the Ministry of Education (improbably, under the Social and Physical Training Grant Regulations).[120] This department was always ambivalent about its association with WAY, which it regarded as a propaganda machine.[121] In 1953, it insisted on severing its connection with WAY on the grounds that this brand of anticommunist work was not in keeping with the ministry's role as "the natural custodians of the young."[122]

The BNC quickly fell into arrears, and was unenthusiastically bailed out by the Foreign Office. There were always major doubts in governmental circles about its utility. In 1954, Treasury refused three applications from the Foreign Office (backed by the Colonial Office and the Commonwealth Relations Office) for aid to the BNC. The *Sunday Times* remarked that this disavowal of WAY seemed "a poor economy in a cold war."[123] Many Cold Warriors pleaded in vain with the Foreign Office to press WAY's case in Parliament.[124] Lady Mountbatten told Anthony Eden, then prime minister, that allowing British influence to fade from WAY was "little short of tragic."[125] As these pleas suggest, WAY did have powerful advocates. Alec Dickson himself was an early supporter. A WAY representative, T. B. Lawson, toured Man O'War Bay in 1952 and was greatly impressed. Lawson emphasized that Dickson should build students' individual consciences, which would better enable them to resist communism; he urged Alec to give the students more time for private reflection.[126]

Many officials doubted WAY's effectiveness as a barrier to communism; one critic dismissed WAY as "a playground for beardless extroverts."[127] The fact that WAY's funding was increasingly drawn from anticolonial American sources also struck many British officials as embarrassing.[128] Although British members of WAY insisted that they exerted considerable influence over African and Asian youth workers, reports from WAY conferences suggested a different balance of power.[129] After the 1960 meeting in Accra, the Foreign Office expressed concern that British representatives had voted for communist resolutions. The British delegation responded that it had been "swamped" by Africans, who had threatened to walk out if their demands were not met.[130]

Although WAY was intended to combat Soviet influence, its own allegiances to left-wing political platforms were always under investigation. Alec Dickson grew disenchanted with WAY as a "kind of junior Bandung, with young men from Africa and Asia passing resolutions denouncing Imperialism and showing a complete disinterest in youth work as we understand it." Alec warned the Colonial Office that the Soviets were dominating youth work, while WAY dissipated its energies on anticolonial theorizing.[131]

Alec's ambivalence toward WAY, which was widely shared, reflected the tensions between Cold War objectives and the processes of decolonization. The desire to mobilize British youths as a political force in the Cold War was continually hampered by Britain's own colonial history. Support for the BNC waned further as the image of young Britons intimidated by African and Asian nationalists circulated in the press. Few were willing to give up on WAY altogether, however, which meant that one of Britain's most prominent organizations for Cold War youth work was consistently hamstrung.

Yet there was more than one way to wage a Cold War. Cabinet also urged the recruitment of African and Asian children to British boarding schools to promote personal contacts among Commonwealth youth.[132] In 1958, just as Alec's first cadets were departing for Sarawak and West Africa, an interdepartmental committee began to plan a Commonwealth Youth Trust to increase Britain's commitment to the Commonwealth as a "live and developing organism."[133] The idea was to promote interracial friendship through scholarships, travel, work camps, and welfare centers.[134] Whereas adults might be inflexibly wedded to the imperial past, young people—who had never really known the empire at all—were more likely to invest in the new Commonwealth. The forging of sentimental ties between young people would strengthen the Commonwealth's economic interconnectedness, and avoid the "ignorance and insularity" that plagued adults.[135]

The trust's supporters emphasized that its commitment to multiracialism must be uncompromising, even if this principle conflicted with previous generation's norms. If the older members of a club threatened to resign if Africans were admitted, then the younger men should refuse to join unless they were.[136] Although such overt demands for racial equality might be dangerous if they were orchestrated by intemperate British youths, it was considered worth the risk to compete with the Soviets— who were happily unencumbered by the weight of colonial history.

The Colonial Office believed that the existing bodies of the Empire Youth Movement, which had flourished in interwar Britain, could be harnessed for this purpose.[137] For example, Major Frederick Ney's Commonwealth Youth Movement brought schoolchildren from different parts of the Commonwealth to tour Britain every summer. Ney, a hero of the First World War, styled these visits grandly as "Quests," during which young people, ages sixteen to nineteen, dined in stately homes, visited historical sites, and attended conferences on chivalry in the modern world.[138] The movement was unabashedly anachronistic; its slogan was, "First unto God and then to the Queen."[139] The Questers wore red blazers with the Union Jack on the shoulder, made by Harrods of specially dyed material. They held overnight vigils in churches, with Hindu, Muslim, and Christian youths praying together that they might dedicate their lives to the service of the great imperial family.[140]

Although the Colonial Office recognized that Ney's movement was unlikely to appeal to the new Commonwealth, the aim of uniting schoolchildren from the different territories was seen as highly valuable.[141] Ney described communism's appeal in uniting a restless, rudderless population of youths after the war. He promised Prime Minister Harold Macmillan that the Commonwealth Youth Movement could offer a countervailing crusade: "what the youth of Nazi Germany and of Communist Russia have done for an evil purpose, the youth of the Commonwealth can be led to do—and just as successfully—for the good of all."[142] In official circles, Ney was widely perceived as a liability, prone to right-wing hysteria.[143] Still, if Ney's rhetoric was overblown, then the government sought to revitalize his aims, not to abandon them.

The Commonwealth Youth Trust's underlying principle was that British youths could be deployed as Cold Warriors in order to compensate for the state's limited financial resources. In 1962, the British government's spending on Commonwealth development was a "pitiful" £140 million, the size of the British Railways' deficit.[144] Many officials conceded that the Commonwealth was largely a matter of sentiment rather than constitutional ties.[145] Given the fragility of the Commonwealth's political and economic bonds, the trust's agenda of crafting social ties meshed with the interests of the decolonizing state. Cabinet warned that emotional attachments between young people might turn out to be all that prevented the Commonwealth from dying of inanition, or breaking up in anger.[146] Such sentiments were to be fomented with the support of the state, as in the Commonwealth Scholarship and Fellowship Plan, launched in 1960 to encourage cohesion through reciprocal programs of education among Commonwealth countries.[147] Yet galvanizing affection in the age of independence was not a task for states alone. Youth was the last, best hope to which the Commonwealth might turn.[148]

The Commonwealth Youth Trust committee was chaired by the famed military commander Sir Gerald Templer (figure 6). The choice of Templer reveals much about the seriousness with which youth politics was treated in Britain, and about the complex afterlives of those who had overseen the violent transition to independence. Templer was best known for his work as High Commissioner of the Federation of Malaya, where he suppressed the guerrillas during the "Emergency." For this undertaking, he was featured on the cover of *Time* magazine in 1952. He was a specialist in counterinsurgency, with extensive experience in psychological warfare and anticommunist propaganda. It was he who spoke so memorably of winning the "hearts and minds" of the people of Malaya.[149] He was, in short, a Cold War hero. But Templer's achievements did not translate at all well when he returned to Britain. One striking element of this story

Figure 6.   Sir Gerald Templer. (Reproduced
by permission of the National Army
Museum)

is the rapidity with which this victor of the early days of decolonization
came to seem entirely out of date. Some forms of expertise had expired
with independence.

Templer's most cherished proposal was for a vast (and vastly expensive)
Commonwealth Youth City to be constructed in the heart of London. The
"city" would house more than 5,000 overseas students, and cost upward
of £10 million.[150] Although the Colonial Office was initially supportive,
it ultimately rejected the project. Instead, it embarked on a £3 million
program of building 5,000 new hostel places across the country. Why
did Templer's vision fail? The Commonwealth Youth City was costly, but
also it segregated overseas students from their British counterparts and
seemed to negate the beneficent influence of metropolitan social mores
upon African and Asian student politics.[151] Furthermore, not everyone
was convinced of the magnitude of the communist threat to African and
Asian youth. The danger of communism had to be weighed against the
high cost of fighting it.[152] Templer's committee was widely criticized for
its overstatement of Britain's continued role in Africa, and its reluctance
to acknowledge the prominence of the United States. Templer gave the

anachronistic, rather wishful impression that Russia and Britain were locked in a two-sided combat for Africa's soul.[153]

In thinking about the successes and failures of these different (and often incompatible) proposals for deploying youth in the service of the Cold War, it appears that an investment in Third World youths trumped anticommunist measures at home. The project of making young Britons into Commonwealth enthusiasts was supplanted by the focus on improving the experience of young Africans and Asians in the metropole.[154] Although many youth organizations had been designed to fight the Cold War, only VSO was able to outlast it, perhaps because anticommunism was always just one of VSO's many ideological threads.

In the 1960s, political upheaval in Africa and Asia, competition from the American Peace Corps, and a more entrenched discourse of development shaped a new generation of VSOs. Although Alec's program had power and purchase for a brief historical moment, these principles did not survive intact. Among these competing visions of how young Britons should operate in the wider world, VSO emerged triumphant, but radically changed.

GROWING UP: VSO IN THE AMERICAN AGE

In 1961, Alec and Mora returned from a trip to the United States to find that Alec had been ousted from the VSO leadership. It is not easy to discern the reasons for this decision. Despite Alec's charisma, he was also an eccentric personality with a reputation for ideological inflexibility.[155] Douglas Whiting, a schoolmaster who had taught multiracial communities in South Africa, took over as director, aided by Robert Birley. Thereafter, VSO won increased Treasury support. But it also lost its focus on the school-leavers program, which Alec had seen as VSO's most politically significant aspect. Indeed, it was partly Alec's refusal to consider trained volunteers that had led to Alec's dismissal. This tension between old and new incarnations of Britain's global attachments would prove characteristic of VSO's next phase.

The critique of development faded quickly at VSO, along with the commitment to an elite group of untrained youths. Development discourse was becoming more unified and univocal. One reason this history of VSO is significant is that it demonstrates that if we trace back the divergent threads of development, we can see that some strands of what were later incorporated into its orbit were initially deeply critical of the idea of development itself. The particular vision of development that emanated from Britain had complex origins, in which development and its critics were closely intertwined.

In 1962, VSO established its graduate volunteer program, which quickly came to dominate the organization. There were practical reasons for the decline of the school leaver program and the rise of graduates. The graduate program brought new levels of financial support from the government, which agreed to provide 50 percent of the funds for the graduate volunteers. The receiving countries were increasingly insistent on hosting only trained volunteers, prompting complaints in Britain that naïve African and Asian politicians (precisely those youthful Third World leaders whom Alec had sought to engage) had been "bedazzled" by the prospect of technical aid from American M.A.s.[156]

This shift, however, should also be taken as a sign of the ephemerality of Alec's valorization of youth. Indeed, the average age of VSOs today is forty-two years old: a stark contrast with the days of the elite teenager.[157] For Alec, the school leaver was valuable because he was the very antithesis of the colonial civil servant, differentiated from other Britons abroad by his ready supply of adolescent affection. For a brief moment, Alec successfully generated a cult around this image of the volunteer, which spoke specifically to metropolitan concerns about the pathologies of the teenager. By the 1960s, the rhetoric about rescuing *British* adolescents through overseas service was declining. With the shift to graduate volunteers, the idea of the mutuality of aid became less visible.

The use of graduate volunteers brought VSO more closely in line with international trends in overseas development. Some were concerned that VSO would no longer be distinctive in the broader world of American-dominated aid without the "spontaneous élan" that came from the extreme youth of its volunteers.[158] Supporters of Alec's original scheme warned that trained graduate volunteers would be more readily associated with the colonial past. Whereas young countries might accept young Britons, they would reject the more paternalistic voices of expertise. Even within VSO, there were conflicting perceptions of how development should operate.

The resistance to the graduate program may have been motivated in part by the vestiges of the elitism that drove Alec's original concept. The shift to the graduate program transformed in the socioeconomic composition of the volunteers, as older volunteers were recruited more heavily from the grammar schools rather than public schools.[159] Robert Birley warned that the graduate scheme would not attract the same "high class" applicants as the school leaver program, because truly elite youths would be engaged with their own professional pursuits by that age.[160]

The graduate volunteer program revitalized VSO's relationship to the state. In 1961, one of the first acts of the new Department of Technical Cooperation was to issue a grant to VSO for £17,500.[161] In 1963, Patrick Gordon Walker, the Labour Party spokesman on foreign affairs, promised that Labour would increase government support for VSO, putting it on a footing more akin to the Peace Corps.[162] Labour pushed the VSO agenda during the general election, and key Labour celebrities such as Michael Young were also strong advocates. When Labour took office in 1964 and transformed the Department of Technical Cooperation into the Ministry of Overseas Development, it stressed its ideological commitment to overseas aid.

Conservatives also backed VSO as a way of revitalizing the imperial mission in a postimperial age. Quoting from the Conservative manifesto "The Next Five Years," one official argued that when the country had been "raising its standard of living and having a bit of a spree," it was impossible to find a sense of national purpose only "by looking inwards upon ourselves in this island." As in the past, the answer to this moral conundrum was to be found in overseas service.[163] The Conservative leader Iain Macleod exhorted parents to send their sons to VSO in order to serve "this new Commonwealth which is becoming a family." The success of VSO could prove that the Commonwealth "has its greatest days ahead."[164] In general, though, the Conservative interest in VSO was overwhelmingly nostalgic. Conservative Prime Minister Harold Macmillan spoke to Robert Birley of using VSO to revive the "missionary" sentiment of earlier eras.[165] One reason for VSO's longevity and success was precisely this ideological flexibility, which allowed it to be perceived by Conservatives as charmingly anachronistic and by Labour as resolutely forward looking.

The use of technical assistance funds for VSO was controversial, especially given Dickson's ongoing critiques of large-scale development. As one representative at the Commonwealth Relations Office said, "It may be an admirable thing for teenage boys to go out into the wilds to teach young Nigerians or Pakistanis how to read and write but this sort of activity is not our reason for being in business."[166] From the government's point of view, it was unclear whether VSO's brand of aid should be considered "technical assistance" that warranted financial support from the Colonial Development and Welfare grant. One Colonial Office document suggested that the psychological effect of Africans seeing young Britons who were willing to work as teachers for low pay might encourage more Africans to take up teaching, but efforts to connect VSO's work to technical aid projects often seemed strained.[167]

In the age of decolonization, VSOs bore an ambiguous relationship to British officialdom. For Alec, VSOs wielded an indirect form of authority, "like being a prefect in a good school."[168] Some volunteers in Nigeria and Northern Rhodesia were deployed as assistant district officers, and were closely associated with the interests of law and order.[169] But many volunteers also celebrated independence with their African peers, and were directly involved with the transfer of power. When Somaliland held its first general election on the eve of independence in 1960, a VSO helped with the polling arrangements. He found it "amusing to be given a most friendly welcome by the villagers, who presented him with a live sheep—and then went on to record a 90 percent vote for the anti-British independence party."[170] Another VSO, a Cambridge undergraduate named William, promised his African peers that he would mark Nigeria's independence by wearing full Yoruba dress when he was back at university. In order to honor his vow without embarrassment, William found himself bicycling furiously around Cambridge at dawn on independence day, dressed in his African robes.[171]

In 1963, volunteers were evacuated from Indonesia after anti-British disturbances in Jakarta, and individual cadets were removed from Cyprus and Cambodia in 1964. The single biggest emergency was prompted by the civil war in Nigeria in 1967, when 150 volunteers were withdrawn.[172] During the war in the Middle East in 1967, there were evacuations from Israel, Lebanon, Algeria, Tunisia, and Jordan.[173] Perhaps the most contentious issue was whether VSO should remain in Rhodesia after Ian Smith's Rhodesian Front party signed the Unilateral Declaration of Independence in 1965, which declared independence from Britain and opposed the advent of black majority rule; the British government promptly condemned the declaration as illegal. The debate about Rhodesia spoke directly to the question of whether VSOs were counted as official aid, because if they were, then they would legally have to be withdrawn from a rebel country. After much anguished debate, VSO elected to keep cadet volunteers at their posts teaching black African students in mission schools.[174] For Mora, countries with virulent racial tensions such as Rhodesia imperiled volunteers with moral corruption as well as physical danger.[175]

By the late 1960s, criticism of VSOs as agents of colonial power had intensified.[176] The supporters of VSO were at pains to distinguish their venture from an older colonial model of service, especially as the number of unskilled school leavers—who looked so unlike colonial servants—declined. As *The Economist* argued, the key difference between the "parasitic" colonialism of the past and the symbiotic system of the present was that if the old colonialism "taught the turbulent young how to govern and how to get the most out of 'their' people, these voluntary excursions have the great merit of teaching them a proper humility and how to get the best out of themselves."[177]

By the 1960s, of course, VSOs were far from alone in the field. From the inception of the Peace Corps in 1961, VSO leaders spoke of being "swamped" by Americans. Alec remarked of the Peace Corps—which dramatically outspent its counterparts in international aid work—that it was "'as though Standard Oil had moved in on the Quakers.'"[178] Given that the Peace Corps received $30 million from Congress for its first year alone, it was impossible for VSO to compete on the same scale. Still, Alec admonished his countrymen for allowing themselves to be so completely outdone. "What thoughts must possess an Englishman," he asked, "on hearing that Jamaica and North Borneo are now among those supplicating for the services of the Peace Corps?"[179] The first Peace Corps mission was to the former British colony of Tanganyika, which heightened the sense of one imperial order replacing another.

Dickson urged VSOs to define themselves against the Peace Corps juggernaut, with "the self-reliance of the Lone Ranger, the solitary courage of Lord Jim, pushing their frontiers of service still further into the forests and higher into the hills."[180] Barbara Castle, Labour's "Red Queen" who would soon serve as the first Minister of Overseas Development, urged the prime minister in 1961 to finance a British "peace corps." The tepid response that such enterprises were best sustained through voluntary bodies prompted an uncomfortable awareness of the contrast between America's "vigorous and youthful leadership" and Britain's "effete gamesmanship."

Alec's followers tended to see his explicit rejection of expertise as a way of differentiating VSO from the Peace Corps, although in fact this principle predated the Peace Corps' foundation. But it is worth asking what was at stake in the assertion that VSOs were strikingly different from Peace Corps volunteers, and whether the gulf between British and American volunteers always was more imagined than real.[181] The age gap between American and British volunteers was never very great: generally, only four or five years. The Peace Corps accepted applications from anyone over the age of eighteen, although the vast majority of its volunteers were twenty-one to twenty-five.[182] Although Peace Corps members were required to offer two years of service, and undeniably received more training—up to ten times as much language instruction, for example— they also often thought of themselves as having an antiprofessional bias, and perhaps were less "expert" than their British counterparts supposed.

President John F. Kennedy offered unequivocal public praise for VSO, but British reactions to the Peace Corps were less universally appreciative. British observers predicted that Americans would be unable to serve in the former colonies without serious adjustment problems, and that American volunteers must be chosen carefully for areas that were vulnerable to communist penetration, such as British Guiana.[183] Compared to the "Robin Hood" quality of British volunteers, one report complained, the Peace Corps seemed over-chaperoned, not to mention hesitant to infuse local elites with their own frontier spirit of service.[184] The British High Commissions kept close tabs on Peace Corps volunteers in regions of former British control, reporting from West Pakistan that a few Americans there looked "distinctly Beatnik."[185]

Despite its insistence that the American model should not be imitated in Britain, VSO debated extending the tenure of service from one year to two, as the Peace Corps had always done. Here, too, some VSO leaders wished to preserve their uniquely British elements. If young American graduates could afford two years of service, then this reflected the greater social mobility they enjoyed upon their return. In the more constrained social atmosphere of Britain, however, such lengthy service amounted to exploitation. As one participant in these debates declaimed, "In this matter, as in so many others surely it would be a mistake to limp lamely after America . . . in base and mediocre imitation!! We may have lost an Empire and not yet found a new road, but it is very questionable that Uncle Sam's path is also the right one for us."[186]

Although VSO rejected the two-year service requirement, the elements that had distinguished the British organization were declining. In crafting its survival for a new era, VSO no longer offered a specifically British—or specifically youthful—solution to the pathologies of the postwar world. Britain's era of overseas aid, such as it ever was, did not last long. In 1966, the government reduced by 10 percent, or £20 million, the amount that it devoted to overseas aid. The Ministry of Overseas Development was dropped from Cabinet shortly thereafter. The idea that overseas aid could redress Britain's *own* discontents was receding.

AFTERLIVES: VSO AT HOME

One key assumption of VSO's early years was that the "problem" of young people in the First and Third Worlds could not be resolved by experts alone. Rather, this problem required mutual rehabilitation that was based on the fundamental equality of these populations. Where expertise failed, volunteers would proffer new solutions to the myriad discontents of affluence and welfare. Much was at stake in the early and explicit denial of expertise at VSO, and the deployment of elite youths whose contributions were assumed to be primarily affective, rather than material. But this model did not last. By the late 1960s, VSO had begun to attract its own brand of experts—as volunteers. New graduates of psychology, sociology, and politics were recruited, and filled posts ranging from the supervision of juvenile delinquents in the Congo to psychiatric social work in Trinidad.[187]

Many VSOs were themselves proto-experts, demonstrating how expertise could be denigrated and revered at nearly the same moment— or, perhaps, how expertise and its critiques constituted less of a true opposition than a continuum for individuals at different times and places.[188] Indeed, we might read the Dicksons themselves as experts who had learned how to market successfully the mythology of anti-expertise, emphasizing the ways in which critiques of expertise served as an important element of postwar politics and social organization.[189]

Despite the eclecticism of their schemes, the Dicksons were neither outliers nor outcasts. At different moments, the Dicksons' agenda of feeling could either mesh or clash with the interests of the decolonizing state, which were themselves constantly shifting. They were often intimately connected to the centers of state power, and highly effective in publicizing their vision of the transnational redemption of youth.[190] One Colonial Office representative spoke of Alec Dickson as embodying "a new sort of romantic evangelism," which he expected to establish a new way of being British in the world.[191] Their organizations have persisted through the present day, with VSO now having sent 33,000 volunteers abroad.[192] The zeal surrounding the Dicksons' schemes illustrates that it may be apt to read this era not in terms of a withdrawal from empire, but rather as a reinvestment in a new internationalism in which the former empire played a significant part.[193] During these decades, Britain did not retreat from the world, but undertook new forms of engagement that were sometimes fearful, sometimes enthusiastic. In this environment, the Dicksons' promise that they could create new Britons—along with new Africans and Asians—held tremendous appeal.

Although VSO thrived, its initial model of forging ties between elite— and equally disorientated—youths, and using these ties as the basis for a critique of technocratic models of development, fell into disuse. This shift took place for a variety of reasons, including changes in the program's leadership, a political shift to a more technocratically oriented Labour government, demands for more usable forms of aid from the postcolonies, and competition with the Peace Corps.

After his expulsion from VSO, Alec Dickson founded the Community Service Volunteers (CSV) in 1962. This organization sought to dedicate British youths to service in their own neighborhoods. Was it really true, Alec asked, that people had it so good in Britain—as their prime minister had proposed—that there were no human needs left to which the young could contribute? The adventure of service could be made as meaningful in the slums of Liverpool as in Sierra Leone, at an approved school in the Midlands as at Aden College in the Middle East.[194] One distinctive element of CSV was its democratization of service: that is, unlike VSO, any young person who wished to volunteer was accepted: "'To serve overseas, in other people's countries, is a privilege—and so selection is inevitable. But to serve Britain, your own country, that is your right.'"[195] Here, the ethos of the youthful anti-expert was reborn, although with a new emphasis on the universality—rather than the elitism—of service.

Like VSO, CSV enjoyed enduring success, although the latter remains closer to its original form. The Home Office used CSV volunteers in the approved schools as auxiliary housemasters, and to inspire social work impulses among the students. CSV youths were also deployed as English instructors for new migrants.[196] Alec's critique of the selfishness of Third World elites lost much of its bite by the 1960s, as he came to focus on the problems of African and Asian youths in Britain who were often significantly less privileged than those he had encountered in Iraq, Sarawak, and Nigeria. Still, he was intent that overseas visitors should undertake social service projects during their time in Britain. His belief that the pathologies of both indigenes and foreigners were best addressed by mutual service lived on in CSV, although the dominant figure in his new scheme was the impoverished migrant rather than the elite school leaver.

Perhaps Dickson's most persistent idea was that both welfare and the end of empire required new forms of affective relations. His projects serve as an important reminder that affect, one of the mainstays of scholarship on colonialism, has been largely left out of the history of decolonization. The history of affect has been presumed to dwell only in very particular sites, and moments, which we might think to diversify. Scholars of colonial history have been consumed only with some kinds of affective ties, with an emphasis on sexual and familial relationships. But although these relationships are of great interest (in this project and elsewhere), it is worth noting that both colonial expansion and its reversal were conducted in multiple emotional and social registers. We might consider friendship, mentorship, and collegiality—as well as the power struggles, and even violence that shaped these dynamics—as topics deserving their own explorations in order to isolate what is distinctive about the affective regimes of decolonization and development.[197]

The reconstruction of personal relationships, in Dickson's view, was crucial to the West's success in the Cold War, to the peaceful management of independence, and to curing the ills of welfare itself. Yet these battles were not to be waged by just anyone. Dickson's critique of development was driven by many factors, but key among them was his focus on reforming the inner lives and social relationships of elites rather than the material conditions of the masses. It was this element of his vision that explained the early success of VSO at a moment when the plight of the teenager in British society appeared to demand a global solution, and the threat of the young African or Asian politician appeared to be accelerating.

Many of the participants in VSO, WAY, and CYT thus drew links between the fortunes of young Britons abroad and students from Africa and Asia in Britain, who were experiencing their own form of "culture shock" in Britain.[198] Overseas students were often quite literally changing places with VSOs, who stepped into the places vacated by ambitious teachers and civil servants eager to earn higher qualifications in Britain. Although these groups met very different fates, both populations were assumed to have a disproportionate influence on the uncertain and unknowable politics of the future. Furthermore, academics and government officials perceived both populations as powerful weapons against communism, and as emblems of postwar mobility. In the next chapter, I turn to the ways in which overseas students in Britain came to embody the hopes and anxieties of a new era of geopolitics.

3.   Problem Learners

Overseas Students and the Dilemmas
of Cold War Education

When John Mensah Sarbah left the Gold Coast (now Ghana) for England in 1937 to study law, no one could have imagined that he would meet such a disastrous end. Sarbah was a member of one of the most prominent Gold Coast families; his father, who bore the same name, was a famed political activist and the first African from the Gold Coast to qualify in Britain as a barrister.[1] Sarbah seemed destined for success. But soon after his arrival in London, Sarbah underwent a frightening transformation. In 1941, he was arrested after yelling "Heil Hitler!" in public. At the Banstead Hospital in Surrey, his delusions became violent; specifically, he believed that he had to kill an Englishman in order to learn English. The Colonial Office, which attributed Sarbah's breakdown to academic stress, proposed that he stay in England, to receive the most advanced psychiatric treatment. But Sarbah's illness persisted, and in 1958 he was repatriated to a mental hospital in Takoradi. He remained there as an invalid, his degree never completed and the bill for his repatriation unpaid.

Despite the bizarre elements of Sarbah's story, his British contacts saw it as all too typical.[2] The case, which spanned Ghana's transition to independence, exemplified the plight of overseas students in the metropole. Like many other cases, it disrupted multiple fictions regarding overseas students: that young elites would be improved by their time in Britain, and that they would speedily return home with new credentials to guarantee the advancement of their families and nations. Sarbah's downfall, and many others like it, gave the lie to these ideals. Education had long represented the supreme paradox of British colonial power, a demonstration of justice in an inherently unjust system.[3] These paradoxes were not resolved, but heightened in the postcolonial metropole. Could education sustain British governance, or simply hasten its dissolution? Education was the last gift that a crumbling empire could bestow. Yet it also seemed to prompt the radicalization or deterioration of those who were supposed to become the ideal liberal subjects. As colonial rule weakened, Britons were no longer confident about turning "Hindoos into Englishmen." Increasingly, they emphasized preparing students for Indianization or Africanization as the doctrine of development supplanted the colonial discourse of improvement.

The experiences of overseas students served as an important area of study for the decolonizing state, as well as psychologists and sociologists. But some groups received more zealous scrutiny than others. The targets of investigation shifted according to the chronology of nationalist agitation and violence. Multiple timelines of independence thus shaped how different student populations in Britain emerged and receded from view. In the early twentieth century, governmental investigations focused on sedition among Indian students.[4] In the 1930s, West Indian students briefly attracted interest, although this was soon eclipsed by attention to West Indian migrant labor during the Second World War. There was a bout of concern about Malayan students in the early 1950s, shaped by the demands of the Malayan "Emergency."

Even in this crowded field, however, it was the African student who ultimately reigned supreme. More than any other figure, the African student served as a global icon of all of the opportunities and anxieties regarding Cold War education. By the 1950s, the intensity of enthusiasm about African successes and the stigma of African failures were equally remarkable. This emphasis reflected the distinctive status of educated Africans in Britain's perception of the Cold War, decolonization, and the relationship between the two. Equally distinctive was the mustering of new forms of expertise—most notably, in the realm of psychology and psychiatry—to conceptualize the experiences of African students. Although other overseas students fell under the watchful eye of the state, the elaboration of new apparatuses of social science brought the maladies of African students into a particularly bright light.

Certain groups of African students were singled out for investigation. Following Ghanaian and Nigerian independence (in 1957 and 1960, respectively), West Africans dominated the overseas student population in Britain. The majority of African students lived in London, but there were also sizable populations in Manchester, Birmingham, Edinburgh, and Glasgow. By 1960, when there were approximately 50,000 overseas students in the United Kingdom, at least 11,000 Africans resided in

Britain as recognized students, plus tens of thousands of "private" students without government scholarships.[5]

For many British observers, understanding how African students in Britain functioned was vital to controlling the trajectory of Britain's empire in Africa. Scholars in Britain were singularly insistent on the theme of pathology, diagnosing a range of "syndromes"—from neuroses to psychoses—that they associated with overseas students. Here, I consider what was at stake in labeling these students "ill," and why their narratives of glittering successes and devastating failures were so compelling to Britain's Cold Warriors.

Overseas students were not simply objects of study for white social scientists, but were future practitioners of social science as well. Some of the most prominent researchers on overseas students were themselves South Asians or West Africans who were educated in Britain.[6] Overseas students were a prominent force in social science units at the LSE and the University of Liverpool, the Department of Social Study at the University of Edinburgh, and the Institute of Education. R. H. Tawney and Harold Laski, the LSE's eminent socialists, attracted many students from the former colonies. The American sociologist Edward Shils, who taught at the LSE from 1946 to 1950, quipped that the LSE was "the most important institution of higher education in Asia and Africa."[7]

Throughout the 1950s and 1960s, the USSR and the United States competed vigorously to attract scholars from the rapidly decolonizing continent. But this rivalry was not merely a bipolar affair. Within this broader contest, Britain had a distinctive role to play as the former "mother country" to many of these students. Furthermore, Britain's uniquely complicated (and constantly evolving) relationships with these students' countries of origin made it a crucial hub of international education, especially for those countries that the superpowers perceived as valuable Cold War prizes.

But overseas education engendered its pains as well as its promises. The overseas student was at once valorized and pathologized, often by the same people, as an emblem of Britain's changing role in the world. In the 1950s, British researchers evinced a cautious optimism about the role that international education might play in the monitoring and management of decolonization. By the 1960s, academics and government officials had come to focus on overseas students' power to disrupt Britain's global interests. In this more anxious climate, research on overseas students intersected with policy shifts regarding migration controls. The overseas student was both emblematic of the larger migrant population and a crucially important exception to it.

We should see here a persistent theme of ambivalence rather than a linear move from optimism to pessimism. Optimism and pessimism intensified simultaneously, and the fear about who these students might "infect" ebbed and flowed according to shifting global imperatives. The images of triumph and defeat that surrounded overseas students rarely mapped neatly onto individual lives. Overseas students galvanized tremendous energy and anxiety. This chapter aims to capture both of these moods, and to explore the disjunctions between them.

EARLY TO SCHOOL: INDIAN STUDENTS IN BRITAIN

The first overseas students to experience any sustained level of surveillance were Indians. Official efforts to ameliorate the conditions of Indian students in Britain began in the late nineteenth century, and peaked at key moments of political agitation in India, especially with the rise of nationalist violence in early-twentieth-century Bengal.[8] British authorities considered not only the dangers of disloyalty for Indian students as a group, but also risks to individual students' characters, health, and respectability. Indian students were never pathologized to the same extent as Africans. But investigations of Indian students established a remarkably durable set of concerns: that overseas students lacked a functional home life, that their social isolation would foment political radicalization, and that they would wield disproportionate influence on their countries of origin.

In 1904, the Government of India introduced scholarships for Indians to study technical subjects in Britain.[9] Shortly thereafter, in 1907, the secretary of state appointed a committee to investigate the problems of Indian students in Britain. Chaired by William Lee-Warner, formerly of the Indian Civil Service, the committee deposed scores of Indian and British witnesses.[10] The findings were so disturbing that the report's publication was suppressed for more than a decade. Many witnesses described the "rapid deterioration" of Indian students in the metropole. A legal scholar argued that "if an Indian 'goes under,' he usually goes beyond hope of redemption . . . The Indian seems to have no power of recovery. He is never able to 'pull himself together.'" He reported how he found an Indian student living in a low house in South London, naked except for his shirt—the rest of his clothes pawned for alcohol. The student was repatriated to India, but returned to London six months later, contracted delirium tremens, was sent home again, and committed suicide in the Red Sea.

Amid these tales of social degradation, the political outlook was equally gloomy. The report estimated that half the Indian student population in Britain was hostile to colonial rule, and that time in Britain strengthened the "seditious virus."[11] What was to be done? There were few options for a liberal imperialist state. Strikingly, the report concluded that the "radical cure" of banning Indian scholars from Britain was not desirable. Instead, it focused on welfare and providing "wholesome and helpful influences."[12] Indian students who held government scholarships were asked to exercise moderation in their political debates. But major restrictions on entry were rejected.

After the Lee-Warner report, British officials articulated what would prove a longstanding mantra. Indian students were seeing "hardly anything of good English life."[13] They socialized with lower-class radicals with "vicious manners and habits" who would harm their chances for advancement in India.[14] The solution was to integrate Indians into bourgeois domestic life. As one Indian student wrote, "The sweet homes of England are indeed the abodes of trust, love and peace. Let not India learn the physical arts and sciences of England only; but let her also carefully study the elements and graces which construct a really pure and sweet English home."[15] This assertion that the intimacy of the home served as a panacea for the ills of overseas students would recur throughout the twentieth century, even though very few families were actually willing to take in students of color.

In 1908, *The Times* reported that more than a hundred Indian students attended a secret meeting to celebrate the fiftieth anniversary of the "Mutiny," and hissed at the name of the king.[16] It was in this climate of discontent that the Government of India established an advisory bureau in London in 1909 to act *in loco parentis* to young Indians. But British fears about the dangers posed by (and to) Indian students were about to escalate. In July of 1909, Madan Lal Dhingra, a Punjabi engineering student, shot and killed Sir William Curzon-Wyllie, formerly the aide-de-camp to the secretary of state for India.[17] Just before the shooting, Dhingra's older brother, a doctor who himself studied in Britain, had pleaded with Curzon-Wyllie to investigate his brother's political activities and to wean him from "pernicious" influences. The murder took place at a formal party at the Imperial Institute for the National Indian Association: a dazzling affair, with many of the Indian guests dressed in native costumes. At the party, Dhingra strode up to Curzon-Wyllie and shot him in the face. The crime was carefully planned; Dhingra was armed with three loaded revolvers and a dagger. He was also carrying an anti-British paper exhorting Indian students to undertake political assassinations.[18] Dhingra was hanged for murder, but public anxiety lingered.[19] Dhingra came from a family of proud loyalists, who were horrified by his actions. If he could be so viciously radicalized in Britain, then the effects of overseas education seemed fearsome indeed.

Scotland Yard watched Indian students more closely after this crime. But even after the murder, British palliatives focused on welfare and surveillance rather than restricted entry. In 1921, the secretary of state for India appointed another committee to investigate the well-being of Indian students. The committee was chaired by the Earl of Lytton, the undersecretary of state for India, and it deposed 180 witnesses in 10 cities.[20] According to the report, Indian students were socializing with their British counterparts and participating more actively in games than they had done in the past.

Despite these heartening signs, there were new menaces.[21] In 1925, a group of Indian students at Oxford was accused of trying to induce other Indians to join the Communist Party.[22] The threat of communism gave a new urgency to earlier concerns about Indian disloyalty, but relied on the same connections between education, radicalization, and social deterioration. Even as surveillance of Indian students intensified, though, the police found little evidence of truly dangerous activity.[23] A document tellingly titled "Tragic Cases of Indian Students Going Wrong" focused less on sedition or communism than debt, failed marriages, and shattered nerves.[24]

Just before the Second World War, then, the state's stance on Indian students was that this population posed more of a social risk to itself than a political risk to the empire. After India became independent in 1947, the reputation of Indian students in the metropole underwent a revival. The precise ways that educated Indians would shape the transition to nationhood seemed less alarming in postindependence reality than they had in the colonial imagination.

In 1952, Lord Chorley argued that the bonds of education had enabled Britain and India to weather painlessly their "constitutional crisis" just five years before. Indians who had studied in Britain, he argued, retained their great affection for it even after independence.[25] For Africans, he dourly predicted, the same experiences might now have the opposite effect. Chorley did not explain this distinction. But in the aftermath of the Second World War, we can see a dramatic intensification of optimism *and* pessimism regarding overseas students, especially Africans. More than ever, these students' triumphs and failures became a matter of state.

THE STUDENT AS STAR: POSTWAR IDEALS
AND SUCCESSES

After the Second World War, research into the achievements and experiences of overseas students became a vital new area of study for psychologists, psychiatrists and sociologists in the United States and Europe. Overseas students, who provided valuable insight into the benefits and drawbacks of immersion into foreign cultures, were perceived as instrumental to the future success of internationalist politics. British researchers focused on students of color, and especially on Africans from territories scheduled for independence. In novels, films, and the popular press, these students figured as new kinds of transnational celebrities.

The *West African Review* reported in 1945, "never have there been so many sons of Chiefs in Great Britain."[26] The Colonial Office supervised these students closely. When Kabaka Edward Mutesa of Buganda came to Cambridge to read history, the Colonial Office urged his relatives to increase his allowance to purchase suitable clothing at Harrods. The kabaka proved distressingly slow to settle his debts, and left behind a hefty bill for a set of Victorian lithographs when he returned to Africa. Still, when the kabaka expressed a desire to vacation in Spain, the Colonial Office rationalized the expense by noting how important it was to future relations between Britain and Uganda that the kabaka be "fully equipped . . . to bring to his government of Buganda a fully matured mind well acquainted with the trends of modern Europe." Given that the Buganda were considered to be among the most advanced peoples in East Africa, it was essential that their ruler be "fully aware of the cultural and economic benefits which European civilization can bring to Africa."[27] Such benefits were worth a few unpaid bills.

These elite young men could prove difficult to manage. When Seepapitso Gaseitsiwe, the son of Chief Bathoen II of Bechuanaland, came to study public and social administration at South Devon Technical College, he seemed wholly unmoved by the Colonial Office's efforts to keep a "fatherly eye" on him. When invited to attend one of Major Ney's anticommunist Quests for Commonwealth youth, Seepapitso declined, noting tartly that he was "not a teenager."[28] Still, Seepapitso's tutors believed that his time in Britain had been worthwhile: "his sense of

Figure 7. "Congrats." When Osigbuyimola Osibogun, son of Chief J. O. Osibogun of Lagos, passed his B.Sc. Economic Degree examination at Hull University in 1959, congratulations poured in and this portrait appeared in *West African Pilot*. (*West African Pilot*, July 11, 1959, p. 2)

responsibility which was a little disorientated . . . has now become more balanced."[29]

Even ordinary students were often treated as celebrities. The *West African Pilot* chronicled large parties at the docks to bid students good luck, and witness their triumphant homecomings, as well as chronicle their achievements and social lives overseas (figures 7–9). Many Indian students recalled the collective excitement surrounding their voyages to Britain. Relatives devoted themselves to fixing an auspicious time for the trip, and threw coconuts into the water to bring the travelers good fortune. One Pakistani student wrote of his departure, "It was a scene of beauty. About hundred people have come to say me good-bye . . . It is difficult to tell all the advices which were whispered in my ears but few I will report. 'Don't indulge in sex and wine. Don't eat Pig. Keep your character clean. You are going alone, Come back alone.' Tears rolled in my eyes as I went towards the plane."[30] In 1953, the *West African Review* began a gossip column called "Agwa's Diary," which charted the social activities of West Africans in Britain. Students also regularly appeared on the cover of the *Review* (figures 10–11) in glamorous poses.[31]

Students conveyed their impressions of life in Britain through radio

In Quest Of "Golden Fleece"

They Return With 'Golden Fleece'

Figure 8 *(top)*. "In Quest of 'Golden Fleece.'" This photograph celebrated Nigerians who were about to pursue studies in the United Kingdom. (*West African Pilot*, October 8, 1959, p. 3)

Figure 9 *(bottom)*. "They Return with 'Golden Fleece.'" Other students were welcomed back when their degrees were completed. (*West African Pilot*, June 24, 1960, p. 3)

Figures 10 and 11.   *(left)* "A Nigerian Ports Authority Instructor Himself Receives Instruction." A Nigerian welding student in North London appeared on the cover of the *West African Review* in 1956. (*West African Review* 27 [October 1956]); *(right)* Mrs. Lake Bakaar and Miss Grimilda Johnson of Freetown, secretarial students at the West London College of Commerce, were photographed for the cover of the *West African Review* in 1961. The women were shown trying on masks from Sierra Leone at an exhibition at the Commonwealth Institute in London. (*West African Review* 33 [November 1961])

addresses, television broadcasts, and articles in the British and African press (figure 12), often with anthropologically savvy titles such as, "I Lived with the People of Britain."[32] T. E. A. Salubi, an Urhobo social anthropologist who studied with Harold Laski, Kenneth Little, and Audrey Richards, recounted how in Britain, "I saw civilization. She stared at me and I looked right into her eyes."[33] As we will see, engagements with British culture by overseas students could be damning. But, especially in the 1940s and early 1950s, many students' reports were glowingly positive. Samuel George Ayi-Bonte, a physical education student from the Gold Coast, delivered a stirring radio address called "A Student Discovers the Full Life." Ayi-Bonte insisted that he had become a better African through encountering racism in Britain: "the people who turned me out of doors soon became my friends . . . Britain has helped me to thrust strong roots into the civilization into which I am born." Ayi-Bonte recalled how he had arrived "a stranger to this Island and had my heart

Calling Nigeria From Belfast

Figure 12.   "Calling Nigeria from Belfast." Joshua Alokan, secretary of the Nigerian Students' Union in Belfast, discussed his script with Mallam Abba Zoro of the Nigerian Broadcasting Corporation before recording a newsletter about student life for the BBC's "Calling Nigeria" program. (*West African Pilot,* November 19, 1959, p. 1)

open and my hands stretched to receive what training Britain could give me . . . today, I feel I am a new man. I have enjoyed to its fullest measure the beauty in human relationships."[34]

By his own account, Ayi-Bonte was a grand success story. But the Colonial Office's vision of success was distinctive and depended on neutralizing the threat of student radicalism. Students who obtained government scholarships were often described as "courteous" or "submissive." One recommendation for a telecommunications student from the Gold Coast noted reassuringly that, "I will be saying just the right thing (as far as my knowledge goes) that young Cyril being docile, painstaking and respectful, carries along a smooth-running character coupled with a strong physique."[35] Another letter for a Ugandan scholar noted that although the candidate was not intellectually outstanding, "his whole outlook is the right sort of outlook for a person going to England; he is not 'clever'; he is thoughtful; he has a mind of his own; and his whole attitude is sound."[36]

Yet even for candidates who seemed politically incendiary, colonial governments were sometimes prepared to trust that time in Britain would have a calming effect. Jean-Marie Seroney, for example, was a Kenyan law student who would later become one of the key voices of opposition to the nationalist leader, Jomo Kenyatta. In 1952, the secretary of state for Kenya sent a secret letter to J. L. Keith, Director of Colonial Scholars, to lobby for Seroney's acceptance to an Inn of Court.:

> [Seroney is] a man of considerable ability with an exceptional command of English and he has already shown that he could be a dangerous political agitator. He appears, however, to be a sincere Catholic and is susceptible to advice and beneficial influences. It has accordingly been decided that it is in the best interests of himself and of this Government that he should be provided with a loan to enable him to visit the United Kingdom with a view to being called to the Bar. It is hoped that by the time he returns here he will have matured and will have had a chance to absorb British ideas.[37]

Seroney was accepted to study in Exeter and London, and reports of his political activity and "erratic personality" were sent back to Kenya. Individuals such as Seroney were crucially valuable assets, whose power could be used for good or ill, and whose future entailed a complex set of calculated hopes and risks.

The Colonial Office was well aware that its imagined trajectory of pacification was not always fulfilled. Its files are rife with cases of students who went awry in Britain, at least from the Colonial Office's perspective. Their experiences involved political radicalization, academic fiascos, debt, ill-fated marriages, mental breakdown, and even death. These problems generated new agencies of surveillance and welfare to bring students into closer contact with the state. The optimistic investment in overseas students was often paired with an equally dramatic—and far more devastating—vision of failure.

LEARNING THE WRONG LESSONS: FAILURE AND DEGRADATION IN THE METROPOLE

When Mr. G. S. Patel, a Hindu district engineer's assistant in Uganda, sent his son to study engineering in London, he had the highest hopes for the young man's future. Narendrekumar was a "very promising boy," in whom his family had invested tremendous financial resources. But shortly after Narendrekumar's arrival in London, he ceased contact with his family, and his father became frantic. All too soon, the terrible truth was revealed: Narendrekumar had fallen in love with his white English landlady, Mrs. Harries, a divorcée with two children. Mr. Patel launched an impassioned campaign to urge his son's liaison officer to intervene: "The Lady is 28 years and my son is 23 years. (Woman five years older than man). Her education is very poor to stand on her foot to maintain herself and her two children . . . I regret I cannot allow my son to marry this English lady even if the British rules have no objection for this inter-cast marriage, as my son is under my debt of Shs. 20,000/- cash and obligations I did to him as a father. I was wonderfully kind to him."[38] Patel summoned Narendrekumar back to Kampala and extracted a written oath from him that he would only marry an Indian woman. He produced letters from religious leaders stating that this proposed marriage would violate the Patels' beliefs. Patel hinted to Mrs. Harries that Narendrekumar had a venereal disease and asked her to honor the "dignity and prestige of English ladies" by calling off the marriage. His friends banned their sons from studying abroad, because "English girls hypnotize our pure boys."[39]

Narendrekumar hastily fled his father's watchful eye to return to London. Claiming that he was now pauperized by the expense of his son's wasted education, Patel bitterly reminded the liaison officer that his son had gone to England "so that he may be useful to this newly developed country. He was not sent to get training in love affairs."[40] The student welfare officers were responsive to Mr. Patel's plight, and warned the couple about the difficulties they would face in Uganda. But as one officer wrote, "the fact is that they are in love and intend to marry and I am afraid that they know there is nothing that can stop them."[41] Instead of the "golden fleece" of a university degree, Narendrekumar would come home only with his white wife, and his father feared that the two of them would live in poverty and isolation.

The Patel story illustrates the incredible variety of ways in which overseas education could go awry. Certainly public anxiety about interracial unions was not confined to students, but such matches could represent a particularly distressing derailment of a family's plan for social advancement.[42] The devastation of unfulfilled expectations plagued not only individual students, but also the relatives and governments who sponsored them.[43] In these cases, elites from Africa and Asia were perceived to have lowered their class position through their time in Britain rather than elevating it.

One interesting element of the Patel case is the intense involvement of the Colonial Office. The supervision of overseas students had a long history in Britain.[44] The office of the director of colonial scholars was created in 1902.[45] The director authorized students' allowances, reported on their conduct, and orchestrated the return home. This post was originally filled by crown agents, who received £3 per year for every scholar under their supervision. In 1940, the welfare section of the Colonial Office took over the supervision of government scholars. When the number of overseas students in Britain spiked after the war, the Colonial Office appointed liaison officers for each colonial territory. Their introduction signaled the vast apparatus that was established after the war to accomplish the twin projects of welfare and surveillance.[46] These officers, who were mostly ex–civil servants, gave advice based on their knowledge of the students' home environment. To their frustration, however, they often found that their expertise failed to translate in the metropole.

In 1948, Cabinet created an Official Committee on Overseas Students.[47] Its chair was C. F. A. Warner, a prominent Cold Warrior who previously served on the Russia Committee of the Foreign Office and researched Soviet influences on British public opinion.[48] Other Cabinet committees on overseas students operated throughout the 1950s.[49] The Church of England helped to establish the Special Committee for Overseas Students in Nigeria in 1947. But most colonial territories lacked any coordinated body to prepare students for life in Britain.[50] In 1950, the British Council took over responsibility for the reception of colonial students. The council described their initial encounters with these young people as extremely daunting. Students arrived carrying "coconuts, yams, dried fish, ground nuts, tinned fruit, sacks filled with cooking powder, carpets, kitchen utensils, bedsteads including a four-poster, perambulators, cycles and a steel lathe." One group turned up in London with malaria and broken bones, some having suffered recent amputations.[51]

The council produced a bestselling £1 booklet, *How to Live in Britain*, which contained useful advice for decoding social interactions: "When British people are introduced to each other, they give a faint smile and say 'How do you do?' There is no answer to this question."[52] It also hosted screenings of quintessentially British films such as *Kind Hearts and Coronets*, along with talks on democracy and advice about battling colds and the flu from World Health Organization. Elite young men and women who enrolled in the council's introductory course were shocked to find themselves being instructed on how to eat with a knife and fork or use the toilet (figure 13).[53] The council denied that it sought to instill a "blind Anglomania."[54] But one African student complained, "'If only they

Preparatory Course For Students

Figure 13. "Preparatory Course for Students." Mrs. B. H. Atkinson, the wife of the acting East regional director of the British Council in Enugu, demonstrated how to use a soup spoon at a British Council course for Nigerian students who were planning to travel overseas. (*West African Pilot*, August 20, 1959, p. 3)

would come out into the open about it and admit that the British Council is a propaganda machine we wouldn't mind. But it makes us very bitter when we think that we have been deceived.'"[55]

Both within and beyond the British Council, student welfare workers had a wide and elastic sphere of responsibility. They loaned money to students, often in remarkably large sums, and negotiated between students and their families. The brother of one Nigerian law student, Nwabufo Uwechia, wrote repeatedly to Nwabufo's liaison officer to ask if his brother was wasting his time with radical activists such as George Padmore. When Nwabufo failed the bar exam, his brother begged the officer to "look into every department of [Nwabufo's] life and use any reasonable measure to correct any imperfections."[56] Because Nwabufo had impressed his British contacts as an "earnest fellow" who was concerned about anti-British activity in Nigeria, they agreed to intercede.

In terms of sexual behavior, overseas students were always under scrutiny.[57] In 1963, the principal of Guildford County Technical College complained to the Home Office about "the libertine response to our freedom" by Kenyan Indians who had impregnated English women at the school: "this is what I have found in quiet peaceful little Guildford—heaven knows what happens in the London Polytechnics!"[58] According to Dame Margery Perham, whose lectures were broadcast on the BBC in 1960, African students in Britain enjoyed "the supreme racial compensation" of sex with white women while they faced shattering incidents of racial discrimination. This combination, she claimed, created a pathological state of mind among educated Africans.[59]

Furthermore, there was the cataclysmic specter of academic failure. One Pakistani student recorded in his diary after failing his exams: "I confess it today! I am finished. I am done with. I am gone. I am ruined. God does not help me any more. I am lost to this world. My life is wreck. I am a dead loss to my parents. I have been reduced to a frustrated middle-aged man from a young ambitious boy by this world. I have no future—I am lost forever."[60] In several cases, overseas students drifted into crime. Dominic Ntawa, a young man from the Southern Cameroons, won a scholarship to study construction at the Brixton Building School in 1961. Two years later, he was convicted of the manslaughter of Mustapha Kannieh, who was burned to death in a building in Brixton. Deeply in debt, and with a damning criminal record, Ntawa wrote to the Colonial Office, "I am sorry I did the crazy thing I did, " and "I am very lonesome, wish to visit people and get to know more about the British places and more important to make friends."[61]

A 1961 photo-essay in the *West African Review,* "Oh Mary, this London" (figures 14–15) depicted this growing sense of disenchantment. Tom Picton's photographs traced a student's progress from his arrival at Euston Station, capturing not only London's amusements, but also the difficulties of negotiating and socializing with whites. The essay's title was taken from William Percy French's song about Irish migrants in London, "The Mountains of Mourne" (1896), and included part of its first stanza:

Oh, Mary, this London's a wonderful sight,
With people here working by day and by night.
They don't sow potatoes, nor barley nor wheat
But there's gangs of them digging for gold in the street.
At least when I asked them that's what I was told
So I just took a hand at this digging for gold.

The photographs' captions referred to "the fading of a rosy dream," revealing the discomfiting gap between the fantasy and reality of overseas edu-

Figure 14.   Tom Picton's 1961 photo-essay for the *West African Review,* "Oh, Mary, This London," showed a student enjoying some of London's charms. (*West African Review* 32 [August 1961]: 4–11)

cation. These images were at odds with the *Review*'s glamour shots of students just a few years before.

Even amidst these darker views, though, the optimism of the late 1940s and early 1950s did not disappear. The value of these students was heightened, even as the dangers they seemed to pose were more acute. During the late 1950s and the 1960s, the problems of the overseas student were cast in a new register driven by the Cold War. As independence movements swept West Africa, the greatest fear was that African students in Britain would fall prey to communism.[62] Next, I explore British responses to overseas student politics, and the careful balance between anxiety and investment that the Cold War engendered.

Figure 15.   Picton also documented the "fading of the rosy dream," as the student negotiated with white landladies, and encountered isolation and racism. (*West African Review* 32 [August 1961]: 4–11)

COMMUNIST LESSONS: OVERSEAS STUDENTS AS COLD WAR ICONS

The governmental fear that overseas students would be radicalized (rather than civilized) in Britain became much more urgent with the advent of the Cold War. For Cold Warriors, the time that students spent in Britain represented an important opportunity—although also a moment of danger. Not every African or Asian leader was reachable in his indigenous environment. The overseas student in Britain was uniquely accessible, and thus presented an ideal population for those who sought to influence the rapidly changing political sentiments of newly independent citizens. Students might be converted to or from Western ideals, but racial discrimination was an obvious factor of disenchantment. My intention here is not to debate the degree to which overseas students were actually engaged in communism. Rather, I want to suggest how the fear of such radical politics drove race relations policies in Britain more generally.

Colonial students were seen as vulnerable to political extremism, especially communism, because they lacked "the corrective home and social influences which help British young people to preserve a sense of balance."[63] Such perceived radicalism often did not survive the trip back home—leading one graduate to note wryly that his fellow West Africans were "'proletarians in Westminster and bourgeois in Lagos'"[64] Still, the Colonial Office urged aggressive interventions to ensure that students were happily integrated into their communities after completing their degrees, as "it is no good our setting them straight if they are going to be treated as 'niggers' when they get home."[65]

The British state had a vested interest in supervising overseas students' experiences in the metropole. Postwar liberals stressed Britain's moral responsibility toward students "from countries whose systems of education we started but never finished."[66] The perceived significance of these students and their impact on global politics was enormous, although many authorities were unsure whether this impact would be positive or negative: "The presence of these thousands of young men and women from abroad, in this country now, is Dynamite—but dynamite rightly directed can be used for good. The possibilities for good in the coming together of this vast assembly of the world's youth are immense. The possibilities of harm, individually and internationally, mainly through students who return home bitter, disillusioned and often impregnated with undigested communist maxims—are also infinite."[67] According to the Colonial Office, the student population was making the path to decolonization more volatile and less predictable. The rapid growth of educated Africans had "upset our calculations and disturbed the even tenor of political development among the slow moving masses." As the Colonial Office emphasized, "the whole political future of the African colonies is bound up with these few men."[68] Specifically, the Colonial Office worried that students of color would be radicalized when they encountered racism in Britain: "we may easily be raising up a body of men who will cause the most serious trouble in the future and breed sedition, irreligion, and discontent."[69] Such warnings raised the stakes for research on overseas students, and underscored the importance of policing racism both in Britain and in Africa.

Metropolitan security agencies kept close watch on students from any region where Britain had economic or defense interests, although Africans received special surveillance. When anti-British riots broke out in Accra in 1948, it was widely suspected that African students had planned these disturbances from London. British security services intensified their scrutiny of overseas students accordingly.[70]

Although communism was feared to be especially virulent among West Africans, there were other populations of concern. Famed nationalists such as Jawaharlal Nehru wrote of first encountering radical political theories in Britain; in Nehru's case, through hearing a Cambridge lecture by George Bernard Shaw on "Socialism and the University Man."[71] Several prominent South Asian communists were educated in Britain.[72] The India Office warned that whereas white undergraduates might recover from communism like the measles, this was "certainly *not* true of the Indians who are likely to be permanently affected."[73] Young Indians from aristocratic families were thought to be especially prone to "plunging" into communist ideology, both to reject their parents' conventionality and to mix more freely with the young girls of the Communist Party, who were "more brilliant than the conservative variety."[74]

The Colonial Office routinely discussed protecting Malayan students from undesirable influences, and considered "pre-indoctrinating" these students before they left Malaya. The Colonial Office was especially concerned by the rumor that Malayan students in Britain were being trained by British Labour leaders, and received requests from the Malayan Special Branch to find out whether these "teachers" were genuine Labour men or communists.[75] One alarmist missive estimated that 80 percent of Malayan students returning from Britain had been indoctrinated.[76] But even during the Malayan "Emergency," the Colonial Office urged a light touch with Malayan students.[77]

Even the most dedicated Cold Warriors acknowledged that communist influence over students should not be exaggerated.[78] Only 2 percent of overseas students were documented as having communist associations.[79] Most overseas students evinced a casually left-wing stance. T. E. A. Salubi reported how he had nearly declined to vote while he was in Britain: "What did the party in power mean to me, a colonial subject? Why must I interest myself actively in British politics?" Salubi decided that his interests were tied to the fate of British policymaking, and cast his vote after all: "Do not ask me for which party! But if you want to know, it was the Labour Party."[80] His diary recorded his delight at the election's outcome: "A most exciting day—Labour Glory. What a victory! May it benefit the Colonies, Nigeria in particular."[81]

In one strikingly racist missive, the Foreign Office reported that the Communist Party had failed to exploit the social grievances of African students; "colored students, even the more advanced, do not take easily to theoretical indoctrination nor to formal organization."[82] A principal in Liverpool argued that his Malayan pupils were far too elitist to associate with communist "wharfies."[83] One tutor noted "how vital the personal relationships are" with overseas students, reiterating that social bonds could cure political extremism.[84] The Cold War heightened the earlier insistence on bringing overseas students into contact with English home life; as one MP suggested, taking an overseas student into one's home aided in "building up the ramparts of the free world against the attacks of the Communists."[85]

The housing question was particularly sensitive, as the Foreign Office had long warned that Communist Party members were prepared to take in lodgers of color who were rejected elsewhere.[86] The rejection of students of color by was sufficiently widespread that even the British Council's register of lodgings used a code of symbols to indicate landladies' racial preferences, thus imposing a "private" color bar.[87] This casual racism was immortalized in the Nigerian author Wole Soyinka's first published poem, "Telephone Conversation" (1962), which Soyinka also read aloud on the BBC. The poem recounted his interaction during his student days with a white landlady who learned that he was an African, and asked him,

"ARE YOU DARK? OR VERY LIGHT?" Revelation came.
"You mean—like plain or milk chocolate?"
Her assent was clinical, crushing in its light
Impersonality. Rapidly, wave-length adjusted,
I chose. "West African sepia"—and as afterthought,
"Down in my passport." Silence for spectroscopic
Flight of fancy, till truthfulness clanged her accent
Hard on the mouthpiece. "WHAT'S THAT?" conceding
"DON'T KNOW WHAT THAT IS." "Like brunette."
"THAT'S DARK, ISN'T IT?" "Not altogether.
Facially, I am brunette, but madam, you should see
The rest of me. Palm of my hand, soles of my feet
Are a peroxide blonde. Friction, caused—
Foolishly madam—by sitting down, has turned
My bottom raven black—One moment madam!"—sensing
Her receiver rearing on the thunderclap
About my ears—"Madam," I pleaded, "wouldn't you rather
See for yourself?"

Communists, on the other hand, were reputedly offering social contacts, entertainment, unconditional support of nationalist objectives, summer tours behind the Iron Curtain, and the "stimulating vision" of a return to Africa armed with funds.[88] Outside of Britain, Cabinet was greatly disturbed by reports that the Soviets were providing lavish facilities— such as expensive laboratories and gymnasia—to lure African and Asian students, and warned that Britain must do its best to "outbid" the Soviets despite the alarming expense.[89]

Like their British colleagues, American social scientists were deeply interested in whether overseas students were radicalized by their experiences abroad.[90] But they struck a far more optimistic tone than their British peers. American researchers took note of the corrosive effects of racial discrimination for overseas students, and of the bitter disappointment that racism could engender.[91] But they also argued that African students in America displayed a keen sense of objectivity, as well as a reassuring lack of vindictiveness against their former colonizers, and that only 8 percent of Africans had acquired "nationalistic ideas" while studying in the United States.[92] Cora Du Bois, the Harvard anthropologist, asked whether overzealous experts had created the "problem" of the foreign student in their own image. "Have we, by adopting the running presumption that the foreign student *must* be a quivering mass of problems, encouraged a jungle-growth of a great, loose-jointed apparatus in this country which makes problems inevitable?"[93]

In 1957, the African-American sociologist and diplomat Hugh Smythe and his wife, the economist and diplomat Mabel Smythe, undertook a major study of Nigerian elites.[94] Sponsored by the Ford Foundation and the Social Science Research Council, they interviewed more than 500 individuals. The Smythes denied that Nigerians who had been educated abroad were disruptive to Nigerian politics. Rather, these students rejected egalitarianism and preserved aristocratic forms of social organization. They acknowledged that returned students could experience discontent, but claimed that their malaise generally took psychosocial, rather than overtly political forms.[95]

One of the more famous African students to enter both American and British institutions of higher learning was Kwame Nkrumah, the future president of Ghana. In 1935, Nkrumah traveled to Lincoln University in Pennsylvania to study theology and anthropology. Praised for his "good grace" when confronted with American racism, he proved exceptionally popular with his Lincoln classmates. They voted him Most Interesting Man of the Year in 1939, and composed these lyrics in his honor: "Africa is the beloved of his dreams, / Philosopher, thinker, with forceful schemes. / In aesthetics, political, all, he's in the field; / Nkrumah, 'très intéressant,' radiates appeal."[96]

When Nkrumah went to read law in London eight years later, his reception was distinctly less glamorous. Nkrumah described his "London Days" as a heady time, in which "there was nothing to stop you getting on your feet and denouncing the whole of the British Empire." But despite finding new friends such as George Padmore and active colleagues at the West African Students' Union (WASU), Nkrumah found that material conditions in London were dire. While he crafted a thesis on logical positivism at University College London, the meeting spots for African and West Indian students suffered an acute heating shortage, so that "much of our time during the winter months was spent walking miles and miles around London in search of lumps of coal."[97]

Within the British press, these controversies about student housing were widely reported as fodder for the "colour bar" debates, and as an exclusively metropolitan concern. But the Foreign Office and Colonial Office archives reveal more fully the high political stakes of this issue, which extended beyond the borders of the metropole. The provision of services for overseas students was one way in which Britain could contribute to Western objectives in the Cold War, although its contribution was complicated by its own ambivalence about educated Africans and Asians.

The Foreign Office proposed two methods of inoculating overseas students against communism: first, allowing their countries of origin to achieve their independence, and second, ensuring that students were not psychologically damaged by episodes of racism during their time in Britain. The first part of this equation—that European governments perceived decolonization as a method of staving off communist threats—is of course well known. The second element, that race relations legislation in the metropole may have been perceived within government channels as serving the same function, has been less often observed. As early as 1949, a top secret Colonial Office file offered disturbing new evidence about how the treatment of "coloured" people in the United Kingdom undermined British efforts at anticommunist publicity in Africa. More strikingly, it introduced the possibility of formulating antidiscrimination legislation specifically in order to oppose communist influence both in Britain and in Africa.[98] The Colonial Information Policy Committee argued forcefully that such measures could serve as powerful antidotes to communism. According to the CIPC, the Russians had a major propaganda advantage in the ideological battles of the Cold War, because there was no color bar in the Soviet Union. Although there was no legal color bar in Britain, the CIPC was aware of the pernicious effects of discrimination.[99]

Speculatively, one might ask whether such documents illuminate the weakness of race relations legislation in Britain. Historians have long characterized measures such as the Race Relations Act as a sign of the failings of liberal activists in the 1960s. The prevailing wisdom is that British liberals were disappointingly complacent about entry controls and offered ineffectual antidiscrimination laws as an unsatisfying palliative for domestic racism instead of vigorously defending the rights of migrants of color.[100] But situating all of this legislation within the global context of the Cold War suggests a new interpretation, in which antidiscriminatory measures were driven not solely by a weak form of liberal guilt, but also by the more immediate demands of anticommunism. Such texts reveal the ways in which race relations law in Britain may have been conceived—in confidential government files, if not in the press—as part of a larger response to communism in Africa and Britain, thus underscoring the internationalist dimension to racial politics in the metropole. These Colonial Office documents provide insight into what one might call the secret history of British race relations, whereby antiracism was shaped not only by the frailty of liberal responses to migration, but also by Cold War imperatives.[101]

British officials acknowledged that the demand for higher education in countries such as Pakistan was simply too great for the government to forbid its citizens to study behind the Iron Curtain, although they were assured that "official care will be taken to select well balanced people for training in the Communist bloc."[102] The Guyanese authorities explicitly rejected British proposals for an exit permit system, and also refused to discourage training in the Soviet Union. As British officials admitted, any other response would lay the Guyana government open to attack on the grounds that "they were behaving on a blatantly discriminatory and 'neo-colonial' manner as well as preventing young Guyanese from taking advantage of opportunities to acquire training overseas which their country badly needed for its development."[103]

Although social scientists around the world took up the theme of international education, the particularity of the colonial ties that were undergoing dissolution meant that the investigation of overseas students had distinctive features in Britain. In contrast to buoyantly confident American scholars, British researchers focused closely on the theme of pathology. Concerns about the psychological weaknesses of overseas students were not easily divorced from Cold War anxieties, because unstable individuals were perceived as more vulnerable to radical political appeals. Again, African students from newly independent countries were characterized as especially susceptible. Their presumed vulnerability was not only to communism, but also to multiple—and previously unknown—forms of mental illness in the metropole.

BREAKING DOWN IN BRITAIN:
OVERSEAS STUDENTS AND "BRAIN-FAG" SYNDROME

Thorold Dickinson's 1946 film, *Men of Two Worlds*, vividly depicts the psychological strains upon the educated African. Here, we witness the valiant struggles of an African music student, Kisenga, to hold on to the rational precepts of his English education when he returns to his homeland. In the opening scene, we see Kisenga giving a concert at the National Gallery in London to wild applause. He learns that he must return to Tanganyika immediately to aid the district commissioner. His community is threatened by sleeping sickness, but the evil medicine man, Magole, stubbornly refuses to evacuate. Kisenga becomes locked in a battle with Magole, and is nearly driven mad by Magole's incessant drumming. His people denounce him as a white man, and he begins to lose his grip on his sanity: "What is fifteen years in England against 10,000 years of Africa in my blood?"

As Kisenga lies in bed, feverish from the primitive sound of the drums, the white district commissioner exhorts him to become a "new African" and "put a bit in Africa's mouth" by combining African sounds with his English training. The commissioner organizes African children to sing Kisenga's own composition, which drowns out Magole's drums. Kisenga recovers, and leads his people to safety. With a moment of white guidance, the question of whether Kisenga's education will "hold" in Africa is happily resolved, and the white bureaucrats are glad to remove themselves back to Britain.

During the 1950s and 1960s, numerous researchers sought to explain what they saw as a growing mental health crisis among overseas students. Generally, groups that were approaching decolonization were described as high risk, whereas those that had already become independent were characterized as more psychologically stable. In particular, the mental health of African students became a veritable obsession, uniting Cold War concerns with a new psychic register.[104] Although many alleged communists were spied upon, African students were far more likely to have their politics described in terms of psychopathology. Part of what was distinctive about the postwar response to African students was the newly psychologized language in which student politics were conceptualized. It was in this realm of psy that we see the most pessimistic stance on overseas education.[105]

Overseas students were thought to be vulnerable to a host of racially coded syndromes, suffering mood swings of "bewildering intensity" and twice as many illnesses as their British peers.[106] One psychiatrist noted that African patients often accused British officials of interfering with their success. A Nigerian law student was hospitalized after he stated that people were plotting to make him fail his exams, and were hiding white girls under his bed to kill him.[107] Physical complaints by overseas students were often taken as signs of their emotional fragility—a long-standing trope of colonial psychiatry.[108]

Not all student populations were equally or consistently concerning. In the 1950s, many social scientists were quite upbeat about the impact of British education on Indians. John Useem and Ruth Hill Useem's 1955 study of 110 foreign-educated Indian men and women reported that 80 percent of Indian students who had earned degrees abroad had lost much of their antagonism toward Britain.[109] Most individuals had shifted from extremist views toward the political center. The Useems reported that American- and British-educated Indian students strengthened their egos in different ways, with those in Britain benefiting from outpacing their former rulers in academic competition. According to J.C. Read, the psychiatric adviser at the LSE and the Institute of Education, Indian students reacted acutely to stress, but also recovered quickly.[110]

The American sociologist Edward Shils wrote movingly of the psychological dilemmas of educated Indians, who bore the weight of ensuring democracy in India. Shils acknowledged the bleak material conditions that Indian students faced in Britain: beetle-infested rooms and meager meals cooked over a gas ring. But, he avowed, Indian intellectuals "told, with a catch in the throat, of the wonderful times they had in London, where life was free and the world was wide open." From the kindness of Laski and the Webbs at the LSE, to the *New Statesman* fresh and crisp on Friday mornings and the theater offering Shaw and Chekhov and Shakespeare, Shils claimed that Indian intellectuals recalled their student days in Britain through a sunny haze of nostalgia and affection.[111]

Shils's own students did not always share this optimism. Amar Kumar Singh's study of 400 Indian students reported that some Indian students suffered nervous breakdowns after only a few days in Britain, and had to return home.[112] Singh claimed that 70 percent of middle-class Indian students and 43 percent of their upper-class counterparts were disappointed in Britain. Both groups mentioned "psychological adaptation" as the most difficult element of their experience, and 44 percent of Indian students felt depressed.[113] Still, Singh favored international education for Indians as a means of combating ethnocentrism, even if he remained anxious about its potential missteps.[114]

Experts were becoming considerably less certain about the value of overseas education for Africans. As decolonization movements peaked in West Africa, the potential for political and psychological derailment seemed vast. In 1957, the *West African Pilot* proclaimed that countless Nigerian students in Britain "have gone dotty, have gone ga-ga . . . gone screamingly and ragingly mad."[115] Reports of suicide were not uncommon. At the same time, British psychologists and psychiatrists who worked with African students defined "mental illness" very broadly, characterizing individuals as "grossly maladjusted" simply for changing their course of study too often.[116] The Colonial Office's list of mentally ill Nigerians included one student who was never hospitalized but "became quite unable to concentrate and was only persuaded to go home with difficulty. He appeared to have no money sense."[117] Many kinds of unruly behavior might land someone on this list, such as interacting aggressively with their liaison officers. Often, West African students who were hospitalized for psychiatric reasons had clashed with the High Commission offices, and the police were involved in at least a quarter of these cases.[118]

One of the most important investigations of African students in Britain was undertaken by T. Adeoye Lambo, the anticolonial psychiatrist who established Nigeria's first outpatient mental health care scheme. Lambo specialized in psychiatry at the University of London after taking his medical degree at the University of Birmingham and completing his training at Maudsley Hospital in London. He conducted two surveys (1952–53 and 1957–58) of mental breakdowns among Nigerian students. This research was closely related to Lambo's work on mental illness in Africa, which firmly rejected somatic explanations for psychotic behavior.[119] He emphasized the environmental stresses that plagued Nigerian students in the metropole: financial worries, restricted social lives, and false preconceptions of Britain's grandeur. These disturbances cut across social strata, and could "spread" from husband to wife.[120]

Lambo's pilot study revealed that eight of the ten students who suffered breakdowns were subsequently repatriated to Nigeria; only two recovered, and the other six broke down again after a few months in Nigeria. Lambo sent questionnaires to hostel wardens in Britain asking how Nigerian students rated in terms of physical and mental health. The replies were unfavorable. One Birmingham warden reported that Nigerian students tended toward "moral collapse . . . their work goes to pieces, their appearance deteriorates, and their willpower appears sapped."[121] Lambo concluded that up to 25 percent of Nigerian students in London were mentally ill, a shockingly high figure.

Both British and African researchers emphasized the political dimension of this mental health "crisis."[122] Lambo argued that African groups in the United Kingdom were becoming pathologically partisan now that Nigeria was regionalized; the emotional unity of Nigerian students was declining.[123] This upsurge of "tribalism," combined with racial discrimination in Britain, could allegedly prompt psychosis. The Nigerian author Dayo Olugboji warned that Nigerians who had studied in Britain were susceptible to bribery and corruption when they returned, because they had invested so much in their success. Thus, the future of a moral Nigerian politics was jeopardized by those who had studied abroad.[124]

In 1960, on the eve of Nigerian independence, the transcultural psychiatrist Raymond H. Prince identified the "'brain-fag' syndrome"—a combination of sensory disorders and intellectual impairment akin to neurasthenia—in Nigerian students in Britain. Sufferers demonstrated the characteristic gesture of passing the hand over the scalp and rubbing the skull when trying to concentrate, as well as an unhappy, tense facial expression. Prince theorized that because the British educational experience required isolated endeavor where the Nigerian craved community, the syndrome constituted an unconscious "revolt" against an alien metropolitan experience.[125]

Two years later, Prince published a more elaborate study of brain-fag syndrome in Nigerian secondary schools, tracing the origins of the problem he had already diagnosed in Britain.[126] Prince was then the chief psychiatrist at the Aro Hospital in Abeokuta, and was aided by T. A. Lambo. They asked boys at six Nigerian secondary schools if they had experienced any unpleasant sensations while studying. Of 844 boys, 54 percent complained of these symptoms.[127] Prince concluded that children of illiterate parents were more likely to develop brain fag.[128] Ultimately, he had no treatment to offer, as he took the syndrome as proof that Nigerians were not suited to academic work and suggested that they developed this disorder as a way of escaping responsibility for the demands of education.[129]

The notion of a syndrome that struck particularly at African students attracted considerable academic attention. One doctor stated he had never seen the syndrome in West Indians, and only rarely in "Orientals."The psychiatrists G. I. Tewfik and A. Okasha characterized the sufferers of brain-fag syndrome as "the rather spoilt sons of wealthy parents who have sent their sons to [Britain] at considerable expense but sometimes not at the recommendation of the university in the home country."[130] Other researchers questioned the very existence of the syndrome, suggesting that the patients so labeled could fit into existing diagnostic categories: anxiety, hysteria, or depression.[131]

Starting in the 1960s, the Nigerian psychiatrist Amechi Anumonye (one of Lambo's protégés) sought to revise Prince's findings.[132] Through his investigations, Anumonye came to believe that Nigerians demonstrated a "special reaction pattern" to education that was akin to trauma.[133] For example, he noted that the first exposure to sexual activity or alcohol could be deeply disturbing to Nigerian students, who generally had a high sense of morals. The reactions of most Nigerians to higher education, he hypothesized, fell "somewhere between mental well being and mental illness."[134]

Whereas Prince's explanation of the syndrome had blamed the imposition of European learning techniques upon the Nigerian personality—Anumonye countered that the concept of a uniform "Nigerian personality" was a myth. The explanation for brain-fag syndrome must be sought elsewhere. Anumonye traced the emergence of brain-fag syndrome to a South African Bushman in 1822. Although the Bushman had not been a "student," he had been engaged in teaching an English visitor a foreign language and thus had been using all of his powers of mental concentration. This finding suggested to Anumonye that the disease was not necessarily linked to the challenges of decolonization, but was rooted instead in early colonial history.

Anumonye concluded that brain-fag syndrome was a curable psychosomatic disorder that caused no structural damage. Indeed, the disorder often acted as a spur to academic success. Although Anumonye did not explicitly link brain fag with the political activities of West African students, he asserted that it was important not to pathologize Nigerian youth culture. Ultimately, Anumonye suggested, very little was wrong with the emotional reactions of "our space-age youths." Instead, psychiatrists should focus their investigative energies on the elders—parents and teachers—who might turn out to be the more pathological individuals in modern African society.[135]

The trajectory of brain-fag syndrome reveals how such diagnoses were tied closely to the chronology of decolonization.[136] Although the syndrome was broadly associated with all African students from its inception, the focus on Nigerians as the main sufferers of this syndrome dovetailed with the evolution of Nigeria's independence. Such ties indicate the complex intermingling of power and pathology at the end of empire. These diagnoses could shape governmental policy toward specific student populations, spurring welfare (but also surveillance) for Nigerians in Britain at a moment when their psychological well-being seemed vital to Britain's global interests.

Other scholars described the pathology of "overintegration," in which students identified too strongly with British culture.[137] This disorder could manifest itself in a desire to marry white Britons; the physician's task was to help these students "face up" to the reality of having to return home.[138] Although overintegration was typically thought to afflict West Indians, Elspeth Huxley also recounted the tale of a Nigerian who left his comfortable digs because "he was *too* happy—over-integrated." The student reported that he was treated like family by a maternal landlady who did his washing and looked after his health. He had departed this idyllic situation because, "'I felt I was becoming English, ceasing to be African—I was losing my Nigerian personality.'"[139] The diagnosis of overintegration underscored how experts pathologized overseas students who wanted to remain in Britain. Those who failed to recognize their temporary status risked being labeled with a psychological disorder.

Compared to other groups of mentally ill migrants, students received greater legal protection from expulsion and, sometimes, an extraordinary level of psychiatric care.[140] Liaison officers recommended that overseas students should be admitted as voluntary patients to private homes rather than to asylums, in order to facilitate their release.[141] Still, the prognosis for these students was remarkably poor. In one study, T. Asuni, the medical superintendent at the Aro Hospital, interviewed eighty-two Nigerian students who had been repatriated from Britain for psychiatric reasons. Asuni noted that neither financial security nor intellectual ability shielded students from psychiatric illness. More surprisingly for those versed in the lexicon of colonial psychiatry, Asuni found no link between the student's degree of urbanization before embarking for Britain and his or her immunity to "culture shock." At least twenty repatriates were readmitted to hospital, five had minor relapses, and four returned to Britain and then broke down again.[142] In Asuni's view, repatriated students were permanently disabled.

During the 1950s and early 1960s, social scientists and state officials proposed numerous solutions to the "problem" of unstable overseas students. But their cures often conflicted with one another. According to British psychologists, the students most likely to break down were unsponsored students who lacked strong academic qualifications. Many psychologists thus urged stricter entry controls to protect and limit this population. But Cabinet resisted stricter selection based on academic criteria because students might then seek education in the Soviet Union.[143] Cold War anxieties thus made it implausible simply to restrict the number of overseas students in Britain. Similarly, the Colonial Office advocated devoting state funds to unsponsored students, who might be especially susceptible to communist proselytizing because of their precarious finances. The Colonial Office was thus willing to subsidize the very students who had been ignored by their home governments, specifically to avoid the communist threat.[144] The risk of these students turning to the Soviets outweighed psychologists' claims that stricter entry qualifications would produce a more stable population. The state's desire to control radical student politics, and to shape the fate of postindependence politics, was at odds with the demands of mental health experts.

Academic researchers and government officials often disagreed about the root causes of overseas students' dysfunction in Britain. State agencies were most concerned with the students' impact when they returned "home" to their countries of origin, whereas social scientists were more preoccupied by the potentially destabilizing effects of these individuals within the metropole itself. But they all eagerly affirmed the political significance of the pathology and the necessity of finding a cure.

By the 1960s, the distinctions and hierarchies between students and other groups of migrants were increasingly difficult to uphold. What did it actually mean to label someone a "student?" This elastic category encompassed everyone from elite university scholars to individuals in technical courses from hairdressing to boot-making and confectionary. Some of these individuals stayed in Britain for a few weeks; others, for more than a decade. Next, I explore how students figured in debates about migration, and how they underscored the contradictions of migration policy.

STAYING ON: STUDENTS VERSUS MIGRANTS?

In 1959, the Central Office of Information's film, *Learning in Britain*, depicted the triumphs of overseas education. A South Asian man in a turban is called to the bar, while the narrator reminds the viewers that

Mohandas Gandhi once stood here too. A Jamaican nursing student cradles a white toddler, as the narrator intones, "with gentle hands and trusting heart, all differences of race and nationality disappear." Students of color are shown with white teachers, whose prowess in textiles and metallurgy is "backed by the skill of generations." Young people from the former colonies study nuclear power, "whose beneficial use Britain teaches the world." Education is intertwined with independence (another gift from Britain), but metropolitan knowledge is valued over the local or indigenous, and Britain is still at the center of all things.

The film is clearly exhortative, offering many rationales for why young people should learn in Britain. Crucially, though, the final scenes show the students walking out of their classrooms, magically reappearing in their home countries. The narrator concludes, "the students come, and they stay and they learn . . . and in the end, they go, to apply in their *own* lands what they have learned in Britain." Ultimately, the students undertake heroic feats in Africa and Asia, framed by gigantic bridges and shining new hospital wards as manifestations of their new skills.

Learning in Britain offers a glorious vision of overseas education, one that depends on the students completing the circuit of developmentalism by returning home. And yet, it was at precisely this moment that British policymakers were most anxious about students who simply would not leave. As immigration authorities were increasingly aware, students and migrants were not always so easy to keep separate. When Commonwealth students entered Britain, they signed declarations of their intention to return home when their studies were complete. They were not, however, compelled to depart. When students stayed on in Britain, becoming indistinguishable from other migrants of color, their sponsors and mentors could feel profoundly betrayed.

Cobina Kessie, a law student from the Gold Coast, caused the Colonial Office no end of consternation. He arrived in London in 1937, failed the bar exam six times, suffered a nervous breakdown, and was accused of falsely styling himself "Prince Kessie of Ashanti" in order to borrow money from unsuspecting friends.[145] Kessie's career in Britain ranged widely; in addition to his legal work, he studied anthropology with Bronislaw Malinowski at the LSE and worked as a BBC broadcaster. He was politically active, serving on the Gold Coast Students' Association and the Scottsboro Defense Committee. The Colonial Office loaned him money for several years, but concluded that he was a bad influence on other West Africans, and should go home. Kessie finally passed the bar and returned to his ranks among the Gold Coast elite in 1945, but not before waging a lawsuit against the director of colonial scholars, and refusing to pay his debts. Still, he wrote, "despite my bitter experiences in this country, there is a sort of sentimental attachment which makes my departure a little bit difficult."[146]

If *Learning in Britain* expressed a fantasy of how overseas education ought to work, then Kessie's case spoke to a more complex reality. Students often refused to return to their countries of origin. Hastings K. Banda, a sponsored medical student from Nyasaland (and the future prime minister of Malawi), informed the Colonial Office that he had lived away from home for such a long time that he had become "thoroughly detribalized" and could not tolerate African living conditions for the five years of service he had promised. Here, Banda used expert language regarding the woes of detribalization to his own advantage. The governor of Nyasaland decided that Banda's attitudes were politically unfavorable, and accepted his offer to repay his scholarship money.[147]

Such cases were troubling because they disrupted the imagined trajectory of development, in which the fruits of British education were borne in the postcolony. They also threatened to increase the ranks of migrants of color in the metropole. British race relations experts sharply differentiated students from other migrants. From Kenneth Little's *Negroes in Britain* (1947) and Michael Banton's *The Coloured Quarter* (1952) to Sheila Patterson's *Dark Strangers* (1963), the most canonical postwar texts on British race relations treated students and workers as separate groups.[148] Sociologists generally characterized African students in Britain as a bourgeois group; they could be "rescued" from immorality as long as they did not merge with the larger black population.[149]

This perceived divide between students and workers had important ethnic overtones. After the Notting Hill and Nottingham riots in 1958, the *Daily Mirror* published profiles on Nigerian students who held prestigious government scholarships to counter the popular notion that all "coloured" individuals were West Indians living off British taxpayers.[150] Such contentions overlooked the longer history of Caribbean intellectuals in Britain, assigning this role only to Africans.[151] Whereas sociological research on West Indians focused on long-term processes of integration, Africans were described as profoundly uninterested in the mechanics of assimilation, focused only on their own nation's independence. African students, then, were "definitely not immigrants" at all.[152] Rather, they were visitors who were always in a hurry to return "home."[153] G. G. C. Rwegellera's study of migrant mental illness in Camberwell revealed that West Africans outpaced West Indians for schizophrenia.[154] He theorized

Figure 16.   Oswald K. Laryea, who came to Britain to study public administration, was photographed at the Lancashire colliery where he worked as a coal miner. (*West African Review* 28 [December 1957]: 1076–81)

that African students must adjust "just enough" to allow them to complete their studies successfully. Because integration was not their goal, their response to British culture was doomed to be disrupted and incomplete.[155]

Although sociologists and psychologists insisted that students and workers represented two completely distinct populations, British politicians worried that the two categories were not so easily separated. Unsuccessful students could easily become ordinary workers, or worse. Ivor Cummings, a student welfare officer who was himself of African descent, lamented that failed students composed up to 75 percent of the "destitute floating population of colored persons" in London.[156] The British Council upheld the division between "learners" and "earners," warning students that, "if you attempt to study and work at the same time, you are heading for trouble and will likely become ill."[157] But for most overseas students, full-time study was unfeasible. In a photo-essay on "Problems of Overseas Students," the *West African Review* included Oswald K. Laryea (figure 16), who came to Britain to study public administration; he was shown at the Lancashire colliery where he worked as a coal miner.[158] Even students from elite families could plunge down the socioeconomic ladder. In one study, 46 percent of Pakistani students said they had "slipped" into a lower social class upon arrival in London.[159]

These taxonomies were alternately embraced and rejected in immigration law. When employment vouchers were introduced with the Commonwealth Immigrants Act in 1962, the category of the "student" as a special type of migrant became more fraught. As one MP noted, it was almost impossible to draft the word "'student' in legal form."[160] Immigration officers were told that students should devote fifteen hours per week to their schoolwork, but were also instructed to be flexible. There was no way to distinguish between the genuine part-time student—a definition that encompassed an enormous sector of the overseas student population—and workers who were merely anxious to evade controls.[161] Indeed, the distinction between students and workers was eroded entirely for certain fields of training; student nurses, for example, had to obtain Ministry of Labour vouchers before they entered their courses. Student trainees who received any cash—even pocket money—for their work were regarded as voucher holders and not as students at all.

Individuals who wished to enter Britain as students were not allowed to profess a general desire to study; they must have a definite intention of taking a specific course at a single institution. But there was strong Parliamentary opposition to using the Commonwealth Immigrants Act 1962 to restrict the entry of overseas students. The Commonwealth Relations Office was concerned about excluding students from territories such as Nigeria, who often had limited credentials and might be unqualified "but whom, in the interest of maintaining the Commonwealth connection, it was desirable not to discourage." Furthermore, the bill might wrongly exclude "those from the white Commonwealth countries who had good family backgrounds and came to study in a more or less informal way."[162] For these reasons, draconian proposals for controlling the entry of students, such as fingerprinting or regular reporting to the police, never received wide support.[163] Despite the problems that overseas students posed, it proved difficult for policymakers to let go of the opportunity they had once seemed to represent.

The survival of unrestricted entry for students in the 1960s represented a holdover from the 1950s, in which students had been both targeted and hypervalued by Cold War officials. International education continued to be prized for its utility in Cold War propaganda battles. The Colonial Office argued that Britain must continue to stand behind a fully liberalized entry policy for students from the former colonies. The rationale was that higher education would prevent the creation of slum conditions abroad and the political unrest that accompanied poverty.[164] On this view, entry controls should be loosened for any group that contributed so materially to Britain's global interests. Students formed just such an ideally supranational population.

In the wake of the Commonwealth Immigrants Act 1962, the special status of the overseas student—which had for more than a decade been zealously, if anxiously embraced as a vital component of Cold War politics—began to unravel. The Home Office grew increasingly concerned about students who remained in Britain after their courses were complete (estimated to be 15 percent of Commonwealth students), "bogus" students seeking to evade entry controls, and "failed" students. By the mid-1960s, the Home Office and local police were allowed to request evidence from colleges that overseas students were progressing with their courses. Colleges were also advised that they should inform the Home Office whenever an overseas student changed his or her course of study, increasing the level of surveillance over this population.[165]

The overseas student remained a pivotal figure who both required the state's attention and served the state's interests. Government authorities sought to obtain the fullest information possible about these students' behavior while still allowing them the greatest ease of access to metropolitan institutions. In this context, new hierarchies of "real" and "false" students emerged. The Home Office described the practice of posing as a student to evade restrictive entry controls as a Nigerian specialty.[166] Some colleges were "inundated" with applications from Nigeria; in 1964, for example, the Kettering College of Technology received up to forty Nigerian applications per day, 90 percent of which were from unqualified students.[167] Elspeth Huxley reported on Nigerians who gained access to Britain by enrolling in an English-language course but never showed up to begin their studies. Because they entered Britain as students, they were "untrammeled by the red tape attached to vouchers, acts of Parliament and other tiresome bureaucratic controls. Then they found the jobs they had always intended to take."[168]

As one immigration official noted, many British educators resented the recent restrictions on Commonwealth migration and favored a more liberal entry policy. These individuals might therefore be willing to accept virtually any Commonwealth student as a method of political protest against the new controls. Such measures placed immigration officials in an awkward position. As one official complained, "I am a layman and not in a strong position to argue positively that Mr. X, aged twenty-four, with one G.C.E. pass in bible knowledge eight years ago, is scarcely likely to pass out as a barrister in three years."[169]

The question, then, was how the state and its institutions of higher education might best distinguish the bona fide student—to whom a responsibility was still owed in the aftermath of empire—from the deceitful worker. By the 1960s, the fiction of this division was constantly exposed. Studentship, Huxley warned, was being falsely used to bypass the racialized entry controls of the Commonwealth Immigrants Act 1962. The act's amendments successively narrowed the definition of studentship in order to close the "student loophole" in immigration control.[170] Proposals to increase fees for overseas students in 1967–68, which sparked widespread protests at the LSE, marked a new phase in the governmental reconceptualization of the student as an ordinary migrant.

Overseas students had once seemed like an exceptional and prized population in Britain. But as their health in the metropole received increasing academic and governmental scrutiny, their privileged status within the broader spectrum of migrants began to decline. If overseas students seemed politically significant in the 1950s because they were supposed to become leaders in their newly independent homelands, then the fear in the 1960s was that they were never going home at all.

As the fiction of temporary migration was increasingly exposed, and students—along, of course, with many other groups from the former colonial territories—married and had families in the metropole—these relationships gave rise to new conceptualizations of intimacy between former colonizers and colonized subjects. As we will see in the next two chapters, the domains of marriage and parenthood offered both opportunities and dangers for imagining and experiencing the afterlife of empire.

4. Much Married Men

Polygamy, Culture, and the State

The postwar years, it seems, were happy days for polygamists in Britain. In 1866, the case of Hyde v. Hyde had defined "marriage" as the voluntary union of one man and one woman, to the exclusion of all others.[1] This doctrine stood until—abruptly, mysteriously—judges began to demonstrate new respect for polygamous unions after the Second World War. In 1946, a polygamous Hindu marriage was recognized as a bar to a subsequent marriage in England, and the House of Lords declared that the first son of a potentially polygamous marriage was entitled to a hereditary position in its chamber.[2] With polygamy's arrival in the House of Lords, its judicial and social embrace seemed imminent.

Why did marriage look so different in the era of decolonization? Ever since the 1960s, legal scholars have argued that as more individuals from polygamous countries entered Britain, the courts rapidly learned—under the pressure of numbers—to accept diverse forms of marriage.[3] Migration, they posit, was an irresistible force that inevitably wrought emotive change, awakening judges to the necessity of acknowledging Asian and African migrants' demands for recognition.[4] If hostility to polygamy had been built on cultural isolation, evangelical convictions, and imperial prejudices, then the postwar era inaugurated the moral edification of the state regarding cultural relativism. Revulsion towards polygamy gave way to tolerance.[5]

In contrast to this view, I argue that the judicial recognition of polygamy was driven less by a rising tide of racial tolerance than by a desire to liberate white women from failed unions with Hindu, Muslim, and Sikh men. Far from accommodating a "new" heterogeneity, recognition of polygamy often constituted an extension of colonial norms, rather than a turn away from them. Polygamy cases were not just about migrants, and interracial and intraracial marriages met very different fates.

One remarkable feature of these cases was the absence of moralizing about different forms of marriage. The perceived danger of polygamy was not about divergent sexual moralities. Rather, British anxieties focused on the ethics and mechanics of postimperial law.[6] Was polygamy legal in Britain? It depended on where one looked. For many participants, the fundamental question was not *whether* polygamy should be recognized, but *for what purpose*.[7]

Polygamy cases were not limited to the courts. They took place in multiple sites, moving back and forth between different venues in the metropole and postcolony. The National Insurance Tribunal, for example, determined whether individuals in polygamous marriages were entitled to claim maternity benefits and widows' benefits. During the 1950s and 1960s, the tribunal heard scores of expert witnesses on African and Asian marriage law, as well as hundreds of men and women making their claims for legitimacy. These tribunals reveal how welfare was intertwined with the legal complexities engendered by the end of empire. Polygamy was recognized variously in different spheres, as individuals encountered widely varying forms of protection depending on their points of contact with the state.

Strikingly, the majority of these cases did not involve individuals who were actually practicing polygamy. Overwhelmingly, they affected people who had moved from places that recognized polygamy to places that did not. The state's interest in controlling entry for migrants of color, which intensified after the Commonwealth Immigrants Act 1962, intersected in unforeseen ways with anthropological knowledge regarding African and Asian marriage customs. Increasingly, immigration authorities drew on scholarly investigations of marriage in the former colonies to debate the feasibility of new controls on dependents. Yet even as the state depended on expert guidance about the parameters of valid marriages, it found itself constrained by these definitions in unanticipated ways. As immigration officers delved into marital practice, polygamy was linked to more controversial forms of union, such as child marriage. The colonial storehouse of knowledge on marriage was redeployed—but also challenged—after the Second World War, giving rise to complex new migration regimes.

The deference of the state to experts, especially in ways that worked against the state's intentions, is one striking aspect of this story. Yet even here, experts' powers of enchantment were not absolute. Polygamy cases were central to the invention of the migrant in Britain. As we saw in chapter 1, the creation of the migrant was an uneasy joint venture and not the monopoly of a single field of knowledge. Rather than being a descriptor of a stable set of experiences or behaviors, the identity of the migrant emerged out of the often awkward intersection of legal systems (imperial and postimperial, metropolitan and postcolonial). Different forms of expertise clashed, as those who insisted on the timelessness of African and Asian marital practices conflicted with the growing body of scholars who worked on assimilation. Expert witnesses were called upon to situate migrants within multiple time frames, assessing their relationship to modernity and various systems of law past and present.

At the same time, expert testimony also opened up a space for critiques of expertise.[8] Polygamy cases involved a highly vocal set of individuals who rejected expert definitions of their experiences. Men and women who sought recognition of their marriages opened a larger debate about the closure or survival of imperial law. Many migrants contested the classification of their marriage as polygamous in the first place.

The subjects of polygamy cases were notoriously difficult for experts to categorize, both in terms of their legal status and in terms of their allegiance to metropolitan or foreign norms of behavior. Judges were not just ruling on individual marriages. They were also defining the borders of Britain's sphere of influence over formerly colonized subjects. Judges were often uncertain whether to treat the individuals as indigenes of Africa and Asia—who could be interpreted through a colonial anthropological lens—or as migrants to Britain, who were more appropriately understood through the burgeoning sociology of the family.[9] Decolonization thus haunted the case law on polygamy. The indeterminacy of who was perceived as a true "migrant" played out in courts and tribunals.

These cases illustrate how welfare in Britain was shaped by the global forces of decolonization. Such forces included not only the experiences of individual migrants and Britons, but also the emergence of new legal regimes in Africa and Asia.[10] In tracing metropolitan responses to polygamous marriage, I ask why (and by whom) polygamy was embraced or denounced, and what this process tells us about the uneven integration of culture into the realm of English law. Furthermore, this chapter describes the dramatic and powerful stories of the men and women who were directly affected by the law on polygamy, and how these individuals negotiated a rapidly changing legal framework. I begin by looking back to imperial days, to trace how marriage and migration became so peculiarly fused in ways that were both sustained and challenged after the Second World War.

GOVERNING MARRIAGE: POLYGAMY IN AN
AGE OF EMPIRE

Laws of marriage operated as points of conflict not only between men and women, but also between nations and races.[11] Nowhere was this more evident than in colonial milieus. Yet official responses to polygamy varied in different sites of empire. Given the demands of indirect rule, which—despite its condescension—credited African culture with some degree of complexity and integrity, British officials in Africa did not wish to be perceived as trying to stamp out polygamy.[12] In a diverse set of locales, however, the British disavowal of polygamy could function as an effective tool of governance, especially at key moments of anticolonial activity.

The case of In Re Bethell (1887) highlighted how polygamy cases were intertwined with colonial expansion. In 1884, Christopher Bethell, an English aristocrat who made his fortune in South Africa as a trader, hunter, and emissary to Chief Montshiwa, was murdered by mercenaries from the Transvaal Republic. Prior to his death, Bethell had married Tepo, a Morolong woman. He had undergone the traditional ceremonies to validate the union under Barolong law, such as slaughtering an ox and sending the head to Tepo's mother. After the marriage, Bethell declared to Montshiwa, "I am now a Barolong."[13] Bethell also signed a document to provide for Tepo in the event of his death, specifying that she should be given thirty heifers, and that their child, if a boy, should be educated. The couple lived together until hostilities broke out in Bechuanaland, whereupon Bethell joined the Bechuana mounted police and was killed.[14]

After Bethell's death, his family in England challenged his will. They argued that English law did not recognize the "marriage" between Bethell and Tepo. The reason was that Barolong custom allowed polygamy, although there was no evidence that this marriage had actually been polygamous. Bethell's family claimed that Tepo was only a paramour, evidenced by the fact that he had hidden her from his relatives and had referred to Tepo in a letter only as "that girl of mine." The court viewed the fact that Bethell had avoided a church wedding, despite the availability of a Methodist minister at Mafeking, as confirmation that he had not viewed the relationship as monogamous. Justice Stirling noted that Bethell had never spoken to another European of Tepo as his wife. Tepo herself did not give testimony, which Stirling took as proof that she did not consider herself to be Bethell's rightful wife.

The Chancery Division of the High Court of Justice determined that Tepo was Bethell's "wife" only in the sense that this term might be used by the polygamous Baralongs. Thus, an English court could not recognize her.[15] Grace, Tepo's daughter, was disinherited, and Bethell's family retained his property in England. The case was widely interpreted to mean that no Englishman could contract a valid polygamous marriage, and that polygamy could be *potential* as well as actual. That is, a marriage was polygamous if the personal laws of the contracting parties allowed polygamy. Whether a man actually exercised his right to take more than one wife was irrelevant.

In the wake of Bethell, polygamous unions were an important area of colonial regulation. In Fiji, the colonial government sought to ban polygamy among Indian indentured workers. Polygamous marriages were characterized as a threat to the social progress of the Fijians, who might otherwise be successfully educated to European standards.[16] In Natal, white European settlers insisted that eradicating polygamy would protect white women from rape by Africans. Their rationale was that the polygamous system enabled only older men to marry, leaving young African men sexually frustrated.[17] In South Africa, where the Indian commercial elite frequently challenged doctrines of white superiority, all Hindu and Muslim marriages were declared polygamous and legally invalid in 1913. Indian wives were reclassified as "concubines," in the hope that they would flee the colony in shame.[18] The anti-polygamy law backfired in South Africa, as it became a focal point of Gandhian resistance.[19]

In most of British Africa, the colonial state relied on economic and social suasion against polygamy instead of legal eradication.[20] Polygamy was recognized for Africans who were under customary law. Secular courts could prosecute men who contracted Christian marriages and then took second wives, but the first wives rarely lodged formal complaints. British missionaries debated how polygamy should be discouraged and the penalties that should be invoked against those who "lapsed" into polygamy after their conversion.[21] Some missions withheld baptism for polygamous Africans, but this was never universal. Anthropologists were generally more interested in whether black Africans were rejecting polygamy as an index of social change than they were in critiquing the practice.[22] These scholars also assured Western readers that polygamy was rare. Lucy Mair, a reader in colonial administration at the University of London, put the monogamy rate for black South Africans in 1921 as high as 89 percent, presumably because most men could not afford multiple wives.[23] Colonial responses to polygamy thus varied by region and department, with missionaries taking the most hostile stance.

The mantra of potential polygamy that had been established

with Bethell survived in Britain throughout the 1950s and 1960s. Controversially, this aspect of the law seemed to exclude the possibility of assimilation. Migrants could be "trapped" in the marital forms that were dictated by their country of origin, regardless of their own intentions or behavior after they moved to Britain. The law of polygamy thus circumscribed the process of assimilation that was championed by race relations experts in other fields, such as sociology.

THE TROUBLE WITH DOMICILE: RACE, GENDER, AND POLYGAMY IN THE METROPOLE

The legal concept at the heart of polygamy cases, the law of domicile, had a long colonial history. The reliance of English courts on this elusive concept shaped the trajectory of polygamy cases—and many individual lives—in unanticipated ways. More broadly, debates about domicile revealed the clash between fantasies and realities of postcolonial migrations.

Starting in the nineteenth century, British scholars debated the relationship between polygamy and monogamy. Were these different forms of the same institution, or entirely distinct? Was it possible to convert polygamous marriages into monogamous ones—for example, by undergoing a second ceremony? What made a marriage monogamous or polygamous? Was it the place of celebration, the form of the ceremony, or the domicile of the individuals? And what was a domicile, exactly? The participants in polygamy cases gave conflicting answers to these questions, which contributed to unpredictable outcomes.

Polygamy cases compelled justices to dwell in the realm of personal law, mostly through their meditations on the deeply problematic law of domicile. Domicile was the relationship between a person and a territorial area subject to one system of law. Every person acquired a domicile at birth (usually the place of birth), which was his or her domicile of origin. Legitimate children took their father's domicile, and illegitimate children followed their mother. No one could have more than one domicile at once.[24] Thus far, the law of domicile seemed straightforward. But the process of acquiring a new domicile—a domicile of choice—was far more opaque. It depended on whether the individual intended to settle *permanently* in the country to which he or she had moved. If this intention existed, then a person could be said to have a new domicile even if they had only lived in the new country for one hour.[25] Conversely, if a person did not intend to settle, then length of residence was irrelevant.

Polygamy cases thus prompted broader investigations into how each individual conceived of their own migration. Colonial authorities had clearly never envisioned the particular population movements that brought polygamy into the heart of the metropole. The legal response to polygamous marriage depended on a complex thicket of factors: namely, whether the individuals involved were actually domiciled in Britain. In the debates about domicile, the clash between imperial law and the realities of postimperial migration became highly visible, opening up a space for individuals to challenge the often unsatisfying ways in which legal experts assigned identity.

Domicile was used to determine the validity of marriages. But there was little consensus in the courts and Home Office regarding how domiciles were acquired. Sometimes, the mere fact of a man marrying a woman from his country of origin was taken as proof that he had not abandoned his domicile in that country.[26] The parties in polygamy cases might be asked how far their "process of settlement" had proceeded in Britain—that is, whether they had purchased property there. But establishing the rule of domicile simply by evaluating material assets could be complicated and unfair, since migrants were so "variously circumstanced."[27] The Home Office typically assumed that the individuals in polygamy cases had maintained their original domiciles, unless there was strong evidence to the contrary.[28]

Which aspects of imperial law should be maintained in the metropole, and for whom? Many legal scholars saw the law of domicile, which had survived unchanged since the 1860s, as outdated. The notion that people could change the system of personal law that applied to them by acquiring a new domicile bore the distinctive hallmarks of laissez-faire individualism.[29] Domicile brought a Victorian legal precept into conflict with the changing parameters of colonial and postcolonial migrations. It was in the realm of gender politics that the vagaries of domicile seemed most antiquated and destructive.[30] The English convention was that a married woman's domicile followed her husband's. Even after married women gained the legal right to dispose of their own property and commit their own torts, they still lacked the capacity to acquire their own domicile: a power that was, in effect, tantamount to the capacity to choose personal law.[31] The question of determining a woman's domicile was especially vexed in cases of polygamous marriage, because if the marriage was held to be invalid, then the woman retained her own domicile. That is, a married woman took her husband's domicile if the marriage was valid, but not when it was void.[32]

In 1900, Sir Dennis Fitzpatrick, the lieutenant governor of the Punjab, argued that English courts should be able to enforce the claims of non-Christian marriages. Given the British empire's vast geographic scope, it was illogical and unjust that "our Courts in England should absolutely ignore all family relations among the great majority of the human race, treating all wives among them as mere concubines, all children as bastards," and their property as ownerless.[33] Fitzpatrick wanted courts to acknowledge the relationships engendered by imperial expansion. But he also insisted that Englishmen could not acquire domiciles in "uncivilized" lands. The marriage laws of "barbarous" countries were personal or customary laws, not territorial ones. Even permanency of settlement could not attract these laws to a civilized outsider. As the law strove to make clear, imperialists never changed their domicile. In this sense, the migrations demanded by imperial service were not migrations at all.

In the early twentieth century, debates about polygamous marriage in Britain focused on white women who married Hindu, Muslim, or Sikh men domiciled in India. Typically, these cases addressed the plight of women who were "trapped" in such marriages and unable to obtain matrimonial relief from English courts. In one sense, we might read these cases as a gendered twist on Bethell. As Bethell was shielded from the embarrassments of colonial liaisons, so too English women began to enjoy the same protection. But public and judicial responses to polygamy cases reflected more than generalized anxiety about interracial marriage. The discomfiture was legal, not exclusively social. Polygamy illuminated metropolitan concerns about bringing seemingly incompatible systems of personal law into contact with one another.

In 1913, *The Times* reported on a young Christian Englishwoman who had married a Parsi from Bombay. The marriage was potentially polygamous according to the husband's domicile. Her husband deserted her shortly after the wedding in London, and she traveled alone to India to urge the courts to order her husband to return to her. The case dramatized the complex links between marriage and migration, as the Parsi husband stayed in England and the English wife journeyed to Bombay to demand her conjugal rights. The first judge ruled in the wife's favor. But the husband appealed to the High Court of Bombay, which ruled that it had no jurisdiction; it dealt with matrimonial issues only when both parties were Christians, and living within the Presidency. This decision provoked angry indignation from the Anglo-Indian community in Bombay, which resented the court's failure to protect a white Englishwoman.[34]

In the metropole, some judges chose to ignore Hyde and offer relief to Englishwomen in potentially polygamous marriages.[35] Another Englishwoman who married an Indian man at a registry office was deserted upon his return to Madras, and she undertook separation proceedings. The husband's defense was that because the marriage was polygamous, it was invalid in England and could not be dissolved. Lord Gorrell, president of the Probate and Divorce Division of the High Court of Justice, overruled the husband's objection, saying that the husband could not marry an Englishwoman and then claim that by virtue of his domicile he was unable to contract this marriage validly.[36]

According to *The Times*, such cases proved the distressing effects of mixed marriages, which typically took place between "persons who hold loosely to the religious or moral codes of their own countries, and who are ill-adapted to bear the strain of a novel situation and conflicting duties." Although the editors acknowledged that it would be impossible to unify the many different systems of law relating to marriage within India and the other colonies, "that such anomalies [i.e. where a valid marriage in one country is deemed invalid in another] should take place within the British Empire seems unfortunate." *The Times* called for jurists to develop new remedies for this "distinctive class" of marriage, which was increasing "under the veneer of cosmopolitanism."[37]

In 1913, the India Office issued a circular for distribution in Register Offices to warn Englishwomen of the legal consequences of marrying Hindu or Muslim men. Three years later, all Register Offices were ordered to report any requests for marriage licenses involving men who were "foreigners, Indians, Egyptians, and Negroes."[38] The dominant theme of these different branches of state was how to protect white Englishwomen from unions that were legally allowable, but socially undesirable.

Legal scholars remained interested in the complications surrounding these marriages, especially as increased facilities for travel and study brought more Indians and Africans to Britain.[39] The case of In the Estate of Abdul Majid Belshah (1926–27) held that people of "polygamous race" could contract valid polygamous marriages in England. Two English women (Kate Belshah and Violet Majid) claimed to be the lawful wife and heir of Abdul Majid Belshah, a Muslim teacher of Eastern languages who died in England. Abdul was legally entitled to four wives. Kate testified before the High Court of Justice that Abdul had introduced her to his friends as his wife, and that she had embraced his faith. Witnesses from the Royal Asiatic Society testified that Belshah had been an exceptionally learned man, but that he had kept his wives sequestered. This type of testimony illuminates what kind of expertise was valued in polygamy cases:

that is, not only evidence about foreign marriage practices, but also the parties' adherence to metropolitan cultural norms. Violet gave evidence that she had undergone a Muslim marriage ceremony; she also solicited a letter from an Indian expert in marriage law stating that her union was valid. Kate and Violet ultimately settled that they would share Abdul's estate.[40] But neither woman was granted the full status of an English wife. Rather, they were both described as "women with whom the intestate had contracted marital relations in accordance with Mahomedan law."[41]

Such cases were crucial in heralding the arrival of legal pluralism in the metropole. By the 1930s, the Lord Chancellor's Office was sufficiently concerned about polygamy in Britain to launch its own investigation, arguing that the existing law constituted "a grave blot upon English jurisprudence."[42] It detailed the tragic cases of Hindu students who deserted their English wives, leaving the women with no legal redress.[43] At the same time, the Colonial Office undertook a related study of polygamous marriages in the colonies. It aimed to verify anthropological claims, as in W. H. R. Rivers' *Social Organization*, that polygamy was disappearing from the colonial world where it had once flourished.[44]

In his work on the Committee on the Marriage Laws as it Affects Marriages between British Subjects and Foreign Nationals, the legal scholar G. C. Cheshire warned that prohibiting marriages between Hindus and English girls would only lead to illicit intercourse, and doubted whether it was "right to protect English girls to that extent." What was needed was a remedy if the marriage turned out badly—a way to "ensure that the girl, once she has discovered her mistake, may be regarded as a spinster by English law, and thus be free to make a fresh start."[45] The other members of the committee enthusiastically championed a ban on marriages between potentially polygamous persons and English citizens. But Cheshire insisted that the courts should simply develop the means to render these marriages void.

Ultimately, Cheshire's view won out. But crafting a mechanism for English women to "escape" polygamous marriages entailed the beginning of the legal recognition of polygamy. The case of *Baindail v. Baindail* (1946) has long been taken as a pivotal moment in the metropolitan recognition of polygamy. The details of the case, however, suggest that the justices were driven less by the dawning of cultural relativism than by the desire to intervene in an interracial marriage. This case highlights the need to avoid equating recognition with tolerance, and to examine the racial and gender politics of recognition more closely.

In 1928, Nawal Kishore Baindail, a Hindu man domiciled in India, married a Hindu woman by Hindu rites in the United Provinces; this marriage was potentially polygamous. In 1939, he married Kathleen Lawson at the Holborn Registry Office while his Indian wife was still living, and Nawal and Kathleen had a daughter the next year. In 1944, after Kathleen became aware of the Indian marriage, she successfully petitioned for custody of the girl and a decree that her marriage to Nawal was null and void. On appeal, Nawal's attorney argued that because the Hindu marriage was potentially polygamous, it was not recognized by English law. Thus, Nawal was legally a single man when he married Kathleen, and their marriage was valid.

Nawal's appeal was dismissed. Significantly, the justices affirmed that Hindu marriages could be recognized in England for specific purposes. But they also noted that the law of domicile was not conclusive. Although the court recognized Baindail's status as a married man according to his domicile, it maintained that there were some practices (such as slavery) that English courts could not tolerate regardless of the law of his domicile. There were, therefore, limits to the law of domicile. The court left open the question of precisely which elements of personal law would be validated in England.

The decision to recognize the Hindu marriage and thus render the English marriage invalid was prompted by a judicial desire to protect Kathleen Lawson, who was possessed of a sizable estate, from the ill effects of her marriage. As the Master of the Rolls argued, if the English ceremony were held valid, "disastrous consequences might flow . . . For, if he [Nawal] decided to return to India, it would be her duty to follow him there, and she [Kathleen] might find herself, under Hindu law, obliged to share her husband with his Indian wife."[46] English courts, he suggested, should never allow virtuous English citizens to suffer such a plight. Regarding the polygamous Indian marriage as an effective bar to a subsequent English marriage thus freed Kathleen Lawson from the bonds of polygamy.

In 1936, Grace Clayton married Narayana Srini Vasan at the Blackburn Registry Office. Srini Vasan was a Hindu domiciled in India, who was studying medicine in England. Unbeknownst to Grace, her husband had already been married for three years to a Hindu girl, whom he had married in India. In 1937, Srini Vasan returned to India alone and ceased to communicate with or support Grace, who petitioned for divorce. Justice Barnard argued that, "it would be strange if English law were to afford no recognition of polygamous marriages when England was the centre of a great Empire whose Mohamedan and Hindu subjects numbered many millions."[47] If Srini Vasan brought his Hindu wife to England, then he would be living in adultery with her. If he lived in England with his English wife for part of the year, and with his Hindu wife in India for the rest of the year, then both marriages would be lawful. Finally, if Srini Vasan deserted both of his wives, then he could be sued for restitution of conjugal rights by both women and could be ordered by two courts to return to two different wives in two different parts of the world.[48] In a widely quoted decision, Barnard ruled that to deny recognition of the Hindu marriage would be "to fly in the face of common sense, good manners, and the ordered system of tolerance on which the Empire was based."[49] Grace was granted a decree of nullity, with costs.

These rulings were crucial in crafting a rhetoric of tolerance in order to undo the pernicious effects of interracial marriage. It is perhaps not surprising that English justices would object to such marriages. It is more striking that they located their remedies in their recognition of polygamy. As subsequent generations have equated this recognition with an embrace of multiculturalism, it is worth remembering that the judicial emphasis was on rescuing white English women from the plight of failed exogamy. Recognition was designed not to accommodate migrants' diverse cultural practices, but rather to free English women from the marital bonds they had unwisely chosen. Legal scholars argued that English women and Hindu or Muslim men understood the marriage ceremony differently. Whereas English women believed that any ceremony gave them the status of a "wife" as they understood the term in England, the men might see the same ceremony merely as a cloak for sexual intercourse until they returned to their own country. English women must be able to seek relief when their definitions of marriage inevitably clashed with those of their wayward husbands.[50]

One striking element of these polygamy cases was the way in which they seemed to reverse colonial legal history. When Britain established courts in India, Africa and Asia, one of the fundamental principles of imperial justice was the complex system of multiple personal laws.[51] The interlocking system of personal laws differentiated metropolitan courts from their colonial counterparts. The recognition of polygamy could be read as an abandonment of the civilizing mission, in which English justices sought to eradicate harmful forms of marriage for Indian women. Instead, the judicial focus was now on protecting English women from being tainted by these same forms of marriage, and being seduced away from their own rights of citizenship.

Polygamy cases composed part of the distinctive catalogue of tasks that were engendered by governing a multiethnic empire. How were these cases perceived once the age of empire drew to a close? Next, I explore how the British state's relationship to polygamy became more complex as the age of formal empire waned, and the independent nations of Africa and Asia formulated new marriage laws and affective regimes.

STATES OF UNION: THE POSTCOLONIAL REJECTION OF POLYGAMY

One remarkable aspect of this history is the fact that the British embrace of polygamy was so notably out of sync with global legal developments. Just as polygamy seemed to be increasingly tolerated in Britain, it was rejected in many of the former colonies that sought to modernize their affective relations. Although many British experts continued to insist that polygamous marriage was exclusively an "African" or "Asian" practice, a few scholars warned that Britain was in danger of becoming a salvage site for polygamy.

After the Hindu Marriage Act 1955, monogamy became the rule of law for all Hindus in India.[52] Individual citizens still contracted polygamous unions in defiance of the act, but their numbers were drastically reduced.[53] British officials were remarkably slow to acknowledge these transformations. As late as 1968, registrars were still warning English girls who were planning to marry Hindu men that "they might be saying 'I do' to a load of trouble when they learn, too late, that they are not wife No. 1."[54] Many Indians were outraged by these ongoing British mischaracterizations of polygamy as a "Hindu practice."[55] Such flawed portrayals of Hindu marriage exposed Britain's reluctance to see polygamy as a metropolitan event as well as its failure to register the scope of social and legal transformations of independence.

Pakistan also proposed new legal constraints on polygamous unions. Husbands were required to seek permission from the local councils before taking new wives, and the first wife's views were consulted.[56] By 1961, polygamous marriages in Pakistan were subject to a special arbitration court; Iran and Iraq enacted restrictions on polygamous unions as well. Singapore debated enforcing monogamy for all subjects except Muslims.[57] For African elites, the rejection of polygamy could function as a marker of social status. Educated men had good reason to limit the number of their dependents, in the hopes of increasing their resources for their family's social mobility.[58] Although the choice of polygamous marriage might have appealed to elites as a form of anticolonial resistance, the educated class embraced "Christian" marriage more than any other segment of the population.[59] Monogamy could be seen as part of a larger commitment to the "enlightenment" to which they aspired, especially as social scientists positioned monogamous marriage as a marker of national modernization.[60]

It was not accurate to describe polygamy as a "foreign" practice, as some British scholars claimed. Rather, diverse forms of marriage existed in both colonial and postcolonial African and Asian societies, each with a multiplicity of rules.[61] In this context, the metropole came to function as a site of marital anachronism: a striking reversal of the colonial laboratory model. The judicial focus on stigmatizing marriages that were potentially, as well as actually polygamous meant that polygamy possessed a strange afterlife in the metropole.

Even as polygamy was disavowed in many of Britain's former colonies, then, it was increasingly recognized in the metropole. The marginalization of polygamy within postcolonial law was accompanied by its metropolitan revival. Why should this asynchronicity have taken place? Was it simply a failure to take note of the impact of decolonization, an effort to freeze colonial cultures at an earlier moment in time and enshrine their difference in law? Next, I trace the evolution of polygamy's recognition after the Second World War. Previously, judicial concern had focused on the hardships of white women who contracted marriages with "foreign" polygamous men. After the war, judges and legal scholars were supplanted by a wider variety of state departments who sought to confront the relationship between polygamy and welfare. Increasingly, they emphasized the plight of women who were domiciled *outside* of Britain and who were denied the benefits of the welfare state.[62]

POSTWAR WIVES: POLYGAMY AND THE WELFARE STATE

The postwar decades are typically characterized as the age of recognition for polygamy in Britain. But the state's approach to polygamous marriage remained complex and contradictory. I focus here on the byzantine dramas of denials and appeals at the National Insurance tribunals, in which polygamous couples negotiated their relationship to the welfare state. By looking closely at the stories of these husbands and wives, and the unforeseen effects of recognition, we can better understand the intimacy, the disjunctures, and the friction between imperial and postimperial law.

Polygamy had long been recognized in colonial milieus as an economic practice, not just a cultural norm. But the Second World War generated new concerns about the economics of polygamy in the metropole: specifically, about pensions for the polygamous wives of Indian and Arabic seamen, who had played an important role in the British victory. In 1952, the Ministry of Pensions generated a complex new calculus of benefits that was designed to acknowledge polygamous families. The formula recognized polygamous marriages that had been contracted in Muslim countries, but not subsequent marriages that took place in Britain. In the case of death of a polygamous man, the ministry promised, "we would pay half the widow's allowance of gratuity to the first widow and if the second widow was considered worthy, we would treat her as an innocent party to a bigamous marriage and as an unmarried dependent and go to Treasury to pay her something."[63] Precisely what made for a "worthy" second wife was not clearly defined, but the files alluded to second wives' sexual histories as well as the length of cohabitation. As such calculations suggest, British officials were defining very narrowly the problem they were trying to solve. Their focus was on limiting the liabilities of the state to polygamous wives, and on circumscribing the state's fiduciary responsibility to the dependents of polygamous marriage.

Throughout the 1950s, the Ministry of Pensions debated allowing benefits for wives who were monogamous in fact. But the same files frequently referenced individuals in potentially polygamous marriages whose benefits were denied.[64] In some cases, the wives were pensioned as unmarried dependents; in others, not at all. The ministry suggested dividing the normal benefit in cases where there were two wives, as long as both had been married in a genuine ceremony according to the insured person's own religious rites. If the insured person was domiciled in a country that permitted polygamy, then his benefits should be shared among his spouses.[65]

As the case of Gbi Anderson (1952) demonstrated, it was neither easy nor straightforward for women to claim the benefits that the ministry promised. Gbi was born in Sierra Leone. Her husband George Anderson, also from Sierra Leone, had served as a seaman in Manchester and died during his service. When Gbi claimed her widow's benefit, a local tribunal ruled that because she and George were both members of the Kru community, which permitted polygamy, Gbi was not a widow as defined by the National Insurance Act 1946 and was not entitled to benefits. The tribunal determined that George and Gbi's decision to live monogamously was irrelevant as long as George was still entitled to take another wife. For the purposes of National Insurance, Gbi had never been a wife; she could not now be a widow.

Gbi proved to be a vocal and resilient opponent of the tribunal. On appeal, she submitted evidence from Kru leaders and from George's sisters stating that her marriage had never been polygamous. Gbi suggested that her husband had absorbed western ideas about monogamy during his voyages in Europe. Although her community recognized polygamy, her husband had personally embraced Christianity, "and it was therefore impossible for him to contemplate a polygamous marriage, not to speak of contracting it."[66] Gbi's advocate argued that denying her benefits contravened the presumably universal provisions of the National Insurance scheme, exposing undesirable gaps in the protective measures of the welfare state. British subjects should not be made to suffer for the "fictive polygamy" of their customary laws. After all, men could marry in their own countries "only as their own law allows; yet on coming here [to Britain] they are compelled under the National Insurance Acts to contribute to secure widowhood and retirement benefits for which . . . their wives will never qualify."

Gbi wrote angrily that Kru husbands had been "practically extorted" by this scheme, and she was made to suffer "just because I happen to be born in a place other than Great Britain with a marriage custom of its own, but my husband's contributions have been unjustly lifted from his small earnings and used to swell the coffers of revenue of Great Britain."[67] Ultimately, Gbi's appeal was rejected, and her widow's benefit denied. She was penalized for the place where her marriage was celebrated and her husband's personal law. The law of domicile trumped marital practice.

Other departments dealt with similarly controversial claims. In 1955, the National Health Service refused to pay the £14 maternity benefit for the seventh child of the wife of a Pakistani, Abdul Mannan, on the grounds that his marriage had been conducted in a place that recognized polygamy; the Mannans (like the Andersons) were monogamous. The Imam of the London Mosque, M. A. Khan, protested publicly, saying that it was legally and morally untenable for the government to deprive tax-paying Muslims who had only one wife of their national allowances.[68] Mrs. Mannan herself also gave evidence to the tribunal. Her husband had joined the National Insurance Scheme on the very day it was introduced, and she invoked the words of James Griffiths, formerly the Minister of National Insurance, that the scheme constituted an act of faith in the British people. By denying her the maternity benefit for which her husband had contributed, Mrs. Mannan suggested, this faith had been violated.[69] She also put forward her own expert witnesses in Muslim law, who asserted that Muslims were commanded to obey the law of the country in which they lived, and thus could not practice polygamy in Britain. As she wrote, "my husband and I are settled here for the last ten years so the polygamy is out of the question."[70] On appeal, the National Insurance Commissioner ruled that Mrs. Mannan did not count as a "wife" under the National Insurance Act.

The Family Allowances and National Insurance Bill, introduced in 1956, provided an increase in widows' benefits and raised the age for children's coverage from sixteen to eighteen. It included a clause proposing that marriages performed outside the United Kingdom under laws permitting polygamy should be valid for insurance and family allowances if these marriages were monogamous in fact. If the husband actually took another wife, then all benefits were lost and neither woman was recognized. Thus, a more expansive definition of marriage emerged in the context of the welfare state.

Various departments generated complicated new formulae to bring polygamous women within the purview of the welfare state. In the 1960s, the Ministry of Social Security introduced new measures to emphasize the length of cohabitation rather than domicile. If a man cohabited with two legal wives, then they were both included in his social security assessment; their resources were aggregated with his. But if one of the wives lived in a separate residence, then she could only claim benefits as a single person. Where both wives resided in the same household, the husband was entitled just to the basic scale laid down for man and wife.[71] The *Daily Mail* quoted one landlady, Mrs. Granby, complaining that, "though illegal for white people, our Government (quietly hoping nobody will notice) allow coloureds to have more than one wife, and no doubt the Social Security benefits to go with them. But nobody, not anybody is going to practice polygamy in any property belonging to me."[72]

Until the 1960s, the character of a marriage was held to be immutable, subject to change only through legislation. But now justices began to consider whether marriages might "mutate" from polygamy to monogamy. This issue was dramatized in the case of Ohochuku v. Ohochuku.[73] The parties were both Nigerian Christians. In 1949, they contracted a potentially polygamous marriage in Eastern Nigeria in accordance with Ibo customary law. In 1950, Vincent Ohochuku, came to England as a student. In 1953, he was joined by his wife, Vidah Chituru, who worked at St. Mary's Hospital in London. Shortly after Mrs. Ohochuku's arrival in England, the couple married again in a registry office because Vidah wished to have a marriage certificate to use in England.[74] Three years later, Vidah petitioned for divorce on the ground of cruelty. Under the

Matrimonial Causes Act, English courts could exercise jurisdiction in divorces even if the husband was not domiciled in England, as long as the proceedings were instituted by the wife and she had been resident in England for three years or more. The case thus underscored how changing migration patterns could affect legal rights in the metropole.

During the trial, Dr. Elias, a member of the English Bar and a barrister of the Federal Supreme Court of Nigeria, testified that Nigeria would recognize any subsequent marriages on the part of Mr. Ohochuku even though both parties were Christian. That is, the law of the land did not forbid polygamy even if it were contrary to the religious tenets of the spouses. Mrs. Ohochuku's claims that she intended that neither party take other partners during their marriage was trumped by this expert account. The marriage was held to be polygamous despite the Christian intentions of the husband and wife. Justice Wrangham held that the court did not have the power to dissolve the Nigerian (polygamous) marriage and could only dissolve the English one.

Wrangham was not arguing that the English ceremony had changed the nature of the original marriage. Rather, it had created an entirely new marriage.[75] If monogamy and polygamy were so different, was it really plausible that a husband and wife could be in both relations to each other at once? Also troubling was the fact that Wrangham's decision left the parties trapped in a limping marriage: still married in Nigeria while divorced in Britain. One scholar referred to the case as an example of the "casuistry into which we are forced by our obstinate refusal to dissolve" polygamous marriages.[76] There was no way to ensure that the English divorce would be recognized in a Nigerian court.

It is striking to note here how mysterious the act of determining an domicile could be. What counted as judicial evidence of domicile? How did proof of domicile intersect with the process of assimilation? These questions proved thorny for English courts, resting as they did on the individual migrant's intentions. The concept of domicile was vital to determining not only the validity of a particular marriage, but also the marriage's relationship to the welfare state. For example, if an Indian-born husband and wife who married in a Muslim ceremony in Pakistan moved to England and intended never to return to their country of origin, then they acquired an English domicile. The husband would lose his legal ability to take a second wife, and the marriage would be valid for the purposes of National Insurance. If the same couple intended to return to Pakistan, either in a few years, or in their old age, then they were said to have retained their original domicile. The marriage was potentially polygamous, and the parties were not entitled to National Insurance benefits.[77]

Profound social and economic consequences thus followed from this frustratingly opaque classificatory system, in which the state typed only certain groups of travelers as permanent settlers. According to the Ministry of Pensions,

> The British Civil servant who spends his whole working life in Nigeria and the Italian waiter who does the same in London do not acquire a domicile of choice in the country where they work if, as is commonly the case, they mean to go "home" in their old age. On the other hand, the emigrant from England who sets foot in New Zealand with the firm intention of living there for the rest of his life acquires New Zealand domicile immediately. The emigrant who goes to "try out" the new country only acquires a domicile of choice there when he has formed the intention to remain for an indefinite period.[78]

Such intentions were extraordinarily difficult for judges to evaluate. Furthermore, they exposed the highly subjective process of classifying individuals as "migrants." Anyone who entered a country for a specified period (for example, in order to complete a degree) could not say legally that they were acquiring a new domicile. But what if they were unsure of their future plans, or if their economic situation required them to work for unspecified periods during their education? The process of *losing* a domicile was similarly fraught, as an individual was said to have lost a domicile only if he or she had left a place of residence and intended never to return. The mysterious category of "intention" remained at the heart of polygamy cases throughout the postwar years. Who could speak with certainty about their intentions in such a highly mobile age? Few participants in these cases were willing to do so.

Domicile did not encompass the realities of many migrants' lives. Nor, as a law that was forged in an age of empire, did it respond to the exigencies of decolonization. Rather, it was used to allow transnational citizenship for some individuals, but not others, in ways that seemed increasingly arbitrary. Domicile assumed that each territory was governed by a single law: an assumption that was not applicable to, for example, postfederation Nigeria.[79] British officials also lamented that the law of domicile was fundamentally at odds with the larger project of assimilation. If Pakistanis, Indians, and Nigerians could continue to be governed by their personal law with regards to marriage, then they were unlikely to conform to English standards of behavior.[80] That is, British officials feared that domicile allowed migrants to reside in Britain without adopting British mores and thus shielded them from the pressures of social conformity.[81] In the wake of the Commonwealth Immigrants Act 1962, British immigration authorities were all the more desirous of maintaining such pressures rather than lessening them.

POLYGAMY AND MIGRATION AFTER THE
COMMONWEALTH IMMIGRANTS ACT

The Commonwealth Immigrants Act 1962, which restricted the rights of entry for individuals from South Asia, Africa, and the Caribbean, further complicated the metropolitan response to polygamy. Under the act, a woman could not be refused admission if she claimed that she was validly married to a Commonwealth citizen. But what was a "valid" marriage in the realm of immigration law? Did provisions for polygamous wives extend to child brides, who were also often polygamous? What about proxy marriages, in which one party was absent from the wedding ceremony? In the wake of the 1962 act, polygamous wives were a distinctive population of entrants. The governance of polygamy functioned as a means to police migrants' entry to Britain. This surveillance, however, was unevenly and often ineffectively executed.

The process of entry to Britain was crucially dependent on anthropological knowledge, as migration regimes and certain forms of expertise were increasingly entwined. Unorthodox forms of marriage posed a host of problems for immigration authorities. When more than one wife sought admission, the immigration officer had to be satisfied that polygamy was indeed the custom of the country of origin, thus relying on anthropological reports regarding these marital norms.[82] Polygamous child brides prompted special concern at the Home Office about conflicts between the Immigrants Act—which appeared to allow child brides free entry—and metropolitan legislation that sought to protect young persons from sexual exploitation, such as the Children and Young Persons Act 1963 and the Sexual Offences Act 1956. Several social workers proposed that newly arrived child brides should be forbidden to cohabit with their husbands and placed in the custody of the welfare authorities. The Home Office rejected these plans as costly and illogical: "there is nothing to be said in favor of letting a child bride enter the country on the basis that she is a wife and then turning around and saying that all the same she must not live with her husband but must be cared for at public expense."[83]

By 1968, there was some Parliamentary demand to limit the number of dependents seeking entry from polygamous marriages.[84] Entry certificate officers were instructed to flag cases where the wife appeared to be under the age of puberty (defined in English law at this time as sixteen), so that these girls would be barred from being admitted as wives.[85] The officer was enjoined to try to dissuade the husband from bringing his wife to Britain until she was older, and to tell the husband that his "neighbors might misunderstand the situation if the girl is obviously very young." Parents in the country of origin were also encouraged to defer their child's departure "in the interest of her assimilation into the community in which she will live." If these measures of suasion failed, then the immigration officers were instructed to alert welfare services.[86]

In all of these ways, the Home Office sought to discourage the entry of child brides into Britain. But it also conceded that under its own controls, which valorized legal marriages, there was no real alternative to admitting the girls as wives.[87] The only option was to convey valuable anthropological information about child marriage to the local authorities when such girls came into their care.

The fact that the Home Office was compelled to accept child brides as legitimate entrants against its stated intentions was yet another unforeseen consequence of the Immigrants Act. The principle of the act was that all marriages that had been legally contracted abroad were recognized for the purposes of entry. Circumscribed rights were granted, for example, to common-law wives from the West Indies.[88] But proxy marriages, which were common among Nigerians when one spouse (typically the husband) was in Britain, disconcerted immigration authorities in that the parties rarely had evidence of a long connection, and frequently had never even met.[89] They seemed to contravene the act's purpose with regard to domestic relations: that is, to preserve the indigenous nuclear family ties that colonial authorities had long sought to generate. Yet these marriages were also clearly legal in Nigeria, and seemed to fall under the act's protection.

African marriage customs, long a vital subject of British anthropological investigation, intersected in new ways with the thicket of immigration controls that emerged in the 1960s. Immigration officials zealously collected information from Lagos regarding marriage customs in Nigeria, putting colonial research about West African kinship practices to new use.[90] The Home Office designated certain regions of Nigeria as having especially "tangled" matrimonial affairs, with citizens who were "most devious" in using marriage to circumvent immigration laws.[91] One frustrated Home Office administrator complained, "it is difficult to know what to do about these odd Nigerian marriages."[92] The Home Office dealt with this problem by admitting proxy wives as if they were fiancées and insisting on new ceremonies after the women traveled to Britain. A couple might be required to submit evidence—such as a letter from a priest setting a date for a wedding—that they had arranged to marry again in Britain.[93] More generally, Nigerian women proved perplexing to immigration officials; they did not always bring their children with them, and frequently planned to undertake their own studies or business ventures, triggering suspicions that they did not plan to function as "wives" in Britain at all.

Accepting proxy marriages as valid for the purposes of immigration appeared to open the door to evasion. When couples claimed to be married by indigenous law, they could be questioned about their knowledge of each other, but in proxy marriages even this form of control was useless.[94] As the Home Office concluded, "to accept that a Nigerian woman acquires this legal right to be admitted to the United Kingdom simply by going through a form of proxy marriage would be to recognize that the control could not be effective against Nigerian women who wished to go round it."[95] The impact of migration controls was unevenly distributed, by gender as well as by race and ethnicity.

At the same time, "Commonwealth mistresses," or common-law wives, were recognized for the purposes of entry, if the woman hailed from the West Indies, and could establish that she had been living in permanent association with a man. The couple was not required to marry in Britain.[96] Denying proxy wives the right of entry would create an explicit hierarchy of migrants, which privileged one unorthodox form of union over another. Ultimately, the Home Office decided to accept the risk of evasion rather than rejecting proxy marriages as invalid. But common-law wives were typically refused welfare benefits whereas proxy wives were not. Proxy wives aroused more controversy as entrants, but their right to claim benefits after they came to Britain was much more widely accepted. The rationale for these distinctions was murky. Government officials cited a wide range of social scientific authorities who overwhelmingly valorized West African family forms over their West Indian counterparts.

There was no government consensus on a single definition of "marriage." Rather, each department legitimated different forms of union, depending on the purpose for which that union was evaluated. Second wives were required to prove that their marriage was lawful in the country where it was contracted. Like proxy wives, they had a clear right of admission, as long as their husband had not claimed to have acquired an

English domicile. In 1964, the Home Office vowed to examine female entrants more strictly.[97] Wives could be asked to submit a recent letter from their husbands, although the Home Office emphasized that the letter was only to prove that the husband was in Britain and need not say that he wished for his wife to join him; "a man cannot escape from his wife by emigrating to Britain, she has an absolute right of entry, whether he wants her or not."[98]

By the 1960s, polygamy cases increasingly involved intraracial marriages, which evoked different forms of anxiety. But interracial cases still held particular sway in the popular press, as in the 1965 article "One Thousand Wives . . . And Not One of Them is Married!" This exposé described weddings between "English girls" and "Moslem boys" in vivid terms: "it can be like something exotic out of *The King and I*, an impressive event in a Midlands mosque . . . or a simple little affair in the front room of a suburban 'semi.'" The trouble was that the law did not feel as happy as the bride: "a Cockney or Brummy girl who gets hitched to an Arab, Pakistani or Indian may not be married at all." Readers were warned that "the best thing an English girl can do, if she's got her eye on an Oriental, is to teach him to say 'I do' . . . the English way. And, if it's a Moslem she's marrying, to make darned sure he hasn't said it before."[99]

As one official from the General Registry Office noted, though, it was not only impressionable British girls who were deceived into "back street moslem marriages." Also at risk were young Muslim women who were permitted to enter Britain in order to contract what they thought was a valid marriage, only to find that the marriage was not recognized in Britain and their children were illegitimate.[100] One vivid example of an intraracial polygamy case was that of the "Much Married Man," Mr. Roggee Goodfellow Sammy-Joe.[101] Sammy-Joe was born in Nigeria in 1930, and married a woman named Victoria in a potentially polygamous ceremony at his home in 1951. The couple had a son, but then parted ways; Sammy-Joe later claimed that Victoria was caught in circumstances of gross impropriety with another man, and that he considered himself divorced. In 1953, Sammy-Joe married another woman named Felicia at the Registry Office in Lagos. Under the Marriage Ordinance, that union would have been monogamous, but because the marriage to Victoria had not been legally terminated, this marriage was invalid.

Sammy-Joe came to Britain as a law student in 1954. Felicia followed him to London, where they lived together for some years. In 1961, Sammy-Joe heard rumors that Victoria was saying he was still married to her. In order to avoid prosecution for bigamy under Lagos's

Marriage Ordinance, he took the Lagos registrar's advice and sought to divorce Victoria by letter. He repaid her dowry money, plus a £32 divorce fee. Victoria replied, "'I have received divorcing. I will not make any trouble.'"[102] He subsequently parted from Felicia, claiming that she had committed adultery, and deposited her in a flat in Kentish Town. Soon after, Sammy-Joe undertook a marriage by proxy to a nineteen-year-old, Catherine, in Benin City. That marriage was arranged by Sammy-Joe's father; Sammy-Joe had only seen Catherine in photographs. Catherine came to England, where she bore Sammy-Joe a child. Soon after, Sammy-Joe wrote Catherine a letter to divorce her, claiming that she did not meet the standard of education he had expected. She signed a letter accepting the divorce. By the end of 1962, Sammy-Joe had married yet again, this time a West Indian woman named Frances at a Register Office in Willesden. At this ceremony, he described himself as a bachelor. He paid what he considered a dowry: the registrar's fee of £3, to validate the marriage under Nigerian law. Frances bore him two children, but he soon wrote her a letter to terminate the marriage.

Sammy-Joe's legal trouble began when Catherine went to the North London magistrates and pursued a maintenance order for herself and her son. She did not disclose that she had already agreed to divorce Sammy-Joe. The court ruled that Sammy-Joe had deserted Catherine, and attached his earnings for £3 per week. Shortly thereafter, Frances won a similar order from the Bow Road magistrates, who ordered Sammy-Joe to pay £5 per week for maintenance. Sammy-Joe protested that these orders were mutually inconsistent; he could not be held liable for two wives at once. Although Sammy-Joe had been in London for eleven years, he argued that he remained a domiciled Nigerian who planned to return to his own country. He was therefore entitled to marry in England in accordance with Nigerian law, and also to dissolve his marriages without recourse to the English courts. He took out his own petitions to nullify his marriage to Frances, and to claim that he had legally divorced Catherine. As the maintenance orders, custody proceedings, and appeals multiplied, Justice Ormrod of the divisional court told Sammy-Joe that it was his fault that two women claimed to be his wife: "You should keep clear of the ladies."[103] Because both women required national assistance, the public was "paying dearly" for Sammy-Joe's matrimonial offences.[104]

The court heard evidence from S. N. Bernstein, a scholar of Nigerian marriage law. Bernstein testified that the letters did not constitute a valid form of divorce in Nigeria, although Sammy-Joe had been advised to take this action by the Lagos registrar. This dispute raised important questions about exactly who had authority over marital relations in the early postcolonial world. Expert witnesses played a pivotal role in polygamy cases, testifying not only about the legality of specific marriage and divorce customs but also about how they these practices might be transformed in the metropole. Experts clung to a largely ahistorical view of African marriage, far removed from the rapidly changing laws of the postcolony. Their testimony revealed a failed effort to imagine the particular postcolonial forms of modernity and mobility that so many of the participants in these cases seemed to embody.

At this point, Sammy-Joe's many marriages had become a matter of state. The court ruled that the original marriage to Victoria was still valid. All subsequent marriages were void. Frances was granted a decree of nullity. Sammy-Joe was ordered to pay Frances's costs. Furthermore, the Director of Public Prosecutions considered charging him with a host of criminal offenses, including bigamy, perjury, and procuring a woman by false pretenses. Sammy-Joe appealed that only Nigerian courts could rule on his marriages. But the court determined that Sammy-Joe had acquired a domicile in England through his long residence there, a finding that highlighted the disunity of legal opinion on how domicile was established. The appeal was dismissed.

By the 1960s, polygamy cases were integrated into larger debates about the secularization of British mores regarding *all* forms of marriage.[105] The case of Mohamed v. Knott (1967–68) illustrated how polygamy cases could be connected to other forms of moral panic. In 1967, Alhaji Mohamed, a Nigerian medical student in his 20s, married a girl, Rabi Mohamed Musa. Mohamed was residing in London, but the ceremony took place in Nigeria after Rabi and Mohamed had exchanged photographs. They had a marriage feast with more than a hundred guests, and declared that they loved each other.[106] The marriage was potentially polygamous under Nigerian law. Mohamed brought Rabi to London, where she was admitted as his wife. Shortly thereafter, Mohamed took Rabi to a doctor to obtain a birth control device. The doctor thought the girl looked young, and reported the case to the police.

Conflicting medical evidence was given before the Southwark North Juvenile Court regarding Rabi's age, and whether she had reached puberty. Although Mohamed claimed that Rabi was thirteen, a pediatrician testified that ten was more likely.[107] The notion that girls should not marry before puberty was enshrined in the Marriage Act 1949, which stated that no marriage should be recognized if either party was under age sixteen, although English girls had been permitted to marry at age twelve as recently as 1929.[108] Rabi herself gave evidence about the marriage ceremony, and about her sexual relationship with Mohamed in Nigeria.

The juvenile court ordered that Rabi should be removed from the family home. She was committed to a children's home under the Children and Young Persons Act 1963 on the grounds that she was being exposed to moral danger by her husband. The justices (wrongly) argued that because the marriage was potentially polygamous, it was invalid under English law. Therefore, Rabi was living with a man who was not her husband. Furthermore, even if the marriage were valid, it was "repugnant to any decent-minded English man or woman" to allow such a young girl to be married.[109]

Mohamed appealed the juvenile court's fit person order. On appeal, Lord Parker, C.J., held that the Southwark justices were wrong to say that polygamous marriage was not valid in England. On the contrary, Rabi had the same status in England as she did in Nigeria, and the court recognized her as a wife.[110] The courts were also divided as to whether the marriage put Rabi in moral danger. The justices at Southwark emphasized that Mohamed had borne illegitimate children with another woman before his marriage; he had also had sex with Rabi before she reached puberty, and had contracted gonorrhea from a prostitute thereafter. They concluded that every time Mohamed had sex with Rabi in England, he was committing a crime under the Sexual Offences Act, 1956, which criminalized intercourse between men and girls under the age of sixteen. Parker took a different view, for which he has long been lauded for his tolerance.[111] Mohamed would be morally endangering Rabi only if he exposed her to drugs or assault. The contraceptive device simply constituted a recognition of Rabi's wifely duties. Predictably, Parker also argued that girls from Nigeria developed at an earlier age than girls in Britain and thus were not morally compromised by marriage.[112]

Parker revoked the fit person order against Mohamed. The couple received a great deal of positive press, including their own photo spread in the *Daily Express*. Here, Mohamed and Rabi's story was depicted in highly romanticized terms. The couple was shown strolling in the park with the caption, "Once more by her husband's side . . . the child bride." The editors noted that Mohamed had visited the children's home every Sunday, and that the "young bride wept with happiness" when her husband was finally allowed to take her for a walk. Recounting her ordeal, Rabi said: "When I came to your country I could not speak English. I could not believe it when two policemen came to our house and took me away. Then

I went to a strange place where people talked very quickly and I could not understand. The worst time was when my husband explained to me that I would have to live away from him with strangers. He said that in time he would get me back. He said the courts would not keep us apart for ever. I am so happy he was right."[113] Mohamed claimed that Parker's ruling had "'restored [his] faith in the British justice I have always admired.'" The couple was reunited after a week's delay to allow Rabi to prepare for the transition from the state-run children's home into married life.

The Mohamed ruling also attracted many critics. The Labour MP Lady Edith Summerskill, characterized the case as "putting the clock back. Our laws were designed to protect little girls of this age. And to say that this child is more mature than European girls of the same age is ridiculous."[114] She asked, "what justification there is for legalizing sexual intercourse between a girl of 14 [sic] and an adult male, since this is contrary to the laws of our country."[115] It was unwise to allow Rabi to live with Mohamed, because "in this country we believe that girls of this age should be protected and because this would be, in my opinion, discrimination on grounds of race."

This clash spoke to the participants' different memories of colonial rule and misrule. Summerskill spoke of Parker "putting the clock back," but colonial authorities might actually have been more prone to shield Rabi from Mohamed than to legitimate her marriage. The legal validation of polygamy had engendered a broader judicial acceptance of child marriage—yet another unforeseen consequence of recognition. Summerskill's reaction might be interpreted simply as a restaging of colonial debates about the responsibility of white British feminists for indigenous women.[116] Yet the relocation of this history to the postcolonial metropole carried with it other significant changes. In contrast to earlier child marriage cases, the courts and media displayed little interest in fetishizing Rabi's innocence, or in demonizing her husband. The key preoccupation here was with the conflict of laws, and the ways in which the law of domicile manifested this conflict through the bodies and lives of migrant women.

THE AFTERLIFE OF RECOGNITION: MIGRANT WIVES AND WAYWARD HUSBANDS

By the 1960s, the judicial emphasis on protecting white Englishwomen from Hindu or Muslim husbands had waned. It was supplanted by a revitalized rhetoric of protection for women from the former colonies. British observers were always concerned that non-recognition allowed polygamous men to behave badly.[117] Polygamous husbands, too, might desert their wives or treat them cruelly. Why should these husbands be allowed to abandon their wives and children? Although the public and judicial image of the polygamous wife changed over the postwar decades—namely, from a white English woman to a migrant woman of color—the depiction of the polygamous husband as someone who required the state's surveillance was remarkably constant.

The scandalous case of Sowa v. Sowa (1961) dramatized how the non-recognition of polygamy was perceived to victimize migrant women. Benjamin Sowa was domiciled in Ghana, but worked in England as a telegraphist for British Railways. In 1955, during a visit to Ghana, he became engaged to a Ga woman named Janet Amberley.[118] Benjamin returned to England, and celebrated a marriage by proxy with Janet. The marriage was potentially polygamous by customary law, though both parties were Christians. The nature of the marriage was complicated by the fact that Benjamin had presented Janet with a ring and a Bible when they became engaged. According to expert testimony, these gifts signified the intention to convert the marriage to a monogamous one. In 1956, Janet joined her husband in England but he refused to fulfill his promise to undergo a new ceremony. In 1960, a Liverpool magistrate granted Janet a custody order for her child as well as maintenance for herself and the child on the grounds of desertion. Benjamin appealed these orders, stating that a polygamous marriage was not amenable to relief in an English court.

The appeal was "reluctantly" granted by the Divisional Court of the Divorce Division, as Hyde appeared to favor the husband's "unmeritorious" behavior.[119] Public sympathy for Mrs. Sowa's plight was enhanced by the fact that both she and her husband were "educated persons." She was employed as a teacher in Ghana, and had worked for the Liverpool Education Committee before the birth of her child.[120] As a member of the African elite, Mrs. Sowa should have been uplifted by her time in the metropole rather than degraded by it. In this sense, the English court had failed her.[121] Why, one legal scholar asked, should a man's responsibility to care for his biological child be tied to the type of marriage ceremony he had? At one point, Mrs. Sowa actually began bastardy proceedings in order to win child support, but was advised to drop them because she did not meet the definition of a "single woman."[122] The absurd result was that the child was neither legitimate for the purpose of maintenance under the Summary Jurisdiction Acts, nor illegitimate for the same purpose under the Affiliation Proceedings Act 1957.[123] Even if the affiliation proceedings had succeeded, scholars were disconcerted that the child should have to be called a bastard in order to wrest support from its legitimate father. Such were the contortions of polygamy laws.

Janet's appeal was dismissed. Lord Justice Pearce denigrated Benjamin's behavior; he regretted that he felt compelled to rule for Benjamin though all the merits of the case were on Janet's side. Lord Justice Harman instructed Mrs. Sowa to seek damages for breach of contract instead of maintenance, as she might prove that Mr. Sowa had failed to fulfill his promise to marry her in a Christian ceremony. She would receive a lump sum, although not the regular payments that maintenance would have offered.[124] This was, he suggested, the only way to extract justice from her wayward husband.[125]

Increasingly, polygamy cases revolved around the husband's duties within the welfare state. In 1948, Imam Din and Rasul Bibi Din married in a polygamous ceremony in Pakistan. Imam Din already had a living wife when he married Rasul Bibi, although the first wife died in 1949. In 1961, Imam Din and Rasul Bibi journeyed to England. Shortly after their arrival, Imam Din abandoned Rasul Bibi and their four children, leaving them destitute. The family began receiving national assistance. In 1966, the National Assistance Board sought to recover the money they had paid out to the family. But Imam Din countered that his family was not in fact his "wife and children" according to the National Assistance Act, because these terms applied only to monogamous marriages. Thus, he was relieved of his economic responsibilities toward his family. The question before the court was whether Rasul Bibi could be construed as Imam Din's "wife" for the purposes of national assistance.[126] The board replied, "it would perhaps be as remarkable as it would be unfortunate, if a man coming from a country where he is lawfully married to a woman and is lawfully the father of her children, may bring them here and leave them destitute, with impunity, so that when the National Assistance Board is obliged to come to their assistance, he can avoid all responsibility and thereby throw the whole burden of maintaining his wife and children upon the public."[127] The divisional court affirmed that Imam Din should pay £6 per week for maintenance.

Everything depended on the purpose for which this marriage was to be recognized. Within the relatively narrow sphere of national assistance, recognition was deemed acceptable. Legal scholars stressed the importance of preventing husbands from using polygamy to evade their matrimonial obligations. One study suggested that polygamous individuals were more likely to conform to metropolitan social practices if they faced the same obligations as monogamous couples. The court's recognition of polygamy would seem to have been wielded here as a coercive tool of assimilation, rather than as an affirmation of cultural relativism.[128]

This illogic was echoed elsewhere, as English courts demanded that polygamous husbands support their wives but still refused to offer the full recognition of polygamy that would allow divorces. The odd result was that although a polygamous wife was unable to obtain maintenance directly from her husband, he could indirectly be made to pay for her maintenance if she had been on national assistance.[129] The Home Office viewed this policy as extremely unsatisfactory: "a millionaire Moslem prince should obviously maintain his wives more generously than the austere standards adopted by the Supplementary Benefits Commission."[130]

Objections to polygamy tended to be couched in terms of unfair benefits that multiple wives gained from the welfare state, rather than a moralistic defense of monogamous marriage. Was polygamy really the worst of Britain's moral woes? The Law Commission on Polygamous Marriages thought not. Recognizing potentially polygamous marriages for specific purposes, the commission argued, "will not produce a very much worse situation in principle than the sundry marital adventures of our white permissive society."[131] The commission proposed that marriages which were monogamous in fact should be accepted for the purposes of divorce and maintenance, as well as for social security benefits.

Ultimately, the commission decided that the recognition of polygamous marriages should be considered separately with regard to each kind of benefit. Marriages that were actually polygamous would still be ignored. As *The Times* noted, the issue of how to award benefits to multiple wives proved the most intractable aspect of reform; "it is now not so much our matrimonial law that is 'wholly inapplicable to polygamy' [as Hyde had proposed] as our social security arrangements." The judiciary might be amenable to the recognition of polygamy where the welfare state was not.[132]

In the wake of the Law Commission's report, the Matrimonial Proceedings (Polygamous Marriages) Act 1972 abolished the rule against relief for polygamous marriages. Potentially polygamous marriages were recognized for the purposes of insurance benefits if they were monogamous in fact. The act was introduced as a private member's Bill by Neville Sandelson, a barrister and Labour MP, and was backed by women members from both sides of the House.[133] Sandelson promised that the bill was intended neither to legalize polygamy nor to indulge the "wildest private fantasies" of socially marginal individuals.[134] Rather, this "impeccably respectable" bill established "English mores and Christian marital obligations" on all who came to live in the metropole. Bringing polygamists into the fold of English law, he argued, would compel them to act like monogamists, as they would rise to the new duties that were demanded of them.[135]

Enshrined in the bill was a triumphalist liberal claim about how the decolonizing state could successfully accommodate cultural difference without sacrificing its own mores. But the various departments of state never came to any consensus regarding polygamy, and the process of recognition was always unevenly distributed across the welfare tribunals and the judiciary. Furthermore, the bill effectively ignored the longer history of polygamy cases, particularly with regard to interracial marriage. Due to postwar legislation in Africa and Asia, the metropolitan embrace of polygamy did not constitute a recognition of minority practices as they were carried out in the countries of origin. Rather, the metropole was opting to preserve a practice that had become far more contentious in a multitude of postcolonial milieus.

The debates about the Polygamous Marriages Act were vital in elaborating the Whig mythology of tolerance. The bill's sponsors relied on the fiction that polygamy cases dealt exclusively with "new" migrants. The language of the bill suggested that the government was only debating how the interests of "foreign" individuals could be reconciled with a monogamous community. Polygamy was defined as a uniquely "Oriental" or "African" practice, obscuring the role that white British women had played in its history. Furthermore, the liberal presentation of polygamy cases as a virtuous struggle of the host community to accommodate unfamiliar practices overlooks the extent to which these cases were shaped by the law of domicile. Especially in the interwar period, the judiciary was certainly concerned with the regulation of interracial marriage in the metropole. But even more compelling was the clash of legal regimes and the ways in which Britons remained encased in imperial law. The contentious survival of the law of domicile—forged in the crucible of empire—was the key recurrent element of these cases.

English law never eliminated polygamy.[136] The function of the law was to cleave the process of recognition into distinct spheres. Polygamous marriages were recognized for the purpose of granting benefits to wives in potentially polygamous unions. Furthermore, they were recognized in the realm of immigration law, particularly with regard to entry controls. The peculiar result was that courts and tribunals would allow (or sometimes compel) polygamous husbands to take responsibility for their families, but would not dissolve the marriages. By the 1970s, polygamous individuals could receive benefits for being married, but, ironically, could not obtain dissolution of these marriages in the English courts.

The complex response to polygamy illustrates the variety of ways that decolonization could make itself known in the metropole. Polygamy was recognized unevenly in different spheres. The tensions between the venues for these cases—not only courts versus tribunals, but also Britain versus Africa and South Asia—underscored the fact that the degree of tolerance one met depended largely on where one was located within the postwar state at a particular moment in time. Furthermore, this response to polygamy was not forged in Britain alone, but grew out of a larger debate about marriage law in the afterlife of empire.

The next chapter moves from marriage to child rearing, exploring how the history of decolonization intersected with metropolitan theories and practices of parenthood.[137] The multiple paths of independence in West Africa, South Asia, and the Caribbean engendered a spate of new public and academic anxieties about how decolonization would affect the structure of child rearing in Britain, offering another angle on the global making of the welfare state.

5. The Postcolonial Family?

Problem Parents and Children

No phase of the life cycle attracted more expert attention than parenthood. During the 1950s and 1960s, all Britons faced new perceptions and policies regarding the shifting demands of motherhood and fatherhood.[1] But certain populations of parents—namely, West African mothers, South Asian fathers, and West Indian mothers—drew especially intense levels of expert scrutiny in the postcolonial metropole. White families, especially working-class mothers, were also drawn into this orbit of debate.

Children served metaphoric and literal functions in the aftermath of empire, prompting specific anxieties about the imagined future of independence in Africa, Asia, and the Caribbean. It was seldom possible to segregate the health of the "metropolitan" family from global crises and transformations. Child care in the metropole required distinctive forms of transracial intimacy, some of which reversed long-held colonial norms. The politics of independence complicated the colonial history of child rearing by undermining the state's confidence in the value and power of its own reforms, and by promoting controversial new forms of intervention and nonintervention. Decolonization created new family forms in Britain, along with new modes and critiques of parenting.

In the 1950s and 1960s, specific forms of child care became an emblem of the carefully calibrated relations between the metropole and its former colonies. The strengths and failures of West African, South Asian, and West Indian parents were understood in relation to particular paths of independence, and the ways in which Britons perceived their ongoing responsibilities toward these countries. British scholars were instrumental in validating or stigmatizing different kinds of child-rearing practices—from day-minding to fostering to single parenting—each with its own tangled colonial history.

164

From the perspective of the British state, some forms of decolonization mattered more than others. As we have seen elsewhere, it was the trajectory of decolonization in West Africa that especially captured the imagination of British experts. The British narrative of economic and political development in this region shaped how metropolitan researchers perceived West African parents and children, and enhanced the status of West Africans relative to other groups: for example, West Indian mothers, or the white, working-class women who frequently fostered African children in Britain. This chapter traces the reasons for inaction, as well as action, on behalf of certain types of families.

EDUCATED HUSBANDS, PRIMITIVE WIVES: AFRICAN MARRIAGE IN THE METROPOLE

In 1955, the child care journal *Nursery World* published its first advertisement for a private foster home for a West African child in Britain.[2] Earlier that year, following a Political and Economic Planning (PEP) report on the psychological problems of overseas students, the Colonial Office had instituted a new policy regarding married students under its purview.[3] Those students who planned to stay in Britain for more than nine months were now encouraged to bring their wives to accompany them.[4] This shift followed more than a decade of Colonial Office debate. The project of educating African men in Britain was expected to revolutionize their domestic, as well as professional lives. The key question was whether husbands only—or their wives, too—should be the agents of change. Gold Coast students had to sign an agreement not to marry in order to take up their scholarships, as married scholars were feared to be "harassed and uninspired individuals who could not devote their full vigor and energies to academic life."[5] One official proposed a ban on marriage for all African students in Britain, although "cases are rare and Young Love is———?"[6]

Young love *was* indeed unpredictable, as was its impact on metropolitan and colonial policy.[7] Rather than barring male students from marrying, the Colonial Office considered the merits of bringing African wives to Britain. With their wives by their side, students need not be so wary of mixing socially with Britons, as they would not be suspected of trying to instigate sexual relationships with white women, and they would be less susceptible to political subversion.[8] Conversely, if these students returned to wives who had not shared their experiences, then they were likely to become frustrated and politically discontented. Secretary of State for the Colonies J. A. G. Griffiths considered the hardships of students who found

Figure 17.   Melvine Stuart of Sierra Leone, who earned her teacher's certificate at Homerton College, Cambridge. Here she was shown spinning yarn on an old English spinning wheel. (*West African Review* 18 [December 1947]: 1282)

"on their return to the Colonies, that their outlook has altered so much that it is rather difficult to live with their former wives."[9] Unworldly wives might encourage their husbands to "revert" to primitive ways and negate the positive effects of education.[10]

By 1950, Jamaica, Malaya, Tanganyika, Sierra Leone, and the Gambia had agreed to fund the passages of scholars' wives and children to Britain.[11] But not all colonial authorities were enthusiastic. On the Gold Coast, wives were interviewed to prove that they would benefit from the trip; some officials considered allowing only literate wives to travel.[12] In Northern Rhodesia, officials doubted whether African women were capable of learning from a stay in the United Kingdom.[13] One tutor warned that a very promising Sudanese student had "regressed" when his wife, who spoke no English, joined him in London; the couple retired to private lodgings and had no social contacts.[14]

In the wake of the Colonial Office's policy change, however, growing numbers of African male students traveled to Britain with their wives. The secretary of state arranged courses for wives in domestic science, dressmaking, secretarial work, teaching, midwifery and infant care. Classes were available in group leadership, club development, tropical nutrition, English, and public speaking.[15] At the same time, unmarried

Figure 18.   Stuart was also shown giving a tea party for her white classmates. The caption read, "'I say, girls, aren't these muffins simply scrumptious?'" (*West African Review* 18 [December 1947]: 1283)

African women undertook their own courses of study in Britain (figures 17 and 18).[16] The *West African Review* published advice from "Jennifer," an eighteen-year-old at Oxford, who instructed her compatriots to invest in a stylish camel coat, expensive woolen underclothes, and a coffee percolator for their student days in Britain.[17]

That same year, the *Review* published a photo essay of prominent West African women, many of whom had been educated abroad. Aduke Moore and Gloria Rhodes, who together opened a law practice in Lagos after qualifying as barristers in London, were pictured, along with Gold Coast policewoman Rosamond Ahiama, who trained in Staffordshire (figures 19 and 20). Rhodes had also appeared in the *Review* during her student days (figure 21), with a glamorous shot of her performing the "sensuous dance of the Caribbean" with a West Indian folk dance group. Here, Rhodes was participating in a transnational black culture that was uniquely accessible in London.

After 1955, there were new opportunities for African husbands and wives to unite in Britain, and for unmarried African men and women to

Beauty allies itself to intellect in the charming persons of Miss Gloria Rhodes (sitting at desk) and Mrs. Aduke Moore, who have set up a joint practice in Lagos after qualifying as barristers of the Middle Temple, London. They have an office in Campos Square, where clients are interviewed and briefs studied in preparation for the morning's courts.

CAREER WOMEN
OF
WEST AFRICA

Care of children, especially on the busy streets of Accra, is one of the duties of the Gold Coast policewoman. In the photograph with a group of Accra children are Sergeant Rosamund Ahiama, who was trained in Staffordshire, England, and P.C. Esther Botchway.

Figure 19 *(top)*.   A 1955 photo-essay on "Career Women of West Africa" included several women who had been educated in Britain, including the barristers Aduke Moore and Gloria Rhodes. (*West African Review* 26 [April 1955]: 290)

Figure 20 *(bottom)*.   The 1955 photo-essay included a Sergeant Rosamund Ahiama, a policewoman from Accra, who trained in Staffordshire, England. (*West African Review* 26 [April 1955]: 296)

Joie de Vivre

When she is not pouring over her law books Miss Gloria Rhodes, daughter of Mr. Justice Rhodes (of the Nigerian Bench) takes time off to join a group of West Indian folk dancers who specialize in the captivating rhythms of the islands. Gloria has been taught by Boscoe Holder, who founded the group and here she practises the " beguine " which, in its original Martinique form, is said to be one of the most sensuous dances of the Caribbean and unlike the version introduced to the modern ballroom through Cole Porter's song. The " Boscoe Holder Troupe ", as it is known, has appeared on television and it is planned to tour the provinces and Europe. Miss Rhodes is studying law at the Inns of Court, London.

Figure 21.   Gloria Rhodes had also appeared in the *West African Review* several years earlier, during her student days in London. (*West African Review* 22 [March 1951]: 253)

meet there (figure 22). But although the Colonial Office had advocated the reunion of African husbands and wives in the metropole, the prospect of large numbers of children resulting from these unions quickly proved troubling. The fate of these children was highly charged, an emblem of the ethics and ambitions of the decolonizing state. As early as 1951, Colonial Office authorities argued that students should be discouraged from bringing their children with them.[18] Regarding children born in

Figure 22.   The wedding photo of Mr. Eyo Ita and Mrs. Olufemia
Jibowu. Mr. Ita was a medical student at King's College, Newcastle,
and his wife was a teacher of domestic science. The couple had been
friends as children in Lagos but became reacquainted at King's
College, and were married in Newcastle. (*West African Review* 28
[October 1957]: 933)

Britain, the Colonial Office's stance was that their mothers should only
study subjects that would aid them in caring for their own babies.

The department's policy was thus deeply contradictory. The unity of
African husbands and wives was essential to the political stability of the
continent after independence. But the presence of African children in
Britain was quickly pathologized in governmental channels. If the influx
of wives could keep male students sexually and politically quiescent, then
the demands of caring for their children could damage the quality of their
education and the children's own psychological and physical health. The
provision of care for African children in Britain exposed rifts among
different forms of expertise, as social workers and foreign policymakers
were increasingly at odds.

MAKING MIGRANT FAMILIES: AFRICAN CHILDREN AS
STATUS SYMBOLS AND VICTIMS

By 1960, there were 11,000 Africans (mostly Nigerians and Ghanaians)
in Britain as recognized students, plus tens of thousands of "private"

students without government scholarships. These students frequently placed their children, both African-born and British-born, in the care of other adults without the official supervision of state or local authorities. Typically, the children were placed with white, working-class families. According to British observers, the children were believed to accrue social and educational benefits in these private foster homes while their biological parents focused on earning their professional qualifications.[19] *The Times* estimated in 1968 that up to 5,000 African children were privately fostered in Britain annually, with their parents paying up to £3 per week for their children's care.[20]

Placements were generally made through word of mouth or "Homes Wanted" advertisements in child care journals. African parents carefully detailed their preferences, specifying, for example, that the foster mother should have no babies of her own, or should reside in a rural area.[21] The African student population was concentrated in London, but children of African students were typically "exported" to Kent, Surrey, East Sussex, Hertfordshire, and Essex because of the capital's housing shortage. By 1964, 768 African children were fostered in Kent alone, and 1,743 Nigerian children were dispersed in homes throughout southeast England.[22] As one social worker put it, "the Home Counties are full of Nigerian babies."[23]

Early press reports often championed this form of transracial fostering.[24] In 1954, the *West African Review* featured three-year-old Sandra Oke, gleefully celebrating a magical Christmas in London with her white foster mother, Ada Wheeler (figures 23–25).[25] Miss Christine Akin, a West African student, publicly praised a Chatham family for being "too good to our children, buying them things from their own pockets."[26] Akin's story stressed the benefits of the healthy, and quintessentially English, "garden counties," where "coloured babies are being tucked into bed each night."[27] On this view, private fostering reflected the unselfish choice of loving African mothers who wished to offer an antidote to London's vices and give their babies a "happy home life" nearby.

Initially, the press depicted fostering as a way to promote interracial harmony.[28] In 1957, the *Empire News* and *Daily Mirror* featured the Shakespearean actor, John Neville, and his wife, who had "successfully introduced one or more coloured children" into their home and had experienced "wonderful pleasure."[29] The transracial family, when so temporally limited, could provide a happy site of sympathy between migrants and citizens. Vivien Biggs, a social worker, noted that many young Africans returned to their childhood foster homes to lodge when they pursued university degrees. She saw these homes as the only

Figure 23.   "A Santa for Sandra." Sandra Oke, age 3, pictured in the *West African Review* in 1954 with Santa Claus and her white foster mother, Mrs. Ada Wheeler. Ada Wheeler was praised in the *Review* for having fostered more than 150 British and overseas children. The photograph was taken at a London department store. (*West African Review* 25 [January 1954]: 30)

locales where Africans might meet British people on equal terms. Foster homes—as a site of intimate transracial contact—offered one solution to the isolation and alienation of Africans in Britain.[30]

But by the late 1960s, the British view of these transracial fostering agreements had become powerfully negative. Headlines such as "Babies for Hire," "Squeezing Gold from Babies," and "White Girls Exploited by City Harpies" articulated a new sense of panic within the welfare establishment and the press. As these headlines suggest, the target of criticism could shift between the African "city harpies" who took advantage of white foster mothers, and the failings of white parents who "exploited" African babies.

Eighteen African children died in private foster homes in Britain between 1961 and 1964, and scandalous cases of abuse and neglect were widely publicized.[31] By 1963, the Kent County Council was spending

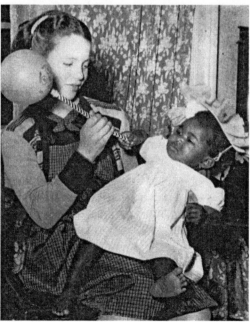

Figure 24 *(top).* Several other foster children appeared in the 1954 *West African Review* article as "A Santa for Sandra"; Ann Bello was shown in a homemade leopard skin singing "Wooden Hut." (*West African Review* 25 [January 1954]: 31)

Figure 25 *(left).* "Even little Bodi Williams, youngest member of the Wheeler 'family' is not forgotten." (*West African Review* 25 [January 1954]: 31)

£15,000 every year on problems related to African children in private foster care.[32] British welfare workers linked private fostering to developmental problems, including delayed speech and an inability to form relationships. Nigerian doctors reported that privately fostered children were returning to Africa in poor physical and mental health.[33] The foster mother of one Nigerian boy said, "He is the delinquent of tomorrow."[34]

By 1968, the Children's Department had urged a reversal of the Colonial Office's policy. Male students who came to the United Kingdom for more than one year were now to be discouraged from bringing their wives and children. Women who wished to pursue their own courses of study were advised to leave their children with relatives. If children were born in Britain, the mother should "in every case put the welfare of the children above her own studies or job" in order to avoid private foster care.[35]

This shift from British sympathy for African student parents in the 1950s to the demonization of private fostering in the 1960s was linked to new border controls. Legislation aimed specifically against Commonwealth children was instituted in 1965; children under sixteen years of age were not to be admitted to join relatives other than their parents, and children over the age of sixteen were barred from admission, even if their parents had already settled in Britain.[36] In 1968, the two-parent rule was introduced, meaning that children under sixteen were now admissible only if both parents were resident in the United Kingdom or were accompanying the child.[37] Migrant families were thus increasingly fractured by the demands of postimperial law.

Immigration laws, however, are only part of the story. The public view of transracial fostering was complicated by shifting definitions of parenthood—especially with regard to expectations of motherhood. Furthermore, the politics of fostering became increasingly divisive between the late 1950s, when numerous African countries were on the verge of independence, and the mid-1960s, when independence was largely a given. These joint chronologies of African and British history—along with the timeline of shifting migration policies—all contributed to the acceleration of anxiety about private fostering in the metropole.

Although sociologists and social workers tended to assume that the fostering of white British children declined as West African fostering rose, there were always white children in private foster care. Of the 10,000 children privately fostered in England in 1974, 6,000 were born to African student parents; the other 4,000 attracted virtually no notice.[38] Furthermore, in the wake of wartime child evacuation programs and emigration schemes, there were multiple ways in which white British children might be separated from their parents.

How, then, did private fostering come to be articulated in Britain as a distinctively "African" problem, a pathological emblem of the newly mobile African family? Sociologists and social workers have analyzed the motives of biological and foster parents, as well as the impact on the children. But the historical conditions in which these relationships emerged has been largely overlooked. This chapter recaptures the role of the state—from individual children's officers to the Home Office and Colonial Office—in creating and responding to the crisis of West African children in Britain, which was in turn complicated by British scholarship on West African fostering practices. The perceived demands of decolonization produced competing agendas for state representatives regarding African children and severely limited the British state's response to West African children within its borders.

The debate about private fostering exposed deep rifts between different government branches about how to aid African children. Liberal scholars of race relations had frequently lamented that British home life seemed impenetrable to migrants of color. The fact that these children were integrated, even temporarily, into the British family spoke powerfully to such concerns. Yet the very process of this integration led these same children—along with their biological and foster parents—into a series of conflicts with the British state, whether through cases of abuse, neglect, or custody disputes.

From sociologists to ex-colonial governors, the participants structured their interactions with African parents and children according to their view of African independence and its impact on British and African families. They disagreed about the quality of African mothering, and the factors that led African parents to foster their children in the first place. British officials experienced profound conflicts between what they saw as their duties to African student parents—the future leaders of independent nations—and to African children, who required the protection of the British state.

It may seem counterintuitive to speak of the role of the state with regard to private foster care, since private fostering explicitly excludes the state from child care arrangements. Officially, West African children in private foster care fell outside the local authority's purview. But private fostering was always a focal point of anxiety for children's officers and policymakers.[39] After the Second World War, governmental concern with child evacuees prompted a new ethos of public safety and inspection.[40]

In 1948, the Children's Department took over responsibility for supervising private foster homes, but the law on private fostering in Britain was still full of loopholes. All foster parents were required to notify the local authority when they took a child, but if the child would be staying less than one month or had been placed in foster care because of an "emergency," then he or she was technically not a foster child at all and was not protected. Against their stated intentions, local authorities often participated in private fostering arrangements by providing lists of unsupervised homes that accepted African children.[41] Children's officers also visited private foster homes, though not with quite the same powers or responsibilities as with a registered home.[42]

Private fostering, then, was never truly "outside" the state's domain at all. Rather, it existed in the space between different state departments and their competing visions of Britain's changing responsibilities toward Africa and Africans. Sociological research and social work often overlapped, as students in sociology and anthropology frequently worked as child care officers.[43] Many of their advisers, such as Esther Goody and Kenneth Little, conducted research on the African family. For British researchers, African children fostered in white families were a unique subject population, who could yield insights into the complex processes of racial identification. One of their key assumptions was that the quality of Africans' domestic lives in Britain would play a vital role in future Anglo-African relations.

Historians of the United States have fruitfully analyzed the politics of transracial adoption. Christina Klein suggests that American citizens who adopted Asian children in the 1950s were encouraged to view their actions as a sentimentalized version of U.S. foreign policy, a Cold War obligation as well as a personal act of rescue.[44] Adoption both deflected attention from U.S. military interventionism and honed a vision of the United States as the savior of "Third World" children in ways that justified further interventions abroad.[45] But controversies about fostering African children in Britain diverged significantly from the liberal internationalism that purified the discourse of adoption in the United States.[46] Whereas American debates typically rendered the biological parents invisible, a practice with deep roots in imperial "rescue" movements for poor and indigenous children, the temporary nature of fostering arrangements meant that African parents in Britain were highly visible indeed.[47] Moreover, metropolitan fostering arrangements were not brokered by an expansionist government. Rather, they were targets of concern for a decolonizing state: a marker of the state's limitations rather than its ascending power.

For many race relations experts, children figured as the key prospect for integration.[48] Several postwar films depicted children's interracial friendships as emblems of the migrant's transformability. *Springtime in an English Village* (1948) depicted a black girl being crowned the Queen of May, applauded by the whole community. This film, produced by the Colonial Film Unit, was screened in Africa and the Caribbean to demonstrate the joys of migration. In a later, more complex example of this genre, Lionel Ngakane's award-winning *Jemima and Johnny* (1966), a young West Indian girl and white boy in Notting Hill become best friends despite the fact that Johnny's father spends his days handing out "Keep Britain White" pamphlets. The racist father is redeemed at the end of the film when the abandoned flat where Jemima and Johnny are playing collapses, and he carries Jemima to safety.[49]

If children represented the greatest hope for liberal race relations theorists, then they were also often pictured as migration's primary victims. The stresses of migration appeared to produce a host of new syndromes in children, all of which required new treatments. Case workers were deeply interested in the intersection between the crisis of the African child and the plight of the white "problem" family, about which professional worries skyrocketed after World War Two.

AFRICAN MOTHERS, BRITISH MOTHERS: THE POLITICS OF FOSTERING IN THE AGE OF BOWLBY

Chapter 3 in this volume described how British experts pathologized African students in the metropole. Mental health studies often explicitly linked the psychopathology of African students in Britain to their familial demands, and specifically to problems that arose from placing their children in foster homes.[50] Female students were reported to suffer intense anxiety about the children they left behind, which disrupted their own studies.[51] The governmental effort to reunite the African family in Britain now appeared to have harmed this family instead.

Was the African family pathological in its indigenous environment, or had it been warped by the process of migration? The mystery for British researchers was how to explain two seemingly contradictory features of West African parenthood: first, the tremendous value placed on parent-child relations and second, the widespread occurrence of practices such as pawning, wardship, and fostering, which involved delegation of the parental role.[52] Social workers in Britain energetically collected statistical evidence about African student parents' emotional ties to their children, measuring the frequency of their visits, and assessing their "active interest" in child rearing.[53]

Scholarship on West African child-rearing practices flourished in the 1950s and 1960s. June Ellis, who taught sociology at the University of Ghana before moving to Birmingham to teach social work, stressed that West African parents took a pessimistic view of their children's behavior and personality. Whereas British parents were increasingly egalitarian, West African parents valued parental authority. Ellis argued that the West African focus on severe methods of child training made West African parents more likely to accept abusive fostering situations in the metropole.[54] Conversely, the psychiatrist T. Adeoye Lambo described early childhood in Nigeria as a "utopian" experience, full of indulgences. Yet he believed that adult Nigerians were plagued by insecurity and resentment. Lambo proposed that Nigerian anxiety resulted from the disconnect between an emotionally satisfying childhood and the multiple frustrations of being a Nigerian adult. He suggested that early childhood experiences were more easily "reactivated" in Nigerians than in Europeans, and that Nigerians overvalued their childhood memories.[55] Such psychiatric insights raised the stakes of the child fostering debates.

Taken as a whole, academic interpretations of the fostering of African children can be divided into "culture" versus "exigency" camps. The "culture" proponents argued that African parents in Britain were drawn to fostering because their traditions encouraged the delegation of parental duties.[56] The parents were thus misapplying an indigenous custom that was benign in its own environment. The parents saw foster care as "perfectly natural" and failed to discriminate between good and bad foster homes because "they think all people who take children will be kind and loving."[57]

According to this camp, African parents saw fostering as a crucial element of the child's moral education. Esther Goody, the Cambridge anthropologist, firmly categorized the placement of African children in Britain not as crisis fostering but as educational fosterage. That is, Goody argued that West African parents in Britain who used private fostering were simply seeking legitimate social advantages for their children. Her research highlighted the positive function of fostering as a way of reinforcing ties between kin. She proposed that West African parents in Britain were engaging in the same parenting practices that they would have used in Africa.[58] Such "cultural" explanations stressed the resiliency of indigenous traditions and underplayed the strains that migration placed on such traditions, as well as the corrosive influence of metropolitan racism. Accordingly, any difficulties pertaining to fostering in Britain were problems of translation: the result of mapping an essentially adaptive practice onto a heartless metropole.[59]

The "exigency" school, on the other hand, claimed that private fostering in Britain bore no resemblance to its African counterpart. In Britain, the children were separated from their biological parents at a much younger age, moved frequently, and were placed with white families with whom the biological parents had no connection.[60] African parents in Britain were thus neither honoring nor extending an indigenous tradition. Rather, they were compelled by economic necessity into an entirely new form of child care.[61] The "exigency" camp was far more negative about private fostering. One social worker described "six year-old [African] twins terrified to use the lavatory because it meant walking along a communal passage shared with the landlord who might jump out and shout at them."[62] She concluded that racial harassment in Britain's cities forced African parents to "export" their children to rural environments.

Outside the academic realm, culture and exigency were not the only possibilities. In the novel *Second Class Citizen*, the Nigerian writer Buchi Emecheta detailed her own struggle to keep her children at home. Her heroine, Adah, is instructed by her husband that in Britain, "only first-class citizens lived with their children, not the blacks." After a disastrous experience with an unethical white day-minder, who moonlights as a prostitute and steals the children's milk, Adah places the children into a state-sponsored nursery. Adah's refusal to foster her children is both personal and political; she proves her own maternal virtue and rejects the presumed superiority of white mothers.

Ultimately, Emecheta suggests that Nigerian mothers fostered their children neither because of economic need nor because of cultural norms. Motherhood in Britain, Adah laments, had become a deeply burdensome affair: "At home in Nigeria, all a mother had to do for a baby was wash and feed him and, if he was fidgety, strap him onto her back and carry on with her work while that baby slept. But in England she had to wash piles and piles of nappies, wheel the child round for sunshine during the day, attend to his feeds as regularly as if one were serving a master, talk to the child, even if he was only a day old! Oh, yes, in England, looking after babies was in itself a full time-job."[63] The fundamental problem was neither indigenous custom nor the pressures of migration. Rather, it was the crushing demands of Bowlbyism.

Starting in the Second World War, the psychologist John Bowlby had influentially stressed the disastrous impact of mother-child separation upon children's physical and moral development. His studies of evacuees noted that children who were deprived of maternal attention posed a grave threat to the civic body, displaying negative social behaviors such as stealing, delinquency, violence, and sexual misdemeanors.[64] Bowlby argued that the more mundane tasks of maternal care—the minutiae of parenting—were crucial to the child's health.[65] In emergencies, foster mothers provided superior care to that available in group homes. But even the very best foster parents lacked the sense of "absolute obligation to the child which all but the worst parents possess."[66]

By the 1960s, Bowlbyism had become a powerful conceptual framework for assessing child care and parent-child relations for all Britons. But even earlier than that, welfare professionals were concerned with the fate of "coloured" children, whose fostering arrangements deviated so markedly from Bowlby's principles. British social workers lamented that African mothers failed to embrace the Bowlbyist gospel of maternal care. West African women were said to express "outright incredulity" when confronted with Bowlbyist principles of childhood development: for example, that infants should be spoken to from an early age.[67]

Different branches of the British government clashed about the potential globalization of Bowlbyism. In particular, the Home Office's demands for peaceful decolonization was explicitly at odds with child protection. At stake here was the larger question of whether Britain's primary duty was to African student parents—the future leaders of the new African nations—or to their children. Mr. Philp, the secretary of the Family Service Units, stressed that young children were psychologically damaged even by satisfactory foster homes; he petitioned the Home Office to see "if something could not be done to 'educate' immigrants about what was now known of the importance of contact between mothers and young children."[68] The Home Office was extremely discouraging: "Most of the emerging countries are jealous of their independence and would . . . resent any suggestion that smacked to them of colonialism and paternalism"; furthermore, "what would emigrants leaving this country say of similar attempts by the receiving country to indoctrinate them before they left these shores?" Here, Philp's Bowlbyist efforts clashed with the Home Office's urgent need to reconcile British and African interests, and risked rousing a political storm in the newly independent countries, a risk that the Home Office was not willing to take.[69] Such conflicts illustrated the choices that particular branches of the decolonizing state undertook, which entailed the rejection of at least some forms of expertise.

These concerns were particularly strong with regard to Nigeria, which had long served in Britain as the paramount example of indirect rule. Colonial authorities in Nigeria had occasionally intervened in indigenous child-rearing practices—for example, criminalizing all street trading by children as "juvenile delinquency" in the 1940s and interceding in the practice of child pawning.[70] The metropolitan government, however, had overwhelmingly disavowed major interventions for families in Nigeria. Given this history, children's officers and the Colonial Office debated whether they could undertake an interventionist policy toward West African families in the metropole—especially because these families were expected to return to an independent Africa. Beryl Watson, a children's officer in Surrey, complained in 1960 that Nigeria House was placing Nigerian children in unsuitable foster homes. She wanted the Nigerian authorities to consult with children's officers about individual homes.[71] But the Colonial Office responded unfavorably: "relations with Nigeria are good, the territory will become independent on October 1st, and it would be inexpedient to make what might be construed as a complaint at official level."[72] At this pivotal moment of Nigerian independence, proposals to protect African children in Britain seemed both impractical and undesirable.

Children's officers frequently urged the Home Office to either strengthen its regulations on private fostering or negotiate more forcefully with West African governments about their exit controls for married students. But both the Home Office and the Colonial Office were reluctant to criticize West African authorities on the question of child protection, and, instead, championed the doctrine of non-intervention. These exchanges (Philp and the Home Office, Watson and the Colonial Office) help to explain the intractability of private fostering in the age of decolonization, and the ways in which anxieties about the end of empire infused the fostering debates. This discomfort with regulating the African family in Britain had powerful—and often powerfully negative—effects on individual families, highlighting both the impossibility of a simple reversal of colonialism's affective relations and the unpredictability of negotiations about how the end of empire played out on metropolitan terrain.

The discussion of private fostering for African children also took place against the backdrop of diagnosing the metropolitan "problem family": a stigmatization of poor families, especially mothers, by the British social services departments from the 1940s to the 1960s. Because destitution was assumed to have been largely eliminated through the welfare state, families with persistent difficulties were now often characterized as psychologically maladjusted. Social workers viewed problem families as poor, but also as unable to manage their poverty in a socially accept-able manner.[73] Complaints regarding problem families included squalor and maternal incompetence, as well as irregular income. The "problem mother" was thus an identifiable social nuisance in postwar Britain, although the emphasis shifted from her failure to provide adequate physical care to a Bowlbyist concern with her psychological maladies. Significantly, it appears that social workers rarely applied the "problem family" label to African student parents, although both West Indian and white families were so designated.[74]

White foster mothers figured prominently in press reports on cases of abuse or neglect. In 1965, Evelyn and Frederick Thornton were tried at Brighton Quarter Sessions for ill-treating Tower Ibikunle, a West African five-year-old boy whom they had fostered since 1961. For much of that time, the couple had allegedly kept the boy locked in their cellar, where he slept with Frederick in a single bed. When he was found, he had scars on his hands and was missing parts of his toes, possibly from frostbite. His biological parents were untraceable. Evelyn Thornton was sentenced to eighteen months' imprisonment; her husband was jailed for only a year. The Recorder explained the discrepancy to Frederick: "I am convinced you were the weakling in this matter . . . but you were the man of the house and it was your duty to do something.'"[75]

Why did social workers and the British press vilify white foster moth-ers? Perhaps because experts considered African students to be tempo-rary sojourners in Britain, they were not evaluated by the same child-rearing standards as white foster parents or as other migrant parents. Furthermore, the Children Act 1958 required the foster parent (not the biological parent) to notify the local authorities about receiving the child. The legal burden of the act therefore rested on foster parents rather than biological ones. At the same time, it was extremely difficult, from the social worker's perspective, to remove children from private foster care. In Kent, only 3 percent of the homes that were deemed unsatisfactory faced removal of the children.[76] The courts' decisions were haphazard, sometimes removing children solely on the basis of a neighbor's accusa-tion of ill treatment, while denying an application for removal when a nine month-old girl had clearly been injured in her foster parents' care.[77]

Social workers' efforts to supervise African foster children entailed contact with white families who had already run afoul of the state. The Commonwealth Students' Children Society (CSCS) estimated that over half of the families who answered advertisements for private foster homes were regarded as "unsuitable" by their local authority.[78] One West African baby girl died in the care of a private foster mother who just a year earlier had been legally debarred from taking children.[79] Although African mothers were challenged in the press for their refusal to keep their children with them, white foster mothers were criticized most strongly within the realm of expertise.

Joan Lawson's 1965 memoir of her work as a child care officer recalled the striking case of a Mrs. Barber, a white, working-class woman who had been repeatedly rejected as a registered foster mother by the Children's Department. Mrs. Barber then answered an advertisement in a newspaper and took in the illegitimate baby of a Nigerian student nurse for £2 a week: ten shillings more than she would have gotten from the Children's Department. She exulted that she had been "approved" as a foster mother at last, blithely ignoring Lawson's distinction between private and registered foster homes. Lawson admits that the baby, Akas, was well treated; "he "prospered, waxed fat, and with a rattle in his hand, most often looked like an African politician in miniature. He was the darling of the neighborhood."[80] When the biological mother, Miss Olumtita, let her payments lapse and ignored her son's second birthday, Mrs. Barber tracked Miss Olumtita down in London and bullied her into disavowing her parental rights. Mrs. Barber then cheerfully adopted Akas, and renamed him Timothy.

Lawson's account is fascinating for her initial stigmatization of the white foster mother, and her parody of Mrs. Barber's efforts to derive social status from fostering an African child.[81] The biological mother, Miss Olumtita, is a cipher in this story. Although Lawson is grudgingly won over by Mrs. Barber's willingness to adopt Akas, she is perturbed by the manipulation of the Children's Department. The professional authority of social workers could easily be thwarted by an African child coming into the care of a woman that the state had deemed unworthy. If welfare experts in the realm of child care denounced the white foster mother, then the decolonizing state still required her services—or at least was unwilling to subject them to systematic regulation.

Postcolonial parenting thus served as a distinctive forum for struggles between experts and their critics. Indeed, one way to interpret this narrative would be as the failure of certain forms of expertise in the face of the demands of decolonization. This split was not neatly divided along racial lines. West African, South Asian, and West Indian parents all articulated their own ideals of child care in an age of decolonization. But for white foster mothers, their work with (and attachments to) African children could serve as a vital assertion of their own powers against the state. Significantly, due to the perceived demands of decolonization, white foster mothers—frequently vilified by child care professionals and the press—nevertheless avoided the surveillance and intervention with African children that they might have undergone at other moments, or with other children. The phenomenon of fostering African children by precisely those mothers whom experts believed fell furthest from the Bowlbyist ideal exposed how mothers might critique experts and dodge their dicta in shaping new kinds of families.[82]

From 1957 to 1964, the Association of Children's Officers detailed "unsatisfactory" placements for African children, ranging from cases of abuse to those in which the foster mother was deemed "neurotic," or "of low intelligence."[83] One white foster mother was criticized for being "eccentric" with a house "like a junk shop." Another woman deserted her husband and biological children to live with the father of her Nigerian foster children.[84] The "crisis" of the African student family highlighted the ways in which many white, working-class Britons also fell short of the nuclear family ideal. Opponents of private fostering mobilized class prejudices to persuade African parents that white foster mothers would undermine their legitimate social aspirations and "corrupt" their children.[85] One Nigerian barrister wrote of African parents who required an interpreter in order to understand children raised by Cockney foster mothers.[86]

Who was a good mother in a postcolonial age? As Wendy Webster has argued, the regulation of motherhood cannot be fully understood outside the history of the orchestration and control of national borders.[87] If white foster mothers were increasingly demonized, then African student mothers played a more complicated role. The 1950s and 1960s were key decades in the emergence of the African bourgeois family, and the uneven renewal of European efforts to inculcate domestic ideology in Africa. In West Africa, the relationship between family and women's work was being reconfigured. This was the age of expanding domestic science educational schemes for women, and an ongoing struggle over the gender politics of wage labor in Nigeria, namely, the increasing identification of wage labor as a male preserve even as women undertook paid employment in greater numbers.[88]

The presumed economic autonomy of West African women played a major role in the British fostering debates, even as this autonomy was jeopardized.[89] Many British researchers spoke wistfully of the high status accorded to working mothers in West Africa, compared to the criticism such women endured in Britain. Kenneth Little's 1961 comparative research on students in Edinburgh and Sierra Leone revealed the much higher percentage of African males who said a girl should have her own career after marriage.[90] Motherhood in Britain was bound to be "a depressing experience for women who, like the Yoruba people of Nigeria, are used to being economically independent. The picture given in Africa of the British way of life always suggests privilege for the woman compared to her oppressed African sister, but the way in which our young mothers are completely tied to home and children is certainly very different from the position of the educated young mother in West Africa."[91] Of the African wives in Goody's sample, 70 percent had come to the United Kingdom hoping to earn their own qualification. Not a single one identified herself as a housewife.[92] Goody concluded that a British couple confronted with a similar conflict would resolve it by the wife giving up her studies. But as one African mother suggested, independence produced new demands on women: "'you don't understand the problems of a young country . . . When we come here [to Britain] with our husbands we want to learn something. Nigeria needs skills.'"[93] From this perspective, the fostering problem could not be resolved simply through better accommodation for overseas students. The deeper issue was the ambitions of African mothers.

By the 1960s, the history of economic independence for West African women had intersected with the more recent process of decolonization to dramatize the political imperative for African women in Britain to seek their own credentials. Children's officers voiced sympathy for African mothers who were pressured by local authorities to give up their courses in order to look after their children. African women would be "at a severe disadvantage socially and in their marriage if they failed to keep pace with their husband's development."[94] The Immigrants Advisory Service suggested that the British state should invest in child care for Africans in the metropole as a form of overseas aid.[95] If Nigerians and Ghanaians were to build "modern states," then they required the participation of educated women to succeed.[96] Thus, even as child care experts denigrated private fostering, African mothers who fostered their children tended to be valorized while white foster mothers were denounced. The fostering debates revealed that the developmentalist state had widened its reach beyond the colony and the postcolony. By the late 1950s, development was happening in Britain as well as overseas. The demands of decolonization, it seemed, fell not only on Africans, but on Britons as well.

Social workers struggled to reconcile the competing interests of

African mothers and African children, and to determine which population had the greater claim on Britain's resources. Mothers from developing countries, most social workers agreed, could not be held to the
same standards as British women—who themselves were being collec-
tively stressed by Bowlbyist demands. The future health of the African
family in Africa seemed to depend on the fracturing of this family in
Britain. The African family was to be sacrificed in the metropole, only to
be restored to unity upon returning to newly independent countries. In
this context of British investment in African development, the "failings"
of African mothers seemed more forgivable than those of white foster
mothers who had already been targeted as problem parents by the state,
which may explain why white foster mothers served as the main culprits
in antifostering campaigns. The imperatives of child welfare in Britain
and economic and political development in Africa were notably out of
joint. As child development and national development seemed increasingly at odds, the demands of the latter triumphed, and harmony with
the former colony was prioritized over the perceived needs of African
children.

When the Colonial Office began to encourage African wives to
join their husbands in Britain, its aim had been to ensure that African
families would remain intact. Within a decade, it had become clear that
this policy's effects were quite the reverse of what the Colonial Office
had intended. Although marital unity might have been achieved, these
couples frequently sent their children into private foster care. The policy
backfired, engendering a new set of British anxieties about the state's
responsibility toward these parents and children.

During the 1950s and 1960s, the state's benefits depended to a large
degree on the faith that all nuclear families were geographically bounded
or united: a proposition that explicitly clashed with the experiences of
many migrant families. For many race relations experts, the extent to
which migrants intended to bring their children to join them in Britain
reflected how these individuals were "settling" in the metropole. But
even as social scientists pressed to reunite families in Britain—and took
these reunions as a positive measure of assimilation—state policies often
worked against this goal.

West African mothers—and their white counterparts in private fostering—were far from the only parental figures targeted by the British state
for surveillance and reform. Child-rearing practices among other groups,
such as South Asians and West Indians, also prompted high levels of
scrutiny, and their own forms of intervention or neglect.

SOUTH ASIAN BOYS AND THE FAILURES OF FATHERHOOD

In general, British experts praised South Asians for the resilience of their family structure.[97] A 1964 guidebook for Indian and Pakistani students, for example, offered detailed instructions on applying for family allowances, and assumed that any children would live with their biological parents.[98] Yet the South Asian family in Britain was typed with pathologies of its own. Social workers who criticized South Asian child-rearing methods focused on fathers and sons: specifically, on the fate of South Asian boys who were brought to all-male households in order to contribute wages or to benefit from Britain's educational system. A.C. Watson of the British High Commission in Karachi complained about Pakistani "false fathers," who called their sons to Britain even when they exceeded the allowed age for child migrants. Because birth certificates were rare in South Asia, and medical exams were inconclusive, the real age of these children was impossible to determine. Fathers might be asked to recite a family tree, or to recognize their child from a photograph, but immigration officers acknowledged that false claims were rampant. Child migrants thus constituted another "loophole" population under the Commonwealth Immigrants Act 1962.[99]

Rachel Scott, a teacher who reported on her work with migrant children for BBC Woman's Hour and Radio Four, described these South Asian boys as "pathetic figures . . . emotionally if not physically neglected and deprived of mothers and affection, as their weary faces, their listlessness, their often chronic anxiety showed all too plainly."[100] These children were thus described in the increasingly familiar Bowlbyist terms of maternal deprivation. But unlike their West African peers, the sufferings of these children did not appear to be warranted by the demands of decolonization. Accordingly, different state policies emerged to address the needs of South Asian children in the metropole.

Throughout the 1960s, the Home Office expressed concern about adolescent Indian and Pakistani boys being left in the care of their paternal uncles while their fathers returned to their countries of origin. In such cases, although the physical standards of care might be satisfactory, "the patterns of the patrilineal society practiced in parts of Asia were found not to prove effective in the highly industrialized, mobile society obtaining in a large conurbation."[101] The Principal Medical Officer of Bradford advocated restricting the entry of children without their mothers, and actively encouraging the mothers of young boys to emigrate to Britain.[102] Thus, the social scientific preoccupation with reforming the all-male,

South Asian household led to new recommendations for liberalized and explicitly maternalist migration regimes.

The homosociality of South Asian families in Britain compared unfavorably with the Bowlbyist doctrine of maternal care. But these "masculine" households attracted far less scrutiny than the apparent dysfunctions of either West African or West Indian families, possibly because of a longstanding tradition within British social science that insisted on the stability of South Asian families.[103] The introduction of the two-parent rule in 1968 effectively curtailed this particular family structure in which male children followed their fathers or uncles to Britain. Thereafter, there was a sharp drop in the number of dependents from Pakistan seeking entry to the United Kingdom.[104]

Ultimately, South Asian fathers and the homosocial household attracted more attention from immigration authorities than from social scientists. Social scientists focused overwhelmingly on child care for migrant families as a "black" problem. By looking closely at social science stereotypes of West Indian mothers, and how their practices were stigmatized in Britain, we can see how their story both intersects with and diverges from that of West African parents. Thus emerged a framework of two maternal pathologies, which demanded different types of intervention and nonintervention.

OTHER MOTHERS: WEST INDIAN DAY-MINDING, LEGITIMACY, AND LOVE

The precondition for any "crisis" of the West Indian family in Britain, of course, was the arrival of children themselves. In the early 1950s, very few West Indian children traveled to Britain.[105] By 1958, however, the number of child and female entrants from the West Indies exceeded the number of men. The Commonwealth Immigrants Act, under the rubric of family reunification, allowed the entry of dependants of migrants who were already in Britain. This shift increased the rates of female migration among South Asians and West Indians.[106] Even more striking was the high proportion of children among Britain's West Indian population by the 1960s. In 1963, almost one-third of West Indian migrants to Britain were children.[107]

The Times initially described the influx of West Indian children as beneficial, as it contributed to the creation of "normal" family units among blacks in Britain.[108] But as the Home Office itself acknowledged, the provisions of the Commonwealth Immigrants Act fundamentally altered the structure of the matrilocal West Indian family. By recognizing the rights of entry for young children, but excluding elder relatives, the act "gave rise to such unlikable attempts to compensate [for the loss of female kin] as illegal baby farming."[109] The new laws encouraged the migration of children, but not the entry of the people who traditionally cared for these children. In the wake of these demographic shifts, British psychologists, social workers, and sociologists became increasingly preoccupied with West Indian child-rearing norms.

Postwar sociologists insisted that private fostering did not exist among West Indians in Britain, and that West Indian mothers only used day-minders.[110] Their collective certainty is puzzling, given the extensive evidence to the contrary. Throughout the 1950s, the League of Coloured Peoples and the British Caribbean Welfare Service handed out names of unregistered foster mothers to West Indian parents.[111] In 1956, Miss Doris Nicholls, a West Indian migrant, appeared on British television and asked for someone to foster her baby; more than 100 people responded.[112] Jamaican and Trinidadian parents also placed "Homes Wanted" advertisements in *Nursery World*, although they were outnumbered by Ghanaians and Nigerians. In 1959, the London County Council devised a scheme for repatriating West Indian children from Britain, precisely because it feared that private foster mothers were endangering these children.[113]

My aim here is not to reject the longstanding view that West Africans dominated the private foster care scene in Britain. Rather, it is to consider what was at stake in seeing private fostering as an exclusively "African" problem. Both West Indian and West African parents experienced periods of separation from their children. But sociologists and social workers perceived these separations very differently, and linked them to broader ideas about both groups' relationships to the decolonizing state.

British scholars had debated the nature of West Indian family systems since the 1930s, prompted by the 1937–38 riots in Barbados and Trinidad.[114] Edith Clarke's *My Mother Who Fathered Me* (1957), Fernando Henriques' *Family and Colour in Jamaica* (1953), and Raymond T. Smith's *The Negro Family in British Guiana* (1956) all characterized the matrilineal family structure in the West Indies as abnormal and deficient, adaptations to the horrors of slavery.[115] British researchers generally assumed that West Indian family practices were derived from African—and specifically West African—antecedents. Fostering by kin in the West Indies was perceived far more negatively than any form of fostering in West Africa. Colonial authorities in the West Indies privileged parents as the only adults who should be responsible for the socialization of their children. The system of kin fostering in the West Indies enlarged the group of adults who might occupy a role of authority toward a child beyond the parameters of the colonial comfort zone.[116]

Was Britain the site of collapse or redemption for the West Indian family? As one report on child-minding put it, "when a West Indian family comes to England, its structural weaknesses are thrown into sharp relief."[117] The race relations specialist Sheila Patterson described the move to Britain as representing the "final breakdown" of Jamaican family life.[118] Yet as West Indians lost their wider kin networks in the process of migration, social scientists also posited that these migrants would be "forced" to construct more conventional nuclear families in Britain.[119] West Indian women in Britain were more likely to marry, to seek affiliation orders when they had children outside of marriage, and to practice birth control. The expert view was that the sexual behavior of West Indians improved upon migration, whereas child-rearing practices worsened.[120]

Two ideas about black families prevailed among British social scientists. First, West Indian and West African families were structurally related. Second, West African fostering by kin was less pathological than West Indian fostering, which had been tainted by the affective distortions of slavery. One key question was why West Africans and West Indians seemed to raise their children so differently after they migrated to Britain. These populations shared an indigenous fostering tradition, as well as a high proportion of women engaged in full-time employment. Why did one group (West Indians) use day-minding, while the other (West Africans) relied on fostering? These differences were largely attributed to the notion that West Indians perceived themselves as permanent residents in Britain and thus were less likely to rely on temporary fostering situations. Such assumptions reveal how British experts sustained the classification of "temporary" and "permanent" migrants, and how they assigned these categories by ethnicity.[121]

Whereas the economic contributions of West African women were vigorously defended, those of West Indian mothers tended to be pathologized. This distinction may reflect the perceived urgency of the demands of decolonization in Africa and the level of British investment in this process.[122] Social scientists characterized West Indian mothers as being compelled to work by financial necessity, rather than pursuing educational ambitions: "the [West Indian] mother is forced to go out to work while leaving the child with a child-minder who will give it no emotional stimulus; the same child is collected by an overtired mother who returns to her overcrowded and expensive home."[123]

Logistically speaking, there were numerous similarities between private fostering and day-minding. Like private fostering, day-minding proved extremely difficult to regulate. Reliance on unsupervised minders was rampant; in 1967, only 30 percent of West Indian children who were minded were in the care of registered caregivers.[124] The Health Services and Public Health Act 1968 mandated that anyone not a relative who looked after a child for more than two hours a day must register with the local health department. But enforcement depended on proving that money had passed between the mother and the minder and this charge was easily denied. Only two illegal minders were prosecuted in 1968, and none at all in 1969.[125]

Unlike private fostering, day-minding was typically not transracial; most minders were West Indian women.[126] West Indian mothers were sometimes praised for maintaining their children within the household: a triumph, of sorts, for Bowlbyism on the cheap.[127] One study detailed the case of a forty-two-year-old Jamaican woman, whose youngest child (aged two and a half) lived with her in London while her other children remained in Jamaica. The psychiatrist described how this mother found her child "too much" for her, believing that "other coloureds" were putting the evil eye on him. She removed the child from his day nursery, and farmed him out instead. The psychiatrist interpreted this shift to private fostering as a sign of the mother's worsening mental condition, diagnosing her as an "unintelligent Jamaican psychopath."[128]

Still, if private fostering was stigmatized because it threatened the class position of elite African children, then day-minding was criticized for hindering West Indian integration. The child who was minded had "no experience of the English children with whom he will later be educated."[129] Day-minding did not provoke quite the same hysteria as private fostering, but it was still a popular subject of academic inquiry.[130] West Indian children in Britain were frequently described as displaying a syndrome akin to autism, in which the children appeared aloof, apathetic and withdrawn.[131] According to G. Stewart Prince, a psychiatrist at King's College Hospital, this phenomenon was unique to West Indian children who had emigrated to Britain—yet another pathology engendered by migration.[132] The Dominican psychiatrist John Royer labeled this cluster of symptoms "Brought Over Child Syndrome," describing how recent arrivals might demonstrate aggression toward siblings, sociocultural retardation, and elective mutism.[133]

West Indian children in Britain thus formed a micro-study of mother-child separation: an ideal population for dissecting Bowlby's attachment theory. In 1967, Margaret Pollak, a family doctor and lecturer in Child Health at King's College Hospital, studied more than 200 English-born and migrant (mostly West Indian) three-year-old children to evaluate the impact of maternal care on the children's development. The mothers received "points" for tasks such as putting the child to bed, and for their ability to describe their child's personality. Pollak concluded that 12 percent of West Indian mothers played with their child for an hour every day, compared to 87 percent of the English-born mothers. The West Indian mother was renowned for high-quality physical care: "her infant is invariably spotlessly clean, as though she were just about to be entered for a baby show."[134] But such achievements were easily trivialized within Bowlbyism. Pollak argued that West Indian mothers failed to provide the Bowlbyist ideal of continuous intimacy between mother and child.[135]

Pollak had highly specific criteria for evaluating child-rearing techniques. She asked if the child had ever seen a live horse, cow, or chicken, whether the parents could produce three toys owned by the child, and if the child had ever been on holiday. She thus explicitly connected the parents' standard of living and their emotional bond with their children. She also asked children to "make tea" in order to measure their degree of Anglicization. This concern with Anglicization as an index of maternal care was mirrored elsewhere. Another study of West Indian mothers in London characterized the mothers' desire to return to the West Indies as a sign of their "failure" to integrate, which might damage their children psychologically.[136]

Pollak's conclusions regarding West Indian children were damning. She claimed that West Indian boys and girls were largely non-verbal, astonished by how few knew their own names and sex.[137] None of this was attributable to mental retardation. Rather, Pollak argued, the problem stemmed from maternal and environmental deprivation. Significantly, West Indian children who were living with their mothers "were just as maternally deprived as those who were minded" because the mothers did not provide stable relationships.[138] The Bowlbyist failure of the West Indian mother was complete.

As all of these studies suggest, there was no consensus on the question of what kind of care was most beneficial—or damaging. One might expect that because private fostering was more often described by British researchers as "voluntary," it would be viewed as a more selfish choice than day-minding. But as we have seen, British social workers and sociologists typically described the ambitions of West African women as essential forces in the successful decolonization of their countries of origin. Their "ambition" was viewed as national, not personal, and therefore morally acceptable. No such allowances were made for West Indian mothers.

This divide underscores the fact that "decolonization" was not a single or monolithic process. Rather, there were multiple decolonizations, each with its own conceptual apparatus. Class prejudices were also likely at work in privileging the acquisition of professional credentials for African women who were largely assumed (probably incorrectly by the 1960s) to be elites over those of West Indian women engaged in lowlier forms of labor. In looking at the disjunctions between the "crisis" of African fostering and the "crisis" of West Indian minding, we can see these divergent forms of decolonization in play. Because of Britain's investment in managing the development of new African nations, West African mothers who did not care for their own children received the most sympathetic reception. The perception of African students as elites also heightened deference toward African parents in the metropole.

Although the debates about day-minding traversed the era of West Indian federation, Britain's relative lack of investment in development in the West Indies meant that there was virtually no discourse about West Indians in Britain improving themselves in order to lead their new nations. Because West Indians were largely assumed to be permanent residents, their parenting practices could wreak more havoc in the metropole, whereas the costs of damage to West African children would be confined to the postcolony. In contrast to British attentiveness to the needs of independent countries in West Africa, West Indian independence and federation barely registered in these discussions.

As West Indians in Britain were continually stigmatized for their "habitual" acceptance of illegitimacy, it is also worth pointing out the role of British law in this process and how metropolitan courts validated particular forms of marital and parental relations. Social scientists rarely considered how Britain's laws contributed to the persistence of illegitimacy for migrant children. Rather, black family structures were overemphasized and the impact of metropolitan racism on family life was downplayed.[139]

Most of the British Caribbean islands made provisions to enforce maintenance orders when parents went abroad. The Jamaican government enforced bastardy and maintenance orders for children residing in Jamaica while their fathers were elsewhere.[140] In Dominica, a married man who left the island and failed to support his wife and children could face legal action if he were traced in Britain. If he were unmarried, and an affiliation order had been made against him, the mother could demand that he appoint a guardian for his child; men who tried to leave without fulfilling this obligation faced arrest. Such principles of paternal responsibility were not always easy to execute. R. B. Davison, a West Indian economist and adviser to the Migrant Services Division of the West Indies Commission in London, reported that the Probation department in Jamaica constantly received applications from women trying to locate their children's fathers after the men had moved to Britain.[141]

This sphere of law was in flux during the postwar years, as the legal distinctions between legitimate and illegitimate children were reduced by West Indian federation.[142] Criticized by metropolitan social scientists for their cavalier attitude toward illegitimacy, migrant parents in Britain were often legally barred from rendering their children legitimate at all. The Legitimacy Act, 1959 allowed fathers to apply for custody of their illegitimate children, and obligated fathers to support these children (albeit at the low rate of 30 shillings per week).[143] But section 2 of the act limited the benefits of the law to children whose fathers were domiciled in England at the time of the child's birth. Thus, many migrant children were automatically excluded from the process of legitimation.[144]

Although British sociologists focused on the matrifocality of the West Indian family, the process of migration drew attention to the complexities of West Indian fatherhood. As the Colonial Office reported, British officials were "unable to appreciate the West Indian's concern for his children even if they are illegitimate. Cases have been reported where the putative West Indian father has been anxious to raise the child himself only to find his application overruled in favor of the mother who desired to have the child adopted." According to workers in migrant welfare, affiliation proceedings were typically overseen by unsympathetic authorities who were "incapable" of understanding the strong emotional connections that West Indian men might have to their illegitimate children.[145] The sociological analysis of the West Indian family overlooked how the laws of Britain prevented migrants from affiliating their children, and how the metropolitan courts contributed to the persistence of illegitimacy. British experts on the West Indian family thus effaced the ways in which their own laws contributed to distinctive family forms. The illegitimate West Indian family was, in part, a recent metropolitan creation.

As we have seen, South Asian fathers and West Indian mothers were important targets of concern in Britain, along with the perceived pathologies of West African families. But only in the West African case was the expert response to parenting techniques explicitly linked to the rhetoric of national independence. This particular historical moment had long-term consequences for generations of black families, as well as the criteria by which *all* families in Britain were evaluated.

GLOBAL RESPONSES TO PRIVATE FOSTERING:
FROM BORDER PATROL TO REPATRIATION

Most British participants agreed that private fostering was harmful to African children, even if justified by the parents' desire for education. But there was little consensus on how to solve this problem. After 1962, the issue of private fostering was often linked to proposals for immigration control.[146] Sir Cyril Osborne publicly described "baby farms" as an inevitable byproduct of Commonwealth immigration.[147] Osborne scored political points by tying his anti-immigration platform to the issue of child protection, and exhorted the Home Office to strengthen the law on private fostering.[148]

Overall, there was more centralized state support for building residential nurseries for African children than for strengthening the legal supervision of private fostering. The fact that private fostering was classed exclusively (and inaccurately) as an "African" problem shaped the government's response. Because most authorities insisted that African children would leave Britain before they reached school age, they saw nurseries— where no substitute mother figure was available—as less psychologically harmful than foster homes. Nurseries would protect children from abuse through state supervision. They would also prevent African children from forming ties to white families that would prove disruptive when the children went "home." For children who were supposed to be in Britain only briefly, integration was not a desirable goal. British and Nigerian social workers both opposed fostering African children with West Indian families: they believed that temporary and permanent migrants should not mix.[149]

The British Council provided larger flats for married students so that these students might choose to keep their children with them, and to give the children "the opportunity of speaking their mother tongue and learning their own culture."[150] In 1964, the British Council and the London County Council opened a new hostel for married overseas students. The Institute of Race Relations described Aban House as a "homelike place" with modernized Victorian apartments and a comfortable lounge where "two small Nigerians played in front of the cheerful fire."[151] Others sought to educate African parents about the dangers of private fostering before they ever left Africa. In 1964, the National Association of Mental Health

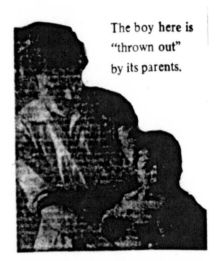

The boy here is "thrown out" by its parents.

Figure 26. "Nigerian Babies 'Banished' by Parents in UK." This picture accompanied an article in the *West African Pilot* lamenting that Nigerian babies were being "banished" by their biological parents. (*West African Pilot*, April 11, 1959, p. 2)

drafted a booklet on private fostering specifically for West African parents. Here, the transcultural psychiatrist Robbina Addis emphasized the emotional risks of fostering: "a child is best looked after by his own mother."[152] She concluded that it was preferable to leave children with relatives in Africa than to foster them in Britain. The National Committee for Commonwealth Immigrants (NCCI) described Addis's pamphlet as "very perturbing," because "it was most invidious for the government to suggest that families should be split up."[153] Although African student families were likely to be divided either through private fostering with white families in Britain or through kinship fostering in Africa, the NCCI believed that the impetus for fracturing African families should never come from the British state.

This literature was echoed in West African newspapers; one headline in the *West African Pilot* demanded, "Leave Your Kids Behind."[154] Another article in the *Pilot*, which was culled from the English newspaper *People*, reported that Nigerian babies were being "'Banished' By Parents in UK," and that British welfare experts were "appalled" by the apparent disregard of Nigerian parents for their children. Here, the ambitions of African student parents were rather less well received than they had been at the Colonial Office and Home Office. The article included a photograph of a young Nigerian boy who had been "thrown out" by his parents with a white English woman leaning protectively over him (figure 26).[155]

One West African mother, Doris Olaofe, explained that she had sent her baby boy, Toks, to a private foster mother in Kent because her husband was busy with his civil engineering course, and she was taking a dressmaking course that would dramatically increase her salary in Nigeria. She had rejected day-minding because she wanted Toks to be out of London, and she did not want him to disturb her husband's studies. Interestingly, the *Pilot* made no mention of fostering practices in Nigeria, writing only that "the basic principle of family life is being violated by Nigerian students," and that "destroying family life is not the way to train for responsible posts in the Commonwealth."[156] The demands of Africanization, the *Pilot* warned, must not be privileged over the survival of the African family itself.

Although the West African authorities did not have a unified stance on private fostering in Britain, their relations with British social workers were often extremely tense.[157] Mrs. Idowu of the Nigeria High Commission was deeply critical of negative British publicity about private fostering. If the local authority was unwilling to find registered homes for Nigerian children, she said, then they should not cause a public furor about the private homes that were found instead. She added that it was rare to find good foster homes for African children, because only the lowest class of people would take them; the children are taken in to "give pin money to housewives who do not want to go out to work."[158] British foster mothers, that is, should earn their own keep rather than making money from African babies.

According to the Kent County Council, Miss D. E. Harvie of the Children's Department in Kent expressed great frustration at her dealings with Mrs. Idowu: "it had been made plain [by a Nigerian social worker] that the Nigerians thought these protests from Kent about the private foster homes were unjustified and the strong implication was made that Miss Harvie wanted to use these foster homes herself for white children."[159] When children's officers recommended that African entrants leave their children at home, they were confidentially instructed to demonstrate that "there was no question of colour bar in these precautions."[160] British authorities were extremely reluctant to give Mrs. Idowu a list of foster mothers who took Nigerian children because it would violate the privacy of politically active African parents. One children's officer wrote, "I suspect that the Nigerian authorities want these addresses only in part for the welfare of the foster children and largely to enable them to keep an eye on the parents."[161]

The Ghana Trustee Society, established in 1961, aided student parents by offering a list of private foster parents and housing African children in its own residential nursery. The society's founder, B. B. Boateng, was a Ghanaian law student who had placed his own son in private care and had to move him abruptly when the foster mother died. Boateng irritated British authorities with his sensationalistic fundraising campaigns; one of his advertisements in British and West African newspapers proclaimed, "African Babies in the U.K. Dying from Lack of Proper Care."[162] Boateng also recommended homes without visiting them or obtaining evaluations.[163] By 1966, the GTS had placed 600 children in private foster homes. The following year, it won a grant from the London Boroughs Association and was renamed the Commonwealth Students' Children Society (CSCS).[164] The London Council of Social Service also provided a full-time social worker, Pat Stapleton, who had previously lived in Nigeria; she gave the society more professional credibility by inspecting individual homes.

The CSCS claimed that it wished to reform private fostering by building "real friendships" between biological and foster families. It reminded British readers that fostering offered the chance to "create a non-racial society," as well as generating incomes of up to £3 per week.[165] But even as the CSCS spoke of improving British private foster care, it also financed programs to repatriate African children. Boateng established branches of the society in Sierra Leone, Ghana and Nigeria, and ran well-publicized fundraising campaigns in these countries as well.[166] Boateng received an annual grant from Ghana, on the condition that any destitute Ghanaian children in Britain be returned either to relatives or to social welfare departments in Africa. Such children, Boateng said, were successfully "rehabilitated" with their extended families.[167] West African social workers also referred to "deprogramming" or "renationalizing" children who had been fostered in British homes. By the mid-1960s, the British Council had developed its own repatriation schemes, and had established a fund for African parents to return their children to Africa.[168]

The fiction that fostering arrangements were temporary and that all African children would eventually return to Africa with their families intact, was largely undone by "tug-of-love" custody cases in the late 1960s and 1970s. The Children Act 1975 eased the process whereby foster parents could be granted custody of children in their care for more than three years; many West Africans in Britain were concerned about how this new legislation might affect their parental rights. In the ensuing cases, white foster parents sought to adopt African children permanently, usually after the biological parents had announced their plans to return to Africa. Thus, judges tended to assume that they must choose between the child living with a white family in Britain or a black family in Africa.

The option that the entire African family might be reunited in Britain was rarely considered. As a result of these cases, a limited number of African children would be brought permanently into a white British family, just as their newly educated, and often newly politicized African parents returned to Africa. Typically, the white adoptive mothers were praised in the press, rather than stigmatized, as foster mothers had been.

Yet even as these cases constituted a formal legal acknowledgement of African foster children as true immigrants, rather than as visitors, both British and African social workers accelerated their demands for repatriation. As June Ellis said, West Africans would likely continue to come to Britain to study, but "it is not in the interests of their children to be here."[169] One CSCS social worker asked whether Africa risked "losing her children through alienation and anglicisation in foster homes . . . Is Africa going to reap the harvest of a generation of disturbed personalities? And what kind of parents will those children make when their turn comes?"[170] Several West African medical workers stressed that if African children were destined for an environment that emphasized group socialization, then the biggest risk to their emotional health was not maternal deprivation, but their alienation from the group.[171] Were the children who had been fostered in Britain "really useful" to newly independent countries such as Nigeria? By the 1970s, the consensus among African social workers appeared to be that they were not.

If the African student in Britain had once represented the hopes of newly independent nations, then the African foster child now represented the fears of failure: the ways in which the former mother country inflicted damage in the age of empire's end. Ellis cautioned social workers that the desire to avoid the taint of "Powellism" must not blind them to the joys of repatriation. She offered with a case study of three children sent "home" from London to Ghana. Instead of being "just three more added to statistics of alienated Black British," Ellis crowed, the children could now be counted as happy Ghanaians.[172] In the charged climate of a decolonizing Britain, this was an outcome that few social workers—or states—would gainsay.

Starting in the 1980s, a combination of factors—the growth of institutions of higher education in Africa, the slump in world oil prices that prompted major recessions in the Nigerian economy—discouraged West African students from pursuing their degrees in Britain. The number of West African students in Britain plummeted, and temporary workers took their place. This generation of African migrants has generally been depicted as poorer, more desperate, and considerably more dangerous than the earlier era of student parents.[173] The African Family Advisory Service (AFAS) reported in 1989 that West African parents were increasingly bringing their children to the United Kingdom on short-stay visas and then leaving the children unsupported, often in breach of immigration rules.[174] In one recent AFAS study, 91 percent of the African children were categorized as "abandoned": that is, both parents were resident in West Africa.[175] In the past decade, sensationalistic press reports about the trafficking, abuse, or murder of African children in Britain have again targeted private fostering—and private fostering as a distinctively "African" practice—as the key source of these children's plight.[176] The BBC recently described the phenomenon of West African children in private foster care as a "modern day slave trade" in which the children are systematically exploited as domestic servants.[177] The question of Britain's responsibility to African parents, which was so vital in the 1950s and 1960s, has disappeared, reflecting a new phase of Britain's investment in (or divestment from) the African future and a new sense of failure regarding Anglo-African relationships.

In such reports, Britain is imagined to serve as an accidental staging ground for what is fundamentally a "Third World" problem. As in the 1960s, the press has referred to immigration control as one solution.[178] The envisioned role of the British state is to protect African children through closer supervision of private fostering and border patrols. One aim of this chapter has been to track the ways in which the private fostering of African children in Britain emerged *in concert* with the state's aims, rather than *in opposition* to it. Private fostering for African children has always been simultaneously deplored and protected by different components of the British state. Perhaps the most striking aspect of the fostering debates has been the juxtaposition of the constancy with which many British participants opposed this practice with their sense of complete futility about eradicating it. The anxiety of social workers that African children would be harmed or socially devalued by their experiences with white, working-class foster mothers was countered by the stronger insistence at the Colonial Office and Home Office that the British government not interfere with the "development" of African mothers, who depended on private fostering arrangements in order both to attain personal independence and to abet national independence.

The various attitudes adopted by the state and by social scientists toward West African mothers, South Asian fathers, West Indian mothers, and white British foster mothers illustrate the durability of colonial taxonomies regarding black families, even as these classificatory systems underwent considerable strain and revision in the postwar metropole. Each group elicited different responses from the decolonizing state, which viewed the relations between parents and children through the lens of its own shifting relations to newly independent countries. One of the enduring themes of this history has been the intractable paralysis of the British state in the afterlife of empire, officially committed to "rescuing" specific groups of children but equally deeply divided about the limitations (political, legal, and moral) on its governance of them.

The intersecting histories of family and decolonization continue to prove combustible. Their apparent insolubility continues to draw expert resources and attention, as well as sparking debates about migration for specific groups of parents and children. At a moment of imperial contraction, the demands for harmony with Britain's former colonies were set directly against the health of families in the metropole. This struggle was never fully resolved in the postwar decades, nor has it been so today. Even as global interests were apparently prioritized over domestic concerns, precisely at the moment when Britain's energies were assumed to be turning inward, we can still see the high stakes of the domestic realm within British foreign policy. The state's choices regarding migrant families reveal how the processes of decolonization have been persistently imprinted upon everyday metropolitan life.

6. Leaving Home

The Politics of Deportation

How does one end a book about an afterlife? Certainly, one can imagine many different conclusions for the story that I have been telling here, even if some are avowedly artificial. The life cycle could be understood as coming to a close in several different ways—old age, retirement, even physical death. I have chosen the legal "death" of deportation. I am concerned with cases of failed migration, and with the moment that most decisively marked this failure: that is, when this category of person now called "the migrant" was forcibly expelled from the metropole. Deportation revealed that the process of migration could always be reversed, and that migration could never truly be said to have come to an end.

Although this is not the only possible endpoint to the story, it is one in which both experts and their critics were crucially invested. In the 1940s, most postwar experts on migration did not believe that their subjects would grow old in Britain. The expectation was that migrants would return "home" after they had completed their studies or earned sufficient wages. In this sense, the deportee only experienced an extreme version of the "normal" trajectory of migration, in which old age and repatriation were happily intertwined. But this vision of the migrant life cycle was changing by the late 1950s and early 1960s, the same years in which the state elaborated deportation provisions for specific populations. In looking at British debates about deportation, we can see how expert opinion on migration came under increasing stress as the formal empire waned. Deportation in Britain was closely engaged with the articulation of responsibilities for former colonial subjects. But there was little consensus among the different elements of the decolonizing state about how these responsibilities might be defined.

Deportation revealed how expertise was especially fragile in the realm of law and order. Criminology, which represented an area of academic growth in the 1950s, forged crucial links between social scientific expertise and government.[1] But although the Home Office drew extensively upon criminological opinion on deportation, it was by no means beholden to its diagnoses and prescriptions. Here, we can see how expertise shaped—and failed to shape—thought and policy about the ultimate marker of the migrant's "difference": that is, his or her liability to deportation.

In some sense, this chapter marks a break with the dominant themes of scholarship on race and migration in modern Britain. Overwhelmingly, historians in this field have been preoccupied with questions of access: which groups have been allowed or forbidden to enter Britain and what conditions have been placed on their entry.[2] The post-1945 period has been characterized by the intensification of restrictions on the rights of British citizenship, as prospective migrants from South Asia, Africa, and the Caribbean faced increasingly discriminatory entry controls. Clearly, governmental anxieties about the acceleration of migrants of color after the Second World War created formidable new barriers to entry for many individuals. But entry is only one part of the story of race and citizenship. This chapter asks what happens if we look at *another* moment in the process of migration—not restricted entry, but forced exit. How did the politics of departure compare to that of arrival?

I respond to these questions by tracing the evolution of thought and practice regarding deportation in Britain. Typically, historians have treated deportation as part of the rule of war: most frequently, as a corollary of the waves of ethnic cleansing and population transfer that characterized postwar Europe. But Britain's deportation policies were generated by the distinctive demands of public order in a collapsing multiethnic empire.[3] These demands produced surprising and often counterintuitive results. Scholars have assumed that as the British state's power to deport was strengthened, people of color from South Asia, Africa, and the Caribbean were the primary targets.[4] That is, the expectation has been that those who faced the harshest entry controls were also more likely to face expulsion, and that the politics of exit mirrored precisely those of entry.[5]

Given these assumptions, it is startling to discover that the group most dramatically affected by deportations in the postwar metropole was not West Indians, Africans, or Asians, but the Irish. Between 1962 and 1969, 60 percent of deportees from Britain were Irish.[6] By way of contrast, West Indians—the archetypal criminals of the popular imagination—constituted only 15 percent of deportees during this same period. In the realm of deportation, at least, the Irish topped the list of Britain's unwanted.

What do these numbers tell us about the politics of deportation? At a time when the absence of barriers for Irish entrants stood in such marked contrast to the controls on populations from the Commonwealth, these findings are all the more striking. The statistics regarding the racial composition of deportees would seem to suggest that the politics of exit were precisely the *reverse* of those of entry: that is, that the Irish—and not migrants of color—were targeted for deportation. Was that indeed the case? And, if so, how might we make sense of this apparent gap between the ideologies of entry and exit?

This chapter explores the multiple, contradictory, and competing agendas that shaped Britain's policies of expulsion. During the 1950s, the government began to consider legislation aimed at deporting Commonwealth immigrants who had been convicted of crimes in Britain. These discussions culminated in part 2 of the Commonwealth Immigrants Act 1962. Under this act, Commonwealth immigrants were liable to deportation by the Home Secretary if they met three criteria: they had been resident in the United Kingdom for less than five years, they were convicted of an offense punishable by imprisonment, and they had been recommended for deportation by a court. This chapter asks how the story of deportation might challenge or counter the prevailing story of entry. More specifically, it treats criminal law as a largely unexplored vector of thought and practice about migration and decolonization in Britain.

The various players in the deportation debates of the 1950s and 1960s—the Home Office, the police, magistrates and judges, legal scholars, criminologists, and the press—identified the key threats to Britain's well-being in different ways. In general, the press, police, and courts perceived deportation as a mechanism for achieving the moral purification of the postwar community and as a means of demographic restructuring. The Home Office focused more on deportation's role in the maintenance of public safety and the elimination of terrorism. Both camps drew on the growing body of research on Irish and West Indian crime. Postwar criminologists often juxtaposed Irish and West Indian migrants in order to highlight their perceived differences. As we will see, the status of criminological expertise was far from secure in the decolonizing state. When, and why, did the state reject expert opinion on migrant crime? What were the consequences of the state adopting or devaluing this particular form of expertise? By examining closely how the law of deportation evolved in the 1950s and the 1960s, we can analyze the complex ways in which race played into the history of forced exit from Britain. Furthermore, we can better evaluate the reasons why the racial politics of deportation seemed to diverge so sharply from the politics of entry.

In order to understand fully the politics of deportation in postwar Britain, we need to explore both the collective—and highly public—fantasy of the West Indian deportee, as well as the reality of Irish deportations. One major influence on the deportation debates was the legacy of the Notting Hill and Nottingham riots of 1958, which helped to articulate the public imagining of the West Indian as the archetypal deportee. But equally important was the longstanding problem of governing Irish crime and violence on the mainland. The Irish occupied a very different role in the politics of forced exit than they did in the realm of voluntary entry. In both cases, though, they illuminated the catalogue of British anxieties about crime, migration, and the end of empire. For many participants, deportation debates were intertwined with questions about Britain's moral responsibilities toward its former colonial subjects and were thus engaged with larger anxieties about how to sustain some form of civilizing mission in a postimperial age.

RACIAL VIOLENCE AND THE FANTASY OF THE WEST INDIAN DEPORTEE

When the question of deporting Commonwealth citizens was raised in Parliament in the late 1950s, the overwhelming public perception—documented widely in the press—was that West Indians would be the main target. The apparent impetus for this proposed legislation was not war with an external enemy, but rather the 1958 riots in Notting Hill and Nottingham. These eruptions of racial violence, in which crowds of up to 4,000 whites attacked West Indian and African residents with knives, razors, bottles, and iron bars, prompted an outpouring of public anxiety about the "degenerate" working-class white youths who were perceived to have instigated the riots.[7] British criminologists sought to understand how postwar affluence had produced a generation of disaffected, racist, and violent thugs.[8] The working-class adolescent white male was increasingly perceived to commit his own distinctive crimes: namely, hooliganism and street violence.

The riots were followed by a severe new penal regime that Home Secretary Richard ("Rab") Butler intended to reorient Britain's youth toward more orderly behavior.[9] But the initial scholarly and governmental

interest in white rioters quickly faded. Many British academics and politicians argued that the misbehavior of recently arrived black migrants had
fueled working-class white violence.[10] Such explanations distinguished
little between criminal acts (such as living on immoral earnings) and
acts that were widely perceived as socially destructive (such as interracial sex). The point was the cumulative effect of these behaviors on the
white psyche. These connections between black misbehavior and white
rioting served to "naturalize" racial antipathy and to place culpability for
both the violence and the failures of assimilation upon the black targets.[11]
Although black crime had only the most tenuous link to the riots—that
is, in offering an appealing explanation for white violence—it became a
compelling framework for understanding the social tensions that seemed
to plague postwar Britain.

After 1958, statistics on immigrant crime were deployed to establish a
genealogy for precisely how whites had been "pushed" to riot by the misbehavior of their black neighbors. Indeed, this era was pivotal in remaking relations between people of color and the police, as the Metropolitan
Police intensified their investigations of West Indian "vice" crimes.[12] The
Home Office suggested that West Indians were especially prone to commit certain kinds of offenses: perjury, stowing away, possessing illegal
weapons, hemp trafficking, brothel keeping, and living off of immoral
earnings.[13]

There are major problems with assessing the statistics on crime, race,
and migration in postwar Britain. Because there was no firm numerical
data regarding the total population of color in Britain, it was impossible
to determine what percentage of this population committed crimes.[14]
Furthermore, there was no consensus on exactly who constituted an
"immigrant" for the purposes of expulsion, because the length of residence that rendered people liable to deportation was constantly debated.
Although the police often collected information on the birthplace of
criminal offenders, these statistics did not reveal how long the individual
had lived in Britain. Statistics on crime divided by race or nationality
were limited and uneven.[15]

The widespread allegations of vice crime among West Indians in
Britain are therefore difficult to confirm or refute. What is clear is that
in the wake of the 1958 riots, the existing (and very limited) crime statistics for migrants were deployed in order to support both entry and
exit controls and to link the deportation process to the criminal justice
system. Prior to the riots, *The Times* had estimated that 10 percent of the
Jamaicans who came to Britain had criminal records.[16] But subsequently,

Norman Manley, the chief minister of Jamaica, assured British audiences that any Jamaican who had been convicted of a violent crime could not travel to Britain without special permission, and that anyone with three convictions for any offense was intensively screened.[17]

The riots thus seemed to serve as a key moment in the racialization of the study of crime, prompting the Metropolitan Police's first attempts to separate crimes by the race of the defendant, and new efforts to consider the "racial significance" of these crimes.[18] In this sense, the deportation policies of the 1950s and 1960s might be seen simply as a direct legislative byproduct of the racial disturbances in Notting Hill and Nottingham: an effort to extirpate those individuals who had presumably provoked white violence.[19] Deportation policy was expanded while the trials of the Notting Hill instigators (and victims) were playing out in the courts and the press.

At this time, legal experts were also weighing the ramifications of the Homicide Act 1957. Of special relevance was section 3, which elaborated the doctrine of the "reasonable man" in relation to the doctrine of provocation. The new act clarified that all evidence pertaining to provocation that might have caused a defendant to lose self-control should be left to the jury, which would determine whether this provocation had been sufficient to reduce the charge against the defendant. Thus, criminal law was potentially made more culturally specific as legal scholars embraced anew the concept that different individuals were provoked by different acts or events.

Could the "reasonable man" be a migrant? The legal scholar Colin Howard argued that it was more complicated to judge Jamaicans or Pakistanis in Britain who committed violent crimes than to judge aborigines in Australia. He suggested that "newcomers" should take their adopted country as they found it, even if they tended to preserve their own customs and language in a separate sub-community. The law would quickly become "overcomplicated if a Jamaican who killed another Jamaican in London were entitled to an inquiry by the jury whether at the time of the killing he was more under the influence of Jamaican than of English customs."[20] The real question was whether the migrant's milieu constituted enough of a "distinct and separate" community to argue that the defendant actually inhabited a different cultural sphere than native-born Britons.

The migrant's relationship to the "reasonable man" was thought to be especially problematic in cases that revealed the offender's inability to adapt to his new surroundings. The example that Basil Nield had given the

Royal Commission on Capital Punishment (1949–53) was that Englishmen were conditioned by "a century of music-hall badinage" to accept the invasion of their privacy by their mothers-in-law, but the Jamaican husband of an English woman would not normally be so conditioned and might be roused by this provocation to violence.[21] Yet if the test of the "reasonable Englishman" gave way in such cases to that of the "reasonable Jamaican," then conflicts of anthropological and psychiatric expertise would inevitably ensue. The migrant thus posed special challenges for the new homicide legislation, as his or her "culture" was so difficult to define.

Debates about deportation policy thus took place against this backdrop of expert contention about the highly charged relationship between race, culture, migration, and crime. Yet if deportation was initially conceived by some parties as a tool for resolving racial tensions after the riots, then it was clearly not always implemented in this fashion. The riots generated a powerful public image of the West Indian criminal, which facilitated debates about deportation. But the vast majority of deportees were *not*, in fact, West Indians or other migrants of color who had been convicted of vice crimes. How might we make sense of the discrepancy between the public image of deportation and its reality? How did a policy that initially seemed to be aimed at West Indians end up targeting another group entirely: that is, the Irish?

If we look closely at the evolution of these debates, we can see that the notion of deportation as a weapon to be used exclusively against West Indian "vice" was never universally shared, nor was it particularly long-lasting. The politics of deportation in postwar Britain were complex and multifaceted. There were always major disagreements—most notably, between the executive and the judiciary—about who should be deported from Britain and why. In order to fully understand the complexities of deportation, we must expand the chronological and geographical parameters of the story to explore the ways in which, by the postwar years, the fiction of West Indian deportation and the subterranean reality of Irish deportation were working in tandem.

ALIENS AND IMMIGRANTS: THE INEQUITIES OF DEPORTATION BEFORE 1962

Until the Commonwealth Immigrants Act 1962, the British government's formal powers of deportation were generally limited to aliens.[22] This limited scope of deportation powers in the metropole contrasted sharply with the sweeping powers that colonial authorities enjoyed.[23] In

Southern Rhodesia, for example, the government could deport anyone convicted of supplying alcohol to "colored" persons, or anyone unable to read and write in a European language.[24] Colonial governments also massively expanded their use of deportations in postwar anticolonial movements, most notably during the Malayan "Emergency." Deportation, then, was one technique for resisting decolonization. One rationale for these contrasting deportation policies in Britain and its colonies was that dangerous outsiders were perceived as more threatening in territories with largely uneducated populations. On this view, Britain could absorb or tolerate criminals more readily than its colonial counterparts.[25]

Prior to the Second World War, the Home Office had generally resisted deportation provisions for colonial subjects, maintaining that, "to deport or exclude any members belonging to the family would only weaken the bonds of Empire."[26] But with the advent of nationalist independence movements in Asia and Africa after 1945—which illustrated all too vividly that the "family bonds" of empire might be loosened without Britain's approval—the Home Office began to investigate an expanded deportation policy for the metropole. In particular, the Home Office was increasingly dissatisfied with the judicial methods employed in lieu of a deportation provision for Commonwealth immigrants. For even before 1962, it was possible to use indirect means of expulsion. Defendants could be bound over, meaning that the convicted person was given a choice of being punished in Britain or returning to his country of origin. If he chose the latter course, he would not be called up for judgment as long as he left Britain for a specified country and stayed there for a certain number of years.[27] English courts also frequently suspended sentences for Irish citizens if they agreed to return to Ireland.[28] This method was especially popular in dealing with young Irishmen. Rather than sending the Irish citizens to Borstal in England and placing the burden of reform upon the English taxpayer, the courts often shipped the defendants back to Ireland instead.[29]

These practices were deplored by the Home Office, because they effectively allowed judges to "blackmail" offenders out of the country. Furthermore, the procedures for enforcement were unclear; if a man were escorted to the boat and he refused at the last minute to go, then the police did not have the power to arrest him. The accused would then simply serve his prison sentence, as he would have done without an order of expulsion in the first place. Furthermore, no authority was specifically empowered to pay the fares home of the accused. If the accused had no money, then he or she was not compelled to leave.[30] For these reasons, neither the executive nor the judiciary were satisfied with the use of binding over orders to expel criminals from the metropole, as these orders seemed both ad hoc and unethical.

The judiciary demand for deportation provisions to be used against Commonwealth immigrants intensified further after the Notting Hill and Nottingham riots. Several justices (along, of course, with numerous fascist groups) stated publicly that they thought deportations of black residents might be an appropriate response to the riots. One justice lamented that he lacked the power to execute deportation orders for "undesirable" or "misplaced" West Indians who were connected with the riots.[31] In another case, the magistrate objected to having to pass two different sentences for aliens and Commonwealth immigrants who had committed comparable crimes. Victor Van Zanta, a West Indian who hired two German au pair girls to work for him as prostitutes out of his flat in Hampstead, was sentenced in 1961 to six months' imprisonment for living on immoral earnings. The magistrate complained to Van Zanta, "'It is a great pity I have no power to deport you,'" and then deported the two German girls instead, telling them, "'the sooner you get back to your native land the better.'"[32]

Discussions of a deportation bill for Commonwealth immigrants initially focused on acts of moral turpitude. Even before the riots, a Conservative lobby mobilized for deportation provisions focused specifically on male pimps.[33] Although deportation provisions for Commonwealth immigrants would ultimately be folded into legislation on immigration controls, they were initially introduced in the venue of criminal law: that is, as an amendment to the Street Offences Act (or "vice" act). The amendment empowered the courts to recommend the deportation of any entrants from the Commonwealth or the Republic of Ireland who were convicted of living on the earnings of prostitution.[34]

The amendment was defeated (by 22 votes to 8) in 1959, on the grounds that it was undesirable to alter so radically the legal status of a whole population in respect of one crime alone. But the Conservative proponents of the amendment were heartened by the breadth of support they had attracted, which had extended even to the Labour members of the Street Offences Bill committee.[35] Thereafter, a new deportation bill was drafted, still focused largely on the drug and sexual offenses in which all Commonwealth immigrants—but especially West Indians— were presumed to "specialize": carrying knives, smoking hemp, pimping white women.[36] The bill would, however, theoretically apply to all Commonwealth immigrants regardless of their race.

Many of these offenses (such as living on immoral earnings) were non-indictable, so a tension existed in the draft bill between its stated focus on crimes punishable by imprisonment and its underlying interest in vice crimes, which were seen as key spurs to racial violence. "Moral obloquy" was considered the best gauge of whether an offense warranted deportation.[37] One participant noted the desirability of using deportation provisions to catch "shady [Maltese and Cypriot] café proprietors whose activities render them liable to criminal conviction but not to imprisonment."[38] Although serious crime would be emphasized in later stages of Parliamentary debate, the draft bill's proponents viewed deportation as a useful mechanism for policing a wide range of misbehaviors.

After the deportation bill was drafted in 1958, the cabinet delayed its introduction in order to obtain the views of colonial and Commonwealth governments. The bill prompted angry protests from officials in West Africa, South Asia, and the West Indies, all of which highlighted the misalignment of metropolitan and colonial (or, increasingly, postcolonial) concerns. One issue of contention was the length of residence in the U.K. that exempted individuals from deportation. M. F. Dei-Anang, Permanent Secretary to Ghana, suggested that the proposed five-year exemption discriminated unfairly against newer residents, who were likely to commit minor crimes because of the racial discrimination they faced in Britain.[39] Pakistan noted that the bill's focus on indictable crime failed to address other "anti-social" residents in Britain—for example, South Asian students under the influence of communism—who were perhaps even more dangerous than convicted offenders.[40]

One noteworthy feature of the draft bill was that it explicitly conceived of deportation as an alternative to entry controls.[41] Although staunch anti-immigrationists Norman Pannell and Cyril Osborne had led the early push for deportation, the draft bill also won qualified support from liberal organizations, such as the Institute of Race Relations.[42] Many liberals were willing to support some version of the deportation bill, which was openly hoped to "save us from a worse fate": that is, restricted entry.[43] In fact, the Dominions Office had initially proposed using the deportation provisions to remove people with forged entry papers, but this suggestion was rejected on the grounds that it would ally the process of deportation too closely with entry controls.[44] Clearly, it was more offensive to liberal opinion to keep targeted populations from entering Britain than to expel individuals once they had violated Britain's legal and social norms.

At this stage, deportation was conceived of not as a solution to immigration problems, but rather as a palliative for the highly vocal anti-immigration lobby, and as a filter to improve the quality of the migrant population. The liberal presumption, soon to be proved entirely false, was that deportation might serve as a cure for white racism: that as Britain's "colored" population was purged of its criminal elements, racial tensions would ease and calls for entry controls would fade away.[45] The Home Office projected that the proposed legislation would result in 500 deportations per year.[46] The rationale, which depended on dichotomizing "good" and "bad" entrants, was that deporting a few hundred convicted criminals *from* Britain would salvage the rights of unfettered access *to* Britain for thousands of others.

In the immediate aftermath of the riots, deportation was largely perceived as an alternative strategy of policing that obviated the need for entry controls. Its focus was on expelling individuals who committed vice crimes, which were closely linked to the incitement of racial violence. In the following decade, deportation policy took a new direction. By the 1960s, deportation was increasingly used as a complement to restricted entry rather than as a substitute for it. The next section of this chapter considers the trajectory of deportation provisions after the Commonwealth Immigrants Act 1962, which marked a dramatic departure from the draft bill of 1958. Entry and exit, which had been decoupled in 1958, were by 1962 firmly intertwined.

SAVING CARMEN BRYAN: CRIME AND THE COMMONWEALTH IMMIGRANTS ACT 1962

By 1962, the draft deportation bill had ended its independent existence and had been folded into the Commonwealth Immigrants Act. As part of the Street Offences Act, it had failed; as part of the Commonwealth Immigrants Act, it would expand and flourish. At this point, the crucial opposition between forced exit and unlimited entry disappeared. Instead of "saving" Britain from entry controls, deportation had itself become part of a restrictive entry system.

The Commonwealth Immigrants Act 1962 has been taken as a watershed in the racialization of British citizenship, and scholars have written powerfully of the ways in which this legislation constrained non-white immigration. But it is important to note that the act actually consisted of two parts: part 1 dealt with the much-discussed entry controls, and part 2 dealt with deportation provisions, specifically for Commonwealth citizens who had been resident in the U.K. for less than five years, were convicted of offenses punishable by imprisonment, and were recommended for deportation by the court. From the inception of the act, parts 1 and 2 operated differently. The powers conferred in part 1 (the entry controls) were temporary, requiring annual renewal by Parliament. But part 2 (the deportation section) was intended as a permanent addition to the statute book. Part 2 was also brought into force first, on May 31, 1962; the entry controls in part 1 were effected more slowly. Historians have focused on part 1 of the Commonwealth Immigrants Act: the vexed question of ingress. But if we look closely at part 2 of the act, we can see just how uneven and complex the racialization of citizenship in postwar Britain really was.

The mechanics of the deportation process under the Commonwealth Immigrants Act were important, because they involved a range of different government branches that actually held contradictory views on the purpose of deportation. In 1962, courts obtained the power to recommend deportations for Commonwealth citizens who met the criteria outlined above. But the final decision to deport these recommended offenders rested with the Home Secretary, who ruled on each deportation order served by the courts. The process of deportation, then, required coordination between the Home Office and the judiciary, which was frequently lacking in the 1960s.

The first deportation cases under the new act involved an Australian who had stolen a bicycle, and an Irishman accused of child neglect.[47] Neither of these cases attracted much public sympathy or attention, in the Australian's case, perhaps because he had fourteen previous convictions in his homeland and had arrived in Britain as a stowaway.[48] But with the Carmen Bryan case—the first to involve a person of color—the Home Office was thrown into a human rights scandal. Bryan was a Jamaican woman, twenty-two years old, who came to Britain in 1960. She worked in a welding factory until she was sacked; thereafter, she lived in on national assistance. In June of 1962, she stole from a shop in Paddington one packet of tomatoes, four tins of milk, two hand tongs, a clothes line, a Pyrex bowl, and five pairs of nylons: the total value of the goods was just over £2.[49] She pleaded guilty to a first offence of petty larceny and was conditionally discharged, then recommended for deportation. Although she had not been sentenced to prison time, she was taken straight to Holloway Gaol to wait for Home Secretary Henry Brooke, who had just taken office, to rule on her case.[50]

Bryan remained in prison for five weeks with no legal advice.[51] She quickly became a *cause célèbre* in the British press, a sympathetic victim of the new legislation. Representatives of the Jamaica Migrants Service and Jamaican High Commission visited the Home Office to plead Bryan's case. They also offered Bryan welfare services so that she could "go straight" and "settle down to a happy and useful life" in Britain.[52] The fact that Bryan was West Indian was discomfiting even at the Home Office, as deporting a Commonwealth citizen had far more dire—and enduring— consequences than deporting an alien au pair girl or foreign domestic: "persons from the West Indies have probably come here to settle, and to require them to return to their country represents a fundamental inter- ference with the plans they had made for their life."[53]

Such statements reveal the often mystifying ways that deportees as well as migrants were categorized in the official mind. The key factor here was the migrant's intention in coming to Britain. By the 1960s, much to the discomfiture of some, the permanency of the West Indian migration was readily apparent. In this case, the facts of migration shaped the different levels of sympathy for deportees. The objections to Bryan's deportation, partly from within the Home Office, illustrate how anti-deportation sentiment could itself stem from a paternalist image of West Indian dependence on the mother country. From this perspective, Britain meant more to the West Indian than it did to the Australian, the European, or the Irishman, and the ethics and feasibility of deporting individuals from any of these groups should be evaluated accordingly.

Bryan was no one's ideal deportee. Even the anti-immigrationist Norman Pannell denounced the deportation order; Bryan was neither a drug trafficker nor a pimp living on immoral earnings (Pannell's two main targets). Certainly, it was never beneath Pannell to grandstand on a question of race relations. But although Bryan may have been some- one Pannell would have sought to keep out of Britain in the first place, she was not the type of person that he wanted to spend political capital on deporting. He had always intended to focus on individuals living on immoral earnings, as well as drug offenses. The ganja-smoking West Indian pimps of Pannell's more inflammatory rhetoric proved to be dif- ficult to locate on the roster of potential deportees. Bryan evoked quite a different stereotype: the vulnerable lone woman migrant.[54] For Pannell and others, the case also represented an abuse of executive privilege.[55] "Rab" Butler, Brooke's predecessor, had promised that deportation would be used only for grave offenses: a promise that Bryan's case seemed to contravene. Across the political spectrum, MPs protested Brooke's treat- ment of Bryan, and even called for Brooke's resignation.[56]

After widespread protests organized by Labour MPs Eric Fletcher and George Brown, Brooke canceled the deportation order for Bryan. He claimed that Bryan's magistrate had believed she was unhappy in England, and that she would benefit from returning to Jamaica.[57] Brooke suggested that Bryan's personal desires were paramount in his decision, as he had changed his mind after learning that Bryan wished to stay in Britain: "Since I have been out of prison I have felt much better and would be very glad if I could be allowed to stay here in England . . . When I was in prison I was so depressed I did not know my own mind and I thought it would be much better to leave the prison and go home rather than stay there. But now that I am out I feel much better."[58] Bryan was released on a restriction order, under which she reported daily to the police.

Carmen Bryan's story had a happy ending of sorts, although it was not precisely the ending that her supporters had anticipated. Upon her release from prison, Bryan married a welder in London. The two returned to Jamaica, stating that they would like to raise their family in the sunshine.[59] Instead of being a forced deportee, then, Carmen Bryan ended up as a voluntarily returned migrant. But what her case revealed about the mechanics of deportation was far more disturbing than her individual fate.

Above all, Bryan's case exposed the divisions within and between the offices that governed the deportation process about who was supposed to be targeted for deportation and why. The episode was a disaster for the Home Office, demonstrating that the new deportation provisions had "gone wrong first crack out of the box."[60] Brooke drew fire for suggesting that deportation was appropriate where the offense—even if relatively minor—was a symptom of difficulty in adjusting to a new country: what several newspapers termed a "benevolent" deportation.[61] On this view, deportation was a privilege rather than a punishment. *The Times* lamented that Brooke was using deportation as a form of social engineering: an instrument of "surveillance over the social conduct of immigrants, weeding out those who in his judgment were not leading useful lives."[62]

Historically, the Home Secretary had always had an uneasy relationship to expertise, and this tension was exemplified in the realm of deportation.[63] For many decades, the Home Secretary had been typed the "arch non-expert," who was as prone to reject expert opinion in the realm of crime and punishment as to embrace it.[64] In terms of Brooke personally, he was maligned during his time in office for his failure to combat crime effectively. His predecessor, "Rab" Butler, had set up a Home Office research unit on the causes of crime in 1956 and spurred the creation of the Institute of Criminology at Cambridge in 1959, as well as urging new programs to alleviate overcrowding in prisons and improved efficiency in criminal courts. But the crime rate continued to climb during Brooke's tenure, and his aggressive—though erratic—handling of deportation cases was likely shaped by the criticism he faced about his response to crime more generally.

Was deportation fundamentally a judiciary decision or an executive one? Sir Charles Cunningham, the Lord Chief Justice, argued that deportation was ultimately an executive act on which courts ought not to have the last word.[65] But the Bryan case had revealed the extraordinary power of magistrates over deportation orders. Because deportation was supposed to be reserved for serious crimes, most MPs had expected that the duty would fall mainly on judges, who were assumed to be less racially prejudiced than magistrates.[66] Indeed, many MPs objected to the scope of the provisions that allowed deportation for any offense punishable by imprisonment, including—for example—traveling on the London Underground without a ticket, precisely because they placed too much power in the hands of magistrates.[67]

This concern about how magistrates were controlling the deportation process was well placed. In the very first month of the Commonwealth Immigrants Act, out of 125 recommendations for deportation, 109 came from magistrates' courts.[68] Brooke refused to offer to circularize magistrates about the government's deportation policy, or to offer the courts any guidelines.[69] Individual magistrates were thus left to craft policies of their own.[70] Yet Brooke also frequently reversed magistrates' decisions. Initially, up to 90 percent of deportation orders were quashed by the Home Office, although by 1963 that rate had dropped to 50–60 percent.[71]

Deportation recommendations depended greatly on the individual magistrate's views of how the criminal justice system in should integrate—or segregate—migrants. Emmanuel Stanley, a twenty-two-year-old Dominican who was convicted of maliciously wounding two youths with a knife, was recommended for deportation by Graham Swanwick, Q.C., the Recorder of Leicester. Stanley was also sentenced to eighteen months' imprisonment, and Swanwick stressed that he had recommended deportation to show that "use of the knife will not be tolerated in this country."[72] But arguments about crime and cultural difference varied by individual court. At the Worcester Quarter Sessions in 1963, the chairman sentenced two Jamaicans for stealing and commented that "other courts would feel you ought to be deported as we have power to do, but this court prefers to deal with accused persons as if they were English offenders."[73]

In a similarly haphazard process, appeals against deportation orders were refused in several cases of theft, but allowed in other cases for rape and the indecent assault of a child.[74] Magistrates were frequently uncertain about which individuals were liable to deportation, and which offenses were deportable.[75] In the case of Vincent Albert Reid, a twenty-seven-year-old Jamaican sentenced for larceny at London Sessions in 1963 to twenty-one months' imprisonment and recommended for deportation, the deportation order was set aside by the Court of Criminal Appeal. Reid should not have been considered for deportation in the first place; he had come to England in 1948, and thus had been in residence for over fifteen years. But the revocation of Reid's deportation order was not based on his legal ineligibility; rather, it was based on his long period of distinguished service with the Royal Air Force, from which he had been discharged in 1957. What saved Vincent Reid from deportation was not the fact that he was legally immune based on length of residence, but that his personal history marked him as a trustworthy individual whose past service to the nation should be recognized.[76]

As these cases suggest, there was no unified policy on deportation. Although the Home Office publicly insisted that it was crafting deportation policy from above, the secretary was dependent on the initiative of courts that constantly sought—and failed to find—executive guidance. Just after Carmen Bryan's deportation order was canceled, a West Indian brickmaker, Emmanuel Joseph, was recommended for deportation for stealing £4 10 s. from a West Indian couple at his lodgings. The Recorder, Charles Henderson, reasoned that, "Where West Indians live cheek by jowl, two or three to a room . . . it is essential that they should be honest for the peace of the whole community. I think it is in the best interests of other West Indians who are overcrowded to saturation that those of them who commit offences should go back where they came from.'"[77] The rationale for deportation was that the courts should protect immigrants from one another, formulating a legal distinction between tolerable and intolerable residents. This deeply paternalistic argument evoked Pannell's claims that deportation was merely a way of policing the boundaries between different types of migrants: the criminal versus the long-suffering laborer.

Not everyone saw deportation as an undesirable punishment. Although Brooke's notion of "benevolent" deportation earned him jeers in Commons, numerous West Indian and African defendants asked to be deported in the early days of the Commonwealth Immigrants Act, and individual magistrates were happy to oblige them.[78] Solomon Fahm was an unemployed Nigerian who had spent fifteen of his eighteen years in Britain in prison. When he was convicted of loitering in 1962, he said that he wanted to go home to Nigeria. The Clerkenwell magistrate, responded, "'That is one way in which we can help you and we are only too delighted to do it.'"[79] The magistrates' view conflicted with that of the Home Office, which feared that fulfilling these requests both undercut the function of deportation as a deterrent to crime and elided deportation with voluntary repatriation.

Fahm did not appear to be legally liable to deportation, as he had resided in Britain for more than five years. But there were always loopholes in the five-year rule. If a defendant had spent more than six months in prison, then that time did not count in calculating the period of residence in Britain. Thus, individuals who had served substantial amounts of prison time could potentially be considered liable to deportation even if they had been continuously resident for long periods.[80] As the Home Office noted, there was nothing "magical" about the five-year period. It had been selected because after five years, a Commonwealth immigrant was allowed to register as a British citizen, and increasing the period of exemption would "alter the whole basis of the present citizenship and nationality law."[81] But as Fahm's case revealed, while five years might mark the time in which a person could become a citizen in legal terms, the processes of cultural transformation were more difficult to measure.

Deportation provisions were thus explicitly linked to the broader question of integration.[82] The question of how much time to give individuals to assimilate before deporting them figured in several criminal cases. Franklyn Rapier, a young man of color from Grenada, was sentenced to nine months in prison and recommended for deportation after he struck a man with a bottle and stole the man's coat during a brawl in 1962. Rapier stated at his trial that in his own country, he would think little of using a bottle to settle a dispute. The trial judge claimed that due to Rapier's behavior, limited intelligence, and poor understanding of English, he was not suited to live in Britain. The Court of Criminal Appeal set aside Rapier's deportation order, noting that deportations were to be linked only to bad behavior, not to intelligence or fluency in English. The assault charge did not justify deporting a man who "had not had sufficient time to settle down in England."[83] This judicial notion that a person might commit a crime through not having had time to adjust to a new country was supported further by the emergent race relations industry, which defined immigrant difference as a problem of environment and setting rather than biology.[84] The act of setting aside a deportation order on the grounds that the defendant had lacked the time to "develop" into a good resident was a way for the judiciary to express confidence in the processes of assimilation rather than disrupting or devaluing them.

Significantly, these cases did not rely on the presumption that the accused lacked knowledge of the law of the land.[85] That is, Rapier needed more time in Britain so that he could overcome the disruptions of migration, not so that he could learn the law. Setting aside deportation orders constituted an optimistic statement, whether by the higher courts by the Home Secretary, about the power of the British environment to overcome the cultural differences that might prompt criminal behavior. Such optimism was not universally shared. In 1963, Norman Pannell sought to strengthen the deportation provisions of the Commonwealth Immigrants Act by scrapping the five-year exemption clause, thus rendering all entrants permanently liable to deportation regardless of the length of their residence. His bid was unsuccessful, but length of residence remained a controversial aspect of deportation policy throughout the 1960s. Deportation cases often involved a meditation on what to do when the trajectory of assimilation appeared to have been derailed.

There were major differences in how the Home Office and the judiciary approached the issue of deportation. But there were other important participants in deportation proceedings. The police played a crucial role by determining who was eligible for deportation in the first place. Although the deportation provisions of 1962 were theoretically blind to race, the likelihood that an accused would be served with deportation orders depended partly on whether the arresting officer thought the accused looked or seemed foreign. Chief constables acknowledged that many defendants—presumably those who were white and spoke unaccented English—might proceed through the courts without anyone guessing that they had been born elsewhere.[86] When an arresting officer did invoke the possibility of deportation, the accused then had seven days to produce proof that he was not eligible for deportation.[87] The early days of the Commonwealth Immigrants Act prompted numerous accounts of "rough justice," in which the police were said to intimidate migrants with threats of deportation and to bully magistrates into deportation orders for minor crimes.[88]

Numerous legal scholars objected to the crucial role of the police in initiating deportation proceedings. They argued that the initiative for deportation ought to come only from the court without police involvement, because the processes of prosecution and punishment should be kept separate.[89] The police generally favored the widest possible deportation powers, proposing that the law should encompass not only convicted criminals, but also "young Commonwealth white girl students living with colored men, or young colored girls living with men and possibly pregnant; girl immigrants obviously heading for the 'streets'; men and women whose mode of livelihood is dubious (living by their wits or engaged in crime); persons who are mentally unsound and are confined in asylums; incorrigible tramps."[90]

In such proposals, criminal behavior was submerged into a larger field of socially maladaptive actions, in which interracial sex was considered the primary offense. Although interracial sex was legal, as all participants acknowledged, the police in particular considered it sufficiently undesirable as to render it deportable. This suggestion that a legal act should be met with expulsion highlights how some participants in these debates sought to link interracial sex and crime more generally.[91] Deportation thus served as a mechanism for policing sexual behavior as well as racial boundaries.

The relationship between punishment and deportation was complicated; the Home Office frequently considered deporting offenders before they had served any part of their prison sentence.[92] Cedric Thornberry, a legal scholar at the LSE, argued that deportation after an individual had already served any part of his or her sentence constituted a double punishment: that is, prison time *plus* exile.[93] Sir Charles Cunningham, the Lord Chief Justice, responded that although it might be attractive to deport Commonwealth citizens immediately, punishment and deportation must be regarded as two separate processes. Deportation, he reminded his critics, was not primarily punitive at all; its aim was not to reform the character of the criminal, but to preserve the physical and moral safety of the country he left behind.

Deportations without prison time were ultimately rejected on the grounds that they represented a selfish abdication of Britain's historic civilizing mission.[94] How could Britain fail to rehabilitate anti-social offenders before letting them loose in their own countries? This problem seemed especially striking when the prisoners in question were citizens of Commonwealth countries, over which Britain had so recently (and unevenly) relinquished control. Those at the Home Office who opposed deportation often did so on the grounds that Commonwealth citizens should still be understood as part of the imperial "family," over whom Britain could never fully abandon its responsibility. Sending these individuals back to their newly independent nations as deportees was thus an admission of British defeat and an unwelcome recognition of other nations' sovereignty over the processes of moral reform. Such consider-ations betrayed a reluctance to forego Britain's status as a moral arbiter of justice after the formal end of empire.[95]

If some participants objected to deportation because they believed it lessened Britain's global status, then Labour barrister George Mikes offered another perspective. He argued that deportation provisions repre-sented a collective British refusal to accept the realities of decolonization, a pathological effort to extend the legal life of empire. Mikes referred explicitly to the pro-deportation lobby as an "imperial hangover," noting that, "We don't have India any more—but still play the master-race game vis-à-vis some Central European refugees and Italian waiters. We can't go out and colonise peoples in five Continents—so let's colonise those who happen to come here . . . Imperialism without an Empire is slightly ridiculous."[96]

Ultimately, deportation procedures in the early days of the Common-wealth Immigrants Act reflected a number of competing interests and agendas, from the management of vice and the policing of sexuality to the extension or rejection of the imperial civilizing mission to the elu-sive—and fictive—dream of demographic control. Overall, the police and magistrates were much more zealous about enforced departure than the Home Office.[97] Charles Royle, the Labour MP for West Salford, suggested that magistrates perceived the act as a chance "to get some coloured people sent out of the country."[98] Royle accused magistrates of unjustly issuing deportation orders as a substitute for stricter entry controls. But there was a significant gap between those whom the court recommended for deportation and those who were actually deported. The rate of deportation for West Indians and Africans who had been served with deportation orders was about 20 percent, whereas that for citizens of the "White Dominions" was 45 percent.[99] If the police and courts sought to use the act to "whiten" Britain's population, then the Home Office con-sistently checked these efforts.

Who, then, were the real targets of the act? Did the Home Office con-ceive of these targets differently from the courts? Although the public discussion of West Indian vice served as a powerful anti-immigration platform, it was less effective in producing executive action on West Indian deportations. The debate about West Indian vice continued into the 1960s, but it was ever more at odds with the underlying facts of expulsion. The gap between real and imagined deportees was increas-ingly vast.

I turn now to the group most profoundly affected by the new deportation provisions of 1962: the Irish. What role did Irish deportees play in a larger discourse about crime and migration? How—and why—did the Irish come to bear the burden of deportations in the 1960s? This section examines the historical trajectory of expulsion for Irish migrants as a means of exploring further the range of competing agendas that shaped postwar deportation policy.

DEPORTING THE IRISH:
THE DILEMMA OF ETERNAL RETURN

More than any other group, the Irish exposed the contradictions of the Commonwealth Immigrants Act. On November 16, 1961, after much tortured debate, Parliament determined that the entry regulations of part 1 would not apply to the Irish.[100] The exclusion of Irish citizens from immigration control was one of the most controversial aspects of the 1962 legislation.[101] It was thereafter impossible to view this part of the bill as anything other than racially restrictive; as *The Times* said, the bill could no longer be accepted "with any shred of decency."[102] The Irish had been included in the deportation debates in 1958 largely for what the Home Office called "presentational" reasons: namely, to avoid the charge that deportation was racially discriminatory. When the draft bill was abandoned, and new legislation proposed in 1961, there was "anguished consideration" of how to apply entry controls to the Irish, but the question of how to include them in part 2 was scarcely mentioned.[103] Thus emerged the curious legal fact that the Irish were eligible for deportation under part 2, but were exempt from immigration control under part 1.[104]

Strikingly, there were no protests raised on behalf of Irish deportees; there was no Irish counterpart to Carmen Bryan.[105] Indeed, there was little public discussion of Irish deportees at all. But the fact that the Irish constituted the dominant group among deportees posed a variety of logistical problems. Because there was no border control between the United Kingdom and the Irish Republic, Irish deportees could easily return to England without interception. In theory, deportees faced a six-month term of imprisonment if they were caught upon their return, but this sentence was not consistently executed, and they were not always deported again.[106]

One Irishman, a painter named Joseph Anthony Burke, was deported from England five times between 1964 and 1969, returning to London after each deportation. On his sixth conviction (this time, for possessing 188 amphetamine tablets), Evelyn Russell of the Old Street Magistrates'

Court wearily informed Burke, "'We do not want you here,'" and recommended him for deportation once more.[107] Irish deportees often brazenly informed their escorting officers that they intended to return to England, sometimes on the very next boat after they arrived in Ireland.[108] Instead of underscoring English authority over Irish criminals, deportation proceedings provided a new opportunity for the Irish to flout this authority. As the Home Office lamented in 1963, "the system of deporting people who come flocking back can be made to look extremely ridiculous."[109] The rate of *known* return for Irish deportees was then up to 27 percent.[110]

Some officials suggested that deportations to Ireland cease altogether under these circumstances.[111] But making the Irish exempt from deportation would create a glaring and politically inexpedient racial inequity. Of course, part 1 of the Commonwealth Immigrants Act already evidenced just such an inequity. The problem of Irish deportees was described at the Home Office as "anomalous and unsatisfactory, but incapable of solution unless we either—(a) treat the Irish better than Commonwealth citizens; or (b) control all traffic across the Irish Sea, including that from Northern Ireland."[112] Faced with these choices, the Home Office was willing to live with the returning deportees.

Irish deportees also posed problems for penal philosophy. The high rate of return for Irish convicts made it difficult to argue that deportation was a deterrent to crime.[113] Furthermore, the frequent use of deportation against Irish criminals in England worked against a cohesive rehabilitation policy for Irish convicts. Rehabilitating someone who was about to be deported seemed pointless.[114]

The postwar era witnessed an intensification of expert concern with Irish vice and crime. Irish prostitutes in England's port cities drew increased attention from vigilance associations, while English welfare agencies repatriated thousands of unmarried Irish mothers in order to reduce immorality on the mainland.[115] By the 1960s, male delinquency had replaced female sexual misbehavior as one of the key concerns regarding Irish migrants in England. F. H. McClintock, a researcher at the Institute of Criminology at Cambridge, argued that after 1950, both Irish and Commonwealth citizens quickly outpaced their English counterparts in convictions for violent crime.

These findings were widely debated. Anthony Bottoms, a criminologist and former probation officer, argued that McClintock's figures were artificially high because they included domestic disputes as "violent crimes."[116] Bottoms claimed that domestic disputes posed no public threat and involved "only technical" amounts of violence. Strikingly, he proposed discounting domestic crimes as "true" violence, which meant that the rate of violent crimes committed by Irish citizens plummeted. The debate about Irish crime rates in England turned on this larger issue of whether domestic violence was violence at all, illustrating how questions of gender and ethnicity could function in tandem in the realm of expertise. Bottoms' own theory was that criminal behavior developed when Irish migrants abandoned their own society—and its strong external controls, such as the Catholic Church—for the fluidity of English mores.

Criminological scholarship on the Irish and West Indians typically set the two groups against one another to determine which had the "worse" degree of criminal behavior. One study conducted in Birmingham under the auspices of the Institute of Race Relations in 1966–67 declared that West Indians were remarkably free from criminal activity, compared to the Irish. West Indian migrants managed to rise above the constraints of their environment, such as poverty, whereas Irish migrants helped to create these constraints in the first place.[117] Interestingly, none of these studies considered discrimination against the Irish in England as a factor that might affect crime statistics. Instead, they underscored the limitations of deportation with regard to crime control. More than half of Irish-born offenders had been in England for more than five years, sometimes since childhood, and were therefore exempt from the deportation provisions of 1962.[118] Criminological scholarship thus highlighted the futility of the Commonwealth Immigrants Act. If the majority of Irish offenders were long-term residents of England rather than recent arrivals, then the threat of deportation could do little to restrain them.

Yet even as the Home Office freely admitted that Irish deportations were ineffective for crime control, it continued to deport the Irish at a high rate relative to other Commonwealth citizens. One motivation might have been to avoid the charge of racial discrimination that was evoked by part 1 of the Commonwealth Immigrants Act. Yet if this were the case, one would expect the Home Office to publicize the rates of Irish deportation in order to show that people of color were not being targeted. Most of the detailed information on Irish deportees is available in confidential Home Office files, which have only recently been declassified. In the press, the archetypal deportee remained the West Indian. Relative to the incredibly active media coverage of West Indian crimes, the high rate of deportations to Ireland was a secret of migration history.

For the most part, the Home Office displayed a remarkable lack of interest in the West Indian pimps and drug traffickers who figured so prominently in the British press. Instead, the Home Office's preoccupation in the 1960s was with a rather different figure: that is, the Irish terrorist. Keeping the public focus on vice crimes, which appeared to be readily governable compared to terrorism, allowed the scope of the threat of political violence on the mainland to be downplayed. The executive thus had a vested interest in keeping the "secret" of Irish deportations. The "secret" was not just that most deportees were Irish rather than West Indian, but also that there were far more dangerous crimes than pimping or drug trafficking with which to contend. Political violence had to be managed, but also public hysteria about it had to be contained. Looking at both the public perception of deportation and its implementation reveals the diversity of agendas and anxieties that shaped deportation policies in the 1950s and 1960s.

In order to understand fully the executive focus on Irish deportees (versus the public and judicial focus on West Indians), we need to consider how the English attitude towards Irish crime—and particularly, the expulsion of Irish criminals—developed prior to the Commonwealth Immigrants Act 1962. In particular, we need to examine the trajectory and legacy of another deportation law that was explicitly concerned with the expulsion of the Irish: the Prevention of Violence (Temporary Provisions) Act 1939. This act responded to 127 IRA terrorist incidents throughout England's major cities in the first half of 1939, fifty-seven of which were in London. The most striking episodes, which aroused public hysteria, were the bombings at the Leicester Square and Tottenham Court Road stations in February and at King's Cross station in July. The bombs at King's Cross, which had been left in the cloakroom, killed one man and left fifteen people injured; a bomb at Victoria Station that same week injured five more. At that time, these were the most serious casualties linked to the IRA.

Neville Chamberlain's government promptly introduced emergency powers against Irish residents in England. Specifically, the bill empowered the Home Secretary to detain, exclude, and deport any persons who he was satisfied were engaged in the IRA campaign; Irish citizens were also required to register with the English police.[119] Notably, the act placed all responsibility for deportation on the executive, as the judiciary could not be held responsible for the public safety. Any Irish citizen who had resided in England less than twenty years was liable to deportation without a court recommendation. The final version of the bill referred to its deportation powers as an alternative to the frankly appealing option of internment without trial, which had long been the preferred solution to political violence within Ireland.[120] Deportation was thus proposed as a "less tyrannical" alternative, as internment was abhorrent to public opinion.

The act swept through both Houses of Parliament in two days.[121] By the end of 1939, 135 expulsion orders had been issued against Irish citizens in England. In order to avoid demonstrations of public sympathy for the accused, these deportations were carried out at night, under close guard, with the deportees placed on a specially curtained and locked carriage of the boat train from Euston Station to Holyhead. But as in the 1960s, Irish deportees always had a nasty habit of reappearing where they were not wanted. The deportees were made known to the local police, but no other special machinery was devised to prevent expelled persons from returning to England.[122] In 1939, James McGuiness was deported from England on a charge of possessing explosives; he then turned up again not only on English soil but actually as a member of the Royal Air Force. When caught, McGuiness asked to stay in England, and claimed that, "it is surely meet and just that I who once sought to destroy your city now ask that I be allowed to help and make good the damage caused by German bombs."[123] Although McGuiness admitted that he had engaged in Republican activities since his first deportation, he promised that it was with "considerably less enthusiasm."[124] More famously, the Republican author Brendan Behan was sentenced to three years' Borstal training for his part in the London and Blackpool bombings in 1939, and was deported after serving part of his sentence.[125] It took him more than a decade—and multiple arrests for trying to enter England illegally—to get his expulsion order revoked.[126]

We may take these cases as emblematic of both the persistence and the limitations of the Prevention of Violence Act. As *The Times* noted, many of the deportees of 1939 were guilty of no great offense under Ireland's law, and would be "quite free to roam the highways and byways of Ireland at their will . . . Ireland's peace may be the sufferer . . . [and] England's opportunity in getting rid of the Irish malcontents has become Ireland's difficulty."[127] As with the deportations of the 1960s, some participants were concerned that expelling criminals from the mainland represented an abdication of England's colonial role as a moral reformer.

The Prevention of Violence (Temporary Provisions) Act was originally scheduled to expire in 1941; it was continued thereafter through the Expiring Laws Continuance Acts. During the Second World War, the flow of people across the Irish Sea was watched more closely.[128] All Irish persons over sixteen years of age traveling to England had to carry a valid identity card issued by the Irish authorities. Despite these controls, the wartime influx of Irish laborers was substantial, and several proposals for letting the Prevention of Violence lapse during this time were rejected; the government was too anxious about the possibility of IRA activity impeding the war effort to cede the power of deportation. Yet in terms of deportations, the war years were not particularly active. After the initial rush in the first year of the act, the rate slowed to one or two expulsion orders every few months.[129] After the war, the act was increasingly described in Parliament as an impediment to good Anglo-Irish relations: a relic of the hysteria prompted by the 1939 bombings. In 1952, the Home Secretary, Sir David Maxwell Fyfe, was pressed to drop the act; he agreed that he would continue it only to maintain expulsion orders already in force. The power to initiate new deportations was removed. The act was continued only in order to target the original criminals of 1939, and not any of their successors.

By the 1950s, then the Prevention of Violence Act was seriously constrained. Under its provisions, 190 expulsion orders had been issued; 113 of these orders, or roughly 60 percent of the total, were issued during the first two months of the bill's life. All orders had been issued by 1944. In 1954, the Prevention of Violence Act was dropped altogether from the Expiring Laws Continuance Bill.[130] The Irish ambassador wrote eloquently of the rehabilitation of the terrorists of 1939, arguing that many of these criminals had severed their IRA associations and had cut themselves "adrift from ways of violence."[131] It was time, he suggested, to declare an end to the "state of emergency" that had developed before the war. On this view, the Prevention of Violence Act was no longer relevant to Anglo-Irish politics. It served only as an unhelpful legislative reminder of more chaotic and antagonistic days.

And yet, not everyone was satisfied with letting the act lapse, nor did all participants agree that the state of emergency was over. The timing of this move was controversial and divisive at the Home Office. The lapsing of the act followed closely on two major IRA raids in Northern Ireland. In June 1954, a group of suspected IRA men (some wearing British uniforms) raided the Royal Irish Fusiliers depot at Gough Barracks, Armagh, and took weapons from the armory in order to smuggle across the border. Unofficial reports suggested that the arsenal was extensive: 250 rifles, 27 Sten guns, 9 Bren guns, and 420 dual purposes rifles.[132] As *The Times* reported, it was shocking that the IRA, "which everyone assumed was more or less moribund, could carry out a raid of such daring."[133] Four months later, a more violent raid took place at the Royal Inniskilling Fusiliers depot in Omagh. No arms were taken, but five soldiers were seriously wounded; eight men were charged with attempted murder and received prison sentences of ten to twelve years.[134]

At the Home Office, there was much debate about whether the Armagh and Omagh raids warranted extending the life of the Prevention of Violence Act, and whether this was an appropriate time for the government to cede its powers of deportation over Irish citizens.[135] Perhaps because the attacks were localized in Northern Irish barracks, the arguments for continued emergency powers throughout Britain (rather than just in Northern Ireland) failed. Between 1954, when the Prevention of Violence Act was allowed to lapse, and 1962, when the Commonwealth Immigrants Act went into effect, the Home Office thus had no power whatsoever to deport citizens of the Irish Republic.[136] From the perspective of anyone concerned about a revival of IRA activity, this was a dangerous position in which to be.

Particularly interesting in the Home Office's discussion of Irish deportation before the Second World War is the recognition of the competing demands of public opinion and public safety. In 1939, Home Secretary Samuel Hoare mulled over the intractable problem of how to target one group for expulsion without the appearance of prejudice. If, he noted, the government's power of deportation were confined to the Irish, this might be seen as an "undesirable discrimination." Furthermore, a deportation provision aimed specifically at the Irish might cause a public panic about IRA terrorism. His solution: "to meet this objection, the power to remove might be made applicable to all British subjects not born in or established in Great Britain for more than x years."[137] As early as 1939, then, Hoare was suggesting that a blanket power of deportation for all British subjects—of any race or ethnicity—who committed crimes would be an ideal mechanism for expelling Irish citizens without either revealing the scope of the threat of terrorism or seeming to target the Irish unfairly. Part 2 of the Commonwealth Immigrants Act (which coincided with a revival of IRA activity in England) met this need precisely: a fulfillment of Hoare's vision for deporting the Irish undetected.

Although there is no direct evidence that the Home Office intended for part 2 of the Commonwealth Immigrants Act to serve as a revival of the deportation measures in the Prevention of Violence Act, it is worth pointing out the bind that the Home Office was in regarding its inability to deport Irish citizens between 1954 and 1962. During this period, the Home Office debated whether it should have allowed the Prevention of Violence Act to lapse in the wake of the Armagh and Omagh raids, and whether new legislation for Irish deportations might be warranted.[138]

Hoare's hope for deportation provisions that could address with Irish violence without arousing public panic or accusations of discrimination would seem to have been well met by the Commonwealth Immigrants Act, intentionally or not.

In trying to understand the disproportionate numbers in which Irish citizens were deported in the 1960s, it is helpful to consider the longer history of governmental efforts to police and manage the Irish migrant population through deportation. Through the 1939 act, deportation had been established as a significant aspect of Anglo-Irish relations. In one sense, the Commonwealth Immigrants Act was even more useful than the Prevention of Violence Act in that it tied the function of removal to the judiciary process and thus avoided the charge of abusing executive power that had plagued the Home Office in 1939. It was just such complaints about excessive executive power that had contributed to the lapsing of the Prevention of Violence Act in 1952.[139] The fact that the deportations of the 1960s were explicitly motivated by the proven criminal actions of the deportee was what made the practice allowable under the Universal Declaration of Human Rights (adopted by the General Assembly of the United Nations in 1948), which forbade arbitrary exile. Deportations for criminal activity might be harsh, but it was difficult to prove that they were arbitrary.[140]

One possible explanation of the disconnect between the public image of the West Indian deportee and the reality of Irish expulsions could be simply that the allegations of vice against West Indians were entirely out of touch with the criminal statistics and that more of these crimes were in fact committed by the Irish. That is, the deportation provisions of 1962 worked much as they had been intended in 1958—to reduce vice—with the major distinction that the relevant population was Irish, rather than West Indian. But by the 1960s, after the Commonwealth Immigrants Act came into force, the earlier focus on vice crimes fell away dramatically. Also, although Irish female prostitutes had been a focal point of concern in the 1950s, the deportation provisions of 1958 that were concerned with vice primarily targeted male pimps, and Irish men were largely believed to be underrepresented in this group.[141]

Most Irish deportees in the 1960s were convicted of crimes against property, especially larceny. This could be explained by poverty or by the prevalence of young single male laborers—the group most likely to commit larceny—within the Irish population in England.[142] But "larceny" also had a more politicized history within Anglo-Irish relations, which again can be traced back to 1939. In stressing the necessity of the Prevention of Violence Act, Hoare had noted that most arrests of IRA members had been made by police straining their powers of search under the Explosives Act 1883. Convictions were secured by linking the accused to a few grains of chlorate of potash, or a balloon such as those used in IRA explosions. But Hoare lamented that by the 1930s the IRA had improved their methods, cleaning their clothes frequently to remove any trace of explosives. A new mechanism of search was needed. This mechanism was to be found in the search procedures for larceny. As Hoare noted, the Larceny Act 1916 allowed exceptional powers of search that might be applied to IRA members in England: in particular, allowing under certain conditions a chief officer of police to authorize a constable to search a premises without a justice's warrant. Larceny accusations were thus potentially useful in the scores of cases in which the police suspected IRA activity but lacked sufficient evidence to proceed under the Explosives Act. To this extent, "larceny" often functioned as a code word for illegal search.[143]

Certainly, this is not to suggest that all Irish citizens in the 1960s who had been convicted of (and deported for) petty larceny were actually terrorists, or suspected terrorists. But it does illustrate that the Home Office had a tradition of borrowing the charge of larceny when they wished to get Irish citizens out of England but lacked the evidence to convict them of more serious charges. It may also explain why the Home Office was so willing to deport Irish citizens who were convicted of larceny while it at the same time generally limited deportations for Commonwealth citizens to more serious offenses, especially after the Carmen Bryan debacle.

This discussion suggests that the Commonwealth Immigrants Act can only be fully understood when read in the context of Anglo-Irish history as well as racial prejudice. According to the press and, to some extent, the judiciary, the deportation provisions of the Commonwealth Immigrants Act were intended to resolve the racial tensions engendered by the Notting Hill riots and to address the threat posed by West Indian drug and sex traffickers. But at the Home Office, the higher priority may well have been to find a legislative substitute for the Prevention of Violence Act and to extend the longstanding practice of governing many forms of Irish crime through deportation.

Although the Commonwealth Immigrants Act was overtly directed towards ordinary crime, it may be a mistake with regard to Ireland to dichotomize the governance of "ordinary" crime and political violence.[144] In the case of Irish deportations in the 1960s, the policing of ordinary individual crime may also have been used to address more serious collective threats. At a moment when the Home Office perceived the IRA as quiet, but not inactive, the deportation provisions of the Commonwealth Immigrants Act were highly tactical. In this sense, deportations were not really a "new" technique at all, but an elaboration of prior modes of action. We might see the deportations of the Irish in the 1960s as continuous with those of the 1920s and 1930s: an extension of, rather than a break with Anglo-Irish tensions over population movements.

In practice, then, if not in explicit intention, the deportations of the Commonwealth Immigrants Act picked up where the Prevention of Violence Act left off, effectively providing a mechanism for deporting Irish citizens without seeming to discriminate against them. Part 2 of the act reflected not only anxiety about West Indian crime (which came to surprisingly little in terms of actual deportations of West Indians), but also the legislative "traces" or sediment of anxiety about Irish terrorism. In the two parts of the Commonwealth Immigrants Act, a highly public campaign to constrict migrants of color meshed uneasily with a longer history of executive concern—and secrecy—about Irish political violence.

RACE AND RACISM IN DEPORTATIONS AFTER 1945

Debates about deportation revolved around the indeterminacy of when colonial relations with both Ireland and the West Indies were to be concluded, which forms of colonial ties should be suspended or sustained, and how the residuum of moral and legal responsibility for former colonial subjects might play out on metropolitan terrain. In this sense, deportation could be seen as the final act or resort of the decolonizing state. Deportation policy evolved out of competing interests and agendas of which racism was only one part, but a crucially functional one. My intention here is not to downplay the crucial role of racism in laws of migration, but to point to the widely varying uses to which racism could be put and how racism may have functioned in the politics of exit. For the Home Office, judicial and public concerns about West Indian crime were extraordinarily useful, providing a legal impetus and mechanism for deporting the Irish while appearing to do something else entirely.

Recognizing that deportation policy primarily affected the Irish, rather than populations of color, is significant for understanding how race did (and did not) figure in the new constraints on British citizenship. If we reduce the Commonwealth Immigrants Act solely to its first part, regarding entry controls, then the Irish certainly look like the victors of migration history. But if we widen the lens to look at the process of *exit*, then the issue of race becomes considerably more complicated. This chapter has revealed how the distinctive processes of entry and exit can highlight different elements of the relationship between individuals and states. Furthermore, it shows that these divergent processes reveal different kinds of prejudices, which are not otherwise visible.

Rather than saying that the Irish were targeted for deportation instead of West Indians, it would be more accurate to say that both groups were targeted at different moments by different actors. Overall, West Indians represented the "public" face of deportation, whereas the history of Irish deportation was submerged. To some extent, the fantasy of West Indian deportation provided cover for the reality of Irish expulsions, which received virtually no scholarly or public attention.

During the postwar era, the Home Office contended with individual magistrates and judges who neither shared nor were even necessarily aware of its agenda. But the structure of deportation law after 1962 allowed the Home Office to revamp magistrates' recommendations for deportation orders, placing the final decision regarding deportation in executive hands. The police and magistrates created the population from which deportees could be drawn, and this population was certainly shaped by judicial concerns about West Indian crime. But the selection of which convicts to expel rested ultimately with the Home Office, and it was precisely at that point—when the Home Office intruded into the deportation process—that the emphasis shifted from West Indian or other Commonwealth residents to Irish ones.[145]

None of this, however, answers what is perhaps the most basic question in this narrative: why did the Home Office ever bother trying to deport people who were known to return so easily? The difficulty of controlling the land border between Northern Ireland and the Republic and the sea border between the Republic and England had been used as public justification for the absence of entry barriers on the Irish throughout the twentieth century.[146] Yet the logistical impossibility of policing these borders did not stop the government from deporting the Irish, despite the obvious futility of such actions. The practical problem of border policing may have saved the Irish from entry controls, or at least provided an excuse to explain this anomaly. But it did not save them from forced expulsion, though the border was surely as porous with regard to exit as it was to entry. Both in the 1930s and in the 1960s, the British state focused its hard-won deportation powers on a group for whom deportation was uniquely meaningless. What was the point of this charade, in which hundreds of Irish citizens were marched down to the docks and sent off on boats to Dublin at great public expense, only to sail right back again? Did these deportations serve any purpose at all?

One might ask whether the most universal theme in this history is actually the failure of deportation to resolve *any* of the problems that its proponents had articulated. British deportation strategies make sense only if one assumes that public safety was not the primary objective. The deportations of the 1960s were entirely ineffective in terms of reducing crime and terrorism. Furthermore, they were admitted to be so by their most ardent proponents. Where they succeeded, in terms of results if not intention, was in destigmatizing deportation itself. In linking deportation explicitly to criminal law, deportation provisions for Commonwealth citizens effectively severed deportation from war and emergency, thus normalizing and routinizing a power previously reserved for crisis. Between 1963 and 1970, the total deportations for *all* groups—aliens, Commonwealth citizens, the Irish—increased by about 60 percent, although the Irish dominated until the very end of this period.[147]

Several key changes after the Commonwealth Immigrants Act further emphasized executive power over the processes of expulsion. In 1965, the White Paper *Immigration from the Commonwealth* proposed that the Home Secretary should be empowered to remove any individual deemed to have entered Britain by evading the act; no court recommendation would be required. The rationale for the 1965 provisions further intertwined the politics of expulsion and demography: "too often a court, having no responsibility for the effectiveness of immigration control, has in mind only the one would-be immigrant before it and cannot see how letting him remain can do the public interest any harm."[148] That is, the courts might be swayed by the claims of individual migrants, whereas the Home Secretary was better able to survey the broader patterns of population movement.

The White Paper thus marked a new phase in the extension of discretionary power over subjects who had already been admitted to Britain (as opposed to those who were still seeking entry). These proposals—which *The Times* characterized as the executive "dispensing with the safeguards of law"—were eventually enshrined in Part 2 of the Immigration Appeals Act 1969, which conferred the power to deport any Commonwealth or Irish citizen who failed to observe the conditions under which he or she was admitted. No court proceedings were required.[149] Shortly thereafter, over the objections of numerous Labour MPs, the Home Secretary was empowered to deport any Commonwealth citizen he considered not conducive to the public good without a court recommendation.[150] At this point, the judiciary was effectively cut out of the deportation process, and deportation became an executive affair.

With regard to the Irish, this new phase of deportation law was strikingly tautological; the Irish were included in the Immigration Appeals Act in name, but were unaffected by deportations for breach of entry conditions precisely because there were no entry controls against them. It is likely for this reason that the statistics for deportations of Commonwealth citizens rose in the early 1970s, finally outpacing Irish deportees.

If we survey the 1950s and 1960s together, we can see that the initial emphasis on vice crimes was relatively short lived and, in any case, never universally shared. In the wake of the Notting Hill and Nottingham riots, public and judicial fears about West Indian vice and crime had provided the impetus for new deportation provisions. In the 1960s, the Irish emerged as the primary victims of deportation law, and the types of crime in question could not be so easily categorized. The arguments marshaled both by proponents and opponents of deportation provisions were always deeply imbued with racialized assumptions about crime and migration. But ultimately it is not possible to delimit the impact of postwar deportation policy to a single racial or ethnic group. The cumulative effect of these decades was to integrate deportation into the ordinary workings of criminal law. The key pattern that emerged by the 1970s was the overall rise in deportation, a pattern that has continued to accelerate ever since.

This integration of deportation into normal migration regimes proved increasingly important by the end of the period under investigation here. Although deportation for ordinary crime was still possible in this period, by far the most common offenses for which individuals were deported by 1967 were actually offenses against part 1 of the Commonwealth Immigrants Act: that is, cases of improper or illegal entry to Britain.[151] No mention was made of the drug and sex offenses that had served as the impetus for the deportation debates in the first place. This earlier focus on vice crimes had been entirely superseded by a new rationale of using deportation to reverse the process of entry.

By the 1980s, the Home Office had begun to use minor breaches of residency conditions—such as doing casual work—as grounds for deportation, although such offenses would previously have resulted in a small fine.[152] At this point, forced exit had become an unexceptional and seemingly unobjectionable response to wrongful entry.[153] Instead of focusing on the crimes of migrants, the Home Office had begun a broader and still ongoing pattern of criminalizing elements of migration itself.

control
of
movement

Conclusion

On October 1, 1960, Nigeria's Independence Day, the Oxford don Margery Perham confessed that when she saw the Union Jack flutter down the post at midnight before the vast crowds at the Lagos race course, "I felt a wholly unexpected, almost physical shock . . . But immediately the Nigerian flag ran up and the assembled Nigerians of all the regions and tribes saluted it with unmeasured pride and hope. I realized then that, whatever our regrets and forebodings, the incalculable force of energy and pride would be harnessed behind the new nation."[1] Shock, regret, anticipation. This catalogue of responses charted a comforting trajectory: a tacit acknowledgment that this was a British defeat dressed up as a victory, and yet also implying that this was precisely what Britain had always hoped and planned.[2]

Envisaging this same transformative moment of independence, Perham's nemesis, the journalist and popular writer Elspeth Huxley, took a bleaker view. Huxley predicted that the end of British rule would kill off the empire's tidy and tiresome virtues, encouraging a reversion to a haphazard and satyric order: "the passions of Saturday night rather than the intentions of Sunday morning." Huxley wrote that "When the British Empire finally crumbles, we might write as its epitaph: 'We bored them to death.'"[3] Whereas Huxley predicted the unleashing of violent, regressive energies, Perham anticipated the birth of a new order, to be welcomed by Britons and Africans alike.

Independence, when it came, proved predictably unpredictable. At the inauguration of Malaysia in 1963, the new governor of Sarawak collapsed under the strain of the event.[4] One official in Eastern Nigeria lamented to his parents that the British flag had been booed when it came down, and that the African Permanent Secretary had muttered "'Good Riddance.'"[5]

Hastily composed national anthems were sung out of key "in falsetto shrieks, " and the new flag of Uganda sported a bird that struck one departing British administrator as looking less like a crested crane than a spavined chicken.[6] A British secretary in Kampala described how rapidly she descended into irrelevance, as shop assistants, ignoring European customers, "managed to convey most convincingly that it was all rather a bore." She was shocked anew in Lusaka, where "African pedestrians, three abreast, remained so, forcing the European to step aside."[7]

Still, these transformations were mostly reported in Britain not as days of infamy and disaster, but as colorful carnivals brimming with good cheer.[8] Andrew Stuart, a longtime administrator in Uganda, spoke with awe of the moments of "rare beauty" when new nations took shape. Independent Africa was "something new and shining, where anything and everything was possible and all the old barriers were swept away."[9] Colonel Eric Hefford, a former army officer whose work as the master of ceremonies for independence celebrations was memorialized in the 1968 film *Ceremonial Man*, declared that he was not a funeral director but a midwife.[10] Former colonial servants recalled returning to a mood of misbegotten cheer about the empire's collapse: "it was all forgotten, as though it had never been, and all that replaced it was an aura of bright optimism about how much better [Africa] was going to be without us."[11]

For some, this is all merely evidence that ordinary Britons would have scoffed at the idea that their lives had been changed by independence abroad—at least, until the denizens of new nations arrived in the metropole.[12] On this view, independence could take the form of chaotic celebration, dignified retreat, or even violence in the former colonies, but barely registered in Britain itself. Such attitudes depended on particular understandings of how decolonization was defined, where it was believed to be happening, and how its effects could be measured—debates that were as controversial in the era in which they began as they have remained in our own.

What, exactly, had decolonization wrought? It depended on where one looked. The question is not only how much decolonization mattered in the metropole, but also what particular form it took there. That is, decolonization unfolded differently when it was staged at home and abroad. Rethinking *where* decolonization happened requires that we rethink what decolonization *is*. Decolonization shaped more than the former colonies (and the new nations that emerged from them), but also Britain itself. It did so not merely by producing sentiments of "loss," "decline," or "melancholia," but by taking part in both the achievements and the failures of welfare. In Britain, decolonization registered as a broadly social process, rather than as an exclusively diplomatic one. My aim has not been to deny or diminish the political import of decolonization, but rather to expand our understanding of the spheres in which it was political.

The question of whether (let alone when) empire came to an end is not simply a political question or a cultural one—to which the answers might be summed up as "yes" and "never," respectively. Rather, the realities and fantasies of independence both seeped into the structures of everyday British life. Independence could not be forgotten in Britain because it was happening on metropolitan terrain: not as a relic or a monument or a memory, but as a living enactment of the ongoing tensions of empire itself.

As all of this suggests, there was not one single decolonization, but many. The 1950s and 1960s witnessed the production of multiple and competing imaginings of the process of decolonization by different players—including, but by no means limited to, the decolonizing state itself. These imaginings, in turn, helped to construct the apparatus of welfare and gave the distinctive shape to the world we now think of as the "postwar." The afterlife of empire, then, was taking place in multiple sites. I have offered one perspective on what will surely become a diverse cacophony of histories. One of my arguments has been that birth and death—beginnings and endings—are not adequate rubrics for describing the wholly unpredictable impact of decolonization on British life in the 1950s and 1960s. The ways in which the consequences of empire's end became entrenched in Britain's political and social structures were persistent, but often spectral or difficult to see: an afterlife, rather than a rebirth.

The absence of a shared vision about the meaning of decolonization explains some of the tensions and fragilities of the postwar state. Dissension about how best to manage decolonization created conflicting policies in multiple domains. In this sense, the end of the empire was reborn in and through what we should now see as a globally manufactured welfare state. Welfare emerged from multiple perspectives, far beyond the local and the metropolitan. Social democracy was not only fractured by race, as is well known, but also shaped by its proponents' and opponents' ever-shifting and urgent sense of which regions of the world were being reconfigured in relation to British interests. For them, decolonization provided an opportunity to expand and critique welfare's aims. We need not reject the familiar themes of postwar history, such as affluence, permissiveness, consensus, and welfare itself. But we do need to call attention to the global conditions in which these themes emerged, and in which—purged of their globality—they have been given historical and historiographical weight.

This book has argued that decolonization was built into the lives of ordinary Britons, reshaping their experiences and identities at the most intimate level. Its impact was not circumscribed by bemoaning or rejoicing over the fate of the Union Jack. It was not momentary or episodic—frozen in time—but ongoing. Decolonization transcended the temporal limits of formal politics to take part in a vast metropolitan experiment of reconstructing social relationships through the guise of welfare. The end of empire conjured new states, but also—in Britain—new categories of identity, from the migrant to the aid worker. Although independence days may have been sedately celebrated—or even ignored—in Britain (and this itself should be taken as a politically vested claim, rather than assumed as a transparent fact), there is a more complicated picture to be drawn beyond these ceremonial moments, one that shows how widely Britons were affected by the real and imagined trajectories of independence.

The histories of decolonization and the welfare state have both been narrated largely in terms of abstractions. Yet one of the key assumptions of their architects was that people's sentiments, and the improvement thereof, were vital to determining the quality of international relations and metropolitan politics. I have sought here to begin to illuminate the joint impact of welfare and decolonization on personal lives and stories, showing how individuals and families, like nations, were reworked in their wake. Part of my hope in bringing together the fields of decolonization and welfare is to humanize them both, and to give a sense of the tremendous individual and familial dramas that were driving and being driven by these processes. These histories deserve to be told in their own—richly flawed and complex—human terms.

Each chapter of this book has dealt with successive problems of welfare, all of which seemed to require their own forms of intervention or withdrawal. These problems, which were forged in global contexts, point to the ways in which decolonization gave rise to the distinctive nature of welfare in 1950s and 1960s Britain. The history of welfare can be understood anew when its relationship to the end—not only the apex—of empire is more fully revealed. Welfare took its particular forms in the context of efforts to rethink Britain's role in the world, and to imagine what kinds of leaders and followers newly independent states might require. Thus, I have proposed, the making of welfare should be viewed through a global, not only a national or local prism. It was deeply inflected by imaginings of global affairs, which were shaped, though not contained, by the map of the former empire.

What kinds of politics have followed from the story I have told here? The debates of the 1950s and 1960s shaped both the idea—and the critique—of multicultural Britain. The Left has typically assumed that the 1950s were not part of their story of race, migration, and collective action, and could be dismissed as insufficiently radical, an age of laissez-faire racism and indifference.[13] Moreover, the specific role that decolonization played in the production of multiculturalism has been forgotten on the Right and the Left. Both sides have tended to discount the years before 1962 (or sometimes 1968), conceiving of decolonization only in terms of its impact on migration patterns.

I would suggest that we might think of the politics of the late twentieth century as having a different genealogy. Multiculturalism in Britain has drawn on the idea of both colonialism and migration as an encounter between distinct cultures. This framework depends on the notion of the coherence and stability of culture: an idea that emanated from postwar studies of "the stranger."[14] Furthermore, the elaboration of the migrant as a legal and political category—namely, through the establishment of racialized entry controls and the radicalization of people of color in the metropole—depended on many of the intellectual frameworks that were established in the 1950s in the context of various trajectories of imperial collapse. Such creations were vital not only for anti-immigrationists, but also for the political mobilization and radicalization of communities of color in Britain. The expert evaluation of different groups in the 1950s according to their levels of community organization was echoed and reworked in the activism of the 1960s, although these continuities have not been readily acknowledged. Ultimately, these problems of welfare would increasingly be seen as rooted in cultural differences that would become a point of celebration: that cultural diversity rather than social homogeneity was the ultimate fate of post-imperial Britain.

The classificatory systems of the 1950s had ongoing effects in terms of the resources available to different groups, how these groups were configured as social "problems" (or as having social value) and how the "Britishness" of these groups was understood. The perceived demands of decolonization played a critical role in the interracial history of black Britain by promoting internal hierarchies for communities of color, and producing incommensurate social identities for its members. The particular constellation of race, welfare, and politics in contemporary Britain—as well as the interpretive frameworks that have been mustered to understand these problems—was forged through a process of decolonization that valued or degraded different groups within Britain, and which encompassed whites as well as people of color. These systems of thought had high stakes, explaining the uneven ground on which multicultural Britain emerged, and the fragmentation of its communities of color. Thus, decolonization was one of the factors that can illuminate how various populations within Britain understood each other, and themselves.

Certain elements of Powellite thought—for example, that the end of empire constituted a catastrophic loss, requiring both palliation and amnesia—have been uncritically adopted into liberal opinion. But decolonization was much more multilayered than this interpretation would suggest. Metropolitan society offered many more possibilities for ways to think about and through the end of empire than the mantra of "loss" can encompass, and a multitude of options for understanding how this apparent ending might resurface and gain new life in Britain.[15] To say this is by no means to idealize the 1950s, but rather to try to understand why only some of its strands of thought survived, and which alternatives were closed down. The 1960s did not represent a break with the earlier decade, but only an elaboration of certain of its elements.

The isolation or division of narratives regarding the end of empire and metropolitan life in the 1950s and 1960s—the segregation of the postwar from the postimperial—was enshrined by experts. For decades, experts anxiously insisted on various forms of separation—of the optimistic 1950s from the pessimistic 1960s, and of the optimistic postwar from the pessimistic postimperial. As we have seen, this was not a process that experts could easily control. Critics of expertise were more likely to integrate these frames, testifying both to the empire's uneasy persistence and to the durability of decolonization's demands. It is this latter perspective, which I have sought to bring into sharper focus, that demands further research. Such research, in turn, requires thinking anew about the location, form, and content of the archives of decolonization.

One hope is that this more global history of the postwar that I have offered here can not only illuminate the 1950s and 1960s, but can also help us rethink the longstanding claim that the immediate postwar years can be severed from the radicalism that followed. More broadly, it can aid in examining what kinds of assertions about continuity and discontinuity have been upheld in narratives of the late twentieth century, and what has been at stake in these chronologies. Acknowledging that what we think started in the 1960s (and, more specifically, after 1968) actually began earlier is important because it raises the question of exactly how the emergence of multicultural Britain might be tied to decolonization and the Cold War: a set of connections that has as yet remained unseen.

Throughout this book, there have been two persistent (if implicit) themes: of defining what has been hard to see about the 1950s and 1960s, and pointing to some directions in which we might look in order to broaden or sharpen our view. I have argued that interweaving these strands of the postwar and the postimperial—chronologically, geographically, and thematically—can yield not only a new view of the period, but also a richer sense of how the most powerfully recurrent images of these decades were created. One aim here has been to investigate the precise nature of connections between histories and historiographies that have either been too easily juxtaposed (such as migration and decolonization), or never integrated at all (such as decolonization and welfare).

To understand why historians have continued to subscribe to the myth that the "postwar" and the "postimperial" were distinct and unrelated, we need to return to the mythmakers of the era under investigation, and find new ways to read both with them and against them. They remind us that although the postwar and the postimperial may have been *felt* or *claimed* to be out of sync, they were *lived* very much in synchrony. Yet simply uniting the postwar and the postimperial is only a beginning; what is equally important is to consider how both might be changed by this union. This book can be only a starting point for exploring the varied ways in which Britain's postwar/postimperial history might be reframed; many other histories are waiting to be told.

Notes

INTRODUCTION

1. Jed Esty, *A Shrinking Island: Modernism and National Culture in England* (Princeton, 2004); Guy Ortolano, *The Two Cultures Controversy: Science, Literature and Cultural Politics in Postwar Britain* (Cambridge, 2009).

2. Anna Davin, "Imperialism and Motherhood," *History Workshop Journal* 5 (1978): 9–66.

3. David Feldman, "Migrants, Immigrants and Welfare from the Old Poor Law to the Welfare State," *Transactions of the Royal Historical Society* 13 (2003): 79–104; Marjorie Levine-Clark, "From 'Relief' to 'Justice and Protection': The Maintenance of Deserted Wives, British Masculinity and Imperial Citizenship, 1870–1920," *Gender and History* 22.2 (2010): 302–21.

4. I am indebted to Seth Koven for this point. See, e.g., Abosede A. George, "Feminist Activism and Class Politics: The Example of the Lagos Girl Hawker Project," *Women's Studies Quarterly* 35 (2007): 128–43; Daniel Gorman, "Empire, Internationalism, and the Campaign against the Traffic in Women and Children in the 1920s," *Twentieth-Century British History* 19.2 (2008): 186–216; and see also Chapter 5.

5. Gail Lewis, *'Race,' Gender, Social Welfare: Encounters in a Postcolonial Society* (Cambridge, 2000); Virginia Noble, *Inside the Welfare State: Foundations of Policy and Practice in Post-War Britain* (London, 2008).

6. James Vernon, *Hunger: A Modern History* (Cambridge, MA, 2007).

7. This account is compatible with recent scholarship that seeks to displace welfare as a central narrative of post-1945 Britain. Although welfare remains crucial to my analysis, I associate it with the energetic recrafting of local and global relationships rather than with declinism. David Edgerton, *Warfare State: Britain, 1920–1970* (Cambridge, 2006).

8. Nicholas Timmins, *The Five Giants: A Biography of the Welfare State* (London, 1995); Richard M. Titmuss, *Social Policy: An Introduction*, ed. Brian Abel-Smith and Kay Titmuss (New York, 1974), 27.

9. Anticolonial violence could also generate colonial welfare schemes,

as in the West Indian development projects that followed the 1937–38 riots. Howard Johnson, "The West Indies and the Conversion of the British Official Classes to the Development Idea," *Journal of Commonwealth and Comparative Politics* 15 (1977): 55–83.

10. Jane Burbank and Frederick Cooper, *Empires in World History: Power and the Politics of Difference* (Princeton, 2010), 413; Frederick Cooper, "Possibility and Constraint: African Independence in Historical Perspective," *Journal of African History* 49.2 (2008): 167–96.

11. Philippa Levine, Laura E. Nym Mayhall, Susan Pedersen, and James Vernon, "Roundtable: Twentieth-Century British History in North America," *Twentieth-Century British History* 21.3 (2010): 375–418; Frank Mort, *Capital Affairs: London and the Making of the Permissive Society* (New Haven, 2010).

12. Brian Harrison, *Seeking a Role: The United Kingdom, 1951–1970* (Oxford, 2009); Peter Hennessy, *Having It So Good: Britain in the 1950s* (London, 2006); David Kynaston, *Family Britain, 1951–1957* (New York, 2009); Mark Jarvis, *Conservative Governments, Morality, and Social Change in Affluent Britain* (Manchester, 2005); and Abigail Wills, "Delinquency, Masculinity and Citizenship in England, 1950–1970," *Past and Present* 187 (2005): 157–85.

13. Nick Thomas, "Will the Real 1950s Please Stand Up? Views of a Contradictory Decade," *Cultural and Social History* 5.2 (June 2008): 227–35; and George Behlmer, *Friends of the Family: The English Homes and Its Guardians, 1850–1940* (Stanford, 1998).

14. Hennessy, *Having It So Good*, 303.

15. Cooper, "Possibility and Constraint"; Cooper, "Reconstructing Empire in British and French Africa," *Past and Present* 210, supplement 6 (2011): 196–210.

16. Martin Lynn, introduction to Martin Lynn, ed., *The British Empire in the 1950s: Retreat or Revival* (Basingstoke, 2006), 1–15.

17. Frederick Cooper, *Africa since 1940: The Past of the Present* (Cambridge, 2002).

18. Burbank and Cooper, *Empires in World History*, 413.

19. David Goldsworthy, *Colonial Issues in British Politics 1945–1961: From 'Colonial Development' to 'Wind of Change'* (Oxford, 1971), 2.

20. This issue of asynchronicity in the history of decolonization—and the ways in which its timing can be out of joint when transnational and transregional comparisons are made—is addressed in Christopher J. Lee, "Between a Moment and an Era: The Origins and Afterlives of Bandung," in Christopher J. Lee, ed., *Making a World after Empire: The Bandung Moment and Its Political Afterlives* (Athens, OH, 2010): 1–42. On transnational histories of colonialism (and their own multiple timelines), see also Marilyn Lake and Peter Reynolds, *Drawing the Global Colour Line: White Men's Countries and the International Challenge of Racial Equality* (Cambridge, 2008).

21. Wm. Roger Louis and Roger Owen, *Suez 1956: The Crisis and Its Consequences* (Oxford, 1989), 9.

22. Focusing on this specific moment highlights how it is more apt to inte-

grate the 1950s and 1960s than to isolate them. Mort, *Capital Affairs*. The specific provisions of the Commonwealth Immigrants Act 1962 are discussed in subsequent chapters.

23. On the domestication of imperial themes, see Alison Light, *Forever England: Femininity, Literature, and Conservatism between the Wars* (New York, 1991); Sonya O. Rose, "From the 'New Jerusalem' to the 'Decline' of the 'New Elizabethan Age': National Identity and Citizenship in Britain, 1945–56," in Frank Biess and Robert G. Moeller, eds., *Histories of the Aftermath: The Legacies of the Second World War in Europe* (New York, 2010), 231–47; Wendy Webster, *Imagining Home: Gender, 'Race' and National Identity, 1945–64* (London, 1998); and Webster, *Englishness and Empire, 1939–1965* (Oxford, 2005). See also Mark Mazower, *No Enchanted Palace: The End of Empire and the Ideological Origins of the United Nations* (Princeton, 2009).

24. Robert Holland, foreword to Frank Heinlein, *British Government Policy and Decolonisation 1945–1963: Scrutinising the Official Mind* (London, 2002), vii–viii; Anthony Kirk-Greene, "Decolonization: The Ultimate Diaspora," *Journal of Contemporary History* 36.1 (2001): 133–51.

25. John D. Kelly and Martha Kaplan, *Represented Communities: Fiji and World Decolonization* (Chicago, 2001), 16.

26. William Roger Louis, "The Dissolution of the British Empire in the Era of Vietnam," in Louis, ed., *Ends of British Imperialism: The Scramble for Empire, Suez and Decolonization—Collected Essays* (New York, 2006), 557–86.

27. I am influenced here by T. M. Luhrmann, *The Good Parsi: The Fate of a Colonial Elite in a Postcolonial Society* (Cambridge, MA, 1996).

28. Although social science forms a crucial nexus of power and contention in this book, I have chosen the more inclusive concept of "expertise" to describe its practitioners and to illuminate the variety of their perspectives. All of the social scientists discussed in this book were experts, but not all experts were academic social scientists. The term "social science" does not fully encompass all of the themes I wish to address. It omits, for example, the fields of law and legal theory, which are essential to my story, and also skirts around the emergence of disciplinary divisions in the first place.

29. Noel Annan, *Our Age: Portrait of a Generation* (London, 1990); Becky Conekin, Frank Mort, and Chris Waters, introduction to Conekin et al., eds., *Moments of Modernity: Reconstructing Britain, 1945–1964* (London, 1999), 1–21. The insights of scholars who work on the global history of social science have been particularly instructive: Jackie Assayag and Véronique Bénï, eds., *At Home in Diaspora: South Asian Scholars and the West* (Bloomington, IN, 2003); Sarah Babb, *Managing Mexico: Economists from Nationalism to Neoliberalism* (Princeton, 2001); Andrew Barshay, *The Social Sciences in Modern Japan: The Marxian and Modernist Traditions* (Berkeley, 2004); Dipesh Chakrabarty, *Provincializing Europe: Postcolonial Thought and Historical Difference* (Princeton, 2000); Gil Eyal, *The Disenchantment of the Orient: Expertise in Israeli Affairs and the Arab State* (Stanford, 2006); Laura Hein, *Reasonable Men, Powerful Words: Political Culture and Expertise in*

Twentieth-Century Japan (Washington, DC, 2004); Timothy Mitchell, *Rule of Experts: Egypt, Techno-Politics, Modernity* (Berkeley, 2002); Gyan Prakash, *Another Reason: Science and the Imagination of Modern India* (Princeton, 1999); Andrew Zimmerman, *Alabama in Africa: Booker T. Washington, the German Empire, and the Globalization of the New South* (Princeton, 2010).

30. On the globalization of welfare, see Richard Titmuss and Brian Abel-Smith (with Tony Lynes), *Social Policies and Population Growth in Mauritius* (London, 1961); Richard M. Titmuss et al., *The Health Services of Tanganyika* (London, 1964).

31. These practitioners had antecedents in nineteenth-century social investigations, although their research involved an increasingly diverse body of disciplines and audiences. Eileen Janes Yeo, *The Contest for Social Science: Relations and Representations of Gender and Class* (London, 1996), 285; see also David Englander and Rosemary O'Day, eds., *Retrieved Riches: Social Investigation in Britain, 1840–1914* (Aldershot, 1995); Oz Frankel, *States of Inquiry: Social Investigations and Print Culture in Nineteenth-Century Britain and the United States* (Baltimore, 2006); Seth Koven, *Slumming: Sexual and Social Politics in Victorian London* (Princeton, 2004); Michael J. Lacey and Mary O. Furner, eds., *The State and Social Investigation in Britain and the United States* (Washington, DC, 1993); and Cyril Smith, "Networks of Influence: The Social Sciences in Britain since the War," in Martin Bulmer, ed., *Essays on the History of British Sociological Research* (Cambridge, 1985), 61–76.

32. Desmond King, "Creating a Funding Regime for Social Research in Britain: The Heyworth Committee on Social Studies and the Founding of the Social Science Research Council," *Minerva* 35.1 (1997): 1–26; Alexandra Nichol, *The Social Sciences Arrive* (Swindon, 2001).

33. Martin Bulmer, "Sociology in Britain in the Twentieth Century: Differentiation and Establishment," in A. H. Halsey and W. G. Runciman, eds., *British Sociology Seen from Without and Within* (Oxford, 2005), 36–53; A. H. Halsey, *A History of Sociology in Britain: Science, Literature, and Society* (Oxford, 2004).

34. Jennifer Platt, *The British Sociological Association; A Sociological History* (Durham, 2003), 16.

35. Quoted in A. H. Halsey, "Provincials and Professionals: The British Post-War Sociologists," in Martin Bulmer, ed., *Essays on the History of British Sociological Research* (Cambridge, 1985), 151–64.

36. Harrison, *Seeking a Role*, 266–68.

37. A. H. Halsey, *No Discouragement: An Autobiography* (Houndmills, 1996).

38. Nikolas Rose, *Inventing Our Selves: Psychology, Power, and Personhood* (Cambridge, 1996), 11.

39. John Gascoigne, *Science in the Service of Empire: Joseph Banks, the British State and the Uses of Science in the Age of Revolution* (Cambridge, 1998); Joseph Morgan Hodge, *Triumph of the Expert: Agrarian Doctrines of*

Development and the Legacies of British Colonialism (Athens, OH, 2007); and Londa Schiebinger and Claudia Swan, eds., *Colonial Botany: Science, Commerce and Politics in the Early Modern World* (Philadelphia, 2005). On early modern experts, see Eric H. Ash, *Power, Knowledge and Expertise in Elizabethan England* (Baltimore, 2004); and Ash, "Expertise and the Early Modern State," *Osiris* 25 (2010): 1–24.

40. Richard Drayton, *Nature's Government: Science, Imperial Britain, and the 'Improvement' of the World* (New Haven, 2000), 220. On postcolonial expertise, see Warwick Anderson and Gabrielle Hecht, eds., "Postcolonial Technoscience," *Social Studies of Science* 32 (2002).

41. Conversely, American social scientists have been described as working against the backdrop of an ascendant, if largely unacknowledged, empire, articulating a newly confident ideology of modernization that emphasized how American foreign aid could fill the void left by the European empires' collapse. Terence Ball, "The Politics of Social Science in Postwar America," in Lary May, ed., *Recasting America: Culture and Politics in the Age of Cold War* (Chicago, 1989), 76–92; and Dorothy Ross, "Changing Contours of the Social Science Disciplines," in Theodore M. Porter and Dorothy Ross, eds., *The Cambridge History of Science. The Modern Social Sciences*, vol. 7 (Cambridge, 2003) 205–37. See also Michael Bernstein and Allen Hunter, "The Cold War and Expert Knowledge: New Essays on the History of the National Security State," *Radical History Review* 63 (1995): 52–85; Noam Chomsky et al., *The Cold War and the University: An Intellectual History of the Postwar Years* (New York, 1997); David C. Engerman, *Modernization from the Other Shore: American Intellectuals and the Romance of Russian Development* (Cambridge, MA, 2003); Engerman, *Know Your Enemy: The Rise and Fall of America's Soviet Experts* (Oxford, 2009); Nils Gilman, *Mandarins of the Future: Modernization Theory in Cold War America* (Baltimore, 2003); Ellen Herman, "Project Camelot and the Career of Cold War Psychology," in Christopher Simpson, ed., *Universities and Empire: Money and Politics in the Social Sciences during the Cold War* (New York, 1988), 97–133; Herman, "The Career of Cold War Psychology," *Radical History Review* 63 (1995): 52–85; Herman, *The Romance of American Psychology: Political Culture in the Age of Experts* (Berkeley, 1995); Michael E. Latham, *Modernization as Ideology: American Social Science and 'Nation Building' in the Kennedy Era* (Chapel Hill, 2000); Rebecca Lemov, *World as Laboratory: Experiments with Mice, Mazes, and Men* (New York, 2005); David H. Price, "Subtle Means and Enticing Carrots: The Impact of Funding on American Cold War Anthropology," *Critique of Anthropology* 23 (2003): 373–401; Price, *Anthropological Intelligence: The Deployment and Neglect of American Anthropology in the Second World War* (Durham, 2008); Ron Robin, *The Making of the Cold War Enemy: Culture and Politics in the Military-Intellectual Complex* (Princeton, 2001); and Christopher Simpson, *Science of Coercion: Communication Research and Psychological Warfare 1945–1960* (New York, 1994). For a useful rejoinder to this scholarship, see Greg Eghigian et al., eds., *The Self as Project: Politics*

and the Human Sciences (Chicago, 2007); Peter Mandler, "Margaret Mead amongst the Natives of Great Britain," Past and Present 204 (2009): 195–233; and Mandler, "One World, Many Cultures: Margaret Mead and the Limits to Cold War Anthropology," History Workshop Journal 68.1 (2009): 149–72.

42. Talal Asad, Anthropology and the Colonial Encounter (London, 1973); Grahame Foreman, "The Power to Exclude: Primitivism and the Persecution of British Social Anthropologists in the 1950s," paper delivered at the Pacific Coast Conference on British Studies, Seattle, 2011; Adam Kuper, "Anthropology," in Porter and Ross, eds., Modern Social Sciences, 354–78; Kuper, Anthropologists and Anthropology: The British School, 1922–1972 (London, 1973).

43. Frederick Cooper, "Decolonizing Situations: The Rise, Fall and Rise of Colonial Studies, 1961–2001," French Politics, Culture and Society 20.2 (summer 2002): 47–76.

44. Mike Savage, Identities and Social Change in Britain since 1940: The Politics of Method (Oxford, 2010), 5. See also Matthew Hilton, "Politics Is Ordinary: Non-Governmental Organizations and Political Participation in Contemporary Britain," Twentieth-Century British History 22.2 (2011): 230–68.

45. Philippa Levine, The Amateur and the Professional: Antiquarians, Historians and Archaeologists in Victorian England, 1838–1886 (Cambridge, 1986); Roy Macleod, ed., Government and Expertise: Specialists, Administrators and Professionals, 1860–1919 (Cambridge, 1988).

46. See, e.g., Harrison, Seeking a Role.

47. Thanks to James Vernon for this observation.

48. Intriguing exceptions are Todd Shepard, The Invention of Decolonization: The Algerian War and the Remaking of France (Ithaca, 2006); and Shepard, "'History Is Past Politics?' Archives, 'Tainted Evidence,' and the Return of the State," American Historical Review 115 (2010): 474–83. On colonial archives, see Anjali Arondekar, For the Record: On Sexuality and the Colonial Archive in India (Durham, 2009); Antoinette Burton, Dwelling in the Archive: Women Writing House, Home, and History in Late Colonial India (Oxford, 2003); Burton, Archive Stories: Facts, Fiction, and the Writing of History (Durham, 2005); Nicholas Dirks, "Colonial Histories and Native Informants: Biography of an Archive," in Carol Breckenridge and Peter van der Veer, eds., Orientalism and the Postcolonial Predicament: Perspectives on South Asia (Philadelphia, 1993), 279–313; Dirks, "The Crimes of Colonialism: Anthropology and the Textualization of India," in Peter Pels and Oscar Salemink, eds., Colonial Subjects: Essays in the Practical History of Anthropology (Ann Arbor, 1999), 153–79; Durba Ghosh, "Decoding the Nameless: Gender, Subjectivity, and Historical Methodologies in Reading the Archives of Colonial India," in Kathleen Wilson, ed., A New Imperial History: Culture, Identity, and Modernity, 1660–1840 (Cambridge, 2004), 297–314; Carolyn Hamilton et al., eds., Refiguring the Archive (Dordrecht, 2002); Saloni Mathur, "History and Anthropology in South Asia: Rethinking the Archive," Annual Review of Anthropology 29 (2000): 89–106.

49. In its methodological and political divisions, this discussion resonates with the ongoing debate about whether Britons cared about the empire. The case for the empire's impact on the metropole is articulated most powerfully in Antoinette Burton, *Burdens of History: British Feminists, Indian Women, and Imperial Culture, 1865–1915* (Chapel Hill, 1994); Burton, "Who Needs the Nation? Interrogating 'British' History," *Journal of Historical Sociology* 10.3 (1997): 227–48; Burton, *At the Heart of the Empire: Indians and the Colonial Encounter in Late-Victorian Britain* (Berkeley, 1998); Catherine Hall, *Civilising Subjects: Colony and Metropole in the English Imagination, 1830–1867* (Chicago, 2002); Catherine Hall and Sonya Rose, *At Home with the Empire: Metropolitan Culture and the Imperial World* (Cambridge, 2006). For an opposing view, see; Bernard Porter, *The Absent-Minded Imperialists: Empire, Society and Culture in Britain* (Oxford, 2004). See also the roundtable on David Cannadine's *Ornamentalism* in *Journal of Colonialism and Colonial History* 3.1 (2002).

50. John Darwin, "British Decolonisation since 1945: A Pattern or a Puzzle," *Journal of Imperial and Commonwealth History* 12.2 (September 1984): 186–208.

51. John Darwin, "Fear of Falling: British Politics and Imperial Decline since 1900," *Transactions of the Royal Historical Society* 36 (1986): 27–43. Similarly, see Paul Addison, *No Turning Back: The Peacetime Revolutions of Post-War Britain* (Oxford, 2010); D. George Boyce, "Decolonisation and the British Empire, 1775–1997* (Houndmills, 1999); John Darwin, *Britain and Decolonisation: The Retreat from Empire in the Post-War World* (Houndmills, 1988); Harrison, *Seeking a Role*; Stephen Howe, "When (if Ever) Did Empire End? Decolonisation in British Culture in the 1950s," in Lynn, *British Empire in the 1950s*, 214–37; Howe, "Internal Decolonization? British Politics since Thatcher as Postcolonial Trauma," *Twentieth-Century British History* 14 (2003): 286–304; Ronald Hyam, *Britain's Declining Empire: The Road to Decolonisation, 1918–1968* (Cambridge, 2006).

52. Nicholas Owen, "Decolonization and the Postwar Consensus," in Harriet Jones and Michael Kandiah, eds., *The Myth of Consensus: New Views on British History, 1945–64* (New York, 1996), 176; see also Alice Ritscherle, "Opting Out of Utopia: Race and Working-Class Political Culture during the Era of Decolonization" (Ph.D. diss., University of Michigan, 2005); Bill Schwarz, "'The Only White Man in There': The Re-Racialisation of England," *Race and Class* 38 (1996): 65–78; Schwarz, "Reveries of Race: The Closing of the Imperial Moment," in Becky Conekin et al., eds., *Moments of Modernity: Reconstructing Britain, 1945–1964* (London, 1999), 189–207; Schwarz, *The White Man's World. Memories of Empire* (Oxford, 2011); Stuart Ward, ed., *British Culture and the End of Empire* (Manchester, 2005); Chris Waters, "'Dark Strangers' in Our Midst: The Discourse of Race Relations," *Journal of British Studies* 36.2 (1997): 207–38; and Webster, *Englishness and Empire*.

53. Bill Schwarz, "Claudia Jones and the *West Indian Gazette*: Reflections

on the Emergence of Post-Colonial Britain," *Twentieth-Century British History* 14. (2003): 264–85.

54. On earlier incarnations of these entanglements, see Susan D. Pennybacker, *From Scottsboro to Munich: Race and Political Culture in 1930s Britain* (Princeton, 2009).

55. Ritchie Ovendale, "The End of Empire," in Richard English and Michael Kenny, eds., *Rethinking British Decline* (Houndmills, 2000), 257–78.

56. Rodney Lowe, "Plumbing New Depths: Contemporary Historians and the Public Record Office," *Twentieth-Century British History* 8.2 (1997): 239–65.

57. Colin Holmes, "Government Files and Privileged Access," *Social History* 6.3 (1981): 333–50.

58. David Vincent, *The Culture of Secrecy: Britain, 1832–1998* (Oxford, 1998); Vincent, "Government and the Modern Management of Information 1844–2009," in Simon Gunn and James Vernon, eds., *The Peculiarity of Liberal Modernity in Imperial Britain* (Berkeley, 2011).

59. On these categories, see Vincent, *Culture of Secrecy.*

60. David Cannadine et al., *Review of the Thirty Year Rule* (London, 2009). The report is published at http://www2.nationalarchives.gov.uk/30yrr/30-year-rule-report.pdf.

61. Holmes, "Government Files"; Lowe, "Plumbing New Depths."

62. On the 2011 landmark High Court case regarding the release of the vast archive pertaining to the violence of decolonization, see the essays on the Hanslope Disclosures in the December 2011 issue (39.5) of the *Journal of Imperial and Commonwealth History*, especially David Anderson, "Mau Mau in the High Court and the 'Lost' British Empire Archives: Colonial Conspiracy or Bureaucratic Bungle" (699–716); Caroline Elkins, "Alchemy of Evidence: Mau Mau, the British Empire, and the High Court of Justice" (731–48); and Stephen Howe, "Flakking the Mau Mau Catchers" (695–97).

63. On sources that pertain specifically to counterinsurgency campaigns, see David Anderson, *Histories of the Hanged: The Dirty War in Kenya and the End of Empire* (New York, 2005); Daniel Branch, *Defeating Mau Mau, Creating Kenya: Counterinsurgency, Civil War, and Decolonization* (Cambridge, 2009); Caroline Elkins, *Imperial Reckoning: The Untold Story of Britain's Gulag in Kenya* (New York, 2005); and Benjamin Grob-Fitzgibbon, *Imperial Endgame: Britain's Dirty Wars and the End of Empire* (Houndmills, 2011).

64. I am speaking primarily of the National Archives; local archives may have very different relationships to secrecy. Deborah Cohen, *Family Secrets* (Oxford, 2013). On individual privacy exemptions that cloak the colonial state's wrongdoings, see David Anderson et al., "A Very British Massacre," *History Today* 56.8 (2006): 20–22.

65. Stephen Brooke, "Twentieth-Century British History: New Directions in Researching and Teaching the Field," roundtable at the North American Conference on British Studies (Baltimore, 2010); Levine et al., "Roundtable."

66. Jennifer Cole and Deborah Durham, "Introduction: Globalization and

the Temporality of Children and Youth," in Jennifer Cole and Deborah Durham, eds., *Figuring the Future: Globalization and the Temporalities of Children and Youth* (Santa Fe, 2008), 3–23; Steven Mintz, "Reflections on Age as a Category of Historical Analysis," *Journal of the History of Childhood and Youth* 1.1 (2008): 91–94.

67. Infantilizing indigenes was complex, in that imperialism also cast its own agency as youthful and rejuvenating. Arrested development could be attributed to individuals and groups on both sides of the colonial divide. Chakrabarty, *Provincializing Europe;* Jed Esty, "The Colonial Bildungsroman: *The Story of an African Farm* and the Ghost of Goethe," *Victorian Studies* 49.3 (2007): 407–30.

68. Mario I. Aguilar, "Gerontocratic, Aesthetic, and Political Models of Age," in Mario I. Aguilar, ed., *The Politics of Age and Gerontocracy in Africa: Ethnographies of the Past and Memories of the Present* (Trenton, NJ, 1998), 3–29; Andrew Burton, "Urchins, Loafers and the Cult of the Cowboy: Urbanization and Delinquency in Dar Es Salaam, 1919–61," *Journal of African History* 42.2 (2001): 199–216; Meredith McKittrick, *To Dwell Secure: Generation, Christianity and Colonialism in Ovamboland* (Portsmouth, NH, 2002).

69. Mario I. Aguilar, "Introduction. The Present and Past of Age Notions: The *Status Quaestionis* within Historical Anthropology," in Mario I. Aguilar, ed., *Rethinking Age in Africa: Colonial, Post-Colonial and Contemporary Interpretations of Cultural Representations* (Trenton, NJ, 2007), 1–7. See also Lynn M. Thomas, *Politics of the Womb: Women, Reproduction and the State in Kenya* (Berkeley, 2003).

70. This research was influenced by E. E. Evans-Pritchard, *The Nuer: A Description of the Modes of Livelihood and Political Institutions of a Nilotic People* (Oxford, 1940), 257.

71. Philippe Ariès, *Centuries of Childhood: A Social History of Family Life* (New York, 1962), 15.

72. B. Seebohm Rowntree, *Poverty: A Study in Town Life* (London, 1901); and Rowntree, *Poverty and Progress: A Second Social Survey of York* (London, 1941). On the implications of Rowntree's research, see Vernon, *Hunger.*

73. Philip Abrams, "Age and Generation," in Paul Barker, ed., *A Sociological Portrait* (London, 1972), 99–111; and see Howard Chudacoff, *How Old Are You? Age Consciousness in American Culture* (Princeton, 1989).

74. Michael Murphy, "Measuring the Family Life Cycle: Concepts, Data and Methods," in Alan Bryman et al., eds., *Rethinking the Life Cycle* (Basingstoke, 1987), 30–50; and David Cheal, "Intergenerational Transfers and Life Course Management," in Bryman et al., eds., *Rethinking the Life Cycle,* 141–54.

75. Michael Anderson, "Emergence of the Modern Life Cycle in Britain," *Social History* 10.1 (1985): 69–87; Stephen Hunt, *The Life Course: A Sociological Introduction* (London, 2005); John Macnicol and Andrew Blaikie, "The Politics of Retirement, 1908–1948," in Margot Jefferys, ed., *Growing Old in the Twentieth Century* (London, 1989), 21–42.

76. Richard Titmuss, *Essays on the Welfare State* (London, 1958).

77. Erik H. Erikson, *Identity and the Life Cycle* (New York, 1980), 18–49; and see also Alan B. Spitzer, "The Historical Problem of Generations," *American Historical Review* 78.5 (December 1973): 1353–85.

78. Sarah Lamb, "Generation in Anthropology," in Neil J. Smelser and Paul B. Baltes, eds., *International Encyclopedia of the Social and Behavioral Sciences*, vol. 9 (Amsterdam, 2001), 6043–46.

79. Arnold Van Gennep, *The Rites of Passage* (Chicago, 1960).

80. Audrey Richards, *Chisungu: A Girls' Initiation Ceremony among the Bemba of Northern Rhodesia* (London, 1956), 162–63.

81. Jennifer Cole and Deborah Durham, "Age, Regeneration, and the Intimate Politics of Globalization," in Jennifer Cole and Deborah Durham, eds., *Generations and Globalization: Youth, Age, and Family in the New World Economy* (Bloomington, IN, 2007), 16; Lamb, "Generation in Anthropology;" and see also Meyer Fortes, "The Significance of Descent in Tale Social Structure," *Africa* XIV (1943–44): 362–85; Fortes, *Oedipus and Job in West Africa* (Cambridge, 1959).

82. Eisenstadt cited intellectual debts to Raymond Firth, Meyer Fortes, Maurice Freedman, Max Gluckman, Isaac Schapera, and Edward Shils, with whom he studied in London before moving to Hebrew University. S. N. Eisenstadt, *From Generation to Generation: Age Groups and Social Structure* (Glencoe, IL, 1956), 21.

83. Ronnie Frankenberg, "Life: Cycle, Trajectory, or Pilgrimage: A Social Production Approach to Marxism, Metaphor and Mortality," in Bryman et al., eds., *Rethinking the Life Cycle*, 122–38. For a provocative analysis of modernization theory and the life cycle, see Lawrence Cohen, *No Aging in India: Alzheimer's, the Bad Family, and Other Modern Things* (Berkeley, 1998).

84. I am influenced here by Mark Bevir, "Rethinking Governmentality: Towards Genealogies of Governance," *European Journal of Social Theory* 13 (2010): 423–41.

85. Feldman, "Migrants, Immigrants and Welfare"; Laura Tabili, "A Homogenous Society? Britain's Internal 'Others,' 1800–Present," in Catherine Hall and Sonya O. Rose, *At Home with the Empire: Metropolitan Culture and the Imperial World* (Cambridge, 2006), 53–76.

86. Ann Laura Stoler, *Along the Archival Grain: Epistemic Anxieties and Colonial Common Sense* (Princeton, 2008), 99; see also Tony Ballantyne and Antoinette Burton, eds., *Moving Subjects: Gender, Mobility, and Intimacy in an Age of Global Empire* (Urbana, 2009); Durba Ghosh, *Sex and the Family in Colonial India: The Making of Empire* (Cambridge, 2006); Philippa Levine, *Prostitution, Race and Politics: Policing Venereal Disease in the British Empire* (New York, 2003); Matt Matsuda, *Empire of Love: Histories of France and the Pacific* (Oxford, 2005); Vicente L. Rafael, *White Love and Other Events in Filipino History* (Durham, 2000); Emma Rothschild, *The Inner Life of Empires: An Eighteenth-Century History* (Princeton, 2011); Stoler, *Carnal Knowledge and Imperial Power: Race and the Intimate in Colonial Rule* (Berkeley, 2002);

Stoler, ed., *Haunted by Empire: Geographies of Intimacy in North American History* (Durham, 2006).

87. Jose Harris, "Tradition and Transformation: Society and Civil Society in Britain, 1945–2001," in Kathleen Burk, ed., *The British Isles since 1945* (Oxford, 2003), 92.

CHAPTER 1

1. Richard English and Michael Kenny, "Interview with Stuart Hall," in Richard English and Michael Kenny, eds., *Rethinking British Decline* (Houndmills, 2000), 104–16. See also Wendy Webster, "The Empire Comes Home: Commonwealth Migration to Britain," in Andrew Thompson, ed., *Britain's Experience of Empire in the Twentieth Century* (Oxford, 2012), 12–60.

2. This view is critiqued by F. Henriques in "Sociology of Immigration," in G .E. W. Wolstenholme and Maeve O'Connor, eds., *Immigration: Social and Medical Aspects* (Boston, 1966): 18–26; Frank Reeves, *British Racial Discourse: A Study of British Political Discourse about Race and Race-Related Matters* (Cambridge, 1983).

3. Ritscherle, "Opting Out of Utopia."

4. On French migration policies and decolonization, see Amelia H. Lyons, "Social Welfare, French Muslims, and Decolonization in France: The Case of the *Fonds d'action sociale*," *Patterns of Prejudice* 43.1 (2009): 65–89; Todd Shepard, "Algeria, France, Mexico, UNESCO: A Transnational History of Anti-Racism and Decolonization, 1939-1962," *Journal of Global History* 6 (2011): 273–97.

5. Kathy Burrell and Panikos Panayi, eds., *Histories and Memories: Migrants and Their History in Britain* (London, 2006).

6. Robert Bickers, *Settlers and Expatriates: Britons Over the Seas* (Oxford, 2010); Elizabeth Buettner, *Empire Families: Britons and Late Imperial India* (Oxford, 2004); Kirk-Greene, "Decolonization."

7. Joanna Lewis, *Empire State-Building: War and Welfare in Kenya, 1925–52* (Athens, OH, 2000), 239.

8. Robert Miles, "Migration Discourse in Post-1945 British Politics," *Migration* 6 (1989): 29–53; Miles, "Whatever Happened to the Sociology of Migration?" *Work, Employment, and Society* 4.2 (June 1990): 281–98; Miles, *Racism after 'Race Relations'* (London, 1993).

9. Savage, *Identities and Social Change.*

10. Michael Banton, "Kenneth Lindsay Little," *Anthropology Today* 7.3 (June 1991): 19–21.

11. Kenneth Little, "The Perils of Pioneering Race Relations," *American Anthropologist* 77.4 (December 1975): 887–88.

12. Kenneth Little to J.L. Keith (CO 876/931, The National Archives, hereafter TNA), March 25, 1942.

13. The term "race relations" was coined in Chicago in 1919, in the wake of race riots in that city. Mark Clapson, "The American Contribution to the

Urban Sociology of Race Relations in Britain from the 1940s to the early 1970s," *Urban History* 33.2 (2006): 253–73.

14. David Mills, *Difficult Folk? A Political History of Social Anthropology* (New York, 2009).

15. In 1960, the social anthropology stream incorporated the study of race in the United States, the West Indies, Brazil, South Africa, and Britain. "Edinburgh University Calendar" (Edinburgh University Library Special Collections, Edinburgh), 1954–55, 350–52; EULSC, 1960–61, 579–80.

16. Michael Banton, "Sociology and Race Relations," *Race* 1.1 (November 1959): 3–14; Banton, "Anthropological Perspectives on Sociology," *British Journal of Sociology* 15.2 (1964): 95–112; Banton, "1960: A Turning Point in the Study of Race Relations," *Daedalus* 103.2 (1974): 31–44.

17. Kenneth Little, "Research Report No. 2 of Department of Social Anthropology," *Sociological Review* 8.2 (December 1960): 255–66.

18. Kenneth Little, "Applied Anthropology and Social Change in the Teaching of Anthropology," *British Journal of Sociology* 11 (1960): 332–47.

19. Interview with Anne Murcott, October 14, 2008.

20. Interview with Suzanne Macgregor, November 19, 2008.

21. Interview with Sandy Robertson, September 22, 2008.

22. On the role of gender in this scholarship, see Mica Nava, *Visceral Cosmopolitanism: Gender, Culture and the Normalisation of Difference* (Oxford, 2007).

23. See also Raymond Firth, "Social Problems and Research in British West Africa," *Africa* 17.2 (1947): 77–92.

24. Quoted in Michael Banton, "The Influence of Colonial Status upon Black-White Relations in England, 1948–58," *Sociology* 17.4 (November 1983), 558n2.

25. Kenneth Little, *Negroes in Britain: A Study of Racial Relations in English Society* (London, 1947), xii.

26. Kenneth Little, "Social Anthropology: The Approaches to Fieldwork," *Man* 52 (November 1952): 176.

27. Kenneth Little, *Contemporary Trends in African Urbanization* (Evanston, 1966), 13.

28. Cooper, *Africa since 1940*, 118–19; W. D. Hammond-Tooke, *Imperfect Interpreters: South Africa's Anthropologists, 1920–1990* (Johannesburg, 1997).

29. James Ferguson, *Expectations of Modernity: Myths and Meanings of Urban Life on the Zambian Copperbelt* (Berkeley, 1999), 27.

30. Kenneth Little, *West African Urbanization: A Study of Voluntary Associations in Social Change* (Cambridge, 1965).

31. Ibid., 77.

32. Michael Banton, "Adaptation and Integration in the Social System of Temne Immigrants in Freetown," *Africa* 26.4 (1956): 354–68; Michael Banton, *West African City: A Study of Tribal Life in Freetown* (London, 1957); Michael Banton, "The Restructuring of Social Relationships," in Aidan Southall, ed., *Social Change in Modern Africa. Studies Presented and Discussed at the First*

International African Seminar, Makerere College, Kampala, January 1959 (London, 1961), 113–25.

33. Kenneth Little, "The Role of Voluntary Associations in West African Urbanization," *American Anthropologist* 59 (1957): 579–96; Little, "Some Traditionally Based Forms of Mutual Aid in West African Urbanization," *Ethnology* 1.2 (1962): 197–211.

34. Sally Falk Moore, *Anthropology and Africa: Changing Perspectives on a Changing Scene* (Charlottesville, 1994); Lyn Schumaker, *Africanizing Anthropology: Fieldwork, Networks, and the Making of Cultural Knowledge in Central Africa* (Durham, 2001).

35. Philip Garigue, "The West African Students' Union: A Study in Culture Contact," *Africa* 23.1 (1953): 55–69.

36. Mills, *Difficult Folk*.

37. Rohit Barot, "Reflections on Michael Banton's Contribution to Race and Ethnic Studies," *Ethnic and Racial Studies* 29.5 (2006): 785–96.

38. Michael Banton, "Questions and Answers: Further Reflections upon My Intellectual Career," unpublished paper, 2008.

39. Michael Banton, "What the Study of Migration Might Contribute to the Study of Community," *International Journal of Social Research Methodology* 11.2 (2008): 117–20.

40. Ibid., 118.

41. Philip Abrams, ed., *The Origins of British Sociology, 1834–1914* (Chicago, 1968); Banton, "Anthropological Perspectives."

42. Interview with Michael Banton, September 22, 2008.

43. Sydney Collins, *Coloured Minorities in Britain: Studies in British Race Relations Based on African, West Indian and Asiatic Immigrants* (London, 1957).

44. Michael Banton, "The Social Groupings of Some West African Workers in Britain," *Man* 53 (1953): 130–33.

45. John Rex and Robert Moore, *Race, Community, and Conflict: A Study of Sparkbrook* (Oxford, 1967).

46. Interview with Michael Banton, September 22, 2008.

47. Philip Mayer, "Migrancy and the Study of Africans in Towns," *American Anthropologist* 64.3 (June 1962): 576–92.

48. See, e.g., the excision of anthropological research in Anthony Richmond, *Migration and Race Relations in an English City: A Study in Bristol* (London, 1973).

49. Robert Moore, "Race Relations and the Rediscovery of Sociology," *British Journal of Sociology* 22.1 (1971): 97–104.

50. Elspeth Huxley, *Back Street, New Worlds: A Look at Immigrants in Britain* (London, 1964), 39 and 87.

51. H. Maddox, "The Assimilation of Negroes in a Dockland Area in Britain," *Sociological Review* 8.1 (July 1960): 5–15.

52. Richmond's mentor, T. S. Simey, worked on race and migration at the University of Liverpool's School of Social Science in the 1930s.

53. See also Michael Banton, "Negro Workers in Britain," *Twentieth Century* 151 (1952): 40–45.

54. Anthony Richmond, *Colour Prejudice in Britain: A Study of West Indian Workers in Liverpool, 1941–1951* (London, 1954), 119–20.

55. Ibid., 121.

56. Kenneth Little, "The Position of Colored People in Britain," *Phylon* 15 (1957): 58–64.

57. Kenneth Little, *Colour and Commonsense* (London, 1958), 23.

58. Ruth Landes, "A Preliminary Statement of a Survey of Negro-White Relationships in Britain," *Man* 52 (1952): 133.

59. Nathan Chio, "'They Are Colonising Us Now 15 Miles from Downing Street: Re-Assessing the Post-Coloniality of Post-War Britain," paper delivered at the Pacific Coast Conference on British Studies, Seattle, 2011.

60. Clapson, "The American Contribution"; and see Antoinette Burton, "When Was Britain? Nostalgia for the Nation at the End of the American Century," *Journal of Modern History* 75.2 (2003): 359–75.

61. Michael Kearney, "From the Invisible Hand to Visible Feet: Anthropological Studies of Migration and Development," *Annual Review of Anthropology* 15 (1986): 331–61.

62. Rose, *Inventing Our Selves*, 11.

63. Gabrielle Hecht, "Negotiating Global Nuclearities: Apartheid, Decolonization, and the Cold War in the Making of the IAEA," *Osiris* 21 (2006): 25–48.

64. J.M. Lee, "British Cultural Diplomacy and the Cold War 1946–61," *Diplomacy and Statecraft* 9.1 (March 1988): 112–34.

65. Peter Catterall, preface to Frank Heinlein, *British Government Policy and Decolonisation 1945–63: Scrutinising the Official Mind* (London, 2002), ix–x. See also William Roger Louis, "American Anti-Colonialism and the Dissolution of the British Empire," *International Affairs* 61.3 (1985): 395–420; William Roger Louis and Ronald Robinson, "The Imperialism of Decolonization," *Journal of Imperial and Commonwealth History* 22.3 (September 1994): 463–511.

66. Antoinette Burton, *The Postcolonial Careers of Santha Rama Rau* (Durham, 2007), 145.

67. Andrew Defty, *Britain, America and Anti-Communist Propaganda, 1945–53: The Information Research Department* (Abingdon, 2004); Anne Deighton, *The Impossible Peace: Britain, the Division of Germany and the Origins of the Cold War* (Oxford, 1990); Anne Deighton, ed., *Britain and the First Cold War* (New York, 1990); Michael F. Hopkins, Michael D. Kandiah, and Gillian Staerck, introduction to Hopkins et al., eds., *Cold War Britain, 1945–1964: New Perspectives* (Houndmills, 2003), 1–4; Michael D. Kandiah, "The Conservative Party and the Early Cold War: The Construction of 'New Conservatism,'" in Hopkins, *Cold War Britain*, 3–38; Marc J. Selverstone, *Constructing the Monolith: The United States, Great Britain, and International Communism, 1945–1950* (Cambridge, MA, 2009); Tony Shaw, "Britain and

the Cultural Cold War," *Contemporary British History* 19.2 (2005): 109–15; D. C. Watt, "Rethinking the Cold War: A Letter to a British Historian," *Political Quarterly* 49.4 (1978): 446–56; Peter Weiler, *British Labour and the Cold War* (Stanford, 1988).

68. Thomas Drapes, "On the Alleged Increase of Insanity in Ireland," *Journal of Mental Science* 40 (October 1894): 519–48; W. R. MacDermott, "The Topographical Distribution of Insanity," *British Medical Journal* 2 (September 26, 1908): 950; D. Hack Tuke, "Increase of Insanity in Ireland," *Journal of Mental Science* 40 (October 1894): 549–61; Oscar Woods, "Discussion," *Journal of Mental Science* 40 (October 1894): 559; and see W. R. Dawson, "The Relation between the Geographical Distribution of Insanity and that of Certain Social and Other Conditions in Ireland," *Journal of Mental Science* 57 (1911): 571–97.

69. Drapes, "Alleged Increase," 532.

70. Isaac Frost, "Home-Sickness and Immigrant Psychoses: Austrian and German Domestic Servants," *Journal of Mental Science* 84 (1938): 802.

71. Jacques Vernant, *The Refugee in the Post-War World* (London, 1953), 357.

72. J. A. Tannahill, *European Volunteer Workers in Britain* (Manchester, 1958), 107–8; Wendy Webster, "Britain and the Refugees of Europe, 1939–50," in Louise Ryan and Wendy Webster, eds., *Gendering Migration: Masculinity, Femininity and Ethnicity in Post-War Britain* (Aldershot, 2008), 35–51.

73. Diana Kay and Robert Miles, *Refugees or Migrant Workers? European Volunteer Workers in Britain, 1946–1951* (London, 1992); F. F. Kino, "Aliens' Paranoid Reaction," *Journal of Mental Science* 97 (1951): 589–94; Andrew Nocon, "A Reluctant Welcome? Poles in Britain in the 1940s," *Oral History* 24.1 (1996): 79–87; Keith Sword, "Their Prospects Will Not Be Bright: British Responses to the Problem of the Polish Recalcitrants, 1946–1949," *Journal of Contemporary History* 21.3 (1986): 367–90.

74. Keith Sword, with Norman Davies and Jan Ciehchanowski, *The Formation of the Polish Community in Great Britain1939–50* (London, 1989); Michelle Winslow, "Oral History and Polish Émigrés in Britain," in Peter D. Stachura, ed., *The Poles in Britain 1940–2000: From Betrayal to Assimilation* (London, 2004), 85–97.

75. Elizabeth Stadulis, "The Resettlement of Displaced Persons in the United Kingdom," *Population Studies* 5.3 (1952): 207–37.

76. Jerzy Zubrzycki, *Polish Immigrants in Britain: A Study of Adjustment* (The Hague, 1956), 187.

77. Ibid., 118–19.

78. Ibid., 188.

79. A. G. Mezey, "Psychiatric Illness in Hungarian Refugees," *Journal of Mental Science* 106 (1960): 628–37.

80. A. G. Mezey, "Personal Background, Emigration, and Mental Disorder in Hungarian Refugees," *Journal of Mental Science* 106 (1960): 618–27.

81. See especially L. Carpenter and I. F. Brockington, "A Study of Mental

Illness in Asians, West Indians, and Africans Living in Manchester," *British Journal of Psychiatry* 137 (1980): 201–5; Errol Francis, "Psychiatric Racism and Social Police: Black People and the Psychiatric Services," in Winston James and Clive Harris, eds., *Inside Babylon: The Caribbean Diaspora in Britain* (London, 1993), 179–205; Roland Littlewood and Maurice Lipsedge, "Acute Psychotic Reactions in Caribbean-Born Patients," *Psychological Medicine* 11 (1981): 303–18; D. McGovern and Rosemarie V. Cope, "First Psychiatric Admission Rates of First and Second Generation Afro Caribbeans," *Social Psychiatry* 22 (1987): 139–49; Barbara Fletchman Smith, *Mental Slavery: Psychoanalytic Studies of Caribbean People* (London, 2000); Christopher S. Thomas et al., "Psychiatric Morbidity and Compulsory Admission among UK-Born Europeans, Afro-Caribbeans, and Asians in Central Manchester," *British Journal of Psychiatry* 163 (1993): 91–99; S. Wessely et al., "Schizophrenia and Afro-Caribbeans: A Case-Control Study," *British Journal of Psychiatry* 159 (1991): 795–801.

82. Leland V. Bell, *Mental and Social Disorder in Sub-Saharan Africa: The Case of Sierra Leone, 1787–1990* (Westport, CT, 1991); Lynette A. Jackson, *Surfacing Up: Psychiatry and Social Order in Colonial Zimbabwe, 1908–1968* (Ithaca, 2005); Kobena Mercer, "Racism and Transcultural Psychiatry," in Peter Miller and Nikolas Rose, eds., *The Power of Psychiatry* (Cambridge, 1986), 112–42; Jonathan Sadowsky, *Imperial Bedlam: Institutions of Madness in Colonial Southwest Nigeria* (Berkeley, 1999); Mathew Thomson, "'Savage Civilisation': Race, Culture and Mind in Britain, 1898–1939," in Waltraud Ernst and Bernard Harris, eds., *Race, Science and Medicine, 1700–1960* (London, 1999): 235–58; Megan Vaughan, *Curing Their Ills: Colonial Power and African Illness* (Cambridge, 1991).

83. Alice Bullard, "Imperial Networks and Postcolonial Independence: The Transition from Colonial to Transcultural Psychiatry," in Sloan Mahone and Megan Vaughan, eds., *Psychiatry and Empire* (Houndmills, 2007), 197–219.

84. Vaughan, *Curing Their Ills*.

85. For critiques of Carothers, see M. J. Field, *Search for Security: An Ethno-Psychiatric Study of Rural Ghana* (Evanston, 1960); Field, "Chronic Psychosis in Rural Ghana," *British Journal of Psychiatry* 114 (1968): 31–33; T. Adeoye Lambo, "The Role of Cultural Factors in Paranoid Psychosis among the Yoruba Tribe," *Journal of Mental Science* 101 (April 1955): 239–66; and T. Adeoye Lambo, "Malignant Anxiety: A Syndrome associated with Criminal Conduct in Africans," *Journal of Mental Science* 108 (1962): 256–64. On Lambo, see chapter 3 in this volume.

86. Jock McCulloch, "The Empire's New Clothes: Ethnopsychiatry in Colonial Africa," *History of the Human Sciences* 6.2 (1993): 35–52; Jock McCulloch, *Colonial Psychiatry and the 'African Mind'* (Cambridge, 1995).

87. J. C. Carothers, "A Study of Mental Derangement in Africans," *Journal of Mental Science* (1947): 548–97.

88. J. C. Carothers, *The Psychology of the Mau Mau* (Nairobi, 1955); and see Sloan Mahone, "The Psychology of Rebellion: Colonial Medical Responses to

Dissent in East Africa," *Journal of African History* 47.2 (July 2006): 241–58; Raymond Prince, "The Changing Picture of Depressive Syndromes in Africa: Is It Fact or Diagnostic Fashion?" *Canadian Journal of African Studies* 1 (1967): 177–92.

89. E. B. Forster, "The Theory and Practice of Psychiatry in Ghana," *American Journal of Psychotherapy* 16 (1962): 7–51.

90. C. V. D. Hadley, "Personality Patterns, Social Class, and Aggression in the West Indies," *Human Relations* 2.4 (1949): 349–62.

91. Aggrey W. Burke, "Socio-Cultural Determinants of Attempted Suicide among West Indians in Birmingham: Ethnic Origin and Immigrant Status," *British Journal of Psychiatry* 129 (1976): 261–66. See also Burke, "Attempted Suicide among Asian Immigrants in Birmingham," *British Journal of Psychiatry* 128 (1976): 528–33; and Burke, "Attempted Suicide among Irish-Born Population in Birmingham," *British Journal of Psychiatry* 128 (1976): 534–37.

92. L. K. Hemsi, "Psychiatric Morbidity of West Indian Immigrants: A Study of First Admissions in London," *Social Psychiatry* 2 (October 1967): 95–100; and see also R. J. F. H. Pinsent, "Morbidity in an Immigrant Population," *Lancet* 1 (February 23, 1963): 437–38.

93. Farrukh Hashmi, "Community Psychiatric Problems among Birmingham Immigrants," *British Journal of Social Psychiatry* 2 (1968): 196–201.

94. H. Burrowes, "The Migrant and Mental Health," in J. S. Dodge, *The Field Worker in Immigrant Health* (London, 1969), 71–76.

95. R. Cochrane, "Mental Illness in Immigrants to England and Wales: An Analysis of Mental Hospital Admissions, 1971," *Social Psychiatry* 12 (1977): 25–35.

96. Christopher Bagley, "The Social Aetiology of Schizophrenia in Immigrant Groups," *International Journal of Social Psychiatry* 17 (1971): 292–304.

97. Christopher Bagley, "Race, Migration, and Mental Health: A Review of Some Recent Research," *Race* 9 (1968): 343–56.

98. Christopher Bagley, "Mental Illness in Immigrant Minorities in London," *Journal of Biosocial Science* 3 (1971): 449–59.

99. Christopher Bagley, "Sequels of Alienation: West Indian Migrants in Britain," in Willem A. Veenhoven et al., ed., *Case Studies on Human Rights and Fundamental Freedoms: A World Survey,* vol. 2 (The Hague, 1975): 55–81.

100. "Repatriation of Coloured Colonial British Subjects" (AST 7/1177, TNA), 1949–1957.

101. "Immigration and Repatriation of Coloured Commonwealth and Colonial Subjects" (AST 7/1212, TNA), May 20, 1949.

102. "Repatriation of Commonwealth and Colonial Immigrants. Extract from Minutes of the Regional Controllers' Conference" (AST 7/1261, TNA), October 21, 1958.

103. "Visiting Officer Circular. Repatriation of Commonwealth Immigrants" (AST 7/1659, TNA), 1963.

104. "Department of Health and Social Security. Supplementary Benefits

Commission. Memorandum 130. Repatriation of Immigrants" (HO 376/131, TNA), February 19, 1969.

105. "Repatriation of Commonwealth Immigrants" (AST 7/1928, TNA), October 14, 1964.

106. National Assistance Board to Henry Brooke, "Measures to Reduce Coloured Commonwealth Immigration" (HO 376/132, TNA), September 11, 1964; "Possibility of the National Assistance Board Repatriating More Commonwealth Citizens" (HO 376/133, TNA), September 14, 1964.

107. "Repatriation of Commonwealth and Colonial Immigrants" (AST 7/1928, TNA), November 2, 1964.

108. "Summary of Dealings with Ministry of Health on Repatriation (AST 35/535, TNA), 1968.

109. B. Hirst to D. H. Fothergill (DO 175/202, TNA), September 16, 1965.

110. Mr. O'Neill, "Minute" (CO 1028/101, TNA), June 28, 1961.

111. L. E. T. Storar, "Minute" (DO 175/93, TNA), March 6, 1963.

112. A. M. Mackintosh, "West Indian Patients in Broadmoor Mental Hospital" (T 277/2460, TNA), December 2, 1960.

113. Miss J. Hope-Wallace to W. A. B. Hamilton (MH 148/337, TNA), February 13, 1963.

114. N. K. Finlayson, "Repatriation. Notes on the Various Discussions of the Subject since 1962," (HO 376/132, TNA), November 26, 1968.

115. Joseph Armatrading to Hon. Frederick Lee (DO 175/202, TNA), May 10, 1966; R. Terrell to S. J. Aspden (DO 175/202, TNA), December 9, 1966.

116. R. W. Taylor to E. M. Baldwin (T 227/2460, TNA), November 9, 1962.

117. "Repatriation of Immigrant Patients on Medical Grounds" (T 227/2460, TNA), 1960–1967.

118. Aggrey W. Burke, "The Consequences of Unplanned Repatriation," *British Journal of Psychiatry* 123 (1973): 109–11.

119. *The People*, December 2, 1963.

120. A. W. Burke, "Epidemiological Aspects of Repatriate Syndrome," *International Journal of Social Psychiatry* 28 (1982): 291–99.

121. Harrison, *Seeking a Role*, 279.

122. Nikolas Rose, "Law, Rights, and Psychiatry," in Miller and Rose, eds., *Power of Psychiatry*, 177–213.

123. *Sunday Telegraph*, March 16, 1969.

124. *Sunday Telegraph*, May 5, 1968.

125. *Daily Telegraph*, June 14, 1969; T. C. Platt, "Repatriation of Commonwealth Immigrants. Revised Note" (HO 376/132, TNA), September 9, 1969.

126. "Repatriation of Commonwealth Immigrants. The Cost" (HO 376/132, TNA), n.d.

127. This program had not been announced in Parliament, and Callaghan was rebuked for exposing the government's inconsistent repatriation policies. *Daily Express*, April 30, 1968, and May 1, 1968; *Sunday Telegraph*, April 28, 1968; *Times* (London), April 30, 1968.

128. Cochrane, "Mental Illness in Immigrants to England and Wales."

129. Anthony W. Clare, "Mental Illness in the Irish Emigrant," *Journal of the Irish Medical Association* 67 (January 12, 1974): 20–24.

130. John Archer Jackson, *The Irish in Britain* (London, 1963), 66–67.

131. Patrick Bracken et al., "Mental Health and Ethnicity: An Irish Dimension," *British Journal of Psychiatry* 172 (1998): 103–5; Liam Greenslade, "White Skins, White Masks: Psychological Distress among the Irish in Britain," in Patrick O'Sullivan, ed., *The Irish in the New Communities* (London, 1992): 201–25; E. Fuller Torrey et al., "Endemic Psychosis in Western Ireland," *American Journal of Psychiatry* 141 (August 1984): 966–70.

132. Liam Greenslade et al., "From Visible to Invisible: The 'Problem' of the Health of Irish People in Britain," in Lara Marks and Michael Worboys, eds., *Migrants, Minorities and Health: Historical and Contemporary Studies* (London, 1997), 147–78.

133. Gerard Leavey, "Suicide and Irish Migrants in Britain: Identity and Integration," *International Review of Psychiatry* 11 (1999): 168–72.

134. S. Harding and R. Balarajan, "Patterns of Mortality in Second Generation Irish Living in England and Wales: Longitudinal Study," *British Medical Journal* 312 (June 1, 1996): 1389–92.

135. John Haskey, "Mortality among Second Generation Irish in England and Wales," *British Medical Journal* 312 (June 1, 1996): 1373–74.

136. R. T. Appleyard, *British Emigration to Australia* (Toronto, 1964), 105.

137. Benjamin Malzberg and Everett S. Lee, *Migration and Mental Disease: A Study of First Admissions to Hospitals for Mental Disease, New York, 1939–1941* (New York, 1956); Malzberg, "Mental Disease among English-Born and Native Whites of English Parentage in New York State, 1949–1951," *Mental Hygiene* 48 (1964): 32–54; Malzberg, "Are Immigrants Psychologically Disturbed?" in Stanley C. Plog and Robert B. Edgerton, eds., *Changing Perspectives in Mental Illness* (New York, 1969), 395–421.

138. James Jupp, *Arrivals and Departures* (Melbourne, 1966), 109–11.

139. James Jupp, *The English in Australia* (Cambridge, 2004), 133; Alan Richardson, "Some Psycho-Social Characteristics of Satisfied and Dissatisfied British Immigrant Skilled Manual Workers in Western Australia," *Human Relations* 10 (1957): 235–48.

140. A. James Hammerton and Alistair Thomson, *Ten Pound Poms: Australia's Invisible Migrants* (Manchester, 2005), 9.

141. James Jupp, *The English in Australia* (Cambridge, 2004), 132.

142. L. B. Brown, "Some Psychological Characteristics of Applicants for Assisted Migration to New Zealand," Ph.D. thesis, University of London, 1954.

143. L. B. Brown, "Applicants for Assisted Migration from the United Kingdom to New Zealand," *Population Studies* 11 (1957): 86–91; Brown, "English Migrants to New Zealand: The Decision to Move," *Human Relations* 13 (1960): 167–74.

144. Alan Richardson, "The Assimilation of British Immigrants in Australia," *Human Relations* 10 (1957): 157–66; Ronald Taft, "The Shared Frame

of Reference Concept Applied to the Assimilation of Immigrants," *Human Relations* 6 (1953): 45–55.

145. Ronald Taft, "Discussion," in C. A. Price, ed., *The Study of Immigrants in Australia* (Canberra, 1960), 207.

146. Alan Richardson, "A Theory and a Method for the Psychological Study of Assimilation." *International Migration Review* 2.1 (1968): 3–30.

147. Alan Richardson, *British Immigrants and Australia: A Psycho-Social Inquiry* (Canberra, 1974); Ronald Taft, *From Stranger to Citizen: A Survey of Studies of Immigrant Assimilation in Western Australia* (Perth, 1965).

148. Ruth Johnston, "A New Approach to the Meaning of Assimilation," *Human Relations* 16 (1963): 295–98.

149. Commonwealth Immigration Advisory Council, *The Incidence of Mental Illness among Migrants* (Canberra, 1961).

150. S. Minc, "Of New Australian Patients, Their Medical Lore, and Major Anxieties," *Medical Journal of Australia* 1 (May 11, 1963): 681–87; and Eric G. Saint, "The Medical Problems of Migrants," *Medical Journal of Australia* 1 (March 9, 1963): 335–38.

151. Ignacy A. Listwan, "Paranoid States: Social and Cultural Aspects," *Medical Journal of Australia* 1 (May 12, 1956): 776–78; Listwan, "Mental Disorders in Migrants: Further Study," *Medical Journal of Australia* 1 (April 25, 1959): 566–68.

152. Ronald Taft, "The Assimilation of Dutch Male Immigrants in a Western Australian Community: A Replication of Richardson's Study of British Immigrants," *Human Relations* 14 (1961): 265–81; and see also L. B. Brown, "The Differential Job Satisfaction of English Migrants and New Zealanders," *Occupational Psychology* 33 (1959): 54–58.

153. Alan Stoller, "Migration and Mental Health in Australia," *British Journal of Social Psychiatry* 1 (1966): 70–77; C. G. Judge and M. M. Glatt, "The Problem of Alcoholism in Australia and England," *Medical Journal of Australia* 1 (April 22, 1961): 586–89.

154. J. F. J. Cade and J. Krupinski, "Incidence of Psychiatric Disorders in Victoria in Relation to Country of Birth," *Medical Journal of Australia* 1 (March 17, 1962): 400–404; J. Krupinski and Alan Stoller, "Family Life and Mental Ill-Health in Migrants," in Alan Stoller, ed., *New Faces: Immigration and Family Life in Australia* (Melbourne, 1966), 136–50.

155. L. B. Brown, "English Migrants to New Zealand: A Pilot Rorschach Study," *Australian Journal of Psychology* 8 (1956): 106–10.

156. Brown, "Psychological Characteristics."

157. Alan Richardson, "British Emigrants to Australia: A Study of Some Psycho-Social Differences between Emigrants and Non-Emigrant Skilled Manual Workers," Ph.D. thesis, University of London, 1956.

158. His research on Poles in Britain is discussed earlier in this chapter. Jerzy Zubrzycki, *Settlers of the Latrobe Valley: A Sociological Study of Immigrants in the Brown Coal Industry in Australia* (Canberra, 1964), 114.

159. Richardson, "Psycho-Social Characteristics."

160. Victor Sanua, "Immigration, Migration and Mental Illness: A Review of the Literature with Special Emphasis on Schizophrenia," in E. B Brody, *Behavior in New Environments: Adaptation of Migrant Populations* (Beverly Hills, 1969), 291–352; and see also J. Hitch, "Culture, Social Structure and the Explanation of Migrant Mental Illness," *Mental Health and Society* 4 (1977): 136–43.

161. Appleyard, *British Emigration*, 171.

162. Richardson, *British Immigrants to Australia*, 15.

163. Zubrzycki, *Settlers of the Latrobe Valley*.

164. J.N. Burgess, "With the Migrants in Europe," *Medical Journal of Australia* 39.2 (September 27, 1952): 438–39; G.M. Redshaw, "Psychiatric Problems amongst Migrants," *Medical Journal of Australia* 43.2 (December 8, 1956): 852–53.

165. J.M. Last, "Culture, Society and the Migrant," *Medical Journal of Australia* 1 (March 18, 1961): 420–24; Sir Harry Wunderly, "A Survey of Immigration and Mental Health in Australia," in C.A. Price, ed., *The Study of Immigrants in Australia* (Canberra, 1960), 183–91.

166. Wunderly, "Immigration and Mental Health."

167. Cade and Krupinski, "Psychiatric Disorders," 403.

168. R.T. Appleyard, "Socio-Economic Determinants of British Emigration from the United Kingdom to Australia," in C.A. Price, ed., *The Study of Immigrants in Australia* (Canberra, 1960), 25–32.

169. J. Krupinski, "Sociological Aspects of Mental Ill-Health in Migrants," *Social Science and Medicine* 1 (1967): 267–81.

170. Richardson, "Psychological Study of Assimilation."

171. F.A. Emery, "A Critique of Some of the Western Australian Studies," *British Journal of Social and Clinical Psychology* 1 (1962): 72–75.

172. Reg Appleyard with Alison Ray and Allan Segal, *The Ten Pound Immigrants* (London, 1988), 97.

173. Jupp, *Arrivals and Departures*, 1 and 13.

174. R.T. Appleyard, "The Return Movement of United Kingdom Migrants from Australia," *Population Studies* 15.3 (1962): 214–55.

175. S.N. Eisenstadt, *The Absorption of Immigrants: A Comparative Study Based Mainly on the Jewish Community in Palestine and the State of Israel* (Westport, CT, 1954); Abraham A. Weinberg, "Mental Health Aspects of Voluntary Migration," *Mental Hygiene* 39 (1955): 450–64; Weinberg, *Migration and Belonging: A Study of Mental Health and Personal Adjustment in Israel* (The Hague, 1961).

176. Kenneth Little, *Race and Society* (Paris, 1958).

177. Michael Banton, "The Changing Position of the Negro in Britain," *Phylon* 14 (1953): 74–83.

178. Jenny Bourne, with A. Sivanandan, "Cheerleaders and Ombudsmen: The Sociology of Race Relations in Britain," *Race and Class* 21.4 (1980): 331–52; Chris Mullard, *Black Britain* (London, 1973), 65–66; A. Sivanandan, "Race and Resistance: The IRR Story," *Race and Class* 50.2 (2008): 1–30.

179. Philip Mason, *A Thread of Silk: Further Memories of a Varied Life* (Salisbury, 1984).

180. H. V. Hodson, "Race Relations in the Commonwealth" (RIIA 8/1804, Chatham House, London), May 4, 1950.

181. "Notes of a Discussion with Sir Hilary Blood" (CO 927/159/6, TNA), October 20, 1950.

182. Mason, *Thread of Silk*, 7.

183. "Race Relations. Correspondence re Donations to the Fund" (Chatham House 3/6/INS, g [1], London), 1952–1958.

184. *Annual Report of the Council 1951–1952* (London, 1952).

185. Mason, *Thread of Silk*, 18.

186. Kenneth Younger to David Astor (Chatham House, London), March 5, 1952.

187. Philip Mason, *Race Relations* (London, 1970), 17.

188. For a shorter version of this study, see Guy Hunter, *New Societies of Tropical Africa* (London, 1962).

189. E. J. B. Rose, "A Myrdal for Britain: A Personal Memoir," *New Community* 14 (1987): 83–88.

190. Jean Comaroff and John Comaroff, "Reflections on Youth from the Past to the Postcolony," in Alcinda Manuel Honwana and Filip de Boeck, eds., *Makers and Breakers: Children and Youth in Postcolonial Africa* (Trenton, NJ, 2005), 19–30; see also Mamadou Diouf, "Engaging Postcolonial Cultures: African Youth and Public Space," *African Studies Review* 46.2 (2003): 1–12; Jane Pilcher, *Age and Generation in Modern Britain* (Oxford, 1995); Lesley Sharp, *The Sacrificed Generation: Youth, History, and the Colonized Mind in Madagascar* (Berkeley, 2002). This research highlights how scholars continue to borrow, even if critically, from the life cycle model.

CHAPTER 2

1. *Times* (London), September 29, 1959; Michael Edwards, ed., *Arriving Where We Started: 25 Years of Voluntary Service Overseas* (London, 1983).

2. Michael Adams, *Voluntary Service Overseas: The Story of the First Ten Years* (London, 1968).

3. David Wainwright, *The Volunteers: The Story of Overseas Voluntary Service* (London, 1965), 33.

4. National Service operated on a reduced scale until 1963. David Lodge, *Ginger, You're Barmy* (London, 1962); Martin S. Navias, "Terminating Conscription? The British National Service Controversy, 1955–56," *Journal of Contemporary History* 24.2 (1989): 195–208; L. V. Scott, *Conscription and the Attlee Governments: The Politics and Policy of National Service, 1945–1951* (Oxford, 1993); Leslie Thomas, *The Virgin Soldiers* (Boston, 1966).

5. Harrison, *Seeking a Role*, 91.

6. Wainwright, *The Volunteers*, 27.

7. On the terminology of First and Third Worlds, see Carl E. Pletsch, "The

Three Worlds, Or The Division of Social Scientific Labor, circa 1950–1975," *Comparative Studies in Society and History* 23.4 (1981): 565–90.

8. On the intersection of decolonization's chronologies with individual life histories, see Burton, *Postcolonial Careers*.

9. Elizabeth Cobbs Hoffman, *All You Need Is Love: The Peace Corps and the Spirit of the 1960s* (Cambridge, MA, 1998), 8 and 15.

10. James Howard Smith, *Bewitching Development: Witchcraft and the Reinvention of Development in Neoliberal Kenya* (Chicago, 2008); and see also Monica Van Beusekom and Dorothy L. Hodgson, "Lessons Learned? Development Experiences in the Late Colonial Period," *Journal of African History* 41.1 (2000): 29–33; Monica M. Van Beusekom, *Negotiating Development: African Farmers and Colonial Experts at the Office du Niger, 1920–1960* (Portsmouth, NH, 2002); Frederick Cooper and Randall Packard, eds., *International Development and the Social Sciences: Essays on the History and Politics of Knowledge* (Berkeley, 1997); David Engerman et al., eds., *Staging Growth: Modernization, Development, and the Global Cold War* (Amherst, 2003); Arturo Escobar, *Encountering Development: The Making and Unmaking of the Third World* (Princeton, 1995); James Ferguson, *The Anti-Politics Machine: "Development," Depoliticization and Democratic Power in Lesotho* (Cambridge, 1990); Colin Leys, *The Rise and Fall of Development Theory* (Bloomington, IN, 1996); Eric Worby, "Discipline without Oppression: Sequence, Timing and Marginality in Southern Rhodesia's Post-War Development Regime," *Journal of African History* 41.1 (2000): 101–25.

11. Hodge, *Triumph of the Expert*, 8.

12. Cooper, *Africa since 1940*, 88.

13. Escobar, *Encountering Development*, 52.

14. Ortolano, *The Two Cultures Controversy*, 18; Harold Perkin, *The Rise of Professional Society: England since 1880* (London, 1989).

15. Abigail Beach, "Forging a 'Nation of Participants': Political and Economic Planning in Labour's Britain," in Richard Weight and Abigail Beach, eds., *The Right to Belong: Citizenship and National Identity in Britain, 1930–1960* (London and New York, 1998), 89–115.

16. Ortolano, *The Two Cultures Controversy*, 251.

17. Jonathon Green, *All Dressed Up: The Sixties and the Counterculture* (London, 1999), 2–3.

18. Lawrence Black, "The Lost World of Young Conservatism," *Historical Journal* 51.4 (December 2008): 991–1024; Catherine Ellis, "No Hammock for the Idle: The Conservative Party, 'Youth' and the Welfare State," *Twentieth-Century British History* 16.4 (2005): 441–70.

19. Catherine Ellis, "The Younger Generation: The Labour Party and the 1959 Youth Commission," *Journal of British Studies* 41.2 (April 2002): 199–231.

20. Green, *All Dressed Up*.

21. "Methods—Views of Mr. Alec Dickson. Reflections on a Possible Commonwealth Youth Trust" (CAB 144/3, TNA), June 12, 1959.

22. "The Role of Commonwealth Youth in the World Today. Notes for

Speech by Mr. J.G.S. Hobson at the Commonwealth Youth Festival" (DO 35/8198, TNA), 1960.

23. "A Memorandum on Youth in the Commonwealth" (BW 1/245, TNA), n.d.

24. "Proposal for the Establishment of a Commonwealth Youth Trust" (CO 859/1036, TNA), December 12, 1957.

25. "Things to Do" (CAB 144/2, TNA), n.d. [1959?].

26. R. Jardine to E.G. Smallman (FCO 68/128, TNA), September 15, 1969; "British Youth Council" (CAB 151/74, TNA), 1968–69.

27. See Cooper, "Possibility and Constraint"; Richard Waller, "Rebellious Youth in Colonial Africa," *Journal of African History* 47.1 (2006): 77–92.

28. Timothy H. Parsons, *Race, Resistance, and the Boy Scout Movement in British Colonial Africa* (Athens, OH, 2004), 22; Carol Summers, "Youth, Elders, and Metaphors of Political Change in Late Colonial Buganda," in Andrew Burton, ed., *Generations Past: Youth in East African History* (Athens, OH, 2010), 175–95.

29. Esty, "The Colonial Bildungsroman."

30. Alec G. Dickson, "Training of Youth Leaders for Work in Fundamental Education," *Fundamental and Adult Education* 10.2 (1958): 45–54.

31. Here, Dickson was at odds with postwar sociological analysis, which focused firmly on working-class subcultures. Richard Ivan Jobs, *Riding the New Wave: Youth and the Rejuvenation of France after the Second World War* (Stanford, 2007), 11. On the pathologies of elite youths, see B.M. Spinley, *The Deprived and the Privileged: Personality Development in English Society* (London, 1953); Frank Musgrove, "Adolescent Status: Rights Withheld Too Long," *Times Educational Supplement* (October 24, 1958); and Musgrove, *Youth and the Social Order* (Bloomington, IN, 1964); and see also David Fowler, *Youth Culture in Modern Britain, c. 1920–1970: From Ivory Tower to Global Movement—A New History* (New York, 2008).

32. Interview with Dick Bird, September 24, 2008.

33. Cobbs Hoffman, *All You Need Is Love.*

34. Mora Dickson, *Portrait of a Partnership* (New York, 2004), 56.

35. Alec Dickson, *A Chance to Serve* (London, 1976), 52.

36. "Training for Citizenship—A Youth Service" (CO 96/811/3, TNA), 1949.

37. "Man O'War Bay Scheme, Nigeria. Report by Mr. Lawson" (CO 554/629, TNA), n.d. [1952?].

38. Dickson, *A Chance to Serve,* 59–60.

39. Alec Dickson, "Man O'War Bay. An Experiment in Education for Citizenship" (BW 90/58, TNA), n.d.

40. The center established a leadership course for women in 1959.

41. The costs of the program were borne primarily by the students' employers, with additional funding from the Community Development Department of Eastern Nigeria.

42. "An Experiment in Education."

43. "The Nigerian Man O'War Bay Scheme for Education in Citizenship" (CO 554/629, TNA), June 25, 1963.

44. "The British National Committee. World Assembly of Youth. Report by Mr. T. Lawson on a Visit to Nigeria and the British Cameroons, as a Special Representative of W.A.Y." (CO 554/629, TNA), 1952.

45. Mora Dickson, *New Nigerians* (London, 1960), 80.

46. Mora Dickson to T. B. Lawson (CO 554/629, TNA), May 5, 1952.

47. "Training for Citizenship—A Youth Service" (CO 96/811/3, TNA), 1949.

48. *Man O'War Bay Training Centre* (London, 1958), 32.

49. Mora Dickson, *New Nigerians*, 119.

50. Dick Bird, *Never the Same Again: A History of the VSO* (Cambridge, 1998), 28.

51. Mora Dickson, *New Nigerians*, 218.

52. Nancy Rose Hunt has argued that this type of "topsy turvy" performance in colonial locales could conceal terror and sadism just beneath the affection it purported to promote. Nancy Rose Hunt, *A Colonial Lexicon: Of Birth Ritual, Medicalization, and Mobility in the Congo* (Durham, 1999).

53. Mora Dickson, *A Season in Sarawak* (Chicago, 1962), 161.

54. Dickson, *A Chance to Serve*, 68.

55. Alec Dickson, "Southeast Asia Training Project in Work Camp Methods and Techniques" (CO 859/1445, TNA), December 5, 1959.

56. Mora Dickson, *Longhouse in Sarawak* (London, 1971).

57. Dickson, *A Chance to Serve*, 61.

58. Cobbs Hoffman, *All You Need Is Love*, 79–80.

59. Musgrove, *Youth and the Social Order*.

60. Dickson, *A Season in Sarawak*, 153.

61. Timmins, *The Five Giants*. On the continued importance of individual philanthropy and voluntary organizations in the era of state-sponsored welfare, see Elizabeth Macadam, *The New Philanthropy: A Study of the Relations between the Statutory and Voluntary Social Services* (London, 1934).

62. Adams, *Voluntary Service Overseas*, 28–29.

63. Harry Hopkins, *The New Look: A Social History of the Forties and Fifties in Britain* (London, 1963); Rodney Lowe, *The Welfare State in Britain since 1945*, 2nd edition (Basingstoke, 1999).

64. Lowe, *Welfare State*, 21; Richard Titmuss, *The Gift Relationship: From Human Blood to Social Policy* (New York, 1971).

65. S. M. Miller, "Introduction: The Legacy of Richard Titmuss," in Brian Abel-Smith and Kay Titmuss, *The Philosophy of Welfare: Selected Writings of Richard Titmuss* (London, 1987), 1–7.

66. *Times* (London), September 29, 1959.

67. Christopher Tipple to Alec Dickson (DO 33/8199, TNA), October 28, 1959[?].

68. Interview with Dick Bird, September 24, 2008.

69. "In Living Memory: VSO" (BBC Radio 4, December 3, 2008), available online at http://www.bbc.co.uk/iplayer/episode/b00fq2xc/In_Living_Memory_Series_9_The_New_Volunteers/.

70. Interview with Chris Tipple, July 12, 2009.

71. Alec Dickson to P. F. Walker (DO 196/19, TNA), May 23, 1961.

72. Alec Dickson, "A Great Voluntary Movement," *Guardian*, January 29, 1962.

73. Report of M. A. Marioghae on William Crawley (CO 859/1445, TNA), July 2, 1960.

74. "Volunteers Sent Abroad in 1959–1960" (OD 10/3, TNA), n.d.

75. J. R. Williams to A. J. Brown (DO 163/22, TNA), December 4, 1961.

76. I am indebted to Susan Pedersen for this point.

77. Birley later became a professor of education at the University of Witwatersrand, and joined the anti-apartheid campaign. Arthur Hearnden, *Red Robert: A Life of Robert Birley* (London, 1984), 163.

78. Robert Birley to Alec Dickson (PREM 11/5007, TNA), November 13, 1962.

79. Bird, *Never the Same Again*, 25.

80. *Times* (London), April 4, 1962.

81. Dickson, *A Season in Sarawak*, 154.

82. Mora Dickson, *A World Elsewhere: Voluntary Service Overseas* (Chicago, 1964).

83. Dickson, *A Season in Sarawak*, 171.

84. *Times* (London), May 26, 1962.

85. Margery Perham, *The Colonial Reckoning: The End of Imperial Rule in Africa in the Light of British Experience* (New York, 1962), 201.

86. Basil Shone to C[harles] Y. Carstairs (CO 859/1445, TNA), October 8, 1960.

87. Dickson, *A Season in Sarawak*, 192.

88. On the psychiatric theory that political independence could engender specific mental health problems, see chapter 1 of this volume.

89. Dickson, *A World Elsewhere*, 22–23.

90. Ibid., 23.

91. Quoted in Bird, *Never the Same Again*, 18.

92. Dickson, *A Season in Sarawak*, 216.

93. High Commissioner of Lagos to Duke of Devonshire (DO 163/22, TNA), February 16, 1963.

94. Adams, *Voluntary Service Overseas*, 56. See also Michael Courage with Dermot Wright, *New Guinea Venture* (London, 1967); and Colin Henfrey, *The Gentle People: A Journey among the Indian Tribes of Guiana* (London, 1964).

95. Alec Dickson, "Southeast Asia Training Project in Work Camp Methods and Techniques" (CO 859/1445, TNA), December 5, 1959.

96. Leela Gandhi, *Affective Communities: Anticolonial Thought, Fin-de-Siècle Radicalism, and the Politics of Friendship* (Durham, 2006), 9–10.

97. Bird, *Never the Same Again*, 70.

98. A tiny minority of VSOs (about 1 percent) experienced breakdowns during their period of service. VSO was occasionally criticized for failing to put its volunteers through the same elaborate psychological screening as their Peace Corps counterparts. Adams, *Voluntary Service Overseas*.

99. J.D.G. Isherwood, "Report of a Field Visit to Zambia, Malawi and Tanzania" (OD 10/79, TNA), January 31–March 12, 1966.

100. Dickson, *A Season in Sarawak*, 173–74.

101. Dickson, "Voluntary Service Overseas. Thomas Holland Memorial Lecture," *Overseas Quarterly* 2.2 (June 1960): 47–48.

102. *Times* (London), April 4, 1962.

103. Dickson, *A World Elsewhere*, 95.

104. Dickson, *A Chance to Serve*, 78.

105. Alec Dickson, "Voluntary Service Overseas," *Oversea Quarterly* 2.2 (June 1960): 47–48.

106. "Volunteers from Industry" (OD 10/3, TNA), n.d. [1961–63].

107. Wainwright, *The Volunteers*, 112.

108. "A Year Abroad for Young Employees," *Guardian*, June 4, 1960.

109. "Volunteers Sent Abroad in 1960–1961" (OD 10/3, TNA), 1961–63[?]

110. *Times* (London), January 13, 1964.

111. Wainwright, *The Volunteers*, 134.

112. Patrick Denison to C[harles] Y. Carstairs (CO 859/1445, TNA), August 24, 1960.

113. Wainwright, *The Volunteers*, 134.

114. C.N.F. Odgers, "Recruitment of Volunteers from Industry" (OD 8/473, TNA), June 30, 1967.

115. Bird, *Never the Same Again*, 38.

116. Van Beusekom, *Negotiating Development*.

117. Susan B. Whitney, *Mobilizing Youth: Communists and Catholics in Interwar France* (Durham, 2009).

118. "World Assembly of Youth Charter" (LCC/EO/HFE/1/164, London Metropolitan Archives, hereafter LMA), 1949.

119. On Peggy Cripps's widely publicized marriage to the Ashanti student and future politician Joe Appiah, see "Activities of J.E. Appiah, Gold Coast" (CO 554/1062, TNA), 1954–1956; and Barbara Caine, "Writing Cosmopolitan Lives: Joseph and Kwame Anthony Appiah," *History Workshop Journal* 70.1 (2010): 152–71.

120. G.W.W. Browne, "World Assembly of Youth" (ED 124/138, TNA), March 21, 1952.

121. "International Youth Conference" (T 220/1210, TNA), August 4, 1948.

122. "World Assembly of Youth" (T 220/1210, TNA), May 18, 1950.

123. *Sunday Times* (London), April 4, 1954.

124. Woodrow Wyatt to Anthony Nutting (FO 924/1039, TNA), May 18, 1954.

125. Lady Mountbatten to Anthony Eden (T 220/2210, TNA), May 5, 1954.

126. *Times Educational Supplement* (London), March 28, 1952.

127. R.J.W. Pimley, "World Assembly of Youth" (T 220/1210, TNA), January 9, 1953.

128. R. Terrell to W.J. Coe (DO 33/8199, TNA), June 21, 1957.

129. O.G. Forster, "Youth Leadership in the British Commonwealth" (DO 33/8199, TNA), March 27, 1957.

130. B. Devan, "WAY Report of Accra Conference" (FO 924/1359, TNA), January 17, 1961; and see also T.C. Barker, "World Assembly of Youth" (FO 1110/1258, TNA), December 18, 1959.

131. Alec Dickson to Alport (DO 33/8199, TNA), April 18, 1957.

132. "Promotion of Commonwealth Links" (CAB 144/3, TNA), May 28, 1959.

133. J.M. Lee, "Commonwealth Students in the United Kingdom, 1940–1960: Student Welfare and World Status," *Minerva* 44 (2006): 1–24.

134. "Comments by Members of the Colonial Office Advisory Committee on Social Developments on the Proposal for the Establishment of a Commonwealth Youth Trust" (CAB 144/3, TNA), June 22, 1959.

135. Interdepartmental Committee on Youth in the Commonwealth, "Draft Memorandum on a Proposal for the Establishment of a Commonwealth Youth Trust" (CO 859/1037, TNA), March 27, 1958.

136. Mr. Peterson, "The Possible Policy of a Commonwealth Youth Trust" (CAB 144/2, TNA), April 2, 1959.

137. Troy Boone, *Youth of Darkest England: Working-Class Children at the Heart of Victorian Empire* (London, 2005); John M. MacKenzie, *Propaganda and Empire: The Manipulation of British Public Opinion, 1880–1960* (Manchester, 1984); John Springhall, *Youth, Empire and Society: British Youth Movements, 1883–1940* (London, 1977).

138. "The Commonwealth Youth Movement. Brief for Prime Minister" (DO 35/8197, TNA), October 1958.

139. O.G. Forster, "Activities of the Commonwealth Youth Movement" (DO 35/8197, TNA), December 20, 1957.

140. "Interview between the Chairman and Major Ney" (CAB 144/2, TNA), April 8, 1959; "Commonwealth Youth Movement. The 21st Anniversary Quest of 1958. Conference Service" (DO 35/8199, TNA), July 13, 1958.

141. "Note for Secretary of State. Major Ney and the Commonwealth Youth Movement" DO 35/8197, TNA), April 25, 1958.

142. "Memorandum Presented by Members of the Commonwealth Youth Movement to the Prime Minister, the Right Hon. Harold Macmillan" (CAB 21/3161, TNA), October 17, 1960.

143. See, e.g., M. Mansherg to N.E. Costar (DO 35/8197, TNA), January 15, 1947.

144. "Memorandum. Commonwealth Youth Movement" (ACC/1888/123, LMA), n.d. [1962?].

145. "A Memorandum on Youth in the Commonwealth" (BW 1/245, TNA), n.d.

146. "Youth. Note by the Commonwealth Office" (CAB 148/86, TNA), June 7, 1968.

147. Hilary Perraton, *Learning Abroad: A History of the Commonwealth Scholarship and Fellowship Plan* (Newcastle upon Tyne, 2009).

148. R.L.D. Jasper to J.H. McEnery (CAB 144/7, TNA), April 28, 1959; *Times* (London), April 11, 1959. On the postimperial rhetoric of the Commonwealth "family," see Annette Kuhn, *Family Secrets: Acts of Memory and Imagination* (London, 1995).

149. Erik Linstrum, "The Truth about Hearts and Minds: Counterinsurgency and Development in the Postwar British Empire," paper delivered at the conference "Burdens: Writing British History after 1945," University of California, Berkeley, 2012.

150. J.M. Lee, "No Peace Corps for the Commonwealth," *Round Table* 336.1 (October 1995): 455–67.

151. Gerald Templer to Duncan (PREM 11/3210, TNA), March 1, 1961.

152. R.L.D. Jasper to J. Chadwick and Costley-White (DO 35/8202, TNA), April 24, 1959; and see also "Group to Study Proposals for the Establishment of a United Kingdom Commonwealth Youth Trust. Weaknesses in Commonwealth Ties and the Methods of Its 'Enemies'" (CAB 144/2, TNA), May 4, 1959.

153. R.L.D. Jasper to J.H. McEnery (CAB 144/7, TNA), April 28, 1959.

154. See chapter 3 in this volume.

155. "In Living Memory: VSO."

156. *Times* (London), May 26, 1962; see also "Voluntary Societies Committee for Service Overseas" (OD 10/40, TNA), January 21, 1963.

157. "In Living Memory: VSO."

158. *Times* (London), January 10, 1963.

159. Bird, *Never the Same Again,* 47.

160. "Notes of a Meeting with a Delegation from the Council of VSO" (OD 10/4, TNA), September 26, 1962.

161. Bird, *Never the Same Again,* 36.

162. *Times* (London), July 15, 1963.

163. Neil Marten to Dennis Vosper (OD 10/35, TNA), May 17, 1962.

164. Iain Macleod, "Years' Voluntary Service," *Common Sense* 160 (June 1961), 1.

165. Robert Birley, "Note on Conversation with the Prime Minister on VSO" (OD 10/50, TNA), May 2, 1963.

166. W.J. Smith, "Voluntary Overseas Movement" (DO 163/22, TNA), July 10, 1961.

167. "Voluntary Service Overseas. CD&W Grant" (CO 859/1447, TNA), n.d.

168. Dickson, *A World Elsewhere,* 31.

169. Bird, *Never the Same Again,* 75.

170. Adams, *Voluntary Service Overseas,* 188–89.

171. Dickson, *A World Elsewhere.*

172. The returned volunteers protested at the VSO's London office. Adams, *Voluntary Service Overseas*, 186.

173. Bird, *Never the Same Again*, 57.

174. W.J. Smith, "VSO and U.D.I." (OD 10/67, TNA), October 6, 1965.

175. Dickson, *A World Elsewhere*, 66.

176. Bird, *Never the Same Again*.

177. *Economist*, April 21, 1962.

178. Quoted in Cobbs Hoffman, *All You Need Is Love*, 45.

179. Dickson, *A Chance to Serve*, 109.

180. Dickson, "A Great Voluntary Movement."

181. Cobbs Hoffman, *All You Need Is Love*, 176; Jonathan Zimmerman, *Innocents Abroad: American Teachers in the American Century* (Cambridge, MA, 2006).

182. Joseph F. Kauffman, "Youth and the Peace Corps," in Erik H. Erikson, ed., *Youth: Change and Challenge* (New York, 1961), 152–60.

183. "United States Peace Corps" (CO 859/1448, TNA), 1960–62.

184. *Times* (London), April 18, 1962.

185. M. Scott to I.T.M. Lucas, British High Commission, Karachi (FO 371/162637, TNA), December 29, 1961.

186. R.L.L. Griffith-Jones, "Memo to the Council for Volunteers Overseas" (OD 10/75, TNA), November 14, 1966. Dickson was paraphrasing a speech delivered by Dean Acheson at West Point in 1962; see Timmins, *The Five Giants*, 214.

187. "Service Overseas by Volunteer Programs" (OD 10/62, TNA), 1966–67.

188. For example, Sebastian Poulter, one of the legal experts on polygamy whose work is cited in chapter 4 in this volume, served as a VSO in Swaziland in 1960–61.

189. Matthew Hilton, Nick Crowson and James McKay, "NGOs and the Professionalization of Politics in Postwar Britain," paper delivered at the North American Conference on British Studies, Baltimore, 2010.

190. The Albemarle Report (1960), which urged a major expansion in spending on youth organizations, praised VSO as a useful form of "social training."

191. R. Terrell to Smith (CO 859/1445, TNA), January 21, 1960.

192. "In Living Memory: VSO."

193. Lynn, ed., *The British Empire in the 1950s*.

194. Dickson, "Voluntary Service Overseas. Thomas Holland Memorial Lecture."

195. Dickson, *A Chance to Serve*, 117.

196. *Times* (London), August 10, 1967.

197. This is an interesting omission, given the centrality of affect in the postcolonial thought and activism of figures ranging from M.K. Gandhi to Frantz Fanon. For a pioneering study in this regard, see Gandhi, *Affective*

Communities. On colonial friendship, see Vanessa Smith, *Intimate Strangers: Friendship, Exchange and Pacific Encounters* (Cambridge, 2010).

198. "Conference of Voluntary Societies on the Welfare of Colonial Students in London" (BW 3/17, TNA), October 14, 1953.

CHAPTER 3

1. The elder John Mensah Sarbah (1864–1910) was an anticolonial nationalist who critiqued the British expropriation of land in the Gold Coast.

2. "John Mensah Sarbah" (CO 981/6, TNA), 1941–58.

3. Gauri Viswanathan, *Masks of Conquest: Literary Study and British Rule in India* (New York, 1989).

4. On earlier generations of overseas students, see Burton, *At the Heart of the Empire;* Paul Deslandes, "'The Foreign Element': Newcomers and the Rhetoric of Race, Nation and Empire in 'Oxbridge' Undergraduate Culture," *Journal of British Studies* 37.1 (January 1998): 54–90; Peter Fryer, *Staying Power: The History of Black People in Britain* (London, 1984); Catherine Hall, "Making Colonial Subjects: Education in the Age of Empire," *History of Education* 37.6 (2008): 773–87; Marc Matera, "Colonial Subjects: Black Intellectuals and the Development of Colonial Studies in Britain," *Journal of British Studies* 49 (2010): 388–418; Ray Jenkins, "Gold Coasters Overseas, 1880–1919: With Specific Reference to Their Activities in Britain," *Immigrants and Minorities* 4 (1985): 5–52; A. Martin Wainwright, *'The Better Class' of Indians: Social Rank, Imperial Identity, and South Asians in Britain, 1858–1914* (Manchester, 2008).

5. "The Problems of Unsponsored Commonwealth Students" (BW 3/53, TNA), February 27, 1961; Mary Trevelyan, "Welfare Services for Overseas Students," *Proceedings of the British Student Health Association* (1961): 51–55.

6. Antoinette Burton, "Cold War Cosmopolitanism: The Education of Santha Rama Rau in the Age of Bandung, 1945–1954," *Radical History Review* 95 (spring 2006): 149–72.

7. Edward Shils, *The Intellectuals and the Powers and Other Essays* (Chicago, 1972), viii. Shils worked for the Office of Strategic Services in London during the Second World War. Beyond his position at the LSE, Shils was instrumental to the development of sociology in Britain. He advised Michael Young in establishing the Institute of Community Studies, and became a fellow of King's College Cambridge in the 1960s and of Peterhouse in 1970, and also conducted seminars in the anthropology department at University College London. He founded the journal *Minerva* in 1962 in London. Martin Bulmer, "Edward Shils as a Sociologist," *Minerva* 34 (1996): 7–21.

8. The anonymous "Lament of an Old Oxonian" (1902) complained that "the married mussalman arrives / With 37 moon-eyed wives / And fills a quad at Oriel." Quoted in Richard Symonds, *Oxford and Empire: The Last Lost Cause?* (Houndmills, 1986), 15.

9. Sumita Mukherjee, *Nationalism, Education and Migration Identities: The England-Returned* (London, 2010).

10. William Lee-Warner, "Report of the Departmental Committee on Indian Students" (IOR/L/PJ/6/845, British Library, London, hereafter BL), November 30, 1907.

11. John Christian, "Indian Students in London," *Times* (London), January 2, 1908.

12. "Indian Students in England," *Times* (London), September 1, 1908.

13. "Memorandum of a Committee of the Council of the East India Association for the Control and Direction of Students and Social Conduct of Indian Students Sent to England" (IOR/L/PJ/6/808, BL), 1907.

14. "Indian Students in England," *Times* (London), September 14, 1908.

15. P. M. Choudry, *British Experiences* (Calcutta, 1889), 7.

16. "Indian Students at Cirencester College" (IOR/L/PJ/6/897, File 3787, BL), 1908; "Indian Students in England," *Times* (London), September 1 and November 4, 1908.

17. Curzon-Wyllie had served on the Lee-Warner Committee in 1907. Dhingra also shot Cawas Lalcaca, a Parsi physician who was trying to intervene. Lalcaca died on his way to the hospital. "Madan Lal Dhingra" (CRIM 1/113/5, TNA), 1909.

18. Dhingra was purportedly influenced by Shyamji Krishnavarma's radical journal *Indian Sociologist*, and its editors were tried for sedition. Krishnavarma was a former student of Balliol College, Oxford.

19. F. H. Brown, "Indian Students in Britain," *Edinburgh Review* 217 (1913): 136–56.

20. *Report of the Committee on Indian Students 1921–1922* (London, 1922).

21. Paul Deslandes, *Oxbridge Men: British Masculinity and the Undergraduate Experience, 1850–1920* (Bloomington, IN, 2005).

22. "Communists at Oxford," *Times* (London), December 9, 1925; "Communist Undergraduates," *Times* (London), January 26, 1926; G. K. Chettur, *The Last Enchantment: Recollections of Oxford* (Mangalore, 1934).

23. "Scotland Yard Reports on Indian Students Hostel and Indian Students Union" (IOR/L/PJ/12/42, BL), 1921–41.

24. "Memorandum on Students" (IOR L/PJ/12/638, File 808/40, BL), 1942.

25. "Commonwealth Students in Britain," *Parliamentary Debates* 175 (March 12, 1952), cols. 663-94.

26. "Open Letter to Britons," *West African Review* 16 (November 1945): 15–17; Central Office of Information, *Students from Overseas in Britain* (London, 1965); Simon Gikandi, "Pan-Africanism and Cosmopolitanism: The Case of Jomo Kenyatta," *English Studies in Africa* 43 (2000): 3–27.

27. D. R. Rees-Williams to Wing Commander Geoffrey Cooper (CO 981/30, TNA), October 28, 1948.

28. Seepapitso Gaseitsiwe to Crook (CO 981/107, TNA), March 10, 1961. On Ney's Quests, see chapter 2 in this volume.

29. G.H. McKay, "Annual Report on Student, Seepapitso Gaseitsiwe" (CO 981/107, TNA), September 1961.

30. Iftikhar Ali, "Effects of Cultural Attitudes on the Adjustment of Pakistani Students in Britain," M.A. thesis, Bedford College, University of London, 1963.

31. See also "Sam Akpabot's Diary," *West African Pilot,* February 4, 1959, May 20, 1959, June 1, 1959.

32. A. Ajose, "I Lived with the People of Britain," *West African Review* 18 (April 1947): 417–20; K. Akinsemoyin, "An Undergraduate in Glasgow," *West African Review* 20 (September 1949): 1005–7.

33. Peter P. Ekeh, ed., *T.E.A. Salubi: Witness to British Colonial Rule in Urhoboland and Nigeria* (Buffalo, NY, 2008), 233.

34. Samuel George Ayi-Bonte to J.L. Keith (CO 981/37, TNA), December 19, 1951.

35. "Cyril Francis Netty" (CO 981/44, TNA), n.d., 1952–57.

36. "Andrew Frederick Mpanga" (CO 981/76, TNA), n.d., 1952–59.

37. Savingram to J.L. Keith (CO 981/86, TNA), March 31, 1952.

38. G.S. Patel to Welfare Officer, Kampala (CO 981/38, TNA), March 21, 1952.

39. G.S. Patel to Mrs. H. Harries (CO 981/38, TNA), December 13, 1952.

40. G.S. Patel to Crook (CO 981/38, TNA), December 12, 1952.

41. Crook to Lucarotti (CO 981/38, TNA), December 23, 1952.

42. A more predictable trajectory was set by the Malik family of Delhi, who in 1935 traveled to Britain to find a suitable match for their daughter. Specifically, they wished to find a Sikh studying at a British university. After this match was successfully arranged, their daughter also undertook a course of study in Britain. Mukherjee, *Nationalism.*

43. On the controversial marriage between Seretse Khama, the future first president of Botswana, who studied law in London and Oxford, and a white clerk, Ruth Williams, see Ronald Hyam, "The Political Consequences of Seretse Khama," *Historical Journal* 29.4 (1986): 921–47; Wilf Mbanga, *Seretse and Ruth: Botswana's Love Story* (Cape Town, 2005); Neil Parsons, "The Impact of Seretse Khama on British Public Opinion," *Immigrants and Minorities* 3 (1993): 195–219; Susan Williams, *Colour Bar: Seretse Khama and His Nation* (London, 2006).

44. J.L. Keith, "African Students in Great Britain," *African Affairs* 45 (1946): 65–72.

45. In 1956, the title of director of colonial scholars was changed to "Head of Students Branch," and the high commissions took on increased responsibility for students from their territories. "The Work of the Colonial Office for Students from Colonial Territories in the UK and Republic of Ireland" (DO 35/7251, TNA), September 12, 1956.

46. A.J. Stockwell, "Leaders, Dissidents and the Disappointed: Colonial Students in Britain as Empire Ended," in Robert Holland and Sarah Stock-

well, eds., *Ambiguities of Empire: Essays in Honour of Andrew Porter* (London, 2009): 144–64.

47. There were also more than twenty voluntary associations for overseas students in London alone. Sheila Kitzinger, "Conditional Philanthropy towards Colored Students in Britain," *Phylon* 21.2 (1960): 167–72.

48. Lee, "Commonwealth Students."

49. The Consultative Committee for the Welfare of Colonial Students in the United Kingdom was established in 1951, and disbanded in 1965.

50. Political and Economic Planning, *Colonial Students in Britain: A Report by PEP, June 1955* (London, 1955), 36. See also "Students from the Colonies," *Planning* 20 (November 29, 1954): 281–300.

51. "Welfare of Colonial Students" (CO 876/256, TNA), 1950.

52. British Council, *How to Live in Britain: A Handbook for Students from Overseas* (London, 1952), 29.

53. J. Ayodele Langley, "Through a Glass Darkly," in Bhikhu Parekh, *Colour, Culture and Consciousness: Immigrant Intellectuals in Britain* (London, 1974), 31–40.

54. *Times* (London), September 5, 1950.

55. J. E. T. Eldridge, "Overseas Students at Leicester University: Some Problems of Adjustment and Communication," *Race* 2 (November 1960): 50–59.

56. Dr. L. O. Uwechia to H. B. Shepheard (CO 981/12, TNA), May 17, 1947.

57. For fictional treatments of this theme, see Peter Abrahams, *A Wreath for Udomo* (1956); Nina Bawden, *Under the Skin* (New York, 1964); William Conton, *The African* (Boston, 1960); E. G. Cousins, *Sapphire* (London, 1959); Dymphna Cusack, *The Sun in Exile* (London, 1955); Mark Freshfield, *The Stormy Dawn* (London, 1946); Mercedes Mackay, *Black Argosy* (London, 1954); Colin MacInnes, *City of Spades* (New York, 1957); John St. John, *A Trick of the Sun* (London, 1956); John Sykes, *The Newcomer* (London, 1956).

58. F. C. Stott to Sir Richard Nugent (BN 29/467, TNA), February 20, 1963.

59. Perham, *Colonial Reckoning*, 40–42. Similarly, see Ezekiel Mphahlele, "The African Intellectual," in Prudence Smith, ed., *Africa in Transition: Some BBC Talks on Changing Conditions in the Union and the Rhodesias* (London, 1958), 149–58; V. S. Naipaul, *The Mimic Men* (New York, 1967); T. S. Simey, "Adjustment Problems of Negro and Immigrant Elites," in Andrew Lind, ed., *Race Relations in World Perspective* (Honolulu, 1954), 289–310; and Philip Z. Zachernuk, *Colonial Subjects: An African Intelligentsia and Atlantic Ideas* (Charlottesville, 2000).

60. Ali, "Effects of Cultural Attitudes," 76.

61. "Dominic Ntawa" (CO 981/112, TNA), 1960–63.

62. *Times* (London), August 3, 1949, January 28, 1956, October 13, 1960, March 13, 1961, September 22, 1967.

63. "Colonial Students' Political Problems" (CO 537/2574, TNA), 1948.

64. Quoted in Hakim Adi, "West African Students in Britain, 1900–1960:

The Politics of Exile," in *Africans in Britain,* ed. David Killingray (London, 1994), 107–28.

65. See Kenneth Little's comments on the Colonial Office paper, "Colonial Students' Political Problems," (Kenneth Little Papers, Edinburgh University Library, Edinburgh).

66. Patrick Lancaster, *Education for Commonwealth Students in Britain* (London, 1962). See also Henri Tajfel and John L. Dawson, *Disappointed Guests: Essays by African, Asian and West Indian Students* (London, 1965).

67. "Outline of a Scheme for an Overseas Students' Bureau" (CAB 134/1313, TNA), October 1955.

68. "The Political Significance of African Students in Great Britain" (CO 537/2574, TNA), 1948.

69. "African Students in London" (T 317/2255, TNA), September 20, 1938. See also "Committee on the Welfare of Overseas Students" (CAB 134/1313, TNA), April 27, 1956; and Hakim Adi, *West Africans in Britain, 1900–1960: Nationalism, Pan-Africanism and Communism* (London, 1998), 3; Adi, "West Africans and the Communist Party in the 1950s," in *Opening the Books: Essays on the Social and Cultural History of British Communism,* ed. Geoff Andrews et al. (London, 1995), 176–94; and G. O. Olusanya, *The West African Students' Union and the Politics of Decolonisation, 1925–1958* (Ibadan, 1982).

70. Lee, "Commonwealth Students."

71. Shompa Lahiri, *Indians in Britain: Anglo-Indian Encounters, Race and Identity, 1880–1930* (London, 2000).

72. "Committee on the Welfare of Overseas Students" (CAB 134/1313, TNA), April 27, 1956.

73. H. L. O. Garrett, "Note on the Situation at Cambridge" (IOR L/PJ/12/638, File 808/40, BL), June 1940.

74. G. Cunningham to Linlithgow (IOR L/PJ/12/638, File 808/40, BL), January 7, 1942.

75. "Malayan Students in the United Kingdom" (CO 1022/197, TNA), February 12, 1953.

76. "Report on the Meeting of the Overseas Students' Committee to Discuss the Reception and Welfare Arrangements for Overseas Students and Apprentices in England" (BW 3/49, TNA), March 28, 1957.

77. John D. Higham to Sir Franklin Gimson (CO 717/193/3, TNA), August 22, 1951; A. T. Carey, "Malayan Students in Britain," *Eastern World* 8 (1954): 36–37.

78. "Communist Training Schools for Indians in Moscow and Elsewhere" (L/PJ/12/412), 1930–36.

79. "Minutes of a Meeting of the Official Committee on Communism (Overseas)" (CAB 134/1313, TNA), May 4, 1955.

80. Ekeh, ed., *Salubi,* 203.

81. Ibid., 208.

82. "British Communist Party Activities among African Students in the United Kingdom" (FO 371/73750, TNA), October 1948–April 1949; and see

also "Communism in the Colonies. Communist Influence on Students in the United Kingdom" (CO 537/4312, TNA), November 11, 1948.

83. G. J. Gurney to Mr. Ward (Mss Eur F168/85, BL), March 15, 1952.

84. W. S. Rankin, "Notes on Spring and Summer Terms" (IE/COL/A/2/1, Institute of Education Archives, London, hereafter IEA), July 1, 1953.

85. "Commonwealth Students in Britain," *Parliamentary Debates* 175 (March 12, 1952), cols. 663–94.

86. "British Communist Party Activities among African Students in the United Kingdom" (FO 371/73750, TNA), October 1948-April 1949; "An Examination of the Student Accommodation Problem" (DO 35/8204, TNA), n.d. [1960?].

87. Huxley, *Back Street, New Worlds*, 137.

88. George T. H. Kimble, *Tropical Africa*, vol. 2 (New York, 1960), 283.

89. "Committee on the Welfare of Overseas Students" (CAB 134/2373, TNA), February 6, 1957. For a less sanguine view, see Julie Hessler, "Death of an African Student in Moscow," *Cahiers du Monde Russe* 47 (2006): 33–63.

90. *African Students in the United States: A Handbook of Information and Orientation* (New York, 1957); Kenneth L. Baer, "African Students in the East and West, 1959–1966: An Analysis of Experiences and Attitudes," *Occasional Paper #54, Program of Eastern African Studies* (July 1970); Cooperative Study of West African Student Opinion, *Nigerian Student Opinions: Tabulations* (Washington, 1959); Daniel Branch, "The Airlift: African Students Overseas in the Era of Decolonization," talk delivered at the National History Center, Washington, DC, 2010; Liping Bu, *Making the World Like Us: Education, Cultural Expansion and the American Century* (Westport, CT, 2003); James M. Davis et al., *IIE Survey of the African Student: His Achievements and His Problems* (New York, 1961); David Engerman, "American Knowledge and Global Power," *Diplomatic History* 31.4 (2007): 599–622; Jane W. Jacqz, *African Students at U.S. Universities. Report of a Conference on the Admission and Guidance of African Students Held at Howard University, Washington, D.C., March 17–18, 1967* (New York, 1967); Paul Kramer, "Is the World Our Campus? International Students and U.S. Global Power in the Long Twentieth Century," *Diplomatic History* 33.5 (2009): 775–806; Richard T. Morris (with Oluf M. Davidsen), *The Two-Way Mirror: National Status in Foreign Students' Adjustment* (Minneapolis, 1960); Claire Sellitz et al., *Attitudes and Social Relations of Foreign Students in the United States* (Minneapolis, 1963); Hans de Wit, *Internationalization of Higher Education in the United States of America and Europe: A Historical, Comparative, and Conceptual Analysis* (Westport, CT, 2002); P. Zalinser, *African Student Opinion* (New Haven, 1957). On Indian students in America, see Ross Bassett, "MIT-Trained Swadeshis: MIT and Indian Nationalism, 1880–1947," *Osiris* 24 (2009): 212–30; George Coelho, *Changing Images of America: A Study of Indian Students' Perceptions* (Glencoe, IL, 1958); Richard D. Lambert and Marvin Bressler, *Indian Students on an American Campus* (Minneapolis, 1956).

91. Norman Kiell, "Attitudes of Foreign Students," *Journal of Higher Education* 22.4 (1951): 188–94.

92. Davis, *IIE Survey*, 36; Zalinser, *African Student Opinion*, 55.

93. Cora Du Bois, *Foreign Students and Higher Education in the United States* (Washington, DC, 1956), 32.

94. Hugh and Mabel Smythe were instrumental in breaking the race barrier at the State Department, and had distinguished academic and foreign service careers. Hugh Smythe had served as a research assistant for W. E. B. Dubois; he was also an ambassador to the Syrian Republic and Malta.

95. Hugh H. Smythe and Mabel M. Smythe, *The New Nigerian Elite* (Stanford, 1960), 100 and 118.

96. Quoted in Elspeth Huxley, *Four Guineas: A Journey through West Africa* (London, 1954), 94. See also Jason Parker, "Made-in-America Revolutions? The 'Black University' and the American Role in the Decolonization of the Black Atlantic," *Journal of American History* 96.3. (2009): 727–50.

97. Kwame Nkrumah, *The Autobiography of Kwame Nkrumah* (New York, 1957), 55–56.

98. "Colonial Information Policy Committee. Note on Treatment of Coloured People in the United Kingdom" (CO 537/5130, TNA), September 1949.

99. "Extract from Minutes of a Meeting of the Colonial Information Policy Committee" (CO 537/5130, TNA), July 21, 1949.

100. Zig Layton-Henry, *The Politics of Immigration: Immigration, 'Race' and 'Race' Relations in Post-War Britain* (Cambridge, MA, 1992); Anthony Lester and Geoffrey Bindman, *Race and Law* (London: Longman, 1972).

101. Historians of the United States have charted how the Cold War influenced the government's response to the civil rights movement, as officials sought to preserve American prestige abroad by containing racial discrimination. Thomas Borstelmann, *The Cold War and the Color Line: American Race Relations in the Global Arena* (Cambridge, MA, 2001); Mary Dudziak, *Cold War Civil Rights: Race and the Image of American Democracy* (Princeton, 2000); Dudziak, "Brown as a Cold War Case," *Journal of American History* 91.1 (June 2004): 32–42; Gerald Horne, *Mau Mau in Harlem? The U.S. and the Liberation of Kenya* (New York, 2009).

102. A. F. G. Hornyold to Mary L. Dooley (FCO 13/296, TNA), May 29, 1967.

103. Ewans to Reid (FCO 13/296, TNA), July 22, 1966.

104. On the psychologizing of other populations, such as homosexuals, see Frank Mort, *Dangerous Sexualities: Medico-Moral Politics in England since 1830* (London, 1987); Chris Waters, "Havelock Ellis, Sigmund Freud and the State: Discourses of Homosexual Identity in Interwar Britain," in Lucy Bland and Laura Doan, eds., *Sexology in Culture: Labelling Bodies and Desires* (Cambridge, 1998), 165–79.

105. See also chapter 1 in this volume.

106. Arthur Stanley Livingstone, *The Overseas Student in Britain* (Manchester, 1960), 4.

107. G. G. C. Rwegellera, "Mental Illness in Africans and West Indians of African Origin Living in London," M.Phil. thesis, University of London, 1970.

108. Peter Gifford, "General Morbidity in Overseas Students," *Proceedings of the British Student Health Association* (1961): 55–58.

109. John Useem and Ruth Hill Useem, *The Western-Educated Man in India: A Study of His Social Roles and Influence* (New York, 1955).

110. J. C. Read, "Psychological Disturbances in Students from Overseas," *Medical World* 90 (January 1959): 18–24.

111. Edward Shils, *The Intellectual between Tradition and Modernity: The Indian Situation* (The Hague, 1961), 80.

112. A. K. Singh, "Indian University Students in Britain," *Planning* 27 (November 13, 1961): 283–313.

113. A. K. Singh, *Indian Students in Britain: A Survey of Their Adjustment and Attitudes* (London: Asia Publishing House, 1963), 99.

114. J. K. Bhatnagar, "The Values and Attitudes of Some Indian and British Students," *Race* 9 (July 1967): 27–36.

115. Nelson Ottah, "Nigerians in U.K.," *West African Pilot*, February 20, 1957; see also G. K. Animashawun, "African Students in Britain," *Race* 5 (July 1963): 38–47.

116. T. Adeoye Lambo, *A Study of Social and Health Problems of Nigerian Students in Great Britain* (Ibadan, [1960?]).

117. "Consultative Committee on the Welfare of Colonial Students in United Kingdom. Action Arising Out of Minutes" (CO 876/270, TNA), n.d., probably 1947–52.

118. J. R. M. Copeland, "Aspects of Mental Illness in West African Students," *Social Psychiatry* 3.1 (1968): 7–13.

119. Lambo, "The Role of Cultural Factors"; Sadowsky, *Imperial Bedlam*.

120. For a critique of Lambo, see George Henry Phills, "Social Perception and Anxiety in Nigerian and British Students," Ph.D. thesis, Bedford College, University of London, 1963.

121. F. D. Hughes to Lambo (BW 3/23, TNA), February 5, 1958.

122. Conversely, the sociologist and economist Ferdynand Zweig found a high rate of neurosis among British-born students, but concluded that they were problems only unto themselves. Ferdynand Zweig, *The Student in the Age of Anxiety: A Survey of Oxford and Manchester Students* (New York, 1963).

123. Lambo, *Social and Health Problems*, 14; and see also Akinsola A. Akiwowo, "The Sociology of Nigerian Tribalism?" *Phylon* 25.2 (1964): 155–63.

124. Dayo Olugboji, *The Problem of Nigerian Students Overseas* (Lagos, 1959); and see Martin Banham, "The Nigerian Student in Britain," *Universities Quarterly* 12 (1958): 363–66.

125. Raymond Prince, "The 'Brain Fag' Syndrome in Nigerian Students," *Journal of Mental Science* 106 (1960): 559–70.

126. Raymond Prince, "Functional Symptoms associated with Study in Nigerian Students," *West African Medical Journal* 11 (1962): 198–206.

127. Ibid., 200.

128. Ibid., 206.

129. McCulloch, *Colonial Psychiatry*, 119.

130. G. I. Tewfik and A. Okasha, "Psychosis and Immigration," *Postgraduate Medical Journal* 41 (1965): 603–12.

131. Rwegellera, "Mental Illness," 48.

132. Amechi Anumonye, *Brain-Fag Syndrome* (Lausanne, 1982[?]). See also Brian Harris, "A Case of Brain-Fag in East Africa," *British Journal of Psychiatry* 138 (1981): 162–63; Olufemi Morakinyo, "A Psychophysiological Theory of a Psychiatric Illness (the Brain-Fag Syndrome) associated with Study among Africans," *Journal of Nervous and Mental Disease* 168 (1980): 84–89; and Morakinyo, "The Brain-Fag Syndrome in Nigeria: Cognitive Defects in an Illness associated with Study," *British Journal of Psychiatry* 146 (1985): 209–10.

133. Amechi Anumonye, *Nigerian Students and Emotional Reactions in Our Space-Age Universities* (Lagos, 1975).

134. Ibid., 11.

135. Ibid., 25.

136. Warwick Anderson, *The Collectors of Lost Souls: Turning Kuru Scientists into Whitemen* (Baltimore, 2008).

137. Bessie Kent, "The Social Worker's Cultural Pattern as It Affects Casework with Immigrants," *Social Work* 22.4 (October 1965): 14–22.

138. R. J. Still, "Mental Health in Overseas Students," *Proceedings of the British Student Health Association* 13 (1961), 73.

139. Huxley, *Back Street, New Worlds*, 140.

140. See chapter 1 in this volume.

141. W. A. R. Walker to LL. Le P. Gardner (CO 876/227, TNA), 1951.

142. T. Asuni, "Review of Nigerian Students Repatriated on Psychiatric Grounds," *West African Medical Journal* 17 (1968): 3–7.

143. "Committee on the Welfare of Overseas Students" (CAB 134/1313, TNA), February 13, 1956.

144. Percy Sillitoe to Sir Orme Sargent (CO 537/4312, TNA), December 23, 1948.

145. "Cobina Kessie" (CO 981/5, TNA), 1942–48; and see also "Cobina Kessie" (CO 96/752/10, TNA), 1938–39; and "Prince Cobina Kessie" (CO 96/768/18, TNA), 1940.

146. Cobina Kessie to Lady Londonderry (CO 981/5, TNA), July 14, 1943.

147. Hastings K. Banda to Colonial Office (CO 981/29, TNA), August 27, 1941; D. M. Kennedy, governor of Nyasaland to Lord Moyne, secretary of state for Colonies (CO 981/29, TNA), October 29, 1941.

148. Michael Banton, *White and Coloured: The Behaviour of British Peo-*

ple towards Coloured Immigrants (London, 1959); Garigue, "The West African Students' Union"; Kitzinger, "Conditional Philanthropy"; Eyo B. Ndem, "The Status of Colored People in Britain," *Phylon Quarterly* 18.1 (1957): 82–87.

149. Paul B. Rich, *Prospero's Return? Historical Essays on Race, Culture, and British Society* (London, 1994), 134.

150. *Daily Mirror,* September 9, 1958.

151. Bill Schwarz, ed., *West Indian Intellectuals in Britain* (Manchester, 2003); see also Lloyd Reckord's 1963 film, *Ten Bob in Winter;* and Sam Selvon's novel, *The Housing Lark* (London, 1965).

152. "The Care of African Children Whose Parents Are Studying in the U.K. (BW 3/52, TNA), 1964–66.

153. Amechi Anumonye, "Psychological Stresses among African Students in Britain," *Scottish Medical Journal* 12 (1967), 318; Kenneth Little's preface to A. T. Carey, *Colonial Students: A Study of the Social Adaptation of Colonial Students in London* (London, 1956); and Anthony McCowan, *Coloured Peoples in Britain* (London, 1952).

154. Rwegellera, "Mental Illness," 173.

155. Asuni, "Review of Nigerian Students."

156. "Colonial Students' Committee Minutes" (CO 323/1416/7, TNA), November 3, 1937.

157. British Council, *How to Live in Britain,* 31.

158. Susan Lester, "West Africa's Students in Britain," *West African Review* 28 (December 1957): 1076–81.

159. Ali, "Effects of Cultural Attitudes," 88 and 104.

160. "Commonwealth Immigrants Bill—Report," *Parliamentary Debates* 654 (February 22, 1962), cols. 748–55.

161. K. B. Paice to Allen (HO 344/48, TNA), January 17, 1962.

162. "Admission of Students under Commonwealth Immigrants Bill" (HO 344/48, TNA), January 31, 1962.

163. J. T. Hughes, "Minute" (DO 163/50, TNA), December 16, 1964.

164. D. M. Smith, "Minute" (CO 1032/333, TNA), November 27, 1961.

165. "Overseas Students—Admission Arrangements" (BW 3/51, TNA), November 1966.

166. "Evasion of Commonwealth Immigration Control by Students" (HO 344/196, TNA), December 1964.

167. "Confidential Notes on a Meeting Held on 22nd December 1964 to discuss problems in connection with Nigerian students going to Britain" (BW 3/51, TNA), 1964–65.

168. Huxley, *Back Street, New Worlds,* 146–47.

169. "Preparation of Bill amending the Commonwealth Immigrants Act 1962. Review of the Definitions of 'Returning Resident' and 'Student'" (HO 344/178, TNA), 1965.

170. "Immigration Control of Overseas Students. 'Loophole' Policy" (ED 188/217, TNA), January 4, 1965.

CHAPTER 4

1. Based on this definition, Penzance refused an English husband's plea to dissolve a marriage that had been celebrated in Utah with a Mormon ceremony. See Hyde v. Hyde and Woodmansee, (1865–69) 1 L.R.P. & D. 130.

2. Baindail v. Baindail, (1946) 1 All ER 342; and Sinha Peerage Claim, (1946) 1 All ER 348.

3. Richard Jones and Gnanapala Welhengama, *Ethnic Minorities in English Law* (Staffordshire, 2000); W. F. Menski, "English Family Law and Ethnic Laws in Britain," *Kerala Law Times* 1 (1988): 56–66; Werner F. Menski, "Asians in Britain and the Question of Adaptation to a New Legal Order: Asian Laws in Britain," in Milton Israel and N. K. Wagle, eds., *Ethnicity, Identity, Migration: The South Asian Context* (Toronto, 1993), 238–68; David Pearl, *Family Law and the Immigrant Communities* (Bristol, 1986); Sebastian Poulter, "African Customs in an English Setting: Legal and Policy Aspects of Recognition," *Journal of African Law* 31 (spring 1987): 207–25.

4. Prakash Shah, "Attitudes to Polygamy in English law," *International and Comparative Law Quarterly* 52 (2003): 369–400.

5. T. C. Hartley, "Polygamy and Social Policy," *Modern Law Review* 32.2 (1969): 155–73; William E. Holder, "Public Policy and National Preferences: The Exclusion of Foreign Law in English Private International Law," *International and Comparative Law Quarterly* 17.4 (1968): 926–52,

6. Eve Darian-Smith and Peter Fitzpatrick, eds., *Laws of the Postcolonial* (Ann Arbor, 1999).

7. Risk v. Risk, (1950) 2 All E.R. 973.

8. Roger Ballard, "Ethnic Diversity and the Delivery of Justice: The Challenge of Plurality," in Werner Menski and Prakash Shah, eds., *Migration, Diasporas, and Legal Systems in Europe* (London, 2006), 29–56; Arnold M. Rose, "The Social Scientist as Expert Witness," *Minnesota Law Review* 40 (1956): 205–18; Lawrence Rosen, "The Anthropologist as Expert Witness," *American Anthropologist* 79 (1977): 555–78.

9. Frederick Cooper, "From Free Labor to Family Allowances: Labor and African Society in Colonial Discourse," *American Ethnologist* 16.4 (1989): 745–65.

10. M. J. Furmston, "Polygamy and the Wind of Change," *International and Comparative Law Quarterly* 10.1 (1961): 180–86; R. H. Webb, "Polygamy and the Eddying Winds," *International and Comparative Law Quarterly* 14 (1965): 273.

11. L. C. Green, "'Civilized' Law and 'Primitive' Peoples," *Osgoode Hall Law Journal* 13 (1975): 233–49.

12. Cooper, "From Free Labor to Family Allowances."

13. Andrew Manson, "Christopher Bethell and the Securing of the Bechuanaland Frontier, 1878–1884," *Journal of Southern African Studies* 24.3 (1998): 485–508.

14. "The Baralong Marriage," *Cape Law Journal* 5 (1888): 182–89.

15. *Times* (London), February 16, 1888.

16. John D. Kelly, "Fear of Culture: British Regulation of Indian Marriage in Post-Indenture Fiji," *Ethnohistory* 36.4 (1989): 372–91.

17. Jeremy Martens, "Polygamy, Sexual Danger, and the Creation of Vagrancy Legislation in Colonial Natal," *Journal of Imperial and Commonwealth History* 31.3 (2003): 24–45.

18. Radhika Mongia, "Gender and the Historiography of Gandhian *Satyagraha* in South Africa," *Gender and History* 18.1 (2006): 130–49.

19. Nancy Rose Hunt, "Noise over Camouflaged Polygamy, Colonial Morality Taxation, and a Woman-Naming Crisis in Belgian Africa," *Journal of African History* 32.3 (1991): 471–94; Joshua Schreier, "Napoléon's Long Shadow: Morality, Civilization and Jews in France and Algeria, 1808–1870," *French Historical Studies* 30.1 (2007): 77–103.

20. Lisa Lindsay, *Working with Gender: Wage Labor and Social Change in Southwestern Nigeria* (Portsmouth, 2003); Arthur Phillips, "Marriage Laws in Africa," in Arthur Phillips, ed., *Survey of African Marriage and Family Life* (Oxford, 1953), 173–327; A. R. Radcliffe-Brown and Daryll Forde, eds., *African Systems of Kinship and Marriage* (London, 1950).

21. Judith Byfield, "Women, Marriage, Divorce and the Emerging Colonial State in Abeokuta (Nigeria), 1892–1904," *Canadian Journal of African Studies* 30.1 (1996): 32–51.

22. Phyllis Kaberry, *Women of the Grassfields: A Study of the Economic Position of Women in Bamenda, British Cameroons* (London, 1952). On the treatment of polygamy in anthropological scholarship, see Elizabeth Fee, "The Sexual Politics of Victorian Anthropology," *Feminist Studies* 3/4 (winter–spring 1973): 23–39.

23. L. P. Mair, "African Marriage and Social Change," in Phillips, ed., *Survey*, 10. See also Jomo Kenyatta, *Facing Mount Kenya* (New York, 1965), 167–68.

24. William Rayden, *Rayden's Practice and Law of Divorce* (London, 1968), 33.

25. Alfred B. Kasunmu and Jeswald W. Salacuse, *Nigerian Family Law* (London, 1966), 111.

26. "Marriage by Proxy in Nigeria" (HO 344/256, TNA), May 5, 1967.

27. R. M. Morris to S. R. Gibson (HO 344/256, TNA), January 19, 1968.

28. R. M. Morris, "Marriage by Proxy in Nigeria" (HO 344/256, TNA), May 18, 1967.

29. R. H. Graveson, "Capacity to Acquire a Domicile," *International Law Quarterly* 3 (1950): 149–63.

30. Laura Tabili, "Empire is the Enemy of Love: Edith Noor's Progress and Other Stories," *Gender and History* 17 (2005): 5–28; Laura Tabili, "Outsiders in the Land of Their Birth: Exogamy, Citizenship and Identity in War and Peace," *Journal of British Studies* 44 (October 2005): 796–815.

31. R. H. Graveson, "Capacity to Acquire a Domicile," 149.

32. Kasunmu and Salacuse, *Nigerian Family Law*, 112.

33. Dennis Fitzpatrick, "Non-Christian Marriage," *Journal of the Society of Comparative Legislation* 2 (1900): 359–87.

34. *Times* (London), May 12 and 14, 1913.

35. Gail Savage, "More than One Mrs. Mir Anwaruddin: Islamic Divorce and Christian Marriage in Early Twentieth-Century London," *Journal of British Studies* 47.2 (2008): 348–74.

36. *Times* (London), May 12, 1913.

37. Ibid.

38. Savage, "More than One Mrs. Mir Anwaruddin."

39. Frederick Robertson, "The Relations between the English Law and the Personal Law of Indians in England with Special Reference to the Marriage Law," *Journal of Comparative Legislation and International Law* 18.2 (1918): 242–59; and see chapter 3.

40. *Times* (London), January 18, 1927.

41. *Times* (London), December 16 and 18, 1926.

42. "Polygamous Marriages" (LCO 2/1148, TNA), December 15, 1933.

43. R. Peel to Sir Claud Schuster (LCO 2/1148, TNA), July 2, 1937. See also the novel in which such a relationship goes awry; John Seymour Eyton, *Mr. Ram: A Story of Oxford and India* (London, 1929).

44. "Marriage Laws. Marriage with Foreigners. Marriages of Foreigners in the UK and Polygamous Marriages" (CO 323/1283/11, TNA), 1935.

45. "Record of Meeting of the Lord Chancellor's Committee on Marriages between British Subjects and Foreign Nationals" (LCO 2/1149, TNA), February 23, 1939; J.H.C. Morris, "The Recognition of Polygamous Marriages in English Law," *Harvard Law Review* 66.6 (April 1953): 961–1012.

46. *Times* (London), January 31, 1946.

47. *Times* (London), May 18, 1945.

48. "Recognition of Polygamous Marriages," *International Law Quarterly* 1 (1947): 64.

49. *Times* (London), May 18, 1945.

50. Morris, "Recognition of Polygamous Marriages."

51. Lauren A. Benton, *Law and Colonial Cultures: Legal Regimes in World History, 1400–1900* (Cambridge, 2002); Elizabeth Kolsky, "Codification and the Rule of Colonial Difference: Criminal Procedure in British India," *Law and History Review* 23.3 (2005): 631–706.

52. Paras Diwan, "The Hindu Marriage Act 1955," *International and Comparative Law Quarterly* 6 (1957): 263–72. There were also new anti-polygamy regulations in China, and polygamy was abolished for Turkish Cypriots. *Times* (London), April 19, 1950, and May 5, 1950.

53. Rochona Majumdar, *Marriage and Modernity: Family Values in Colonial Bengal* (Durham, 2009); Prakash Shah, *Legal Pluralism in Conflict: Coping with Cultural Diversity in Law* (London, 2005).

54. *People*, October 13, 1968.

55. "Law Commission—Working Paper on Polygamous Marriages. Mat-

rimonial Proceedings (Polygamous Marriages) Bill" (RG 48/3126, TNA), 1968–73.

56. "Restricting Polygamy," *Times* (London), March 8, 1961.

57. *Times* (London), April 7, 1960.

58. Kristin Mann, *Marrying Well: Marriage, Status and Social Change among the Educated Elite in Colonial Lagos* (Cambridge, 1985), 58.

59. Mann, *Marrying Well*, 44. On the "modernity" of monogamy, see Emwinma Ogieriaikhi, *My Wife or My Wives* (Benin City, 1965); Ogieriaikhi, *The Marriage Couldn't Continue* (Benin City, 1965); and Kobina Nortey, *The Man with Two Wives* (Accra, 1964).

60. Lindsay, *Working with Gender*.

61. Stephan F. Miescher, *Making Men in Ghana* (Bloomington, 2005); Sean Hawkins, "'The Woman in Question': Marriage and Identity in the Colonial Courts of Northern Ghana, 1907–1954," in Jean Allman, Susan Geiger, and Nakanyike Musisi, eds., *Women in African Colonial Histories* (Bloomington, 2002), 116–43; Dorothy Dee Vellenga, "Attempts to Change the Marriage Laws in Ghana and the Ivory Coast," in Philip Foster and Aristide R. Zolberg, eds., *Ghana and the Ivory Coast: Perspectives on Modernization* (Chicago, 1971), 125–50; Isaac Schapera, *Married Life in an African Tribe* (New York, 1941).

62. On the suggestion that welfare departments ran ahead of other domains of law and civil society in terms of their relatively progressive definitions of family, see Pat Thane, "Happy Families? Varieties of Family Life in Twentieth-Century Britain," plenary address delivered at the North American Conference on British Studies, Denver, 2011.

63. F. H. Johnstone to J. P. Carswell (PIN 15/4092, TNA), March 5, 1952.

64. "Draft. Marriage in a Foreign Country" (PIN 15/4092, TNA), n.d. [1952–58].

65. "Verification of Births, Marriages, and Deaths. Moslems, etc." (PIN 15/4092, TNA), February 27, 1952.

66. Gbi Anderson to National Insurance Tribunal (CT 7/49, TNA), September 11, 1952.

67. Gbi Anderson to National Insurance Tribunal (CT 7/49, TNA), November 11, 1952.

68. *Times* (London), August 10, 1955.

69. B. Mannan to National Insurance Tribunal (PIN 62/135, TNA), December 6, 1954.

70. B. Mannan to National Insurance Tribunal (PIN 62/135, TNA), March 24, 1955.

71. J. J. Barnes to E. A. Paterson (AST 36/213, TNA), June 22, 1967.

72. *Daily Mail*, April 17, 1968; and see *Express and Star*, September 2, 1967.

73. *Times* (London), October 28, 1959; Ohochuku v. Ohochuku, (1960) 1 W.L.R. 183.

74. "Ohochuku v. Ohochuku," *Journal of African Law* 4.1 (1960): 56–57.

75. Furmston, "Polygamy and the Wind of Change."

76. R.H. Webb, "Ohochuku v. Ohochuku. A Variation of Thynne v. Thynne," *Modern Law Review* 23.3 (1960): 327–31.

77. "Ministry of Pensions and National Insurance. Pensions Procedure. Validity of Marriage. General" (PIN 61/24, TNA), n.d. [1956?].

78. "Age Marriage Death etc. Marriage. Hindu Marriage Act" (PIN 61/24, TNA), February 1956.

79. Kasunmu and Salacuse, *Nigerian Family Law*, 112.

80. N. Hellon, "Polygamous Marriages" (PIN 21/603, TNA), September 3, 1968.

81. On the doctrine of conversion, see the case of Ali v. Ali (1966), discussed in J.M. Eekelaar, J.L.R. Davis, and R.H. Webb, "The Dissolution of Initially Polygamous Marriages," *International and Comparative Law Quarterly* (1966): 1181–89; Michael Higgins, "Conflict of Laws. Conversion of Polygamous Marriage into Monogamous Union," *Modern Law Review* 26.2 (1963): 205–8; J.H.C. Morris, "Ali v. Ali," *International and Comparative Law Quarterly* 17 (1968): 1015–16; Dimitry Tolstoy, "The Conversion of a Polygamous Union into a Monogamous Marriage," *International and Comparative Law Quarterly* 17.3 (July 1968): 721–29.

82. J.J. Barnes to E.A. Paterson (AST 36/213, TNA), June 22, 1967.

83. A.D. Gordon-Brown to Miss A. Cox (HO 344/256, TNA), August 30, 1967.

84. "Immigrants (Dependents)," *Parliamentary Debates* 765 (May 30, 1968), col. 254W.

85. R.M. Morris, "Proxy Marriage" (HO 344/256, TNA), n.d. [1967?].

86. "Nigerian Marriages. Circular No. 21 to Entry Certificate Officers" (HO 344/256, TNA), January 1968.

87. R.M. Morris, "Marriage by Proxy in Nigeria" (HO 344/256, TNA), May 18, 1967, and January 3, 1968.

88. J. Saunders to Home Office (HO 344/256, TNA), April 15, 1966; R.M. Morris to K. Hedderly (HO 344/256, TNA), June 10, 1966.

89. R.M. Morris to K. Hedderly (HO 344/299, TNA), June 10, 1966.

90. See, e.g., "Marriage by Proxy in Nigeria" (HO 344/299, TNA), 1964–67.

91. Saunders to Young (HO 344/299, TNA), November 28, 1966.

92. D.R. Birleson, "Marriage by Proxy in Nigeria" (HO 344/299, TNA), October 18, 1966.

93. M.C. Gathercole to E.O. Nwankwo-Ntah (HO 344/299, TNA), July 9, 1966.

94. D.R. Birleson, "Marriage by Proxy in Nigeria" (HO 344/299, TNA), June 2, 1966.

95. "Marriage by Proxy in Nigeria" (HO 344/256, TNA), June 15, 1967.

96. W.M. Lee, "Marriage Act 1949. Amendment Bill" (HO 342/106, TNA), February 11, 1966.

97. A. Pover to Le Bailly (HO 344/299, TNA), August 10, 1964.

98. J.W.G. Tait to A. Pover (HO 344/299, TNA), August 31, 1964.

99. *Weekend*, October 13–19, 1965.

100. F. Rooke-Matthews to K. P. Witney (HO 342/106, TNA), September 1, 1965.

101. *Times* (London), June 9, 1966.

102. *Times* (London), November 26, 1964.

103. Ibid.

104. "Sammy-Joe, Roggee Goodfellow (Nigerian)" (DPP 2/4162, TNA), April 4, 1966.

105. Jarvis, *Conservative Governments*, 104. On British attitudes to marriage after 1945, see Marcus Collins, *Modern Love: Personal Relationships in Twentieth-Century Britain* (Newark, DE, 2006); Hera Cook, *The Long Sexual Revolution: English Women, Sex, and Contraceptions, 1800–1975* (Oxford, 2004); Martin Francis, "A Flight from Commitment? Domesticity, Adventure and the Masculine Imaginary in Britain after the Second World War," *Gender and History* 19.1 (April 2007): 163–85; Claire Langhamer, "Adultery in Post-War England," *History Workshop Journal* 62.1 (2006): 86–115; and O. R. McGregor, *Divorce in England: A Centenary Study* (Melbourne, 1957).

106. *Daily Express*, March 29, 1968.

107. Nigerian's Child-Bride Puzzles UK Home Office," *Daily Times* (Lagos), May 5, 1967.

108. I. G. F. Karsten, "Child Marriages," *Modern Law Review* 32.2 (1969): 212–17.

109. "Alhaji Mohamed. Police Report of Proceedings Taken under Children and Young Persons Act 1963 (HO 344/256, TNA), 1967.

110. Karsten, "Child Marriages"; *Times* (London), March 29, 1968; Poulter, "African Customs in an English Setting."

111. Sebastian Poulter, "Ethnic Minority Customs, English Law, and Human Rights," *International and Comparative Law Quarterly* 36 (1987): 589–615.

112. Similarly, see "Sentence on Jamaican Cut—'Exceptional Course,'" *Times* (London), April 19, 1967.

113. *Daily Express*, April 1, 1968.

114. *Daily Express*, April 4, 1968.

115. "Case of Nigerian Girl Wife" (HO 344/299, TNA), n.d.

116. See, e.g., Burton, *Burdens of History*; Burton, "From Child Bride to 'Hindoo Lady': Rukhmabai and the Debate on Sexual Respectability in Imperial Britain," *American Historical Review* 103.4 (October 1998): 1119–46; Lata Mani, *Contentious Traditions: The Debate on Sati in Colonial India* (Berkeley, 1998); and Tanika Sarkar, "Rhetoric against Age of Consent: Resisting Colonial Reason and Death of a Child-Wife," *Economic and Political Weekly* 28.36 (September 4, 1993): 1869–78.

117. For a contemporary version of this debate, see Susan Moller Okin, *Is Multiculturalism Bad for Women?* (Princeton, 1999).

118. R. H. Webb, "Polygamous Marriages Again," *Modern Law Review* 24.1 (1961): 183–85.

119. Ibid.

120. *Times* (London), February 10, 1961.

121. O. M. Stone, "Ninth Report of the Law Reform Committee (Liability in Tort between Husband and Wife)," *Modern Law Review* 24.4 (1961): 481–86.

122. Valentine L. Korah, "England," *International and Comparative Law Quarterly* 10.1 (1961): 190–93.

123. O. M. Stone, "Sowa v. Sowa: Maintenance of Family Dependents," *Modern Law Review* 24.4 (1961): 500–502.

124. "Polygamous Marriages" (AST 36/311, TNA), November 17, 1961.

125. *Times* (London), February 11, 1961.

126. *Times* (London), November 22, 1966.

127. "Liable Relatives. Polygamous Marriage" (AST 36/311, TNA), November 21, 1966.

128. Ian Saunders and Jerry Walter, "The Matrimonial Proceedings (Polygamous Marriages) Act 1972," *International and Comparative Law Quarterly* 21.4 (1972): 781–89.

129. *Times* (London), August 3, 1968.

130. "Law Commission Proposals on Family Law; Further Papers Relating to Financial Relief in the Case of Polygamous Marriages" (HO 342/125, TNA), 1967–68.

131. "Law Commission Working Paper on Polygamous Marriages" (AST 36/213, TNA), August 26, 1968.

132. *Times* (London), August 3, 1968.

133. Lady Summerskill had introduced the same measure in Lords the previous summer. The bill had an unopposed second reading, but was "counted out" for want of time.

134. *Times* (London), January 19, 1972; and see also *Times* (London), January 21, 1972.

135. *Times* (London), July 10, 1971.

136. Shah, *Legal Pluralism in Conflict.*

137. On the intersection of British debates about parenting and the "twilight of empire," see Pat Thane, "Population Politics in Post-War British Culture," in Conekin et al., *Moments of Modernity,* 114–34.

CHAPTER 5

1. David Kynaston, *Family Britain.*

2. Laurie Joshua, "Private Fostering: A Migrant Worker's Dilemma," *African Woman* (autumn 1991): 6–9.

3. Political and Economic Planning, *Colonial Students in Britain.*

4. "Students—General Welfare. Wives of Students" (CO 876/116, TNA), 1951–53; Marjorie Stewart, "Courses for Overseas Women in London, *African Women* 1 (1955): 32–33. On the longer history of this policy, see Karen

Tranberg Hansen, ed., *African Encounters with Domesticity* (New Brunswick, 1999); and Thomas, *Politics of the Womb*.

5. "Notes of Discussions between Mr. W. A. R. Walker, Gold Coast Students Liaison Officer and Mr. L. L. Le P. Gardner, Senior Assistant Secretary, Accra and Others" (CO 876/116, TNA), n.d. [1951–53]; "Minutes of the Central Advisory Committee on Education, Fourth Session" (CO 876/221, TNA), 1951.

6. J. E. W. Hood to G. Creasy (CO 859/20/18, TNA), February 26, 1940; and see also Jennifer Cole and Lynn M. Thomas, eds., *Love in Africa* (Chicago, 2009).

7. By 1953, a group of young, educated Nigerian women in Britain was sufficiently concerned about the welfare needs of their compatriots to establish the Nigerian Women's League of Great Britain and Ireland, which was to be run on the lines of *egbe* societies in Nigeria. LaRay Denzer, *Folayegbe M. Akintunde-Ighodalo: A Public Life* (Ibadan, 2001).

8. J. L. Keith to R. Rogers (CO 876/116, TNA), December 5, 1951. See also J. E. S. Heyford, "White Brides and Black Husbands," *West African Review* 20 (September 1949): 1009; Kunle Akinsemoyin, "Tragedy of Mixed Marriages," *West African Review* 20 (October 1949): 1125; and Rosemary Uwemedimo, *Mammy-Wagon Marriage* (London, 1961).

9. "Colonial Students, United Kingdom," *Parliamentary Debates* 484 (February 28, 1951), cols. 2063–65.

10. R. Rogers, "Students—General Welfare. Wives of Students" (CO 876/116, TNA), November 17, 1951.

11. "Students-General Welfare. Wives of Students" (CO 876/116, TNA), 1951–53.

12. "Minutes of the Central Advisory Committee on Education, Fourth Session (CO 876/221, TNA), 1951.

13. Hutt to J. Griffiths (CO 876/116, TNA), May 17, 1951.

14. "Report on Activities by Mr. J. Wilson" (IE/COL/A/2/4, IEA), 1959–60.

15. Stewart, "Courses for Overseas Women."

16. See, e.g., Cheryl Johnson-Odim and Nina Emma Mba, *For Women and the Nation: Fumilayo Ransome-Kuti of Nigeria* (Urbana, 1997).

17. Enid Gwynne, "The Wardrobe Problem: Clothes for the West African Student in Britain," *West African Review* 26 (February 1955): 185–87.

18. B. Shepherd, "Minute" (CO 876/116, TNA), April 13, 1951.

19. Robert Holman, *Trading in Children; A Study in Private Fostering* (London, 1973); Hale Gabriel Longpet, "Private Fostering of Children of West African Origin in England" (Ph.D. diss., University of Bristol, 2000). See also Precious Williams, *Color Blind: A Memoir* (New York, 2010).

20. *Times* (London), October 25, 1968.

21. *Kent Messenger*, April 10, 1964.

22. C. Duff to E. N. Oba (BN 29/1965, TNA), November 9, 1964.

23. Miss M. L. Harford, "Nigerian Students and Fostering Conditions for Their Children" (BW 3/52, TNA), March 19, 1964.

24. *Daily Mirror*, January 2, 1958, and January 7, 1958.

25. The article noted that Mrs. Wheeler had fostered 150 British and overseas children; she was fostering 14 children when this photograph was taken. "A Santa for Sandra," *West African Review* 25 (January 1954): 30–31.

26. *Evening Standard*, May 26, 1961.

27. *Times* (London), April 10, 1962.

28. R. Washbourn to Lady Reading (BW 3/52, TNA), April 16, 1964.

29. *Daily Mirror*, December 6, 1957; *Empire News*, December 1, 1957; *Daily Mirror*, January 1 and 7, 1958. One white English woman, Barbara McBride, recalled of her childhood in Lancashire in the 1950s that her white neighbors were given an award by the queen for fostering four black babies. Quoted in France Winddance Twine, *A White Side of Black Britain: Interracial Intimacy and Racial Literacy* (Durham, 2010), 107.

30. See chapter 3 in this volume.

31. "Deaths of Nigerian Children in Private Foster Homes" (BN 29/1947, TNA), 1961–66.

32. *Observer*, February 24, 1963.

33. "Confidential: Nigerian Children in Foster Homes" (BW 3/52, TNA), March 17, 1964.

34. Holman, *Trading*, 146.

35. "Some Suggestions concerning Overseas College Entrants" (BN 29/1970, TNA), April 8, 1968.

36. Kathleen Paul, *Whitewashing Britain: Race and Citizenship in the Postwar Era* (Ithaca, 1997), 175.

37. James Hampshire, *Citizenship and Belonging: Immigration and the Politics of Demographic Governance in Postwar Britain* (Houndmills, 2005), 147; Ian R. G. Spencer, *British Immigration Policy since 1939: The Making of Multi-Racial Britain* (London, 1997), 139.

38. *Times* (London), November 20, 1973.

39. Behlmer, *Friends of the Family*.

40. Longpet, "Private Fostering."

41. Holman, *Trading*, 172.

42. Olive Stevenson, *Someone Else's Child: A Book for Foster Parents of Young Children* (London, 1965), 16.

43. See, e.g., Alan Marsh, "Awareness of Racial Differences in West African and British Children," *Race* 11 (1970): 289–302. Marsh conducted his research while he was employed as a child care officer by the East Sussex County Council. This pattern typified the 1950s and 1960s, in which specialists moved easily between undertaking social work with migrants, and executing academic research about them.

44. Christina Klein, "Family Ties and Political Obligation: The Discourse on Adoption and the Cold War Commitment to Asia," in Christian G. Appy, ed., *Cold War Constructions: The Political Culture of United States Imperial-*

ism, 1945–1966 (Amherst, 2000), 35–66. See also Ann Anagnost, "Scenes of Misrecognition: Maternal Citizenship in the Age of Transnational Adoption," *positions* 8.2 (2000): 389–421; Paula S. Fass, *Kidnapped: Child Abduction in America* (New York, 1997); Fass, *Children of a New World: Society, Culture, and Globalization* (New York, 2007); Linda Gordon, *The Great Arizona Orphan Abduction* (Cambridge, MA, 2001); Ellen Herman, *Kinship by Design: A History of Adoption in the Modern United States* (Chicago, 2008); Elaine Tyler May, *Homeward Bound: American Families in the Cold War Era* (New York, 1988); Sandra Patton, *BirthMarks: Transracial Adoption in Contemporary America* (New York, 2000); and Frederick Noel Zaal, "The Ambivalence of Authority and Secret Lives of Tears: Transracial Child Placements and the Historical Development of South African Law," *Journal of Southern African Studies* 18.2 (1992): 372–404.

45. Laura Briggs, "Mother, Child, Race, Nation: The Visual Iconography of Rescue and the Politics of Transnational and Transracial Adoption," *Gender and History* 15.2 (2003): 179–200.

46. Laura Briggs, "Making 'American' Families: Transnational Adoption and U.S. Latin America Policy," in Ann Laura Stoler, ed., *Haunted by Empire: Geographies of Intimacy in North American History* (Durham, 2006), 344–65.

47. On the longer history of child "rescue" campaigns, see Misty L. Bastian, "'The Demon Superstition': Abominable Twins and Mission Culture in Onitsha History," *Ethnology* 40.1 (2001): 13–27; Behlmer, *Friends of the Family*; Buettner, *Empire Families*; Davin, "Imperialism and Motherhood"; Laurent Fourchard, "Lagos and the Invention of Juvenile Delinquency in Nigeria, 1920–60," *Journal of African History* 47.1 (2006): 115–37; Margot Hillel and Shurlee Swain, *Child, Nation, Race and Empire: Child Rescue Discourse, England, Canada, and Australia, 1850-1915* (Manchester, 2010); Margaret Jacobs, *White Mother to a Dark Race: Settler Colonialism, Maternalism, and the Removal of Indigenous Children in the American West and Australia, 1880–1940* (Lincoln, NE, 2009); Koven, *Slumming*; Jon Lawrence and Pat Starkey, eds., *Child Welfare and Social Action in the Nineteenth and Twentieth Centuries: International Perspectives* (Liverpool, 2000); Lydia Murdoch, *Imagined Orphans: Poor Families, Child Welfare, and Contested Citizenship in London* (New Brunswick, 2006); Fiona Paisley, "Childhood and Race: Growing Up in the Empire," in Philippa Levine, ed., *Gender and Empire* (Oxford, 2004): 240–59; Susan Pedersen, "The Maternalist Moment in British Colonial Policy: The Controversy over 'Child Slavery' in Hong Kong," *Past and Present* 171 (2001): 161–202; Satadru Sen, *Colonial Childhoods: The Juvenile Periphery of India, 1850–1945* (London, 2005); and Tara Zahra, "'Each Nation Only Cares for Its Own': Empire, Nation, and Child Welfare Activism in the Bohemian Lands, 1900–1918," *American Historical Review* 111.5 (December 2006): 1378–1402.

48. Graham Thomas, "The Integration of Immigrants: A Note on the Views of Some Local Government Officials," *Race* 9 (1967): 239–48.

49. Similarly, see Jim O'Connolly's film *The Little Ones* (1965).

50. "The Problems of Unsponsored Commonwealth Students" (BW 3/53,

TNA), February 27, 1961; Amechi Anumonye, *African Students in Alien Cultures* (Buffalo, NY, 1970).

51. Gifford, "General Morbidity."

52. Esther Goody, "Some Theoretical and Empirical Aspects of Parenthood in West Africa," in Christine Oppong et al., eds., *Marriage, Fertility and Parenthood in West Africa*, (Canberra, 1978), 227. On African fostering, see Caroline Bledsoe and Uche Isiugo-Abanihe, "Strategies of Child Fosterage among Mende Grannies in Sierra Leone," in Ron Lestheaghe, ed., *Reproduction and Social Organization in Sub-Saharan Africa* (Berkeley, 1989), 442–75; Caroline Bledsoe, "'No Success without Struggle': Social Mobility and Hardship for Foster Children in Sierra Leone," *Man* 25.1 (1990): 70–88; Uche C. Isiugo-Abanihe, "Child Fosterage in West Africa," *Population and Development Review* 11 (March 1985): 53–73; Mary H. Moran, "Civilized Servants: Child Fosterage and Training for Status among the Glebo of Liberia," in Hansen, ed., *African Encounters with Domesticity*, 98–115; Elisha P. Renne, "Childhood Memories and Contemporary Parenting in Ekiti, Nigeria," *Africa* 75 (March 2005): 63–83.

53. Miss D. E. Harvie, "Information Required by the Home Office about the Fostering of Nigerian Children under Private Arrangements" (BN 29/1965, TNA), 1964.

54. June Ellis, "The Fostering of West African Children in England," *Social Work Today* 2.5 (1971): 21–24; and see Barrington Kaye, *Child Training in Ghana: An Impressionistic Survey* (Legon, 1960).

55. T. Adeoye Lambo, "Characteristic Features of the Psychology of the Nigerian," *West African Medical Journal* 9 (June 1960): 95–104; Lambo, "The Vulnerable African Child," in E. James Anthony, ed., *The Child in His Family: Children at Psychiatric Risk* (New York, 1977): 259–77. See also chapter 3 in this volume.

56. Bledsoe, "'No Success without Struggle'"; Bledsoe (with contributions by Fatoumatta Banja), *Contingent Lives: Fertility, Time, and Aging in West Africa* (Chicago, 2002); D. K. Fiawoo, "Some Patterns of Foster Care in Ghana," in Christine Oppong et al., eds., *Marriage, Fertility and Parenthood*, 273–88.

57. D. E. Harvie to Patricia Allington-Smith (BW 3/52, TNA), 1964.

58. Esther Goody, "Kinship Fostering in Gonja: Deprivation or Advantage?" in Philip Mayer, ed., *Socialization: The Approach from Social Anthropology* (London, 1970): 51–74.

59. Goody, "Some Theoretical and Empirical Aspects."

60. Goody acknowledged that West African children in London were fostered at younger ages than they would have been in Africa, and that their parents (as educated elites) would have been unlikely to seek fostering arrangements at home. Rather, they would themselves have been ideal foster parents for their relatives' children. Christine Muir and Esther Goody, "Student Parents: West African Families in London," *Race* 13 (1972): 329–36.

61. Holman, *Trading;* Amina Mama, "Black Women, the Economic Crisis, and the Welfare State," *Feminist Review* 17 (1984): 21–35.

62. Pat Stapleton, "Living in Britain," in June Ellis et al., eds., *West African Families in Britain: A Meeting of Two Cultures* (London, 1978), 61.

63. Buchi Emecheta, *Second Class Citizen* (New York, 1975), 45–46.

64. Harry Hendrick, *Child Welfare: England, 1872–1989* (London, 1994), 11.

65. Nikolas Rose, *Governing the Soul: The Shaping of the Private Self* (London, 1999), 167–68.

66. John Bowlby, *Maternal Care and Mental Health* (New York, 1966); Bowlby, *Child Care and the Growth of Love* (London, 1953); Jane Lewis, "Anxieties about the Family and the Relationships between Parents, Children and the State in 20th-Century England," in Martin Richards and Paul Light, eds., *Children of Social Worlds: Development in a Social Context* (Cambridge, 1986), 31–54; Denise Riley, *War in the Nursery: Theories of the Child and Mother* (London, 1983).

67. June Ellis, "The Child in West African Society," in Ellis, ed., *West African Families,* 39–55.

68. W. N. Hyde, "Commonwealth Immigrants Advisory Council. The Effects on Immigrant Children of Being Placed in Foster Homes" (BN 29/561, TNA), June 12, 1963.

69. Miss Jones and K. Dawson, "Commonwealth Immigrants Advisory Council. Immigrant Children Placed in Foster Homes" (BN 29/561, TNA), June 12 and 28, 1963.

70. Fourchard, "Lagos."

71. Miss Beryl Watson to S. A. Gwynn (BN 29/1946, TNA), July 29, 1960.

72. "Child Protection General. Placement of Coloured Babies with Unsuitable Foster Mothers" (BN 29/1946, TNA), August 30, 1960.

73. Rose, *Governing the Soul,* 177–78.

74. Pat Starkey, "The Medical Officer of Health, the Social Worker, and the Problem Family," *Social History of Medicine* 11.3 (1998): 421–41; Starkey, "The Feckless Mother: Women, Poverty and Social Workers in Wartime and Post-War England," *Women's History Review* 9 (2000): 539–57.

75. *Daily Sketch,* March 13, 1965. See also "Tower Ibikunle" (BN 29/1966, TNA), 1965; *Daily Mirror,* January 8, 1965; *Guardian,* January 8, 1965; *Times* (London), March 9, March 13, and June 3, 1965.

76. "African Children in Private Foster Homes" (BN 29/1965, PRO), August 20, 1964.

77. D. E. Harvie, "Information Required by the Home Office about the Fostering of Nigerian Children under Private Arrangements" (BN 29/1965, TNA), 1964.

78. June Ellis, "Differing Conceptions of a Child's Needs: Some Implications of Social Work with West African Children and Their Parents," *British Journal of Social Work* 7 (1977): 155–71.

79. *Times* (London), May 8, 1969.

80. Joan Lawson, *Children in Jeopardy: The Life of a Child Care Officer* (Reading, 1965), 82.

81. The pediatrician Bruno Gans lamented that "it has become a status symbol to foster a coloured toddler." Bruno Gans, "Fostering" (HO 231/19, TNA), November 21, 1966.

82. On American mothers' critiques of child care experts, see Julia Grant, *Raising Baby by the Book: The Education of American Mothers* (New Haven, 1998).

83. "Examples of Unsatisfactory Placements" (BN 29/1946, TNA), 1957–64.

84. Miss D. E. Harvie, "Information Required by the Home Office about the Fostering of Nigerian Children under Private Arrangements" (BN 29/1965, TNA), September 1964.

85. Holman, *Trading*, 257; Abiola Ogunsola, "Meeting the Childcare Needs of West African Families," *African Woman* (autumn 1991): 10–11.

86. Animashawun, "African Students."

87. Wendy Webster, "Transnational Journeys and Domestic Histories," *Journal of Social History* 39.3 (2006): 651–66.

88. LaRay Denzer, "Domestic Science Training in Colonial Yorubaland, Nigeria," in Hansen, ed., *African Encounters with Domesticity*, 116–39; Lindsay, *Working with Gender*; T. Peter Omari, "Changing Attitudes of Students in West African Society toward Marriage and Family Relationships," *British Journal of Sociology* 11 (1960): 197–210. On the Belgian colonies, see Nancy Rose Hunt, "Domesticity and Colonialism in Belgian Africa: Usumbura's *Foyer Social*, 1946–1960," *Signs* 15.3 (1990): 447–74.

89. Ifi Amadiume, *Male Daughters, Female Husbands: Gender and Sex in an African Society* (London, 1987); Lisa A. Lindsay, "Money, Marriage, and Masculinity on the Colonial Nigerian Railway," in Lindsay and Stephan F. Miescher, eds., *Men and Masculinities in Modern Africa* (Portsmouth, NH, 2003), 138–55; Mann, *Marrying Well*; Claire Robertson, *Sharing the Same Bowl? A Socioeconomic History of Women and Class in Accra, Ghana* (Bloomington, 1984); Niara Sudarkasa, *Where Women Work: A Study of Yoruba Women in the Marketplace and in the Homes* (Ann Arbor, 1973).

90. Kenneth Little, "Attitudes towards Marriage and the Family among Educated Young Sierra Leoneans," in C. Lloyd, ed., *The New Elites of Tropical Africa* (Oxford, 1966), 139–60.

91. Pat Stapleton, "Children of Commonwealth Students—The Parents' Dilemma," *Institute of Race Relations Newsletter* (January 1969): 20–24.

92. Esther N. Goody, *Parenthood and Social Reproduction: Fostering and Occupational Roles in West Africa* (Cambridge, 1982).

93. *Observer*, February 24, 1963.

94. Kathleen Proud, correspondence (ACC/1888/222/28, LMA), August 6, 1967.

95. M. Dines, "Overseas Students and Their Families in London" (ACC/1888/399, LMA), February 1968.

96. "The Care of African Children Whose Parents Are Studying in the United Kingdom" (BW 3/52, TNA), 1964–66.

97. A.M. Kallarackal and Martin Herbert, "The Happiness of Indian Immigrant Children," *New Society* (February 26, 1976): 422–24.

98. A. Dhall, *An Introduction to Living in England for Indian and Pakistani Students and Their Wives* (Manchester, 1964).

99. J.F. Moss to E.W. Giles (HO 344/183, TNA), May 25, 1964. On Nigerian wives as another "loophole" population, see chapter 4 in this volume.

100. Rachel Scott, *A Wedding Man Is Nicer Than Cats, Miss: A Teacher at Work with Immigrant Children* (New York, 1971), 24.

101. "Bradford County Borough. Care of Children of Commonwealth Immigrants" (BN 29/2600, TNA), January–March 1969.

102. F.N. Bamford, "Children Separated from Their Families," in J.S. Dodge, *The Field Worker in Immigrant Health* (London, 1969), 94–98.

103. See, e.g., Farrukh Hashmi, *The Pakistani Family in Britain* (London, 1967).

104. Spencer, *British Immigration Policy since 1939*, 139.

105. Laurence Brown, "Afro-Caribbean Migrants in France and the United Kingdom," in Leo Lucassen, David Feldman, and Jochen Oltmer, eds., *Paths of Integration: Migrants in Western Europe, 1880–2004* (Amsterdam, 2006), 177–97.

106. Addison, *No Turning Back*.

107. R.B. Davison, *Black British: Immigrants to England* (London, 1966), 26.

108. *Times* (London), December 1, 1959.

109. George E. Sinclair, "Final Report" (HO 376/135, TNA), 1965–67.

110. *Times* (London), April 10, 1962.

111. Dorothy Watkins to D.M. Rosling (BN 29/1946, TNA), April 2, 1958.

112. J.K. Thompson to D.M. Rosling (BN 29/1946, TNA), April 22, 1958.

113. "Special Groups of Children in Care" (LCC/CH/M/46/2, LMA), 1959–62.

114. Mary Chamberlain, "Small Worlds: Childhood and Empire," *Journal of Family History* 27.2 (2002): 186–200; Chamberlain, *Family Love in the Diaspora: Migration and the Anglo-Caribbean Experience* (New Brunswick, 2006).

115. This scholarship is reviewed in Goody, *Parenthood and Social Reproduction;* see also Madeleine Kerr, *Personality and Conflict in Jamaica* (London, 1963).

116. Chamberlain, "Small Worlds."

117. Sonia Jackson, *The Illegal Child-Minders: A Report on the Growth of Unregistered Child-Minding and the West Indian Community* (Cambridge, 1972), 6.

118. Sheila Patterson, "Family and Domestic Patterns of West Indian Immigrants," *Proceedings of the Royal Society of Medicine* 57 (1964): 321–28.

119. Inspectorate Working Party on Immigrants, "Immigrants and the

Child Care Service" (MSS.378/ACCO/C/15/3/57, Modern Records Centre, Warwick), 1969.

120. Ari Kiev, "The Family and Mental Illness in Rapid Social Change Situations," in *Deuxième Colloquie Africain de Psychiatrie* (Paris, 1968), 142–49.

121. See, e.g., "Commonwealth Immigrants Child Care" (HO 361/16, TNA), June 14, 1966.

122. Nancy Foner, "Male and Female: Jamaican Migrants in London," *Anthropological Quarterly* 49.1 (1976): 28–35.

123. Violet Moody and C. Eric Stroud, "One Hundred Mothers: A Survey of West Indians in Britain," *Maternal and Child Care* 3 (June 1967): 487–90.

124. I. B. Pless and C. Hood, "West Indian One-Year Olds," *Lancet* 1 (June 24, 1967): 1373–76.

125. Jackson, *Illegal Child-Minders,* 7.

126. When West Indian women used white day-minders, childcare experts expressed concern about the minders' racism. One illegal white childminder interviewed in 1966 reported that, "the smelly black bottoms of children she minds fair make her sick." Brian Jackson, "The Childminders," *New Society* (November 29, 1973): 521–23.

127. "Happy Families of West Indians," *Times* (London), March 28, 1966.

128. Rwegellera, "Mental Illness in Africans and West Indians."

129. Moody and Stroud, "One Hundred Mothers," 489–90.

130. Michael Rutter et al., "Children of West Indian Immigrants—III. Home Circumstances and Family Patterns," *Journal of Child Psychology and Psychiatry* 15 (1974): 241–62.

131. G. Stewart Prince, "Mental Health Problems in Pre-School West Indian Children," *Maternal and Child Care* 3 (1967): 483–86. Similarly, see J. Graham and C. E. Meadows, "Psychiatric Disorder in the Children of West Indian Immigrants," *Journal of Child Psychiatry and Psychology* 8 (1967): 105–16; and Jef Smith, "The Early History of West Indian Immigrant Boys," *British Journal of Social Work* 1.1 (1971): 73–84; Rex Walcott, "The West Indian in the British Casework Setting," *Probation Journal* 14.2 (1968): 45–47; Anneliese Walker, "Social Influences on Disturbed Immigrant Children," *Case Conference* 15 (1968): 231–38.

132. See chapter 1 in this volume.

133. Royer also noted a related phenomenon among children in Indian or Pakistani families in which the father had held a high-status position in his country of origin but was reduced in Britain to menial labor. Royer theorized that the children, often under pressure to speak several languages and to achieve high levels of success, might develop anxiety, stuttering, and language problems. John Royer, *Black Britain's Dilemma: A Medico-Social Transcultural Study of West Indians,* vol. I (Roseau, 1977), 101.

134. Bruno Gans, "Experiences in a Coloured Children's Welfare Clinic," *Proceedings of the Royal Society of Medicine* 57 (1964): 327.

135. Margaret Pollak, *Today's Three-Year Olds in London* (Lavenham, 1972), 35.

136. Moody and Stroud, "One Hundred Mothers."

137. Pollak, *Today's Three-Year Olds*, 98.

138. Ibid., 142.

139. Ravinder Barn, "The Caribbean Family and the Child Welfare System in Britain," in Harry Goulbourne and Mary Chamberlain, eds., *Caribbean Families in Britain and the Trans-Atlantic World* (London, 2001), 204–18.

140. Lloyd Braithwaite, "Social and Economic Changes in the Caribbean," in *Children of the Caribbean—Their Mental Health Needs. Proceedings of the Second Caribbean Conference for Mental Health, April 10–16, 1959, Saint Thomas, Virgin Islands* (San Juan, 1961), 50–58.

141. R. B. Davison, *West Indian Migrants: Social and Economic Facts of Migration from the West Indies* (London, 1962) , 76–77.

142. K. W. Patchett, "English Law in the West Indies: A Conference Report," *International and Comparative Law Quarterly* (1963): 922–66.

143. H. J. Hudson, "The Commission in the United Kingdom for West Indies, British Guiana and British Honduras, Migrant Services Division" (LCC/CH/M/46/2, LMA), November 19, 1959; Gareth Jones, "The Legitimacy Act, 1959," *International and Comparative Law Quarterly* 8.4 (October 1959): 722–26; O. Kahn-Freund, "Legitimacy Act, 1959," *Modern Law Review* 23.1 (January 1960): 56–60; and Dominic Lasok, "Legitimation, Recognition, and Affiliation Proceedings (A Study in Comparative Law and Legal Reform)," *International and Comparative Law Quarterly* 10.1 (January 1961): 123–42.

144. See, e.g., the case of Buckeridge v. Hall in *Times* (London), December 13, 1962, and January 24, 1963.

145. "Establishment of a Legal Aid Service for West Indian Immigrants in the United Kingdom (CO 1031/4886, TNA), July 1963.

146. "Child Protection. Advertisements" (BN 29/1970, TNA), May 14, 1968.

147. "Immigrants (Foster-Homes")" *Parliamentary Debates* 695 (June 4, 1964), cols. 1226–27.

148. *Times* (London), June 4, 1966.

149. "Commonwealth Immigrants Child Care. The Ghana Trustee Society" (HO 361/16, TNA), June 14, 1966.

150. Hilda Porter to British Council (BW 3/52, TNA), March 1964.

151. *Institute of Race Relations Newsletter* (November 1964): 31–32.

152. R. S. Addis, "Private Fostering of Nigerian Children" (BN 29/1965, TNA), 1965.

153. R. Morris to K. Dawson (BN 29/1965, TNA), April 29, 1966, and reply on May 6, 1966.

154. *West African Pilot*, December 17, 1964.

155. *West African Pilot*, November 4, 1959.

156. *West African Pilot*, April 11, 1959. The original article appeared in *People*, February 22, 1959.

157. R. Washbourn, "Nigerian Children in Foster Care" (BW 3/52, TNA), October 7, 1964.

158. *Times* (London), June 4, 1966.

159. Kent County Council, "African Children in Private Foster Homes" (BN 29/1965, TNA), August 20, 1964.

160. "Confidential: Nigerian Children in Foster Homes" (BW 3/52, TNA), March 17, 1964.

161. R. J. Whittick to Miss Watson (BN 29/1946, TNA), April 12, 1962.

162. "African Babies in the U.K." (BW 3/52, TNA), November 26, 1964.

163. Amicia Carroll to C. P. Huggard (HO 361/16, TNA), February 28, 1966.

164. In 1975, the CSCS was featured in "Student Problems," a television program sponsored by the Central Office of Information. The program included interviews with a white foster mother who spoke of the joys of raising African children. It also showed African children eating ice cream and singing at Kotoko House, a building of modernized flats with daycare for African parents who wished to keep their children with them. "Student Problems" (London Line Series 497, British Film Institute, London), 1975.

165. *Guardian*, July 5, 1968.

166. B. B. Boateng, "Visit to West Africa" (ACC 1888/222/17-19, LMA), January–February 1969.

167. B. B. Boateng, "The History, Problems and Prospects of the CSCS," in Commonwealth Students' Children Society, *The African Child in Great Britain* (Ibadan, 1975), 5–7.

168. S. N. Adams, "Care of African Children" (BW 3/52, TNA), December 1, 1966.

169. June Ellis, "Conclusions," in Ellis, *West African Families*, 110.

170. Vivien Biggs, "The Realities of Private Fostering," in CSCS, *African Child*, 20–24.

171. Dr. Asante, "Medical Implication of Fostering," in CSCS, *African Child*, 15–17.

172. Ellis, "Conclusions," 115.

173. Chris Atkinson and Addie Horner, "Private Fostering—Legislation and Practice," *Adoption and Fostering* 14.3 (1990): 17–22; Anne Nesbitt and Margaret A. Lynch, "African Children in Britain," *Archives of Diseases in Childhood* 67 (1992): 1402–5; Terry Philpot, *A Very Private Practice: An Investigation into Private Fostering* (London, 2001).

174. Margaret Jervis, "Cashing In on the Hopes of Black Children," *Social Work Today* 20 (March 2, 1989): 14–15; B. Olsuanya and D. Hodes, "West African Children in Private Foster Care in City and Hackney," *Child: Care, Health, and Development* 26.4 (2000): 337–42.

175. Carol Woollard, "Private Fostering: Racial and Health Implications," *Health Visitor* 64 (October 1991): 343–44.

176. See, for example, the recent cases of Victoria Climbié and "Adam," West African children who were killed in Britain under the care of people

who were not their biological parents. Organizations in Britain, such as the Lost African Child Project, have galvanized to reunite families who have been affected by private fostering. Edwina Peart, "The Experience of Being Privately Fostered," *Adoption and Fostering* 29.3 (2005): 57–67; Philpot, *A Very Private Practice;* Todd Sanders, "The Torso in the Thames: Imagining Darkest Africa in the United Kingdom," in Anne Meneley and Donna J. Young, eds., *Auto-Ethnographies: The Anthropology of Academic Practices* (Peterborough, 2005), 126–42.

177. Patrick Butler, "Risk of Abuse in Private Fostering Arrangements," *Guardian,* November 12, 2001. See also, "Trafficking Nightmare for Nigerian Children," *BBC News,* January 10, 2001; "African Trafficking Ring Linked to UK," *BBC News,* August 7, 2003.

178. "Girls Smuggled to UK for Flats," *BBC News,* May 9, 2006.

CHAPTER 6

1. Harrison, *Seeking a Role,* 215.

2. Randall Hansen, *Citizenship and Immigration in Post-War Britain: The Institutional Origins of a Multicultural Nation* (Oxford, 2000); Colin Holmes, *John Bull's Island: Immigration and British Society, 1871–1971* (Basingstoke, 1988); Layton-Henry, *The Politics of Immigration;* Kenneth Lunn, ed., *Hosts, Immigrants and Minorities: Historical Responses to Newcomers in British Society, 1870–1914* (Folkestone, 1980); Panikos Panayi, *Immigration, Ethnicity, and Racism in Britain, 1815–1945* (Manchester, 1994); Paul, *Whitewashing Britain.*

3. I am indebted to Susan Pedersen for this point.

4. Alice Bloch and Liza Schuster, "At the Extremes of Exclusion: Deportation, Detention, and Dispersal," *Ethnic and Racial Studies* 28.3 (May 2005): 491–512.

5. I take the concept of a "politics of exit" from Nancy Green, although she focuses exclusively on voluntary emigration. Nancy L. Green, "The Politics of Exit: Reversing the Immigration Paradigm," *Journal of Modern History* 77.2 (June 2005): 263–89.

6. In some years, the Irish represented up to 72 percent of the total pool of deportees. "Statistics of Deportation" (HO 344/72, PRO), 1962–72.

7. The widely-held assumption that the riots were instigated by teddy boys, popularly imagined as antisocial, working-class adolescent thugs (visually distinguished by their drainpipe trousers and ducktail haircuts), is difficult to substantiate. The majority of the rioters were indeed teenagers—60 percent of those arrested were under twenty years old—but they often acted with their parents' tacit approval. Edward Pilkington, *Beyond the Mother Country: West Indians and the Notting Hill White Riots* (London, 1988), 129.

8. Ritscherle, "Opting Out of Utopia."

9. Pilkington, *Beyond the Mother Country,* 137.

10. Frank Mort, "Scandalous Events: Metropolitan Culture and Moral

Change in Post-Second World War London," *Representations* 93 (winter 2006): 106–37. See also Kennetta Hammond Perry, "'Little Rock' in Britain: Jim Crow's Transatlantic Topographies," *Journal of British Studies* 51.1 (2012): 155–77.

11. Michael Rowe, *The Racialisation of Disorder in Twentieth-Century Britain* (Aldershot, 1998), 123.

12. James Whitfield, *Unhappy Dialogue: The Metropolitan Police and Black Londoners* (Cullompton, 2004).

13. "Statistics of Coloured Persons Convicted of Certain Offences. Consideration of Question Whether Statistics of Crime amongst Immigrants Should Be Collected" (HO 344/160, TNA), 1961; Hampshire, *Citizenship and Belonging*, 129.

14. W.N. Hyde to John Mackay (HO 344/258, TNA), March 26, 1964; Mackay to Hyde (HO 344/258, TNA), April 3, 1964.

15. Hampshire, *Citizenship and Belonging*, 129.

16. *Times* (London), October 18, 1954.

17. *Times* (London), September 10, 1958.

18. "Coloured Persons" (MEPO 2/9991, TNA), June 18, 1959.

19. *Glasgow Herald*, October 30, 1958. This was not the first time that race riots had led to calls for expelling Britain's black population. After the race riots of 1919, the Home Office, the Colonial Office, and the Ministry of Labour coordinated a series of largely unsuccessful repatriation schemes for black residents in Britain's port cities. White wives were initially barred from accompanying the returnees. Even after a subsequent provision allowed white wives to join their repatriated husbands, the Colonial Office feared that mixed-race families might damage white prestige in colonial locales, and tried to convince the women to stay in Britain. Jacqueline Jenkinson, "The Black Community of Salford and Hull," *Immigrants and Minorities* 7.2 (1988): 166–83; Jenkinson, *Black 1919: Riots, Racism, and Resistance in Imperial Britain* (Liverpool, 2009); Michael Rowe, "Sex, 'Race' and Riot in Liverpool, 1919," *Immigrants and Minorities* 19.2 (2000): 53–70.

20. Colin Howard, "What Colour Is the Reasonable Man?" *Criminal Law Review* (1961), 47.

21. Bernard J. Brown, "The 'Ordinary Man' in Provocation: Anglo-Saxon Attitudes and 'Unreasonable Non-Englishmen,'" *International and Comparative Law Quarterly* 13 (1964): 204–35.

22. Exceptions included counterterrorist measures, such as the Prevention of Violence Act 1939, which I discuss in this chapter.

23. See, e.g., Caroline Elkins, "Race, Citizenship and Governance: Settler Tyranny and the End of Empire," in Elkins and Susan Pedersen, eds., *Settler Colonialism in the Twentieth Century: Projects, Practices, Legacies* (Routledge, 2005): 203–22.

24. "Secret Memorandum. Powers of Commonwealth Governments to Deport British Subjects" (DO 35/10420, TNA), 1955.

25. "Deportation from UK and Colonies—Re Powers for Dealing with Subversive Activities" (DO 35/4185, TNA), 1949–50.

26. "IRA Outrages: Memorandum for the Home Secretary," (HO 144/21316, TNA), June 30, 1939.

27. Ian A. Macdonald, Race Relations and Immigration Law (London, 1969), 78.

28. H. Lintott to Sir A. Clutterbuck (DO 35/7997, TNA), January 11, 1960.

29. "Binding over British Subjects to Leave the U.K." (HO 344/162, TNA), November 3, 1958; Times (London), July 31, 1958.

30. "Binding over British Subjects."

31. Pilkington, Beyond the Mother Country, 146.

32. Times (London), March 17, 1961.

33. Times (London), November 22, 1957.

34. Times (London), April 9, 1959.

35. Patricia Hornsby-Smith to "Rab" Butler (DO 35/7997, TNA), April 8, 1959; "Commonwealth Immigrants Act. Deportation" (HO 213/1713, TNA).

36. "Colonial and Commonwealth Prisoners. Deportation Bill" (HO 291/984, TNA), August 14, 1961.

37. Times (London), August 20, 1962.

38. M.J. Moriarity, "Deportation of Commonwealth Citizens. Qualifying Offenses other than Offenses Carrying a Penalty of Imprisonment" (HO 291/984, TNA), August 11, 1961.

39. M.F. Dei-Anang to A.W. Snelling (DO 35/7997, TNA), November 9, 1959.

40. J.D.B. Shaw to Sir Charles Dixon (DO 35/7997, TNA), February 5, 1960; J.M. Ross to Dixon (DO 35/7997, TNA), February 29, 1960. On overseas students and communism, see chapter 3 in this volume.

41. Times (London), September 4, 1958.

42. "Crime and the Immigrant" (HO 344/258, TNA), 1964.

43. Lintott to Clutterbuck (DO 35/7997, TNA), January 11, 1960.

44. J.M. Ross to G.W. St. J. Chadwick (DO 35/7997, TNA), November 5, 1959.

45. A. Townsend, "Confidential. Bill for Deportation of British Subjects" (MEPO 2/9773, TNA), 1958?

46. W.N. Hyde, "Deportation" (HO 291/984, TNA), September 7, 1961.

47. Daily Telegraph, June 14, 1962; Times (London), July 21, 1962.

48. "Richard Anthony Sargent" (HO 344/38, TNA), n.d.

49. "Miss Carmen Bryan. Timetable of Events" (HO 344/38, TNA), n.d. [1962?].

50. The imprisonment was unusual, because the Commonwealth Immigrants Act had given courts the authority to release potential deportees on their own recognizance.

51. E.G. Norris to L.J.D. Wakely (DO 175/90, TNA), July 23, 1962.

52. R.F. Wood, "Carmen Bryan" (HO 344/38, TNA), July 5, 1962.

53. "Deportation under Part II of the Commonwealth Immigrants Act" (HO 344/38, TNA), July 17, 1962.

54. Chamberlain, *Family Love in the Diaspora*; Foner, "Male and Female"; Harry Goulbourne and Mary Chamberlain, eds., *Caribbean Families in Britain and the Trans-Atlantic World* (London, 2001).

55. *Times* (London), July 24, 1962; *Guardian*, July 24, 1962.

56. On Brooke's other deportation cases, see Bernard Levin, *The Pendulum Years: Britain and the Sixties* (London, 1970), 174–76.

57. *Guardian*, July 20, 1962.

58. *Times* (London), July 24, 1962.

59. *People*, February 2, 1963.

60. *Times* (London), November 15, 1962. See also *Daily Herald*, July 21, 1962; *Daily Telegraph*, July 23, 1962; K. B. Paice, "Carmen Bryan" (HO 344/38, TNA), July 6, 1962; and Wood to Paice (HO 344/38, TNA), July 23, 1962.

61. Cedric Thornberry, "A Note on the Legal Position of Commonwealth Immigrants and the White Paper Proposals," *Race* 7 (October 1965): 177–84. See also *Daily Telegraph*, August 28, 1962; *Daily Mail*, September 26, 1962.

62. *Times* (London), November 15, 1962.

63. Jarvis, *Conservative Governments, Morality, and Social Change.*

64. Jill Pellew, "Law and Order: Expertise and the Victorian Home Office," in Roy Macleod, ed., *Government and Expertise: Specialists, Administrators and Professionals, 1860–1919* (Cambridge, 1988), 59–72.

65. Sir Charles Cunningham to Sir Reginald Manningham-Buller (HO 344/162, TNA), November 14, 1958.

66. Leonard M. Tomlinson, "Report on the Carmen Bryan Case" (HO 344/38, TNA), July 30, 1962. On magistrates' role in deportation cases, see also *Daily Herald*, July 21, 1962; *Times* (London), August 3, 1962; *Times* (London), August 17, 1962; *Times* (London), March 26, 1963, and the entire file, "Magistrates' Recommendation in Deportation: Role in Immigration Control" (HO 344/93, TNA), 1966–72.

67. Matthew Russell, "The Irish Delinquent in England," *Studies* 53 (1964): 136–48.

68. *Times* (London), August 15, 1962. On the unevenness of magistrates' decisions, see Matt Houlbrook, *Queer London: Perils and Pleasures in the Sexual Metropolis, 1918–1957* (Chicago, 2005).

69. Harry Street, *Freedom, the Individual, and the Law* (Harmondsworth, 1963), 270.

70. Eric Fletcher, the Labour MP, referred to this situation as a judiciary left in ignorance of the wishes of the executive. *Times* (London), August 17, 1962.

71. Colin Rickards, "How the Migrant Deportation Act Is Working," *Daily Gleaner*, February 7, 1963; see also *Times* (London), November 15, 1962.

72. *Times* (London), August 3, 1962.

73. *Birmingham Post*, March 14, 1963.

74. Rickards, "Migrant Deportation Act"; *Times* (London), July 31, 1962; *Times* (London), October 15, 1963.

75. *Times* (London), June 27, 1962.

76. *Times* (London). January 16, 1963.

77. *Daily Herald*, July 21, 1962.

78. *Daily Mail*, September 26, 1962; *Daily Telegraph*, August 28, 1962; and *Times* (London); August 11, 1962.

79. *Times* (London), August 11, 1962, and October 4, 1963.

80. *Times* (London), March 6, 1968.

81. "Deportation" (HO 344/66, TNA), 1965.

82. Mae M. Ngai, *Impossible Subjects: Illegal Aliens and the Making of Modern America* (Princeton, 2004), 1–2.

83. R v Rapier, *Criminal Law Review* 212 (1963); *Times* (London), January 16, 1963.

84. Mort, "Scandalous Events," 128.

85. Martin J. Wiener, "Homicide and 'Englishness': Criminal Justice and National Identity in Victorian England," *National Identities* 6.3 (2004): 203–13.

86. "Minutes of the 78th Central Conference of Chief Constables. Deportation of British Immigrants" (MEPO 2/9773, TNA), November 12, 1958; Home Office Circular No. 81/1962, "Commonwealth Immigrants Act, 1962" (HO 213/1713, TNA), n.d.

87. "Commonwealth Immigrants" (HO 291/984, TNA), August 22, 1961, and see *Times* (London), March 26, 1963, and October 27, 1964.

88. *Daily Mirror*, July 23, 1962. See also Derrick Sington, "The Policeman and the Immigrant," *New Society* (February 24, 1966): 13–15.

89. Theobald Matthew to J.M. Ross (HO 344/162, TNA), November 6, 1958.

90. S.J. Hobson, "Bill for Deportation of British Subjects" (MEPO 2/9773, TNA), November 4, 1958.

91. Bill Schwarz, "Black Metropolis, White England," in Mica Nava and Alan O'Shea, eds., *Modern Times: Reflections on a Century of English Modernity* (London, 1996), 175–207. See also Elizabeth Buettner, "'Would You Let Your Daughter Marry a Negro?': Race and Sex in 1950s Britain," in Philippa Levine and Susan R. Grayzel, eds., *Gender, Labour, War and Empire* (London, 2009), 219–37; Marcus Collins, "Pride and Prejudice: West Indian Men and Racial Prejudice in Mid-Twentieth-Century Britain," *Journal of British Studies* 40.3 (2001): 391–418; Ritscherle, "Opting Out of Utopia"; Waters, "'Dark Strangers'"; Webster, *Englishness and Empire*.

92. C.T.H. Morris, "Special Remission of Sentence for Prisoners to be Deported (HO 344/72, TNA), May 2, 1963.

93. Cedric Thornberry, "Law, Opinion and the Immigrant," *Modern Law Review* (1962): 654–71; and see also R.B. Davison, *Commonwealth Immigrants* (London, 1964), 76.

94. C.T.H. Morris, "Special Remission of Sentence."

95. For a fictional treatment of these issues, see Mervyn Jones, *A Set of Wives* (London, 1965).

96. George Mikes, "Address to Labour Lawyers" (Box 1, File 4, Society of Labour Lawyers Papers, London School of Economics Archives, London), November 28, 1963.

97. Sir Charles Cunningham to Sir Reginald Manningham-Buller (HO 344/162, TNA), November 14, 1958. See also Manningham-Buller's reply in "Colonial Immigrants" (LCO 2/6957, TNA), November 27, 1958.

98. Royle was co-chairman of the British Caribbean Association, an all-party organization of MPs to combat racial prejudice, and was himself a magistrate. Rickards, "Migrant Deportation Act," and see also L. M. Tomlinson, "Report on the Carmen Bryan Case" (HO 344/38, TNA), July 30, 1962.

99. "Deportation of Commonwealth Citizens under the Commonwealth Immigrants Act" (DO 175/90, TNA), 1962–63.

100. Paul, *Whitewashing Britain*, 108–10, and see also John Corbally, "The Jarring Irish: Postwar Immigration to the Heart of Empire," *Radical History Review* 104 (2009): 103–25.

101. Hansen, *Citizenship and Immigration*, 117.

102. *Times* (London), November 17 and December 4, 1961.

103. R. F. Wood, "Deportations to Ireland—General Policy" (HO 344/74, TNA), March 13, 1963.

104. "Deportation of Commonwealth Citizens under the Commonwealth Immigrants Act 1962" (DO 175/90, TNA), April 19, 1963.

105. See the contrast between the treatment of an Irish deportee, Edward McCord, and Carmen Bryan in *Daily Herald*, July 21, 1962.

106. "Deportation to Ireland—General Policy" (HO 344/74, TNA), June 28, 1966.

107. *Times* (London), December 31, 1969.

108. Central Police Office to R. F. Wood (HO 344/74, TNA), November 21, 1963.

109. "Deportation to Ireland—General Policy" (HO 344/74, TNA), March 14, 1963.

110. K. P. Paice, "Minutes" (HO 344/74, TNA), March 22, 1963.

111. "Revision of Background Note on Deportation" (HO 344/72, TNA), August 8, 1963.

112. "Memorandum on Returning Irish Deportees" (HO 344/74, TNA), n.d.

113. A. E. Bottoms, "Delinquency amongst Immigrants," *Race* 8 (April 1967): 357–83; F. H. McClintock, *Crimes of Violence: An Enquiry by the Cambridge Institute of Criminology into Crimes of Violence Against the Person in London* (London, 1963); T. E. St. Johnston, County Police H.Q., Lancashire, to R. F. Wood (HO 344/74, TNA), November 14, 1963.

114. R. F. Wood to Morris (HO 344/72, TNA), October 2, 1963.

115. Paul Michael Garrett, "The Hidden History of the PFIs: The Repatriation of Unmarried Mothers and Their Children from England to Ireland in

the 1950s and 1960s," *Immigrants and Minorities* 19 (2000): 25–44; Garrett, "The Abnormal Flight: The Migration and Repatriation of Irish Unmarried Mothers," *Social History* 25 (2000): 330–44.

116. Bottoms, "Delinquency amongst Immigrants."

117. John R. Lambert, *Crime, Police, and Race Relations: A Study in Birmingham* (London, 1970), 54.

118. McClintock, *Crimes of Violence*, 126.

119. Laura K. Donohue, *Counter-Terrorist Law and Emergency Powers in the United Kingdom, 1922–2000* (Dublin, 2001); Charles Townshend, *Making the Peace: Public Order and Public Security in Modern Britain* (Oxford, 2003).

120. "Prevention of Violence (Temporary Provisions) Bill" (HO 144/21316, TNA), 1939.

121. Donohue, *Counter-Terrorist Law*, 208–9.

122. Irish entrants could not obtain ration books if they had not registered with the police, so it was difficult (though not impossible) for them to evade detection. Michael Hassett, "The British Government's Response to Irish Terrorism, c. 1867–c. 1979" (Ph.D. thesis, Open University, 2007).

123. "James Pierce McGuiness" (HO 144/22146, TNA), 1939.

124. James McGuiness to Home Office (HO 144/22146), March 20, 1945.

125. Brendan Behan, *Borstal Boy* (New York, 1959); Behan, *Confessions of an Irish Rebel* (London, 1965).

126. Colin Holmes, "The British Government and Brendan Behan, 1941–1954: The Persistence of the Prevention of Violence Act," *Saothar* 14 (1989): 125–28.

127. *Times* (London), July 31, 1939.

128. Enda Delaney, "'Almost a Class of Helots in an Alien Land': The British State and Irish Immigration, 1921–45," *Immigrants and Minorities* 18 (1999): 240–65.

129. "Copy of Report by the Secretary of State as to the Expulsion, Registration, and Prohibition Orders Made under the Act" (Prevention of Violence [Temporary Provisions] Act 1939 papers, House of Lords Record Office, London), 1939–54.

130. The act was formally repealed in 1973.

131. "Question of the Inclusion of the Prevention of Violence (Temporary Provisions) Act 1939. Expiring Laws Continuance Bill, 1954" (HO 45/25530, TNA), 1954.

132. *Times* (London), October 18, 1954.

133. *Times* (London), June 14, 1954.

134. *Times* (London), October 18 and December 16, 1954.

135. See, e.g., "Michael Fleming (Preston)—Subject of a Prohibition Order under the Prevention of Violence Act, 1939" (HO 45/25531, TNA), 1954.

136. F. A. K. Harrison to L. B. Walsh-Atkins (HO 45/25530, TNA), January 14, 1956.

137. Quoted in "Immigration Bill: Deportation of Irish Citizens" (HO 394/5, TNA), February 8, 1971.

138. See, e.g., F. A. K. Harrison to Le Tocq, Commonwealth Relations Office (HO 45/25530, TNA), January 3, 1956.

139. "The Expiring Laws Continuance Bill" (HO 45/25530, TNA), October 22, 1952.

140. J. M. Ross to A. W. Snelling (DO 35/7997, TNA), October 31, 1958.

141. Russell, "Irish Delinquent."

142. Bottoms, "Delinquency amongst Immigrants": Russell, "Irish Delinquent."

143. Samuel Hoare, "IRA Outrages. Memorandum by the Home Sec'y" (HO 144/21316, TNA), June 30, 1939.

144. On the relationship between ordinary crime and terrorism in Ireland, see John D. Brewer, Bill Lockhart, and Paula Rodgers, *Crime in Ireland, 1945–95: 'Here Be Dragons'* (Oxford, 1997).

145. "Deportation of Commonwealth Citizens under the Commonwealth Immigrants Act" (DO 175/90, TNA), 1962–63.

146. Paul, *Whitewashing Britain*, 109.

147. "Statistics of Deportation" (HO 344/72, TNA), 1963–71.

148. "Deportation without the Recommendation of a Court" (HO 344/79, TNA), 1965?

149. "Revision of Background Note on Deportation" (HO 344/72, TNA), 1972.

150. The Home Secretary was also empowered to expel the deportee's dependents. *Times* (London), January 7, 1971.

151. "Minutes of Evidence Taken before the Committee on Race Relations and Immigration" (HO 376/159, TNA), December 12, 1968.

152. In the first year of the 1988 Immigrants Act, the official deportation figures rose by 50 percent. "Tough Deportation Regime for Immigrants Angers Lawyers," *New Law Journal* 139 (May 12, 1989): 634–35.

153. "Unobjectionable," that is, only in terms of the Home Office's perspective. The 1980s also saw the mobilization of anti-racism campaigns specifically around the issue of opposing deportation. The West Midlands Anti-Deportation Campaign and the Hackney Anti-Deportation Campaign focused on high-profile deportation cases as a way of protesting Conservative immigration laws: a recoupling of the politics of entry and exit.

CONCLUSION

1. Perham was reader in Colonial Administration at Oxford, and, from 1945 to 1948, director of the Oxford Institute of Colonial Studies. Perham, *Colonial Reckoning*, 198.

2. Robert Holland, Susan Williams, and Terry Barringer, preface to Holland et al., *The Iconography of Independence: 'Freedoms at Midnight'* (London, 2010), ix–xix; David Cannadine, "Introduction: Independence Day Ceremonials in Historical Perspective," in Holland et al., eds. *Iconography of Independence*, 1–17.

3. Huxley, *Four Guineas*, 140–41. Perham and Huxley carried on a contentious correspondence about British settlers in Kenya: *Race and Politics in Kenya: A Correspondence between Elspeth Huxley and Margery Perham* (London, 1956); Wendy Webster, "Elspeth Huxley: Gender, Empire, and Narratives of Nation, 1935–64," *Women's History Review* 8.3 (1999): 527–45.

4. Cannadine, "Introduction."

5. Robert Graham, "Memories of Independence 1960," in Ronnie Anderson, ed., *Palm Wine and Leopard's Whiskers: Reminiscences of Eastern Nigeria* (Otago, 1999), 410.

6. Andrew Stuart, *Of Cargoes Colonies and Kings: Diplomatic and Administrative Service from Africa to the Pacific* (London, 2001), 59.

7. Vivienne Bell, *Blown by the Wind of Change* (Sussex, 1986), 111–12 and 117.

8. Dominic Sandbrook, *Never Had It So Good: A History of Britain from the Suez to the Beatles* (London, 2005), 288–89.

9. Stuart, *Cargoes*, 62–63.

10. *Ceremonial Man* and its sequel, *Ceremonial Man—Retired* (1973), were both shown on the BBC television series *Man Alive*.

11. Quoted in Charles Allen, ed., *Tales from the Dark Continent* (New York, 1979), 149.

12. Sandbrook, *Never Had It So Good*, 288–89.

13. See, e.g., Nadine Peppard, "Into the Third Decade," *New Community* 1.2 (1972): 93–98; A Sivanandan, *A Different Hunger: Writings on Black Resistance* (London, 1982); Sivanandan, *Communities of Resistance: Writings on Black Struggles for Socialism* (London, 1990).

14. Sara Ahmed, *Embodied Others in Post-Coloniality* (London, 2000); Waters, "'Dark Strangers.'"

15. Sara Ahmed, "Multiculturalism and the Problem of Happiness," *New Formations* 63 (2008): 121–37; Paul Gilroy, *After Empire: Melancholia or Convivial Culture* (London, 2004).

Bibliography

ARCHIVES CONSULTED

British Film Institute, London
House of Lords Record Office, London
India Office Records, British Library, London
Institute of Education Archives, London
Kenneth Little Papers, Special Collections, Edinburgh University Library
London Metropolitan Archives
London School of Economics Archives
Modern Records Centre, University of Warwick
National Archives, Kew
Nottinghamshire Archives
Royal Institute of International Affairs, Chatham House, London
Wellcome Archives and Manuscripts, Wellcome Library, London

WORKS CITED

Abrahams, Peter. *A Wreath for Udomo.* London: Faber and Faber, 1956.
Abrams, Philip. "Age and Generation." In *A Sociological Portrait,* ed. Paul Barker. London: Penguin, 1972, 99–111.
———, ed. *The Origins of British Sociology, 1834–1914.* Chicago: University of Chicago Press, 1968.
Adams, Michael. *Voluntary Service Overseas: The Story of the First Ten Years.* London: Faber, 1968.
Addison, Paul. *No Turning Back: The Peacetime Revolutions of Post-War Britain.* Oxford: Oxford University Press 2010.
Adi, Hakim. "West African Students in Britain, 1900–1960: The Politics of Exile." In *Africans in Britain,* ed. David Killingray. London: Frank Cass, 1994, 107–28.
———. "West Africans and the Communist Party in the 1950s." In *Opening the*

Books: Essays on the Social and Cultural History of British Communism, ed. Geoff Andrews et al. London: Pluto Press, 1995, 176–94.

———. *West Africans in Britain, 1900–1960: Nationalism, Pan-Africanism and Communism.* London: Lawrence and Wishart, 1998.

African Students in the United States: A Handbook of Information and Orientation. New York: s.n., 1957.

Aguilar, Mario I. "Gerontocratic, Aesthetic, and Political Models of Age." In *The Politics of Age and Gerontocracy in Africa: Ethnographies of the Past and Memories of the Present,* ed. Mario I. Aguilar. Trenton, NJ: Africa World Press, 1998, 3–29.

———. "Introduction. The Present and Past of Age Notions: The *Status Quaestionis* within Historical Anthropology." In *Rethinking Age in Africa: Colonial, Post-Colonial and Contemporary Interpretations of Cultural Representations,* ed. Mario I. Aguilar. Trenton, NJ: Africa World Press, 2007, 1–7.

Ahmed, Sara. "Multiculturalism and the Problem of Happiness." *New Formations* 63 (2008): 121–37.

———. *Strange Encounters: Embodied Others in Post-Coloniality.* London: Routledge, 2000.

Ajose, A. "I Lived with the People of Britain." *West African Review* 18 (April 1947): 417–20.

Akinsemoyin, Kunle. "Tragedy of Mixed Marriages." *West African Review* 20 (October 1949): 1125.

———. "An Undergraduate in Glasgow," *West African Review* 20 (September 1949): 1005–7.

Akiwowo, Akinsola A. "The Sociology of Nigerian Tribalism?" *Phylon* 25.2 (1964): 155–63.

Allen, Charles, ed. *Tales from the Dark Continent.* New York: St. Martin's Press, 1979.

Ali, Iftikhar. "Effects of Cultural Attitudes on the Adjustment of Pakistani Students in Britain." M.A. thesis, Bedford College, University of London, 1963.

Amadiume, Ifi. *Male Daughters, Female Husbands: Gender and Sex in an African Society.* London: Zed Books, 1987.

Anagnost, Ann. "Scenes of Misrecognition: Maternal Citizenship in the Age of Transnational Adoption." *positions* 8.2 (2000): 389–421.

Anderson, David. *Histories of the Hanged: The Dirty War in Kenya and the End of Empire.* New York: Norton, 2005.

———. "Mau Mau in the High Court and the 'Lost' British Empire Archives: Colonial Conspiracy or Bureaucratic Bungle?" *Journal of Imperial and Commonwealth History* 39.5 (2011): 699–716.

Anderson, David, et al. "A Very British Massacre," *History Today* 56.8 (2006): 20–22.

Anderson, Michael. "Emergence of the Modern Life Cycle in Britain." *Social History* 10.1 (1985): 69–87.

Anderson, Warwick. *The Collectors of Lost Souls: Turning Kuru Scientists into Whitemen*. Baltimore: Johns Hopkins University Press, 2008.

Anderson, Warwick, and Gabrielle Hecht, eds. "Postcolonial Technoscience," *Social Studies of Science* 32 (2002).

Animashawun, G. K. "African Students in Britain." *Race* 5 (July 1963): 38–47.

Annan, Noel *Our Age: Portrait of a Generation*. London: Weidenfeld and Nicolson, 1990.

Anumonye, Amechi. *African Students in Alien Cultures*. Buffalo: Black Academy Press, 1970.

———. *Brain-Fag Syndrome*. Lausanne: International Council on Alcohol and Addictions, 1982?

———. *Nigerian Students and Emotional Reactions in Our Space-Age Universities*. Lagos: University of Lagos, 1975.

———. "Psychological Stresses among African Students in Britain." *Scottish Medical Journal* 12 (1967).

Appleyard, R. T. *British Emigration to Australia*. Toronto: University of Toronto Press 1964.

———. "The Return Movement of United Kingdom Migrants from Australia." *Population Studies* 15.3 (1962): 214–55.

———. "Socio-Economic Determinants of British Emigration from the United Kingdom to Australia." In *The Study of Immigrants in Australia*, ed. C. A. Price. Canberra: Department of Demography, Australian National University, 1960, 25–32.

Appleyard R. T., with Alison Ray and Allan Segal. *The Ten Pound Immigrants*. London: Boxtree, 1988.

Ariès, Philippe. *Centuries of Childhood: A Social History of Family Life*. New York: Knopf, 1962.

Arondekar, Anjali *For the Record: On Sexuality and the Colonial Archive in India*. Durham, NC: Duke University Press, 2009.

Asad, Talal. *Anthropology and the Colonial Encounter*. London, 1973.

Asante, Dr. "Medical Implications of Fostering." In *The African Child in Great Britain*, ed. Commonwealth Students' Children's Society. Ibadan: Department of Sociology, University of Ibadan, 1976, 15–17.

Ash, Eric H. "Expertise and the Early Modern State." *Osiris* 25 (2010): 1–24.

———. *Power, Knowledge and Expertise in Elizabethan England*. Baltimore: Johns Hopkins University Press, 2004.

Assayag, Jackie, and Véronique Bénéï, eds. *At Home in Diaspora: South Asian Scholars and the West*. Bloomington, IN: Indiana University Press, 2003.

Asuni, T. "Review of Nigerian Students Repatriated on Psychiatric Grounds," *West African Medical Journal* 17 (1968): 3–7.

Atkinson, Chris, and Addie Horner. "Private Fostering—Legislation and Practice." *Adoption and Fostering* 14.3 (1990): 17–22.

Babb, Sarah. *Managing Mexico: Economists from Nationalism to Neoliberalism*. Princeton, NJ: Princeton University Press, 2001.

Baer, Kenneth L. "African Students in the East and West, 1959–1966: An

Analysis of Experiences and Attitudes." *Occasional Paper #54, Program of Eastern African Studies* (July 1970).

Bagley, Christopher. "Mental Illness in Immigrant Minorities in London." *Journal of Biosocial Science* 3 (1971): 449–59.

——. "Race, Migration, and Mental Health: A Review of Some Recent Research." *Race* 9 (1968): 343–56.

——. "Sequels of Alienation: West Indian Migrants in Britain." In *Case Studies on Human Rights and Fundamental Freedoms: A World Survey*, vol. 2, ed. Willem A. Veenhoven. The Hague: Nijhoff, 1975, 55–81.

——. "The Social Aetiology of Schizophrenia in Immigrant Groups." *International Journal of Social Psychiatry* 17 (1971): 292–304.

Ball, Terence. "The Politics of Social Science in Postwar America." In *Recasting America: Culture and Politics in the Age of Cold War*, ed. Lary May. Chicago: University of Chicago Press, 1989, 76–92.

Ballantyne, Tony, and Antoinette Burton, eds. *Moving Subjects: Gender, Mobility, and Intimacy in an Age of Global Empire.* Urbana: University of Illinois Press, 2009.

Ballard, Roger. "Ethnic Diversity and the Delivery of Justice: The Challenge of Plurality." In *Migration, Diasporas and Legal Systems in Europe*, ed. Werner Menski and Prakash Shah. London: Routledge-Cavendish, 2006, 29–56.

Bamford, F. N. "Children Separated from Their Families." In *The Field Worker in Immigrant Health*, ed. J. S. Dodge. London: Staples, 1969, 94–98.

Banham, Martin. "The Nigerian Student in Britain." *Universities Quarterly* 12 (1958): 363–66.

Banton, Michael. "Adaptation and Integration in the Social System of Temne Immigrants in Freetown." *Africa* 26.4 (1956): 354–68.

——. "Anthropological Perspectives on Sociology." *British Journal of Sociology* 15.2 (1964): 95–112.

——. "The Changing Position of the Negro in Britain." *Phylon* 14 (1953): 74–83.

——. "Kenneth Lindsay Little." *Anthropology Today* 7.3 (June 1991): 19–21.

——. "The Influence of Colonial Status upon Black-White Relations in England, 1948–58." *Sociology* 17.4 (November 1983): 546–669.

——. "Negro Workers in Britain." *Twentieth Century* 151 (1952): 40–45.

——. "1960: A Turning Point in the Study of Race Relations," *Daedalus* 103.2 (1974): 31–44.

——. "Questions and Answers: Further Reflections upon My Intellectual Career," Unpublished paper, 2008.

——. "The Restructuring of Social Relationships." In *Social Change in Modern Africa. Studies Presented and Discussed at the First International African Seminar, Makerere College, Kampala, January 1959*, ed. Aidan Southall. London: International African Institute, 1961, 113–25.

——. "The Social Groupings of Some West African Workers in Britain." *Man* 53 (1953): 130–33.

——. "Sociology and Race Relations." *Race* 1.1 (November 1959): 3–14.

——. *West African City: A Study of Tribal Life in Freetown.* London: International African Institute, 1957.

——. "What the Study of Migration Might Contribute to the Study of Community." *International Journal of Social Research Methodology* 11.2 (2008): 117–20.

——. *White and Coloured: The Behaviour of British People towards Coloured Immigrants.* London: J. Cape, 1959.

"The Baralong Marriage." *Cape Law Journal* 5 (1888): 182–89.

Barn, Ravinder. "The Caribbean Family and the Child Welfare System in Britain." In *Caribbean Families in Britain and the Trans-Atlantic World,* ed. Harry Goulbourne and Mary Chamberlain. London: Caribbean, 2001, 204–18.

Barot, Rohit. "Reflections on Michael Banton's Contribution to Race and Ethnic Studies." *Ethnic and Racial Studies* 29.5 (2006): 785–96.

Barshay, Andrew. The *Social Science in Modern Japan: The Marxian and Modernist Traditions.* Berkeley: University of California Press, 2004.

Bassett, Ross. "MIT-Trained Swadeshis: MIT and Indian Nationalism, 1880–1947." *Osiris* 24 (2009): 212–30.

Bastian, Misty L. "'The Demon Superstition': Abominable Twins and Mission Culture in Onitsha History." *Ethnology* 40.1 (2001): 13–27.

Bawden, Nina. *Under the Skin.* New York: Harper and Row, 1964.

Beach, Abigail. "Forging a 'Nation of Participants': Political and Economic Planning in Labour's Britain." In *The Right to Belong: Citizenship and National Identity in Britain, 1930–1960,* ed. Richard Weight and Abigail Beach. London: I. B. Tauris, 1998, 89–115.

Behan, Brendan. *Borstal Boy.* New York: Knopf, 1959.

——. *Confessions of an Irish Rebel.* London: Hutchinson, 1965.

Behlmer, George. *Friends of the Family: The English Homes and Its Guardians, 1850–1940.* Stanford, CA: Stanford University Press, 1998.

Bell, Leland V. *Mental and Social Disorder in Sub-Saharan Africa: The Case of Sierra Leone, 1787–1990.* Westport, CT: Greenwood, 1991.

Bell, Vivienne. *Blown by the Wind of Change.* Sussex: Book Guild, 1986.

Benton, Lauren A. *Law and Colonial Cultures: Legal Regimes in World History, 1400–1900.* Cambridge: Cambridge University Press, 2002.

Bernstein, Michael, and Allen Hunter. "The Cold War and Expert Knowledge: New Essays on the History of the National Security State." *Radical History Review* 63 (1995): 52–85.

Bevir, Mark. "Rethinking Governmentality: Towards Genealogies of Governance." *European Journal of Social Theory* 13 (2010): 423–41.

Bhatnagar, J. K. "The Values and Attitudes of Some Indian and British Students." *Race* 9 (July 1967): 27–36.

Bickers, Robert, ed. *Settlers and Expatriates: Britons Over the Seas.* Oxford: Oxford University Press, 2010.

Biggs, Vivien. "The Realities of Private Fostering." In *The African Child in*

Great Britain, ed. Commonwealth Students' Children's Society. Ibadan: Department of Sociology, University of Ibadan, 1976, 20–24.

Bird, Dick. *Never the Same Again: A History of the VSO*. Cambridge: Lutterworth, 1998.

Black, Lawrence."The Lost World of Young Conservatism." *Historical Journal* 51.4 (December 2008): 991–1024.

Bledsoe, Caroline H. (with contributions by Fatoumatta Banja). *Contingent Lives: Fertility, Time, and Aging in West Africa*. Chicago: University of Chicago Press, 2002.

Bledsoe, Caroline, and Uche Isiugo-Abanihe. "'No Success without Struggle': Social Mobility and Hardship for Foster Children in Sierra Leone." *Man* 25.1 (1990): 70–88.

———. "Strategies of Child Fosterage among Mende Grannies in Sierra Leone." In *Reproduction and Social Organization in Sub-Saharan Africa*, ed. Ron Lestheaghe. Berkeley: University of California Press, 1989, 442–75.

Bloch, Alice, and Liza Schuster. "At the Extremes of Exclusion: Deportation, Detention, and Dispersal." *Ethnic and Racial Studies* 28.3 (May 2005): 491–512.

Boateng, B.B. "The History, Problems and Prospects of the CSCS." in Commonwealth Students' Children Society, *The African Child in Great Britain* (Ibadan: Department of Sociology, University of Ibadan, 1975), 5–7.

Boone, Troy. *Youth of Darkest England: Working-Class Children at the Heart of Victorian Empire*. London: Routledge, 2005.

Borstelmann, Thomas. *The Cold War and the Color Line: American Race Relations in the Global Arena*. Cambridge, MA: Harvard University Press, 2001.

Bottoms, A.E. "Delinquency amongst Immigrants," *Race* 8 (April 1967): 357–83.

Bourne, Jenny, with A. Sivanandan. "Cheerleaders and Ombudsmen: The Sociology of Race Relations in Britain." *Race and Class* 21.4 (1980): 331–52.

Bowlby, John. *Child Care and the Growth of Love*. London: Penguin, 1953.

———. *Maternal Care and Mental Health*. New York: Schocken, 1966.

Boyce, D. George. *Decolonisation and the British Empire, 1775–1997*. Houndmills: Macmillan, 1999.

Bracken, Patrick, et al. "Mental Health and Ethnicity: An Irish Dimension." *British Journal of Psychiatry* 172 (1998): 103–5.

Braithwaite, Lloyd. "Social and Economic Changes in the Caribbean." In *Children of the Caribbean—Their Mental Health Needs. Proceedings of the Second Caribbean Conference for Mental Health, April 10–16, 1959, Saint Thomas, Virgin Islands*. San Juan: Treasury Dept., 1961, 50–58.

Branch, Daniel. "The Airlift: African Students Overseas in the Era of Decolonization." Talk delivered at the National History Center, Washington, DC, 2010.

———. *Defeating Mau Mau, Creating Kenya: Counterinsurgency, Civil War, and Decolonization*. Cambridge: Cambridge University Press, 2009.

Brewer, John D., Bill Lockhart, and Paula Rodgers. *Crime in Ireland, 1945–95: 'Here Be Dragons.'* Oxford: Clarendon, 1997.

Briggs, Laura. "Making 'American' Families: Transnational Adoption and U.S. Latin America Policy," In *Haunted by Empire: Geographies of Intimacy in North American History,* ed. Ann Laura Stoler. Durham, NC: Duke University Press, 2006, 344–65.

———. "Mother, Child, Race, Nation: The Visual Iconography of Rescue and the Politics of Transnational and Transracial Adoption." *Gender and History* 15.2 (2003): 179–200.

British Council. *How to Live in Britain: A Handbook for Students from Overseas.* London: The Council, 1952.

Brooke, Stephen. "Twentieth-Century British History: New Directions in Researching and Teaching the Field," Roundtable at the North American Conference on British Studies, Baltimore, 2010.

Brown, Bernard J. "The 'Ordinary Man' in Provocation: Anglo-Saxon Attitudes and 'Unreasonable Non-Englishmen." *International and Comparative Law Quarterly* 13 (1964): 204–35.

Brown, F. H. "Indian Students in Britain." *Edinburgh Review* 217 (1913): 136–56.

Brown, Laurence. "Afro-Caribbean Migrants in France and the United Kingdom." In *Paths of Integration: Migrants in Western Europe, 1880–2004,* ed. Leo Lucassen, David Feldman, and Jochen Oltmer. Amsterdam: Amsterdam University Press, 2006, 177–97.

Brown, L. B. "Applicants for Assisted Migration from the United Kingdom to New Zealand." *Population Studies* 11 (1957): 86–91.

———. "The Differential Job Satisfaction of English Migrants and New Zealanders." *Occupational Psychology* 33 (1959): 54–58.

———. "English Migrants to New Zealand: A Pilot Rorschach Study." *Australian Journal of Psychology* 8 (1956): 106–10.

———. "English Migrants to New Zealand: The Decision to Move." *Human Relations* 13 (1960): 167–74.

———. "Some Psychological Characteristics of Applicants for Assisted Migration to New Zealand." Ph.D. thesis, University of London, 1954.

Bu, Liping. *Making the World Like Us: Education, Cultural Expansion and the American Century.* Westport, CT: Praeger, 2003.

Buettner, Elizabeth. *Empire Families: Britons and Late Imperial India.* Oxford: Oxford University Press, 2004.

———. "'Would You Let Your Daughter Marry a Negro?': Race and Sex in 1950s Britain." In *Gender, Labour, War and Empire: Essays on Modern Britain,* ed. Philippa Levine and Susan R. Grayzel. London: Palgrave Macmillan, 2009, 219–37.

Bullard, Alice. "Imperial Networks and Postcolonial Independence: The Transition from Colonial to Transcultural Psychiatry." In *Psychiatry and Empire,* ed. Sloan Mahone and Megan Vaughan. Houndmills: Palgrave Macmillan, 2007, 197–19.

Bulmer, Martin. "Edward Shils as a Sociologist." *Minerva* 34 (1996): 7–21.
——. "Sociology in Britain in the Twentieth Century: Differentiation and Establishment." In *British Sociology Seen from Without and Within*, ed. A. H. Halsey and W. G. Runciman. Oxford: Oxford University Press for the British Academy, 2005, 36–53.
——, ed. *Essays on the History of British Sociological Research*. Cambridge: Cambridge University Press, 1985.
Burbank, Jane, and Frederick Cooper. *Empires in World History: Power and the Politics of Difference*. Princeton, NJ: Princeton University Press, 2010.
Burgess, J. N. "With the Migrants in Europe." *Medical Journal of Australia* 39.2 (September 27, 1952): 438–39.
Burk, Kathleen, ed. *The British Isles since 1945*. Oxford: Oxford University Press, 2003.
Burke, Aggrey W. "Attempted Suicide among Asian Immigrants in Birmingham." *British Journal of Psychiatry* 128 (1976): 528–33.
——. "Attempted Suicide among Irish-Born Population in Birmingham." *British Journal of Psychiatry* 128 (1976): 534–37.
——. "The Consequences of Unplanned Repatriation." *British Journal of Psychiatry* 123 (1973): 109–11.
——. "Epidemiological Aspects of Repatriate Syndrome." *International Journal of Social Psychiatry* 28 (1982): 291–99.
——. "Socio-Cultural Determinants of Attempted Suicide among West Indians in Birmingham: Ethnic Origin and Immigrant Status." *British Journal of Psychiatry* 129 (1976): 261–66.
Burrell, Kathy, and Panikos Panayi, eds. *Histories and Memories: Migrants and Their History in Britain*. London: Tauris, 2006.
Burrowes, H. P. "The Migrant and Mental Health." In *The Field Worker in Immigrant Health*, ed. J. S. Dodge. London: Staples, 1969, 71–76.
Burton, Andrew. "Urchins, Loafers and the Cult of the Cowboy: Urbanization and Delinquency in Dar Es Salaam, 1919–61." *Journal of African History* 42.2 (2001): 199–216.
Burton, Antoinette. *At the Heart of the Empire: Indians and the Colonial Encounter in Late-Victorian Britain*. Berkeley: University of California Press, 1998.
——. *Burdens of History: British Feminists, Indian Women, and Imperial Culture, 1865–1915*. Chapel Hill: University of North Carolina Press, 1994.
——. "Cold War Cosmopolitanism: The Education of Santha Rama Rau in the Age of Bandung, 1945–1954." *Radical History Review* 95 (spring 2006): 149–72.
——. *Dwelling in the Archive: Women Writing House, Home, and History in Late Colonial India*. Oxford: Oxford University Press, 2003.
——. "From Child Bride to 'Hindoo Lady': Rukhmabai and the Debate on Sexual Respectability in Imperial Britain." *American Historical Review* 103.4 (October 1998): 1119–46.

———. *The Postcolonial Careers of Santha Rama Rau*. Durham, NC: Duke University Press, 2007.

———. "When Was Britain? Nostalgia for the Nation at the End of the American Century." *Journal of Modern History* 75.2 (2003): 359–75.

———. "Who Needs the Nation? Interrogating 'British' History." *Journal of Historical Sociology* 10.3 (1997): 227–48.

———, ed. *Archive Stories: Facts, Fiction, and the Writing of History*. Durham, NC: Duke University Press, 2005.

Byfield, Judith. "Women, Marriage, Divorce and the Emerging Colonial State in Abeokuta (Nigeria), 1892–1904." *Canadian Journal of African Studies* 30.1 (1996): 32–51.

Carey, A.T. *Colonial Students: A Study of the Social Adaptation of Colonial Students in London*. London: Secker and Warburg, 1956.

———. "Malayan Students in Britain." *Eastern World* 8 (1954): 36–37.

Cade, J.F.J., and J. Krupinski. "Incidence of Psychiatric Disorders in Victoria in Relation to Country of Birth." *Medical Journal of Australia* 1 (March 17, 1962): 400–404.

Caine, Barbara. "Writing Cosmopolitan Lives: Joseph and Kwame Anthony Appiah." *History Workshop Journal* 70.1 (2010): 152–71.

Cannadine, David. "Introduction: Independence Day Ceremonials in Historical Perspective." In *The Iconography of Independence: 'Freedoms at Midnight,'* ed. Robert Holland et al. London: Routledge, 2010, 1–17.

———. *Ornamentalism: How the British Saw Their Empire*. London: Allen Lane, 2001.

Cannadine, David, et al. *Review of the Thirty Year Rule*. London, 2009. The full text is available at http://www2.nationalarchives.gov.uk/30yrr/30-year-rule-report.pdf.

"Career Women of West Africa." *West African Review* 26 (April 1955): 290–96.

Carothers, J.C. *The Psychology of the Mau Mau*. Nairobi: Government Printer, 1955.

———. "A Study of Mental Derangement in Africans." *Journal of Mental Science* (1947): 548–97.

Carpenter, L., and I.F. Brockington. "A Study of Mental Illness in Asians, West Indians, and Africans Living in Manchester." *British Journal of Psychiatry* 137 (1980): 201–5.

Catterall, Peter. Preface to *British Government Policy and Decolonisation 1945–1963: Scrutinising the Official Mind*, by Frank Heinlein. London: Frank Cass, 2002, ix–x.

Chakrabarty, Dipesh. *Provincializing Europe: Postcolonial Thought and Historical Difference*. Princeton, NJ: Princeton University Press, 2000.

Chamberlain, Mary. *Family Love in the Diaspora: Migration and the Anglo-Caribbean Experience*. New Brunswick, NJ: Transaction, 2006.

———. "Small Worlds: Childhood and Empire," *Journal of Family History* 27.2 (2002): 186–200.

Cheal, David. "Intergenerational Transfers and Life Course Management." In

Rethinking the Life Cycle, ed. Alan Bryman et al. Basingstoke: Macmillan, 1987, 141–54.

Chettur, G.K. *The Last Enchantment: Recollections of Oxford.* Mangalore: The B.M. Bookshop, 1934.

Chio, Nathan. "They Are Colonising Us Now 15 Miles from Downing Street: Re-Assessing the Post-Coloniality of Post-War Britain." Paper delivered at the Pacific Coast Conference on British Studies, Seattle, 2011.

Chomsky, Noam, et al. *The Cold War and the University: Toward An Intellectual History of the Postwar Years.* New York: W.W. Norton, 1997.

Choudry, P.M. *British Experiences.* Calcutta: Shorne, 1889.

Chudacoff, Howard P. *How Old Are You? Age Consciousness in American Culture.* Princeton, NJ: Princeton University Press, 1989.

Clapson, Mark. "The American Contribution to the Urban Sociology of Race Relations in Britain from the 1940s to the Early 1970s." *Urban History* 33.2 (2006): 253–73.

Clare, Anthony W. "Mental Illness in the Irish Emigrant." *Journal of the Irish Medical Association* 67 (January 12, 1974): 20–24.

Cochrane, R. "Mental Illness in Immigrants to England and Wales: An Analysis of Mental Hospital Admissions, 1971." *Social Psychiatry* 12 (1977): 25–35.

Coelho, George. *Changing Images of America: A Study of Indian Students' Perceptions.* Glencoe, IL: Free Press, 1958.

Cohen, Deborah. *Family Secrets.* Oxford: Oxford University Press, 2013.

Cohen, Lawrence. *No Aging in India: Alzheimer's, the Bad Family, and Other Modern Things.* Berkeley: University of California Press, 1998.

Cole, Jennifer, and Deborah Durham. "Age, Regeneration, and the Intimate Politics of Globalization." In *Generations and Globalization: Youth, Age, and Family in the New World Economy,* ed. Jennifer Cole and Deborah Durham. Bloomington: Indiana University Press, 2007, 1–28.

———. "Introduction: Globalization and the Temporality of Children and Youth." In *Figuring the Future: Globalization and the Temporalities of Children and Youth,* ed. Jennifer Cole and Deborah Durham. Santa Fe: School for Advanced Research Press, 2008, 3–23.

Cole, Jennifer, and Lynn M. Thomas, eds. *Love in Africa.* Chicago: University of Chicago Press, 2009.

Collins, Marcus. *Modern Love: Personal Relationships in Twentieth-Century Britain.* Newark, DE: University of Delaware Press, 2006.

———. "Pride and Prejudice: West Indian Men and Racial Prejudice in Mid-Twentieth-Century Britain." *Journal of British Studies* 40.3 (2001): 391–418.

Collins, Sydney. *Coloured Minorities in Britain: Studies in British Race Relations Based on African, West Indian and Asiatic Immigrants.* London: Lutterworth, 1957.

Comaroff, Jean, and John Comaroff. "Reflections on Youth from the Past to the Postcolony." In *Makers and Breakers: Children and Youth in Postcolo-*

nial Africa, ed. Alcinda Manuel Honwana and Filip de Boeck. Trenton, NJ: Africa World Press, 2005, 19–30.

Commonwealth Immigration Advisory Council, *The Incidence of Mental Illness among Migrants*. Canberra: The Council, 1961.

Conekin, Becky, Frank Mort, and Chris Waters. Introduction to *Moments of Modernity: Reconstructing Britain, 1945–1964*, ed. Becky Conekin, Frank Mort, and Chris Waters. London: Rivers Oram, 1999, 1–21.

Conton, William. *The African*. Boston: Little, Brown, 1960.

Cook, Hera. *The Long Sexual Revolution: English Women, Sex, and Contraception, 1800–1975*. Oxford: Oxford University Press, 2004.

Cooper, Frederick. *Africa since 1940: The Past of the Present*. Cambridge: Cambridge University Press, 2002.

———. "Decolonizing Situations: The Rise, Fall and Rise of Colonial Studies, 1961–2001." *French Politics, Culture and Society* 20.2 (summer 2002): 47–76.

———. "From Free Labor to Family Allowances: Labor and African Society in Colonial Discourse." *American Ethnologist* 16.4 (1989): 745–65.

———. "Possibility and Constraint: African Independence in Historical Perspective." *Journal of African History* 49.2 (2008): 167–96.

———. "Reconstructing Empire in British and French Africa." *Past and Present* 210, Supplement 6 (2011): 196–210.

Cooper, Frederick, and Randall Packard, eds. *International Development and the Social Sciences: Essays on the History and Politics of Knowledge*. Berkeley: University of California Press, 1997.

Cooperative Study of West African Student Opinion, *Nigerian Student Opinions: Tabulations*. Washington, D.C.: Bureau of Social Science Research, 1959.

Copeland, J. R. M. "Aspects of Mental Illness in West African Students." *Social Psychiatry* 3.1 (1968): 7–13.

Corbally, John. "The Jarring Irish: Postwar Immigration to the Heart of Empire." *Radical History Review* 104 (2009): 103–25.

Courage, Michael, with Dermot Wright, *New Guinea Venture*. London: Hale, 1967.

Cousins, E. G. *Sapphire*. London: Panther, 1959.

Cusack, Dymphna. *The Sun in Exile*. London: Constable, 1955.

Darian-Smith, Eve, and Peter Fitzpatrick, eds. *Laws of the Postcolonial*. Ann Arbor: University of Michigan Press, 1999.

Darwin, John. *Britain and Decolonisation: The Retreat from Empire in the Post-War World*. Houndmills: Macmillan, 1988.

———. "British Decolonisation since 1945: A Pattern or a Puzzle." *Journal of Imperial and Commonwealth History* 12.2 (September 1984): 186–208.

———. "Fear of Falling: British Politics and Imperial Decline since 1900." *Transactions of the Royal Historical Society* 36 (1986): 27–43.

Davin, Anna. "Imperialism and Motherhood." *History Workshop Journal* 5 (1978): 9–66.

Davis, James M., et al. *IIE Survey of the African Student: His Achievements and His Problems*. New York: Institute of International Education, 1961.

Davison, R. B. *Black British: Immigrants to England*. London: Oxford University Press for the Institute of Race Relations, 1966.

———. *Commonwealth Immigrants*. London: Oxford University Press, 1964.

———. *West Indian Migrants: Social and Economic Facts of Migration from the West Indies* (London: Oxford University Press, 1962).

Dawson, W. R. "The Relation between the Geographical Distribution of Insanity and that of Certain Social and Other Conditions in Ireland." *Journal of Mental Science* 57 (1911): 571–97.

Defty, Andrew. *Britain, America and Anti-Communist Propaganda, 1945–53: The Information Research Department*. Abingdon: Taylor and Francis, 2004.

Deighton, Anne. *The Impossible Peace: Britain, the Division of Germany and the Origins of the Cold War*. Oxford: Oxford University Press, 1990.

———, ed. *Britain and the First Cold War*. New York: St. Martin's, 1990.

Delaney, Enda. "'Almost a Class of Helots in an Alien Land': The British State and Irish Immigration, 1921–45." *Immigrants and Minorities* 18 (1999): 240–65.

Denzer, LaRay. "Domestic Science Training in Colonial Yorubaland, Nigeria." In *African Encounters with Domesticity*, ed. Karen Tranberg Hansen. New Brunswick, NJ: Rutgers University Press, 1992, 116–39.

———. *Folayegbe M. Akintunde-Ighodalo: A Public Life*. Ibadan: Sam Bookman, 2001.

Deslandes, Paul. "'The Foreign Element': Newcomers and the Rhetoric of Race, Nation and Empire in 'Oxbridge' Undergraduate Culture." *Journal of British Studies* 37.1 (January 1998): 54–90.

———. *Oxbridge Men: British Masculinity and the Undergraduate Experience, 1850–1920*. Bloomington: Indiana University Press, 2005.

de Wit, Hans. *Internationalization of Higher Education in the United States of America and Europe: A Historical, Comparative, and Conceptual Analysis*. Westport, CT: Greenwood, 2002.

Dhall, A. *An Introduction to Living in England for Indian and Pakistani Students and Their Wives*. Manchester: Manchester University Press, 1964.

Dickson, Alec. *A Chance to Serve*. London: D. Dobson, 1976.

———. "Training of Youth Leaders for Work in Fundamental Education." *Fundamental and Adult Education* 10.2 (1958): 45–54.

———. "Voluntary Service Overseas. Thomas Holland Memorial Lecture." *Overseas Quarterly* 2.2 (June 1960): 47–48.

Dickson, Mora. *Longhouse in Sarawak*. London: Gollancz, 1971.

———. *New Nigerians*. London: Dobson, 1960.

———. *Portrait of a Partnership*. New York: International Partnership for Service-Learning and Leadership, 2004.

———. *A Season in Sarawak*. Chicago: Rand McNally, 1962.

———. *A World Elsewhere: Voluntary Service Overseas.* Chicago: Rand McNally, 1964.

Diouf, Mamadou. "Engaging Postcolonial Cultures: African Youth and Public Space." *African Studies Review* 46.2 (2003): 1–12.

Dirks, Nicholas. "Colonial Histories and Native Informants: Biography of an Archive." In *Orientalism and the Postcolonial Predicament: Perspectives on South Asia,* ed. Carol Breckenridge and Peter van der Veer. Philadelphia: University of Pennsylvania Press, 1993, 279–313.

———. "The Crimes of Colonialism: Anthropology and the Textualization of India." In *Colonial Subjects: Essays in the Practical History of Anthropology,* ed. Peter Pels and Oscar Salemink. Ann Arbor: University of Michigan Press, 1999, 153–79.

Diwan, Paras. "The Hindu Marriage Act 1955." *International and Comparative Law Quarterly* 6 (1957): 263–72.

Donohue, Laura K. *Counter-Terrorist Law and Emergency Powers in the United Kingdom, 1922–2000.* Dublin: Irish Academic Press, 2001.

Drapes, Thomas. "On the Alleged Increase of Insanity in Ireland." *Journal of Mental Science* 40 (October 1894): 519–48.

Drayton, Richard. *Nature's Government: Science, Imperial Britain, and the 'Improvement' of the World.* New Haven, CT: Yale University Press, 2000.

Du Bois, Cora. *Foreign Students and Higher Education in the United States.* Washington, D.C.: American Council on Education, 1956.

Dudziak, Mary. "Brown as a Cold War Case." *Journal of American History* 91.1 (June 2004): 32–42.

———. *Cold War Civil Rights: Race and the Image of American Democracy.* Princeton, NJ: Princeton University Press, 2000.

Edgerton, David. *Warfare State: Britain, 1920–1970.* Cambridge: Cambridge University Press, 2006.

Edwards, Michael, ed. *Arriving Where We Started: 25 Years of Voluntary Service Overseas.* London: VSO and IT Publications, 1983.

Eekelaar, J. M., J. L. R. Davis, and P. R. H. Webb. "The Dissolution of Initially Polygamous Marriages." *International and Comparative Law Quarterly* (1966): 1181–89.

Eghigian, Greg, et al., eds. *The Self as Project: Politics and the Human Sciences.* Chicago: University of Chicago Press, 2007.

Eisenstadt, S. N. *The Absorption of Immigrants: A Comparative Study Based Mainly on the Jewish Community in Palestine and the State of Israel.* Westport, CT: Greenwood Press, 1954.

———. *From Generation to Generation: Age Groups and Social Structure.* Glencoe, IL: Free Press, 1956.

Ekeh, Peter P., ed. *T. E. A. Salubi: Witness to British Colonial Rule in Urhoboland and Nigeria.* Buffalo: Urhobo Historical Society, 2008.

Eldridge, J. E. T. "Overseas Students at Leicester University: Some Problems of Adjustment and Communication." *Race* 2 (November 1960): 50–59.

Elkins, Caroline. "Alchemy of Evidence: Mau Mau, the British Empire, and the High Court of Justice." *Journal of Imperial and Commonwealth History* 39.5 (2011): 731–48.

———. *Imperial Reckoning: The Untold Story of Britains' Gulag in Kenya.* New York: Henry Holt, 2005.

———. "Race, Citizenship and Governance: Settler Tyranny and the End of Empire." In *Settler Colonialism in the Twentieth Century: Projects, Practices, Legacies,* ed. Caroline Elkins and Susan Pedersen. London: Routledge, 2005, 203–22.

Ellis, Catherine. "No Hammock for the Idle: The Conservative Party, 'Youth' and the Welfare State." *Twentieth-Century British History* 16.4 (2005): 441–70.

———. "The Younger Generation: The Labour Party and the 1959 Youth Commission." *Journal of British Studies* 41.2 (April 2002): 199–231.

Ellis, June. "The Child in West African Society." In *West African Families in Britain: A Meeting of Two Cultures,* ed. June Ellis et al. London: Routledge and K. Paul, 1978, 39–55.

———. "Conclusions." In *West African Families in Britain: A Meeting of Two Cultures,* ed. June Ellis et al. London: Routledge and K. Paul, 1978, 109–18.

———. "Differing Conceptions of a Child's Needs: Some Implications of Social Work with West African Children and Their Parents." *British Journal of Social Work* 7 (1977): 155–71.

———. "The Fostering of West African Children in England." *Social Work Today* 2.5 (1971): 21–24.

Emecheta, Buchi. *Second Class Citizen.* New York: Braziller, 1975.

Emery, F. A. "A Critique of Some of the Western Australian Studies." *British Journal of Social and Clinical Psychology* 1 (1962): 72–75.

Engerman, David C. "American Knowledge and Global Power." *Diplomatic History* 31.4 (2007): 599–622.

———. *Know Your Enemy: The Rise and Fall of America's Soviet Experts.* Oxford: Oxford University Press, 2009.

———. *Modernization from the Other Shore: American Intellectuals and the Romance of Russian Development.* Cambridge, MA: Harvard University Press, 2003.

Engerman, David C., et al., eds. *Staging Growth: Modernization, Development, and the Global Cold War.* Amherst: University of Massachusetts Press, 2003.

Englander, David, and Rosemary O'Day, eds. *Retrieved Riches: Social Investigation in Britain, 1840–1914.* Aldershot: Scolar Press, 1995.

English, Richard, and Michael Kenny. "Interview with Stuart Hall." In *Rethinking British Decline,* ed. Richard English and Michael Kenney. Houndmills: Macmillan, 1988, 104–16.

———, eds. *Rethinking British Decline.* Houndmills: Macmillan, 2000.

Erikson, Erik H. *Identity and the Life Cycle.* New York: Norton, 1980.

Escobar, Arturo. *Encountering Development: The Making and Unmaking of the Third World.* Princeton, NJ: Princeton University Press, 1995.

Esty, Jed. "The Colonial Bildungsroman: *The Story of an African Farm* and the Ghost of Goethe." *Victorian Studies* 49.3 (2007): 407–30.

———. *A Shrinking Island: Modernism and National Culture in England*. Princeton, NJ: Princeton University Press, 2004.

Evans-Pritchard, E. E. *The Nuer: A Description of the Modes of Livelihood and Political Institutions of a Nilotic People*. Oxford: Clarendon, 1940.

Eyal, Gil. *The Disenchantment of the Orient: Expertise in Israeli Affairs and the Arab State*. Stanford, CA: Stanford University Press, 2006.

Eyton, John Seymour. *Mr. Ram: A Story of Oxford and India*. London: Arrowsmith, 1929.

Fass, Paula S. *Children of a New World: Society, Culture, and Globalization*. New York: New York University Press, 2007.

———. *Kidnapped: Child Abduction in America*. New York: Oxford University Press, 1997.

Fee, Elizabeth. "The Sexual Politics of Victorian Anthropology." *Feminist Studies* 3/4 (winter-spring 1973): 23–39.

Feldman, David. "Migrants, Immigrants and Welfare from the Old Poor Law to the Welfare State." *Transactions of the Royal Historical Society* 13 (2003): 79–104.

Ferguson, James. *The Anti-Politics Machine: "Development," Depoliticization and Democratic Power in Lesotho*. Cambridge: Cambridge University Press, 1990.

———. *Expectations of Modernity: Myths and Meanings of Urban Life on the Zambian Copperbelt*. Berkeley: University of California Press, 1999.

Fiawoo, D. K. "Some Patterns of Foster Care in Ghana." In *Marriage, Fertility and Parenthood in West Africa*, ed. Christine Oppong, et al. Canberra: Australian National University, 1978, 273–88.

Field, M. J. "Chronic Psychosis in Rural Ghana." *British Journal of Psychiatry* 114 (1968): 31–33.

———. *Search for Security: An Ethno-Psychiatric Study of Rural Ghana*. Evanston: Northwestern University Press, 1960.

Firth, Raymond. "Social Problems and Research in British West Africa." *Africa* 17.2 (1947): 77–92.

Fitzpatrick, Dennis. "Non-Christian Marriage." *Journal of the Society of Comparative Legislation* 2 (1900): 359–87.

Foner, Nancy. "Male and Female: Jamaican Migrants in London." *Anthropological Quarterly* 49.1 (1976): 28–35.

Foreman, Grahame. "The Power to Exclude: Primitivism and the Persecution of British Social Anthropologists in the 1950s," Paper delivered at the Pacific Coast Conference on British Studies, Seattle, 2011.

Forster, E. B. "The Theory and Practice of Psychiatry in Ghana." *American Journal of Psychotherapy* 16 (1962): 7–51.

Fortes, Meyer. *Oedipus and Job in West Africa*. Cambridge: Cambridge University Press, 1959.

———. "The Significance of Descent in Tale Social Structure." *Africa* XIV (1943–44): 362–85.

Fourchard, Laurent. "Lagos and the Invention of Juvenile Delinquency in Nigeria, 1920–60." *Journal of African History* 47.1 (2006): 115–37.

Fowler, David. *Youth Culture in Modern Britain, c. 1920–1970: From Ivory Tower to Global Movement—A New History.* New York: Palgrave Macmillan, 2008.

Frankel, Oz. *States of Inquiry: Social Investigations and Print Culture in Nineteenth-Century Britain and the United States.* Baltimore: Johns Hopkins University Press, 2006.

Francis, Errol. "Psychiatric Racism and Social Police: Black People and the Psychiatric Services." In *Inside Babylon: The Caribbean Diaspora in Britain,* ed. Winston James and Clive Harris. London: Verso, 1993, 179–205.

Francis, Martin. "A Flight from Commitment? Domesticity, Adventure and the Masculine Imaginary in Britain after the Second World War." *Gender and History* 19.1 (April 2007): 163–85.

Frankenberg, Ronnie. "Life: Cycle, Trajectory, or Pilgrimage: A Social Production Approach to Marxism, Metaphor and Mortality." In *Rethinking the Life Cycle,* ed. Alan Bryman, et al. Basingstoke: Macmillan, 1987, 122–38.

Freshfield, Mark. *The Stormy Dawn.* London: Faber and Faber, 1946.

Frost, Isaac. "Home-Sickness and Immigrant Psychoses: Austrian and German Domestic Servants." *Journal of Mental Science* 84 (1938).

Fryer, Peter. *Staying Power: The History of Black People in Britain.* London: Pluto, 1984.

Furmston, M. J. "Polygamy and the Wind of Change." *International and Comparative Law Quarterly* 10.1 (1961): 180–86.

Gandhi, Leela. *Affective Communities: Anticolonial Thought, Fin-de-Siècle Radicalism, and the Politics of Friendship.* Durham, NC: Duke University Press, 2006.

Gans, Bruno. "Experiences in a Coloured Children's Welfare Clinic." *Proceedings of the Royal Society of Medicine* 57 (1964): 321–28.

Garigue, Philip. "The West African Students' Union: A Study in Culture Contact." *Africa* 23.1 (1953): 55–69.

Garrett, Paul Michael. "The Abnormal Flight: The Migration and Repatriation of Irish Unmarried Mothers." *Social History* 25 (2000): 330–44.

———. "The Hidden History of the PFIs: The Repatriation of Unmarried Mothers and Their Children from England to Ireland in the 1950s and 1960s." *Immigrants and Minorities* 19 (2000): 25–44.

Gascoigne, John. *Science in the Service of Empire: Joseph Banks, the British State and the Uses of Science in the Age of Revolution.* Cambridge: Cambridge University Press, 1998.

George, Abosede A. "Feminist Activism and Class Politics: The Example of the Lagos Girl Hawker Project." *Women's Studies Quarterly* 35 (2007): 128–43.

Ghosh, Durba. "Decoding the Nameless: Gender, Subjectivity, and Historical

Methodologies in Reading the Archives of Colonial India." In *A New Imperial History: Culture, Identity, and Modernity, 1660–1840*, ed. Kathleen Wilson. Cambridge: Cambridge University Press, 2004, 297–316.

———. *Sex and the Family in Colonial India: The Making of Empire*. Cambridge: Cambridge University Press, 2006.

Gifford, Peter. "General Morbidity in Overseas Students." *Proceedings of the British Student Health Association* (1961): 55–58.

Gikandi, Simon. "Pan-Africanism and Cosmopolitanism: The Case of Jomo Kenyatta." *English Studies in Africa* 43 (2000): 3–27.

Gilman, Nils. *Mandarins of the Future: Modernization Theory in Cold War America*. Baltimore: Johns Hopkins University Press, 2003.

Gilroy, Paul. *After Empire: Melancholia or Convivial Culture*. London: Routledge, 2004.

Goldsworthy, David. *Colonial Issues in British Politics 1945–1961: From 'Colonial Development' to 'Wind of Change.'* Oxford: Clarendon, 1971.

Goody, Esther. "Kinship Fostering in Gonja: Deprivation or Advantage?" In *Socialization: The Approach from Social Anthropology*, ed. Philip Mayer. London: Tavistock, 1970, 51–74.

———. *Parenthood and Social Reproduction: Fostering and Occupational Roles in West Africa*. Cambridge: Cambridge University Press, 1982.

———. "Some Theoretical and Empirical Aspects of Parenthood in West Africa." In *Marriage, Fertility and Parenthood in West Africa*, ed. Christine Oppong, et al. Canberra: Australian National University, 1978, 222–72.

Gordon, Linda. *The Great Arizona Orphan Abduction*. Cambridge, MA: Harvard University Press, 2001.

Gorman, Daniel. "Empire, Internationalism, and the Campaign against the Traffic in Women and Children in the 1920s." *Twentieth-Century British History* 19.2 (2008): 186–216.

Goulbourne, Harry, and Mary Chamberlain, eds. *Caribbean Families in Britain and the Trans-Atlantic World*. London: Caribbean, 2001.

Graham, P. J., and C. E. Meadows. "Psychiatric Disorder in the Children of West Indian Immigrants." *Journal of Child Psychiatry and Psychology* 8 (1967): 105–16.

Graham, Robert. "Memories of Independence 1960." In *Palm Wine and Leopard's Whiskers: Reminiscences of Eastern Nigeria*, ed. Ronnie Anderson, ed. Otago: R. G. Anderson, 1999, 408–11.

Grant, Julia. *Raising Baby by the Book: The Education of American Mothers*. New Haven, CT: Yale University Press, 1998.

Graveson, R. H. "Capacity to Acquire a Domicile." *International Law Quarterly* 3 (1950): 149–63.

Green, Jonathon. *All Dressed Up: The Sixties and the Counterculture*. London: Pimlico, 1999.

Green, L. C. "'Civilized' Law and 'Primitive' Peoples." *Osgoode Hall Law Journal* 13 (1975): 233–49.

Green, Nancy L. "The Politics of Exit: Reversing the Immigration Paradigm." *Journal of Modern History* 77.2 (June 2005): 263–89.

Greenslade, Liam. "White Skins, White Masks: Psychological Distress among the Irish in Britain." In *The Irish in the New Communities*, ed. Patrick O'Sullivan. London: Leicester University Press, 1992, 201–25.

Greenslade, Liam, et al. "From Visible to Invisible: The 'Problem' of the Health of Irish People in Britain." In *Migrants, Minorities and Health: Historical and Contemporary Studies*, ed. Lara Marks and Michael Worboys. London: Routledge, 1997, 147–78.

Gwynne, Enid. "The Wardrobe Problem: Clothes for the West African Student in Britain." *West African Review* 26 (February 1955): 185–87.

Hadley, C. V. D. "Personality Patterns, Social Class, and Aggression in the West Indies." *Human Relations* 2.4 (1949): 349–62.

Hall, Catherine. *Civilising Subjects: Colony and Metropole in the English Imagination, 1830–1867* (Chicago: University of Chicago Press, 2002).

———. "Making Colonial Subjects: Education in the Age of Empire." *History of Education* 37.6 (2008): 773–87.

Hall, Catherine, and Sonya Rose. *At Home with the Empire: Metropolitan Culture and the Imperial World*. Cambridge: Cambridge University Press, 2006.

Halsey, A. H. *A History of Sociology in Britain: Science, Literature, and Society*. Oxford,: Oxford University Press, 2004.

———. *No Discouragement: An Autobiography*. Houndmills: Macmillan, 1996.

———. "Provincials and Professionals: The British Post-War Sociologists." In *Essays on the History of British Sociological Research*, ed. Martin Bulmer. Cambridge: Cambridge University Press, 1985, 151–64.

Halsey, A. H., and W. G. Runciman. *British Sociology Seen from Without and Within*. Oxford: Oxford University Press for the British Academy, 2005.

Hamilton, Carolyn, et al., eds. *Refiguring the Archive*. Dordrecht: Kluwer, 2002.

Hammerton, A. James, and Alistair Thomson. *Ten Pound Poms: Australia's Invisible Migrants*. Manchester: Manchester University Press, 2005.

Hammond-Tooke, W. D. *Imperfect Interpreters: South Africa's Anthropologists, 1920–1990*. Johannesburg: Witwatersrand University Press, 1997.

Hampshire, James. *Citizenship and Belonging: Immigration and the Politics of Demographic Governance in Postwar Britain*. Houndmills: Palgrave, 2005.

Hansen, Karen Tranberg, ed. *African Encounters with Domesticity*. New Brunswick, NJ: Rutgers University Press, 1999.

Hansen, Randall. *Citizenship and Immigration in Post-War Britain: The Institutional Origins of a Multicultural Nation*. Oxford: Oxford University Press, 2000.

Harding, S., and R. Balarajan. "Patterns of Mortality in Second Generation Irish Living in England and Wales: Longitudinal Study." *British Medical Journal* 312 (June 1, 1996): 1389–92.

Harris, Brian. "A Case of Brain-Fag in East Africa." *British Journal of Psychiatry* 138 (1981): 162–63.

Harris, Jose. "Tradition and Transformation: Society and Civil Society in Britain, 1945–2001." In *The British Isles since 1945,* ed. Kathleen Burk. Oxford: Oxford University Press, 2003, 91–125.

Harrison, Brian. *Seeking a Role: The United Kingdom, 1951–1970.* Oxford: Oxford University Press, 2009.

Hartley, T. C. "Polygamy and Social Policy." *Modern Law Review* 32.2 (1969): 155–73.

Hashmi, Farrukh. "Community Psychiatric Problems among Birmingham Immigrants." *British Journal of Social Psychiatry* 2 (1968): 196–201.

———. *The Pakistani Family in Britain.* London: National Committee for Commonwealth Immigrants, 1967.

Haskey, John. "Mortality among Second Generation Irish in England and Wales." *British Medical Journal* 312 (June 1, 1996): 1373–74.

Hassett, Michael. "The British Government's Response to Irish Terrorism, c. 1867–c. 1979." Ph.D. thesis, Open University, 2007.

Hawkins, Sean. "'The Woman in Question': Marriage and Identity in the Colonial Courts of Northern Ghana, 1907–1954." In *Women in African Colonial Histories,* ed. Jean Allman, Susan Geiger, and Nakanyike Musisi, Bloomington: Indiana University Press, 2002, 116–43.

Hearnden, Arthur. *Red Robert: A Life of Robert Birley.* London: H. Hamilton, 1984.

Hecht, Gabrielle. "Negotiating Global Nuclearities: Apartheid, Decolonization, and the Cold War in the Making of the IAEA." *Osiris* 21 (2006): 25–48.

Hein, Laura. *Reasonable Men, Powerful Words: Political Culture and Expertise in Twentieth-Century Japan.* Washington, DC: Woodrow Wilson Center, 2004.

Hemsi, L. K. "Psychiatric Morbidity of West Indian Immigrants: A Study of First Admissions in London." *Social Psychiatry* 2 (October 1967): 95–100.

Hendrick, Harry. *Child Welfare: England, 1872–1989.* London: Routledge, 1994.

Henfrey, Colin. *The Gentle People: A Journey among the Indian Tribes of Guiana.* London: Hutchinson, 1964.

Hennessy, Peter. *Having It So Good: Britain in the 1950s.* London: Penguin, 2006.

Henriques, F. "Sociology of Immigration." In *Immigration: Social and Medical Aspects,* ed. G. E. W. Wolstenholme and Maeve O'Connor. Boston: Churchill, 1966, 18–26.

Herman, Ellen. "The Career of Cold War Psychology." *Radical History Review* 63 (1995): 52–85.

———. *Kinship by Design: A History of Adoption in the Modern United States.* Chicago: University of Chicago Press, 2008.

———. "Project Camelot and the Career of Cold War Psychology." In *Universi-*

ties and Empire: Money and Politics in the Social Sciences during the Cold War, ed. Christopher Simpson. New York: New Press, 1988, 97–133.

——. *The Romance of American Psychology: Political Culture in the Age of Experts*. Berkeley: University of California Press, 1995.

Hessler, Julie. "Death of an African Student in Moscow." *Cahiers du Monde Russe* 47 (2006): 33–63.

Heyford, J. E. S. "White Brides and Black Husbands." *West African Review* 20 (September 1949): 1009.

Higgins, Michael. "Conflict of Laws. Conversion of Polygamous Marriage into Monogamous Union." *Modern Law Review* 26.2 (1963): 205–8.

Hillel, Margot, and Shurlee Swain. *Child, Nation, Race and Empire: Child Rescue Discourse, England, Canada, and Australia, 1850–1915*. Manchester: Manchester University Press, 2010.

Hilton, Matthew. "Politics Is Ordinary: Non-Governmental Organizations and Political Participation in Contemporary Britain." *Twentieth-Century British History* 22.2 (2011): 230–68.

Hilton, Matthew, Nick Crowson and James McKay. "NGOs and the Professionalization of Politics in Postwar Britain." Paper delivered at the North American Conference on British Studies, Baltimore, 2010.

Hitch, P. J. "Culture, Social Structure and the Explanation of Migrant Mental Illness." *Mental Health and Society* 4 (1977): 136–43.

Hodge, Joseph Morgan. *Triumph of the Expert: Agrarian Doctrines of Development and the Legacies of British Colonialism*. Athens, OH: Ohio University Press, 2007.

Hoffman, Elizabeth Cobbs. *All You Need Is Love: The Peace Corps and the Spirit of the 1960s*. Cambridge, MA: Harvard University Press, 1998.

Holder, William E. "Public Policy and National Preferences: The Exclusion of Foreign Law in English Private International Law." *International and Comparative Law Quarterly* 17.4 (1968): 926–52.

Holland, Robert. Foreword to *British Government Policy and Decolonisation 1945–1963: Scrutinising the Official Mind*, by Frank Heinlein. London: Frank Cass, 2002, vii-viii.

Holland, Robert, Susan Williams, and Terry Barringer. Preface to *The Iconography of Independence: 'Freedoms at Midnight,'* ed. Robert Holland et al. London: Routledge, 2010, ix–xix.

Holman, Robert. *Trading in Children: A Study in Private Fostering*. London: Routledge and Kegan Paul, 1973.

Holmes, Colin. "The British Government and Brendan Behan, 1941–1954: The Persistence of the Prevention of Violence Act." *Saothar* 14 (1989): 125–28.

——. "Government Files and Privileged Access." *Social History* 6.3 (1981): 333–50.

——. *John Bull's Island: Immigration and British Society, 1871–1971*. Basingstoke: Macmillan, 1988.

Hopkins, Harry. *The New Look: A Social History of the Forties and Fifties in Britain*. London: Secker and Warburg, 1963.

Hopkins, Michael F., Michael D. Kandiah, and Gillian Staerck, Introduction to *Cold War Britain, 1945–1964: New Perspectives*, ed. Michael Hopkins et al. Houndmills: Palgrave Macmillan, 2003, 1–4.

Horne, Gerald. *Mau Mau in Harlem? The U.S. and the Liberation of Kenya*. New York: Palgrave Macmillan, 2009.

Houlbrook, Matt. *Queer London: Perils and Pleasures in the Sexual Metropolis, 1918–1957*. Chicago: University of Chicago Press, 2005.

Howard, Colin. "What Colour Is the Reasonable Man?" *Criminal Law Review* (1961): 41–48.

Howe, Stephen. "Flakking the Mau Mau Catchers." *Journal of Imperial and Commonwealth History* 39.5 (2011): 695–97.

———. "Internal Decolonization? British Politics since Thatcher as Postcolonial Trauma." *Twentieth-Century British History* 14 (2003): 286–304.

———. "When (if Ever) Did Empire End? Decolonisation in British Culture in the 1950s." In *The British Empire in the 1950s: Retreat or Revival*, ed. Martin Lynn. Basingstoke: Palgrave Macmillan, 2006, 214–37.

Hunt, Nancy Rose. *A Colonial Lexicon: Of Birth Ritual, Medicalization, and Mobility in the Congo*. Durham, NC: Duke University Press, 1999.

———. "Domesticity and Colonialism in Belgian Africa: Usumbura's *Foyer Social*, 1946–1960." *Signs* 15.3 (1990): 447–74.

———. "Noise Over Camouflaged Polygamy, Colonial Morality Taxation, and a Woman-Naming Crisis in Belgian Africa." *Journal of African History* 32.3 (1991): 471–94.

Hunt, Stephen. *The Life Course: A Sociological Introduction*. New York: Palgrave Macmillan, 2005.

Huxley, Elspeth. *Back Street, New Worlds: A Look at Immigrants in Britain*. London: Chatto and Windus, 1964.

———. *Four Guineas: A Journey through West Africa*. London: Reprint Society, 1954.

Hyam, Ronald. "The Political Consequences of Seretse Khama." *Historical Journal* 29.4 (1986): 921–47.

"In Living Memory: VSO." BBC Radio 4, December 3 2008. http://www.bbc.co.uk/iplayer/episode/b00fq2xc/In_Living_Memory_Series_9_The_New_Volunteers/

Institute of Race Relations Newsletter (November 1964): 31–32.

Isiugo-Abanihe, Uche C. "Child Fosterage in West Africa." *Population and Development Review* 11 (March 1985): 53–73.

Jacobs, Margaret. *White Mother to a Dark Race: Settler Colonialism, Maternalism, and the Removal of Indigenous Children in the American West and Australia, 1880–1940*. Lincoln, NE: University of Nebraska Press, 2009.

Jackson, Brian. "The Childminders." *New Society* (November 29, 1973): 521–23.

Jackson, John Archer. *The Irish in Britain*. London: Routledge and Paul, 1963.

Jackson, Lynette A. *Surfacing Up: Psychiatry and Social Order in Colonial Zimbawe, 1908–1968.* Ithaca: Cornell University Press, 2005.

Jackson, Sonia. *The Illegal Child-Minders: A Report on the Growth of Unregistered Child-Minding and the West Indian Community.* Cambridge: Priority Area Children for the Cambridge Educational Development Trust, 1972.

Jacqz, Jane W. *African Students at U.S. Universities. Report of a Conference on the Admission and Guidance of African Students Held at Howard University, Washington, D.C., March 17–18, 1967.* New York: African American Institute, 1967.

Jarvis, Mark. *Conservative Governments, Morality, and Social Change in Affluent Britain.* Manchester: Manchester University Press, 2005.

Jefferys, Margot, ed. *Growing Old in the Twentieth Century.* London: Routledge, 1992.

Jenkins, Ray. "Gold Coasters Overseas, 1880–1919: With Specific Reference to Their Activities in Britain." *Immigrants and Minorities* 4 (1985): 5–52.

Jenkinson, Jacqueline. "The Black Community of Salford and Hull." *Immigrants and Minorities* 7.2 (1988): 166–83.

———. *Black 1919: Riots, Racism and Resistance in Imperial Britain* (Liverpool: Liverpool University Press, 2009).

Jervis, Margaret. "Cashing in on the Hopes of Black Children." *Social Work Today* 20 (March 2, 1989): 14–15.

Jobs, Richard Ivan. *Riding the New Wave: Youth and the Rejuvenation of France after the Second World War.* Stanford, CA: Stanford University Press, 2007.

Johnson, Howard. "The West Indies and the Conversion of the British Official Classes to the Development Idea." *Journal of Commonwealth and Comparative Politics* 15 (1977): 55–83.

Johnson-Odim, Cheryl, and Nina Emma Mba. *For Women and the Nation: Fumilayo Ransome-Kuti of Nigeria.* Urbana: University of Illinois Press, 1997.

Johnston, Ruth. "A New Approach to the Meaning of Assimilation." *Human Relations* 16 (1963): 295–98.

"Joie de Vivre." *West African Review* 22 (March 1951):

Jones, Gareth. "The Legitimacy Act, 1959." *International and Comparative Law Quarterly* 8.4 (October 1959): 722–26.

Jones, Mervyn. *A Set of Wives.* London: J. Cape, 1965.

Jones, Richard, and Gnanapala Welhengama. *Ethnic Minorities in English Law.* Staffordshire: Trentham Books, 2000.

Joshua, Laurie. "Private Fostering: A Migrant Worker's Dilemma." *African Woman* (autumn 1991): 6–9.

Judge, C.G., and M.M. Glatt. "The Problem of Alcoholism in Australia and England." *Medical Journal of Australia* 1 (April 22, 1961): 586–89.

Jupp, James. *Arrivals and Departures.* Melbourne: Cheshire-Lansdowne, 1966.

———. *The English in Australia*. Cambridge: Cambridge University Press, 2004.

Kaberry, Phyllis. *Women of the Grassfields: A Study of the Economic Position of Women in Bamenda, British Cameroons*. London: H.M.S.O., 1952.

Kahn-Freund, O. "Legitimacy Act, 1959." *Modern Law Review* 23.1 (January 1960): 56–60.

Kallarackal, A. M., and Martin Herbert. "The Happiness of Indian Immigrant Children." *New Society* (February 26, 1976): 422–24.

Kandiah, Michael D. "The Conservative Party and the Early Cold War: The Construction of 'New Conservatism." In *Cold War Britain, 1945–1964: New Perspectives*, ed. Michael Hopkins et al. Houndmills: Palgrave Macmillan, 2003, 3–38.

Karsten, I. G. F. "Child Marriages." *Modern Law Review* 32.2 (1969): 212–17.

Kasunmu, Alfred B., and Jeswald W. Salacuse, *Nigerian Family Law*. London: Butterworths, 1966.

Kauffman, Joseph F. "Youth and the Peace Corps." In *Youth: Change and Challenge*, ed. Erik H. Erikson. New York: Basic Books, 1961, 152–60.

Kay, Diana, and Robert Miles. *Refugees or Migrant Workers? European Volunteer Workers in Britain, 1946–1951*. London: Routledge, 1992.

Kaye, Barrington. *Child Training in Ghana: An Impressionistic Survey*. Legon: Institute of Education, 1960.

Kearney, Michael. "From the Invisible Hand to Visible Feet: Anthropological Studies of Migration and Development." *Annual Review of Anthropology* 15 (1986): 331–61.

Keith, J. L. "African Students in Great Britain." *African Affairs* 45 (1946): 65–72.

Kelly, John D. "Fear of Culture: British Regulation of Indian Marriage in Post-Indenture Fiji." *Ethnohistory* 36.4 (1989): 372–91.

Kelly, John D., and Martha Kaplan, *Represented Communities: Fiji and World Decolonization*. Chicago: University of Chicago Press, 2001.

Kent, Bessie. "The Social Worker's Cultural Pattern as It Affects Casework with Immigrants." *Social Work* 22.4 (October 1965): 14–22.

Kenyatta, Jomo. *Facing Mount Kenya: The Tribal Life of the Gikuyu*. New York: Vintage, 1965.

Kerr, Madeleine. *Personality and Conflict in Jamaica*. London: Collins, 1963.

Kiell, Norman. "Attitudes of Foreign Students." *Journal of Higher Education* 22.4 (1951): 188–94.

Kiev, Ari. "The Family and Mental Illness in Rapid Social Change Situations." In *Deuxième Colloquie Africain de Psychiatrie*. Paris: Association Universitaire pour de Développement de l'enseignement et de la culture en Afrique et à Madagascar, 1968, 142–49.

Kimble, George T. H. *Tropical Africa*, vol. 2. New York: Twentieth Century Fund, 1960.

King, Desmond. "Creating a Funding Regime for Social Research in Britain: The Heyworth Committee on Social Studies and the Founding of the Social Science Research Council." *Minerva* 35.1 (1997): 1–26.

Kino, F. F. "Aliens' Paranoid Reaction." *Journal of Mental Science* 97 (1951): 589–94.

Kirk-Greene, Anthony. "Decolonization: The Ultimate Diaspora." *Journal of Contemporary History* 36.1 (2001): 133–51.

Kitzinger, Sheila. "Conditional Philanthropy towards Colored Students in Britain." *Phylon* 21.2 (1960): 167–72.

Klein, Christina. "Family Ties and Political Obligation: The Discourse on Adoption and the Cold War Commitment to Asia." In *Cold War Constructions: The Political Culture of United States Imperialism, 1945–1966,* ed. Christian G. Appy. Amherst: University of Massachusetts Press, 2000, 35–66.

Kolsky, Elizabeth. "Codification and the Rule of Colonial Difference: Criminal Procedure in British India," *Law and History Review* 23.3 (2005): 631–706.

Korah, Valentine L. "England," *International and Comparative Law Quarterly* 10.1 (1961): 190–93.

Koven, Seth. *Slumming: Sexual and Social Politics in Victorian London.* Princeton, NJ: Princeton University Press, 2004.

Kramer, Paul. "Is the World Our Campus? International Students and U.S. Global Power in the Long Twentieth Century." *Diplomatic History* 33.5 (2009): 775–806.

Krupinski, J. "Sociological Aspects of Mental Ill-Health in Migrants." *Social Science and Medicine* 1 (1967): 267–81.

Krupinski, J., and Alan Stoller. "Family Life and Mental Ill-Health in Migrants." In *New Faces: Immigration and Family Life in Australia,* ed. Alan Stoller. Melbourne: Victorian Family Council, 1966, 136–50.

Kuhn, Annette. *Family Secrets: Acts of Memory and Imagination.* London: Verso, 1995.

Kuper, Adam. *Anthropologists and Anthropology: The British School, 1922–1972.* London: Routledge, 1973.

———. "Anthropology." In *The Cambridge History of Science. The Modern Social Sciences,* vol. 7, ed. Theodore M. Porter and Dorothy Ross. Cambridge: Cambridge University Press, 2003, 354–78.

Kynaston, David. *Family Britain, 1951–1957.* New York: Walker and Company, 2009.

Lacey, Michael J., and Mary O. Furner, eds. *The State and Social Investigation in Britain and the United States.* Washington, D.C.: Woodrow Wilson Center, 1993.

Lahiri, Shompa. *Indians in Britain: Anglo-Indian Encounters, Race and Identity, 1880–1930.* London: Frank Cass, 2000.

Lake, Marilyn, and Peter Reynolds. *Drawing the Global Colour Line: White Men's Countries and the International Challenge of Racial Equality.* Cambridge: Cambridge University Press, 2008.

Lamb, Sarah. "Generation in Anthropology." In *International Encyclopedia of the Social and Behavioral Sciences,* vol. 9, ed. Neil J. Smelser and Paul B. Baltes. Amsterdam: Elsevier, 2001, 6043–46.

Lambert, John R. *Crime, Police, and Race Relations: A Study in Birmingham.* London: Institute of Race Relations, 1970.

Lambert, Richard D., and Marvin Bressler. *Indian Students on an American Campus.* Minneapolis: University of Minnesota Press, 1956.

Lambo, T. Adeoye. "Characteristic Features of the Psychology of the Nigerian." *West African Medical Journal* 9 (June 1960): 95–104.

——. "Malignant Anxiety: A Syndrome associated with Criminal Conduct in Africans." *Journal of Mental Science* 108 (1962): 256–64.

——. "The Role of Cultural Factors in Paranoid Psychosis among the Yoruba Tribe." *Journal of Mental Science* 101 (April 1955): 239–66.

——. *A Study of Social and Health Problems of Nigerian Students in Great Britain.* Ibadan: University College, 1960?.

——. "The Vulnerable African Child." In *The Child in His Family: Children at Psychiatric Risk,* ed. E. James Anthony. New York: Wiley-Interscience, 1977, 259–77.

Lancaster, Patrick. *Education for Commonwealth Students in Britain.* London: Fabian Commonwealth Bureau, 1962.

Landes, Ruth. "A Preliminary Statement of a Survey of Negro-White Relationships in Britain." *Man* 52 (1952): 133.

Langhamer, Claire. "Adultery in Post-War England." *History Workshop Journal* 62.1 (2006): 86–115.

Langley, J. Ayodele. "Through a Glass Darkly." In *Colour, Culture and Consciousness: Immigrant Intellectuals in Britain,* ed. Bhikhu Parekh. London: G. Allen and Unwin, 1974, 31–40.

Lasok, Dominic. "Legitimation, Recognition, and Affiliation Proceedings (A Study in Comparative Law and Legal Reform)." *International and Comparative Law Quarterly* 10.1 (January 1961): 123–42.

Last, J. M. "Culture, Society and the Migrant." *Medical Journal of Australia* 1 (March 18, 1961): 420–24.

Latham, Michael E. *Modernization as Ideology: American Social Science and 'Nation Building' in the Kennedy Era.* Chapel Hill: University of North Carolina Press, 2000.

Lawrence, Jon, and Pat Starkey, eds. *Child Welfare and Social Action in the Nineteenth and Twentieth Centuries: International Perspectives.* Liverpool: Liverpool University Press, 2000.

Lawson, Joan. *Children in Jeopardy: The Life of a Child Care Officer.* Reading: Educational Explorers, 1965.

Layton-Henry, Zig. *The Politics of Immigration: Immigration, 'Race' and 'Race' Relations in Post-War Britain.* Cambridge, MA,: Blackwell, 1992.

Leavey, Gerard. "Suicide and Irish Migrants in Britain: Identity and Integration." *International Review of Psychiatry* 11 (1999): 168–72.

Lee, Christopher J. "Between a Moment and an Era: The Origins and Afterlives of Bandung." In *Making a World after Empire: The Bandung Moment and Its Political Afterlives*, ed. Christopher J. Lee. Athens, OH: Ohio University Press, 1–42.

Lee, J. M. "British Cultural Diplomacy and the Cold War 1946–61." *Diplomacy and Statecraft* 9.1 (March 1988): 112–34.

———. "Commonwealth Students in the United Kingdom, 1940–1960: Student Welfare and World Status." *Minerva* 44 (2006): 1–24.

———. "No Peace Corps for the Commonwealth." *Round Table* 336.1 (October 1995): 455–67.

Lemov, Rebecca. *World as Laboratory: Experiments with Mice, Mazes, and Men*. New York: Hill and Wang, 2005.

Lester, Anthony, and Geoffrey Bindman. *Race and Law*. London: Longman, 1972.

Lester, Susan. "West Africa's Students in Britain." *West African Review* 28 (December 1957): 1076–81.

Levin, Bernard. *The Pendulum Years: Britain and the Sixties*. London: Cape, 1970.

Levine, Philippa. *The Amateur and the Professional: Antiquarians, Historians and Archaeologists in Victorian England, 1838–1886*. Cambridge: Cambridge University Press, 1986.

———. *Prostitution, Race and Politics: Policing Venereal Disease in the British Empire*. New York: Routledge, 2003.

Levine, Philippa, Laura E. Nym Mayhall, Susan Pedersen, and James Vernon. "Roundtable: Twentieth-Century British History in North America," *Twentieth-Century British History* 21.3 (2010): 375–418.

Levine-Clark, Marjorie. "From 'Relief' to 'Justice and Protection': The Maintenance of Deserted Wives, British Masculinity and Imperial Citizenship, 1870–1920." *Gender and History* 22.2 (2010): 302–21.

Lewis, Gail. *'Race,' Gender, Social Welfare: Encounters in a Postcolonial Society*. Cambridge: Polity, 2000.

Lewis, Jane. "Anxieties about the Family and the Relationships between Parents, Children and the State in 20th-Century England." In *Children of Social Worlds: Development in a Social Context*, ed. Martin Richards and Paul Light. Cambridge: Polity, 1986, 31–54.

Lewis, Joanna. *Empire State-Building: War and Welfare in Kenya, 1925–52*. Athens, OH: Ohio University Press, 2000.

Leys, Colin. *The Rise and Fall of Development Theory*. Bloomington, IN: Indiana University Press, 1996.

Light, Alison. *Forever England: Femininity, Literature, and Conservatism between the Wars*. New York: Routledge, 1991.

Lindsay, Lisa. "Money, Marriage, and Masculinity on the Colonial Nigerian Railway." In *Men and Masculinities in Modern Africa*, ed. Lisa A. Lindsay and Stephan F. Miescher. Portsmouth, NH: Heinemann, 2003, 138–55.

———. *Working with Gender: Wage Labor and Social Change in Southwestern Nigeria*. Portsmouth, NH: Heinemann, 2003.

Linstrum, Erik. "Winning Hearts and Minds: Counterinsurgency and Development in the Postwar British Empire." Paper delivered at the conference "Burdens: Writing British History after 1945," University of California, Berkeley, 2012.

Listwan, Ignacy A. "Mental Disorders in Migrants: Further Study." *Medical Journal of Australia* 1 (April 25, 1959): 566–68.

———. "Paranoid States: Social and Cultural Aspects." *Medical Journal of Australia* 1 (May 12, 1956): 776–78.

Little, Kenneth. "Applied Anthropology and Social Change in the Teaching of Anthropology." *British Journal of Sociology* 11 (1960): 332–47.

———. "Attitudes towards Marriage and the Family among Educated Young Sierra Leoneans." In *The New Elites of Tropical Africa,* ed. P. C. Lloyd. Oxford: International African Institute, 1966, 139–60.

———. *Colour and Commonsense.* London: Fabian Society and Commonwealth Bureau, 1958.

———. *Contemporary Trends in African Urbanization.* Evanston: Northwestern University Press, 1966.

———. *Negroes in Britain: A Study of Racial Relations in English Society.* London: K. Paul, Trench, Trubner, 1947.

———. "The Perils of Pioneering Race Relations." *American Anthropologist* 77.4 (December 1975): 887–88.

———. "The Position of Colored People in Britain." *Phylon* 15 (1957): 58–64.

———. *Race and Society.* Paris: UNESCO, 1958.

———. "Research Report No. 2 of Department of Social Anthropology." *Sociological Review* 8.2 (December 1960): 255–66.

———. "The Role of Voluntary Associations in West African Urbanization." *American Anthropologist* 59 (1957): 579–96.

———. "Social Anthropology: The Approaches to Fieldwork." *Man* 52 (November 1952).

———. "Some Traditionally Based Forms of Mutual Aid in West African Urbanization." *Ethnology* 1.2 (1962): 197–211.

———. *West African Urbanization: A Study of Voluntary Associations in Social Change.* Cambridge: Cambridge University Press, 1965.

Littlewood, Roland, and Maurice Lipsedge. "Acute Psychotic Reactions in Caribbean-Born Patients." *Psychological Medicine* 11 (1981): 303–18.

Livingstone, Arthur Stanley. *The Overseas Student in Britain.* Manchester: University Press, 1960.

Lodge, David. *Ginger, You're Barmy.* London: Penguin, 1962.

Longpet, Hale Gabriel. "Private Fostering of Children of West African Origin in England." Ph.D. thesis, University of Bristol, 2000.

Louis, William Roger. "American Anti-Colonialism and the Dissolution of the British Empire." *International Affairs* 61.3 (1985): 395–420.

———. "The Dissolution of the British Empire in the Era of Vietnam." In *Ends of British Imperialism: The Scramble for Empire, Suez and Decolonization—Collected Essays,* ed. Wm. Roger Louis. New York: I. B. Tauris, 2006, 557–86.

Louis, William Roger, and Roger Owen. *Suez 1956: The Crisis and Its Conse-quences.* Oxford: Clarendon, 1989.
Louis, William Roger, and Ronald Robinson. "The Imperialism of Decoloni-zation." *Journal of Imperial and Commonwealth History* 22.3 (September 1994): 463–511.
Lowe, Rodney. "Plumbing New Depths: Contemporary Historians and the Public Record Office." *Twentieth-Century British History* 8.2 (1997): 239–65.
———. *The Welfare State in Britain since 1945,* 2nd edition. Basingstoke: Mac-millan 1999.
Luhrmann, T.M. *The Good Parsi: The Fate of a Colonial Elite in a Postcolonial Society.* Cambridge, MA: Harvard University Press, 1996.
Lunn, Kenneth, ed. *Hosts, Immigrants and Minorities: Historical Responses to Newcomers in British Society, 1870–1914.* Folkestone: Dawson, 1980.
Lynn, Martin. Introduction to *The British Empire in the 1950s: Retreat or Revival,* ed. Martin Lynn. Basingstoke: Palgrave Macmillan, 2006, 1–15.
Lyons, Amelia H. "Social Welfare, French Muslims, and Decolonization in France: The Case of the *Fonds d'action sociale.*" *Patterns of Prejudice* 43.1 (2009): 65–89.
Macadam, Elizabeth. *The New Philanthropy: A Study of the Relations between the Statutory and Voluntary Social Services.* London: G. Allen and Unwin, 1934.
MacDermott, W.R. "The Topographical Distribution of Insanity." *British Medical Journal* 2 (September 26, 1908): 950.
Macdonald, Ian A. *Race Relations and Immigration Law.* London: Butter-worths, 1969.
MacInnes, Colin. *City of Spades.* New York: Macmillan, 1957.
Mackay, Mercedes. *Black Argosy* (London: Putnam, 1954).
MacKenzie, John M. *Propaganda and Empire: The Manipulation of British Public Opinion, 1880–1960.* Manchester: Manchester University Press, 1984.
Macleod, Roy, ed. *Government and Expertise: Specialists, Administrators and Professionals, 1860–1919.* Cambridge: Cambridge University Press, 1988.
Macnicol, John, and Andrew Blaikie. "The Politics of Retirement, 1908–1948." In *Growing Old in the Twentieth Century,* ed. Margot Jefferys. London: Routledge, 1989, 21–42.
Maddox, H. "The Assimilation of Negroes in a Dockland Area in Britain." *Sociological Review* 8.1 (July 1960): 5–15.
Mahone, Sloan. "The Psychology of Rebellion: Colonial Medical Responses to Dissent in East Africa." *Journal of African History* 47.2 (July 2006): 241–58.
Mair, L.P. "African Marriage and Social Change. In *Survey of African Mar-riage and Family Life,* ed. Arthur Phillips. Oxford: Oxford University Press, 1953, 1–171.
Majumdar, Rochona. *Marriage and Modernity: Family Values in Colonial Ben-gal.* Durham, NC: Duke University Press, 2009.

Malzberg, Benjamin. "Are Immigrants Psychologically Disturbed?" In *Changing Perspectives in Mental Illness*, ed. Stanley C. Plog and Robert B. Edgerton. New York: Holt, Rinehart and Winston, 1969, 395–421.

———. "Mental Disease among English-Born and Native Whites of English Parentage in New York State, 1949–1951." *Mental Hygiene* 48 (1964): 32–54.

Malzberg, Benjamin, and Everett S. Lee. *Migration and Mental Disease: A Study of First Admissions to Hospitals for Mental Disease, New York, 1939–1941*. New York: Social Science Research Council, 1956.

Mama, Amina. "Black Women, the Economic Crisis, and the Welfare State." *Feminist Review* 17 (1984): 21–35.

Mandler, Peter. "Margaret Mead amongst the Natives of Great Britain." *Past and Present* 204 (2009): 195–233.

———. "One World, Many Cultures: Margaret Mead and the Limits to Cold War Anthropology." *History Workshop Journal* 68.1 (2009): 149–72.

Mani, Lata. *Contentious Traditions: The Debate on Sati in Colonial India*. Berkeley: University of California Press, 1998.

Mann, Kristin. *Marrying Well: Marriage, Status and Social Change among the Educated Elite in Colonial Lagos*. Cambridge: Cambridge University Press, 1985.

Manson, Andrew. "Christopher Bethell and the Securing of the Bechuanaland Frontier, 1878–1884." *Journal of Southern African Studies* 24.3 (1998): 485–508.

Marsh, Alan. "Awareness of Racial Differences in West African and British Children." *Race* 11 (1970): 289–302.

Martens, Jeremy. "Polygamy, Sexual Danger, and the Creation of Vagrancy Legislation in Colonial Natal." *Journal of Imperial and Commonwealth History* 31.3 (2003): 24–45.

Mason, Philip. *Race Relations*. London: Oxford University Press, 1970.

———. *A Thread of Silk: Further Memories of a Varied Life*. Salisbury: M. Russell, 1984.

Matera, Marc. "Colonial Subjects: Black Intellectuals and the Development of Colonial Studies in Britain." *Journal of British Studies* 49 (2010): 388–418.

Matsuda, Matt. *Empire of Love: Histories of France and the Pacific*. Oxford: Oxford University Press, 2005.

Mathur, Saloni. "History and Anthropology in South Asia: Rethinking the Archive." *Annual Review of Anthropology* 29 (2000): 89–106.

May, Elaine Tyler. *Homeward Bound: American Families in the Cold War Era*. New York: Basic Books, 1988.

Mayer, Philip. "Migrancy and the Study of Africans in Towns." *American Anthropologist* 64.3 (June 1962): 576–92.

Mazower, Mark. *No Enchanted Palace: The End of Empire and the Ideological Origins of the United Nations*. Princeton, NJ: Princeton University Press, 2009.

Mbanga, Wilf. *Seretse and Ruth: Botswana's Love Story*. Cape Town: Tafelberg, 2005.

McClintock, F. H. *Crimes of Violence: An Enquiry by the Cambridge Institute of Criminology into Crimes of Violence against the Person in London*. London: Macmillan, 1963.

McCowan, Anthony. *Coloured Peoples in Britain*. London: Bow Group, 1952.

McCulloch, Jock. *Colonial Psychiatry and the 'African Mind.'* Cambridge: Cambridge University Press, 1995.

———. "The Empire's New Clothes: Ethnopsychiatry in Colonial Africa." *History of the Human Sciences* 6.2 (1993): 35–52.

McGovern, D., and Rosemarie V. Cope. "First Psychiatric Admission Rates of First and Second Generation Afro Caribbeans." *Social Psychiatry* 22 (1987): 139–49.

McGregor, O. R. *Divorce in England: A Centenary Study*. Melbourne: Heinemann, 1957.

McKittrick, Meredith. *To Dwell Secure: Generation, Christianity and Colonialism in Ovamboland*. Portsmouth, NH: Heinemann, 2002.

Menski, W. F. "Asians in Britain and the Question of Adaptation to a New Legal Order: Asian Laws in Britain." In *Ethnicity, Identity, Migration: The South Asian Context*, ed. Milton Israel and N. K. Wagle. Toronto: University of Toronto, 1993, 238–68.

———. "English Family Law and Ethnic Laws in Britain." *Kerala Law Times* 1 (1988): 56–66.

Mercer, Kobena. "Racism and Transcultural Psychiatry." In *The Power of Psychiatry*, ed. Peter Miller and Nikolas Rose. Cambridge: Polity, 1986, 112–42.

Mezey, A. G. "Personal Background, Emigration, and Mental Disorder in Hungarian Refugees." *Journal of Mental Science* 106 (1960): 618–27.

———. "Psychiatric Illness in Hungarian Refugees." *Journal of Mental Science* 106 (1960): 628–37.

Miescher, Stephan F. *Making Men in Ghana*. Bloomington, IN: Indiana University Press, 2005.

Miles, Robert. "Migration Discourse in Post-1945 British Politics." *Migration* 6 (1989): 29–53.

———. *Racism after 'Race Relations.'* London: Routledge, 1993.

———. "Whatever Happened to the Sociology of Migration?" *Work, Employment, and Society* 4.2 (June 1990): 281–98.

Miller, S. M. "Introduction: The Legacy of Richard Titmuss." In *The Philosophy of Welfare: Selected Writings of Richard Titmuss*, ed. Brian Abel-Smith and Kay Titmuss. London: Allen and Unwin, 1987, 1–7.

Mills, David. *Difficult Folk? A Political History of Social Anthropology*. New York: Bergahn, 2009.

Minc, S. "Of New Australian Patients, Their Medical Lore, and Major Anxieties." *Medical Journal of Australia* 1 (May 11, 1963): 681–87.

Mintz, Steven. "Reflections on Age as a Category of Historical Analysis." *Journal of the History of Childhood and Youth* 1.1 (2008): 91–94.

Mitchell, Timothy. *Rule of Experts: Egypt, Techno-Politics, Modernity.* Berkeley: University of California Press, 2002.

Mongia, Radhika. "Gender and the Historiography of Gandhian *Satyagraha* in South Africa." *Gender and History* 18.1 (2006): 130–49.

Moody, Violet, and C. Eric Stroud. "One Hundred Mothers: A Survey of West Indians in Britain." *Maternal and Child Care* 3 (June 1967): 487–90.

Moore, Robert. "Race Relations and the Rediscovery of Sociology." *British Journal of Sociology* 22.1 (1971): 97–104.

Moore, Sally Falk. *Anthropology and Africa: Changing Perspectives on a Changing Scene.* Charlottesville: University Press of Virginia, 1994.

Morakinyo, Olufemi. "The Brain-Fag Syndrome in Nigeria: Cognitive Defects in an Illness associated with Study." *British Journal of Psychiatry* 146 (1985): 209–10.

———. "A Psychophysiological Theory of a Psychiatric Illness (the Brain-Fag Syndrome) associated with Study among Africans." *Journal of Nervous and Mental Disease* 168 (1980): 84–89.

Moran, Mary H. "Civilized Servants: Child Fosterage and Training for Status among the Glebo of Liberia." In *African Encounters with Domesticity,* ed. Karen Tranberg Hansen. New Brunswick, NJ: Rutgers University Press, 1992, 98–115.

Morris, J.H.C. "Ali v. Ali." *International and Comparative Law Quarterly* 17 (1968): 1015–16.

———. "The Recognition of Polygamous Marriages in English Law." *Harvard Law Review* 66.6 (April 1953): 961–1012.

Morris, Richard T. (with Oluf M. Davidsen). *The Two-Way Mirror: National Status in Foreign Students' Adjustment.* Minneapolis: University of Minnesota Press, 1960.

Mort, Frank. *Capital Affairs: London and the Making of the Permissive Society.* New Haven, CT: Yale University Press, 2010.

———. *Dangerous Sexualities: Medico-Moral Politics in England since 1830.* London: Routledge and Kegan Paul, 1987.

———. "Scandalous Events: Metropolitan Culture and Moral Change in Post-Second World War London." *Representations* 93 (winter 2006): 106–37.

Mphahlele, Ezekiel. "The African Intellectual." In *Africa in Transition: Some BBC Talks on Changing Conditions in the Union and the Rhodesias,* ed. Prudence Smith. London: M. Reinhardt, 1958, 149–58.

Muir, Christine, and Esther Goody. "Student Parents: West African Families in London." *Race* 13 (1972): 329–36.

Mukherjee, Sumita. *Nationalism, Education and Migrant Identities: The England-Returned.* London: Routledge, 2010.

Mullard, Chris. *Black Britain.* London: Allen and Unwin, 1973.

Murdoch, Lydia. *Imagined Orphans: Poor Families, Child Welfare, and Contested Citizenship in London.* New Brunswick, NJ: Rutgers University Press, 2006.

Murphy, Michael. "Measuring the Family Life Cycle: Concepts, Data and

Methods." In *Rethinking the Life Cycle,* ed. Alan Bryman et al. Basingstoke: MacMillan, 1987, 30–50.

Musgrove, Frank. *Youth and the Social Order.* Bloomington, IN: Indiana University Press, 1964.

Naipaul, V. S. *The Mimic Men.* New York: Macmillan, 1967.

Nava, Mica. *Visceral Cosmopolitanism: Gender, Culture and the Normalisation of Difference.* Oxford: Berg, 2007.

Navias, Martin S. Terminating Conscription? The British National Service Controversy, 1955–56." *Journal of Contemporary History* 24.2 (1989): 195–208.

Ndem, Eyo B. "The Status of Colored People in Britain." *Phylon Quarterly* 18.1 (1957): 82–87.

Nesbitt, Anne, and Margaret A. Lynch. "African Children in Britain." *Archives of Diseases in Childhood* 67 (1992): 1402–5.

Ngai, Mae M. *Impossible Subjects: Illegal Aliens and the Making of Modern America.* Princeton, NJ: Princeton University Press, 2004.

Nichol, Alexandra. *The Social Sciences Arrive.* Swindon: Economic and Social Research Council, 2001.

Nkrumah, Kwame. *The Autobiography of Kwame Nkrumah.* New York: Thomas Nelson, 1957.

Noble, Virginia *Inside the Welfare State: Foundations of Policy and Practice in Post-War Britain.* London: Routledge, 2008.

Nocon, Andrew. "A Reluctant Welcome? Poles in Britain in the 1940s," *Oral History* 24.1 (1996): 79–87.

Nortey, Kobina. *The Man with Two Wives.* Accra: Peacock, 1964.

Ogieriaikhi, Emwinma. *The Marriage Couldn't Continue.* Benin City: Language Press, 1965.

———. *My Wife or My Wives.* Benin City: Language Press, 1965.

Ogunsola, Abiola. "Meeting the Childcare Needs of West African Families." *African Woman* (autumn 1991): 10–11.

"Ohochuku v. Ohochuku." *Journal of African Law* 4.1 (1960): 56–57.

Okin, Susan Moller. *Is Multiculturalism Bad for Women?* Princeton, NJ: Princeton University Press, 1999.

Olugboji, Dayo. *The Problem of Nigerian Students Overseas.* Lagos: C.M.S. Press, 1959.

Olusanya, B., and D. Hodes. "West African Children in Private Foster Care in City and Hackney." *Child: Care, Health, and Development* 26.4 (2000): 337–42.

Olusanya, G. O. *The West African Students' Union and the Politics of Decolonisation, 1925–1958.* Ibadan: Daystar, 1982.

Omari, T. Peter. "Changing Attitudes of Students in West African Society toward Marriage and Family Relationships." *British Journal of Sociology* 11 (1960): 197–210.

"Open Letter to Britons." *West African Review* 16 (November 1945): 15–17.

Ortolano, Guy. *The Two Cultures Controversy: Science, Literature and Cultural Politics in Postwar Britain.* Cambridge: Cambridge University Press, 2009.

Ovendale, Ritchie. "The End of Empire," In *Rethinking British Decline*, ed. Richard English and Michael Kenny. Houndmills: Macmillan, 2000, pp. 257–78.

Owen, Nicholas. "Decolonization and the Postwar Consensus." In *The Myth of Consensus: New Views on British History, 1945–64*, ed. Harriet Jones and Michael Kandiah. New York: St. Martin's Press, 1996), 157–81.

Paisley, Fiona. "Childhood and Race: Growing Up in the Empire." In *Gender and Empire*, ed. Philippa Levine. Oxford: Oxford University Press, 2004, 240–59.

Panayi, Panikos. *Immigration, Ethnicity, and Racism in Britain, 1815–1945*. Manchester: Manchester University Press, 1994.

Parker, Jason. "Made-in-America Revolutions? The 'Black University' and the American Role in the Decolonization of the Black Atlantic." *Journal of American History* 96.3. (2009): 727–50.

Parsons, Neil. "The Impact of Seretse Khama on British Public Opinion." *Immigrants and Minorities* 3 (1993): 195–219.

Parsons, Timothy H. *Race, Resistance, and the Boy Scout Movement in British Colonial Africa*. Athens, OH: Ohio University Press, 2004.

Patchett, K. W. "English Law in the West Indies: A Conference Report." *International and Comparative Law Quarterly* (1963): 922–66.

Patterson, Sheila. "Family and Domestic Patterns of West Indian Immigrants." *Proceedings of the Royal Society of Medicine* 57 (1964): 321–28.

Patton, Sandra. *BirthMarks: Transracial Adoption in Contemporary America*. New York: New York University Press, 2000.

Paul, Kathleen. *Whitewashing Britain: Race and Citizenship in the Postwar Era*. Ithaca: Cornell University Press, 1997.

Pearl, David. *Family Law and the Immigrant Communities*. Bristol: Family Law, 1986.

Peart, Edwina. "The Experience of Being Privately Fostered." *Adoption and Fostering* 29.3 (2005): 57–67.

Pedersen, Susan. *Family, Dependence, and the Origins of the Welfare State: Britain and France, 1914–1945*. Cambridge: Cambridge University Press, 1993.

———. "The Maternalist Moment in British Colonial Policy: The Controversy over 'Child Slavery' in Hong Kong." *Past and Present* 171 (2001): 161–202.

Pellew, Jill. "Law and Order: Expertise and the Victorian Home Office." In *Government and Expertise: Specialists, Administrators and Professionals, 1860–1919*, ed. Roy Macleod. Cambridge: Cambridge University Press, 1988, 59–72.

Pennybacker, Susan D. *From Scottsboro to Munich: Race and Political Culture in 1930s Britain*. Princeton, NJ: Princeton University Press, 2009.

Peppard, Nadine. "Into the Third Decade," *New Community* 1.2 (1972): 93–98.

Perham, Margery. *The Colonial Reckoning: The End of Imperial Rule in Africa in the Light of British Experience*. New York: Knopf, 1962.

Perkin, Harold. *The Rise of Professional Society: England since 1880.* London: Routledge, 1989.

Perraton, Hilary. *Learning Abroad: A History of the Commonwealth Scholarship and Fellowship Plan.* Newcastle upon Tyne: Cambridge Scholars Publications, 2009.

Perry, Kennetta Hammond. "'Little Rock' in Britain: Jim Crow's Transatlantic Topographies." *Journal of British Studies* 51.1 (2012): 155–77.

Phillips, Arthur. "Marriage Laws in Africa." In *Survey of African Marriage and Family Life,* ed. Arthur Phillips. Oxford: Oxford University Press for the International African Institute, 1953, 173–327.

Phills, George Henry. "Social Perception and Anxiety in Nigerian and British Students," Ph.D. thesis, Bedford College, University of London, 1963.

Philpot, Terry. *A Very Private Practice: An Investigation into Private Fostering.* London: British Agencies for Adoption and Fostering, 2001.

Pilcher, Jane. *Age and Generation in Modern Britain.* Oxford: Oxford University Press, 1995.

Pilkington, Edward. *Beyond the Mother Country: West Indians and the Notting Hill White Riots.* London: I. B. Tauris, 1988.

Pinsent, R. J. F. H. "Morbidity in an Immigrant Population." *Lancet* 1 (February 23, 1963): 437–38.

Platt, Jennifer. *The British Sociological Association; A Sociological History.* Durham, NC: Sociologypress, 2003.

Pletsch, Carl E. "The Three Worlds, Or The Division of Social Scientific Labor, circa 1950–1975." *Comparative Studies in Society and History* 23.4 (1981): 565–90.

Pless, I. B., and C. Hood. "West Indian One-Year Olds." *Lancet* 1 (June 24, 1967): 1373–76.

Political and Economic Planning. *Colonial Students in Britain: A Report by PEP, June 1955.* London: PEP, 1955.

Pollak, Margaret. *Today's Three-Year Olds in London.* Lavenham: Heinemann, 1972.

Porter, Bernard. *The Absent-Minded Imperialists: Empire, Society and Culture in Britain.* Oxford: Oxford University Press, 2004.

Porter, Theodore M., and Dorothy Ross, eds. *The Cambridge History of Science. The Modern Social Sciences,* vol. 7. Cambridge: Cambridge University Press, 2003.

Poulter, Sebastian. "African Customs in an English Setting: Legal and Policy Aspects of Recognition." *Journal of African Law* 31 (spring 1987): 207–25.

———. "Ethnic Minority Customs, English Law, and Human Rights." *International and Comparative Law Quarterly* 36 (1987): 589–615.

Prakash, Gyan. *Another Reason: Science and the Imagination of Modern India.* Princeton, NJ: Princeton University Press, 1999.

Price, David H. *Anthropological Intelligence: The Deployment and Neglect of American Anthropology in the Second World War.* Durham, NC: Duke University Press, 2008.

———. "Subtle Means and Enticing Carrots: The Impact of Funding on American Cold War Anthropology." *Critique of Anthropology* 23 (2003): 373–401.

Prince, G. Stewart. "Mental Health Problems in Pre-School West Indian Children." *Maternal and Child Care* 3 (1967): 483–86.

Prince, Raymond. "The 'Brain Fag' Syndrome in Nigerian Students." *Journal of Mental Science* 106 (1960): 559–70.

———. "The Changing Picture of Depressive Syndromes in Africa: Is It Fact or Diagnostic Fashion?" *Canadian Journal of African Studies* 1 (1967): 177–92.

———. "Functional Symptoms associated with Study in Nigerian Students." *West African Medical Journal* 11 (1962): 198–206.

Race and Politics in Kenya: A Correspondence between Elspeth Huxley and Margery Perham. London: Faber and Faber, 1956.

Radcliffe-Brown, A. R., and Daryll Forde, eds. *African Systems of Kinship and Marriage.* London: Oxford University Press, 1950.

Rafael, Vicente L. *White Love and Other Events in Filipino History.* Durham, NC: Duke University Press, 2000.

Rayden, William. *Rayden's Practice and Law of Divorce.* London: Butterworths, 1968.

Read, J. C. "Psychological Disturbances in Students from Overseas." *Medical World* 90 (January 1959): 18–24.

"Recognition of Polygamous Marriages." *International Law Quarterly* 1 (1947): 64.

Redshaw, G. M. "Psychiatric Problems a British Government Policy and Decolonisation 1945–1963: Scrutinising the Official Mind amongst Migrants." *Medical Journal of Australia* 43.2 (December 8, 1956): 852–53.

Reeves, Frank. *British Racial Discourse: A Study of British Political Discourse about Race and Race-Related Matters.* Cambridge: Cambridge University Press, 1983.

Renne, Elisha P. "Childhood Memories and Contemporary Parenting in Ekiti, Nigeria." *Africa* 75 (March 2005): 63–83.

Report of the Committee on Indian Students 1921–1922. London: H.M.S.O., 1922.

Rex, John, and Robert Moore. *Race, Community, and Conflict: A Study of Sparkbrook.* Oxford: Oxford University Press for the Institute of Race Relations, 1967.

Rich, Paul B. *Prospero's Return? Historical Essays on Race, Culture, and British Society.* London: Hansib, 1994.

Richards, Audrey. *Chisungu: A Girls' Initiation Ceremony among the Bemba of Northern Rhodesia.* London: Faber and Faber, 1956.

Richardson, Alan. "The Assimilation of British Immigrants in Australia." *Human Relations* 10 (1957): 157–66.

———. "British Emigrants to Australia: A Study of Some Psycho-Social Differences between Emigrants and Non-Emigrant Skilled Manual Workers." Ph.D. thesis, University of London, 1956.

———. *British Immigrants and Australia: A Psycho-Social Inquiry.* Canberra: Australian National University Press, 1974.

———. "Some Psycho-Social Characteristics of Satisfied and Dissatisfied British Immigrant Skilled Manual Workers in Western Australia." *Human Relations* 10 (1957): 235–48.

———. "A Theory and a Method for the Psychological Study of Assimilation." *International Migration Review* 2.1 (1968): 3–30.

Richmond, Anthony H. *Colour Prejudice in Britain: A Study of West Indian Workers in Liverpool, 1941–1951.* London: Routledge and Kegan Paul, 1954.

———. *Migration and Race Relations in an English City: A Study in Bristol.* London: Oxford University Press for the Institute of Race Relations, 1973.

Rickards, Colin. "How the Migrant Deportation Act Is Working." *Daily Gleaner,* February 7, 1963.

Riley, Denise. *War in the Nursery: Theories of the Child and Mother.* London: Virago, 1983.

Ritscherle, Alice. "Opting Out of Utopia: Race and Working-Class Political Culture during the Era of Decolonization." Ph.D. diss., University of Michigan, 2005.

Robertson, Claire. *Sharing the Same Bowl? A Socioeconomic History of Women and Class in Accra, Ghana.* Bloomington, IN: Indiana University Press, 1984.

Robertson, Frederick. "The Relations between the English Law and the Personal Law of Indians in England with Special Reference to the Marriage Law." *Journal of Comparative Legislation and International Law* 18.2 (1918): 242–59.

Robin, Ron. *The Making of the Cold War Enemy: Culture and Politics in the Military-Intellectual Complex.* Princeton, NJ: Princeton University Press, 2001.

Rose, Arnold M. "The Social Scientist as Expert Witness." *Minnesota Law Review* 40 (1956): 205–18.

Rose, E. J. B. "A Myrdal for Britain: A Personal Memoir." *New Community* 14 (1987): 83–88.

Rose, Nikolas. *Governing the Soul: The Shaping of the Private Self.* London: Free Association Books, 1999.

———. *Inventing Our Selves: Psychology, Power, and Personhood.* Cambridge: Cambridge University Press, 1996.

———. "Law, Rights, and Psychiatry." In *The Power of Psychiatry,* ed. Peter Miller and Nikolas Rose. Cambridge: Polity, 1986, 177–213.

Rose, Sonya O. "From the 'New Jerusalem' to the 'Decline' of the 'New Elizabethan Age': National Identity and Citizenship in Britain, 1945-56." In *Histories of the Aftermath: The Legacies of the Second World War in Europe,* ed. Frank Biess and Robert Moeller. New York: Bergahn, 2010, 231–47.

Rosen, Lawrence. "The Anthropologist as Expert Witness." *American Anthropologist* 79 (1977): 555–78.

Ross, Dorothy. "Changing Contours of the Social Science Disciplines." In

The Cambridge History of Science. The Modern Social Sciences, vol. 7, ed. Theodore M. Porter and Dorothy Ross. Cambridge: Cambridge University Press, 2003, 205–37.

Rothschild, Emma. *The Inner Life of Empires: An Eighteenth-Century History.* Princeton, NJ: Princeton University Press, 2011.

Roundtable on *Ornamentalism. Journal of Colonialism and Colonial History* 3.1 (2002).

Rowe, Michael. *The Racialisation of Disorder in Twentieth-Century Britain.* Aldershot: Ashgate, 1998.

———. "Sex, 'Race' and Riot in Liverpool, 1919." *Immigrants and Minorities* 19.2 (2000): 53–70.

Rowntree, B. Seebohm. *Poverty: A Study in Town Life.* London: Macmillan, 1901.

———. *Poverty and Progress: A Second Social Survey of York.* London: Longmans, Green, 1941.

Royer, John. *Black Britain's Dilemma: A Medico-Social Transcultural Study of West Indians,* vol. 1. Roseau: Tropical Printers, 1977.

Russell, Matthew. "The Irish Delinquent in England." *Studies* 53 (1964): 136–48.

Rutter, Michael, et al. "Children of West Indian Immigrants—I. Home Circumstances and Family Patterns." *Journal of Child Psychology and Psychiatry* 15 (1974): 241–62.

Rwegellera, G. G. C. "Mental Illness in Africans and West Indians of African Origin Living in London." M.Phil. thesis, University of London, 1970.

Sadowsky, Jonathan. *Imperial Bedlam: Institutions of Madness in Colonial Southwest Nigeria.* Berkeley: University of California Press, 1999.

Saint, Eric G. "The Medical Problems of Migrants." *Medical Journal of Australia* 1 (March 9, 1963): 335–38.

Sandbrook, Dominic. *Never Had It So Good: A History of Britain from the Suez to the Beatles* (London: Little, Brown, 2005).

Sanders, Todd. "The Torso in the Thames: Imagining Darkest Africa in the United Kingdom." In *Auto-Ethnographies: The Anthropology of Academic Practices,* ed. Anne Meneley and Donna J. Young. Peterborough: Broadview, 2005, 126–42.

"A Santa for Sandra." *West African Review* 25 (January 1954): 30–31.

Sanua, Victor. "Immigration, Migration and Mental Illness: A Review of the Literature with Special Emphasis on Schizophrenia." In *Behavior in New Environments: Adaptation of Migrant Populations,* ed. E. B. Brody. Beverly Hills: Sage, 1969, 291–352.

Sarkar, Tanika. "Rhetoric against Age of Consent: Resisting Colonial Reason and Death of a Child-Wife." *Economic and Political Weekly* 28.36 (September 4, 1993): 1869–78.

Saunders, Ian, and Jerry Walter. "The Matrimonial Proceedings (Polygamous Marriages) Act 1972." *International and Comparative Law Quarterly* 21.4 (1972): 781–89.

Savage, Gail. "More than One Mrs. Mir Anwaruddin: Islamic Divorce and Christian Marriage in Early Twentieth-Century London," *Journal of British Studies* 47.2 (2008): 348–74.

Savage, Mike. *Identities and Social Change in Britain since 1940: The Politics of Method.* Oxford: Oxford University Press, 2010.

Schapera, Isaac. *Married Life in an African Tribe.* New York: Sheridan, 1941.

Schiebinger, Londa, and Claudia Swan, eds. *Colonial Botany: Science, Commerce and Politics in the Early Modern World.* Philadelphia: University of Pennsylvania Press, 2005).

Schreier, Joshua. "Napoléon's Long Shadow: Morality, Civilization and Jews in France and Algeria, 1808–1870." *French Historical Studies* 30.1 (2007): 77–103.

Schumaker, Lyn. *Africanizing Anthropology: Fieldwork, Networks, and the Making of Cultural Knowledge in Central Africa.* Durham, NC: Duke University Press, 2001.

Schwarz, Bill. "Black Metropolis, White England." In *Modern Times: Reflections on a Century of English Modernity,* ed. Mica Nava and Alan O'Shea. London: Routledge, 1996, 175–207.

———. "Claudia Jones and the *West Indian Gazette:* Reflections on the Emergence of Post-Colonial Britain." *Twentieth-Century British History* 14. (2003): 264–85.

———. "'The Only White Man in There': The Re-Racialisation of England," *Race and Class* 38 (1996): 65–78.

———. "Reveries of Race: The Closing of the Imperial Moment." In *Moments of Modernity: Reconstructing Britain, 1945–1964,* ed. Becky Conekin et al. London: Rivers Oram, 1999, 189–207.

———. *The White Man's World. Memories of Empire,* vol. 1. Oxford: Oxford University Press, 2011.

———, ed. *West Indian Intellectuals in Britain.* Manchester: Manchester University Press, 2003.

Scott, L. V. *Conscription and the Attlee Governments: The Politics and Policy of National Service, 1945–1951.* Oxford: Clarendon, 1993.

Scott, Rachel. *A Wedding Man Is Nicer than Cats, Miss: A Teacher at Work with Immigrant Children.* New York: St. Martin's Press, 1971.

Sellitz, Claire, et al. *Attitudes and Social Relations of Foreign Students in the United States.* Minneapolis: University of Minnesota Press, 1963.

Selverstone, Marc J. *Constructing the Monolith: The United States, Great Britain, and International Communism, 1945–1950.* Cambridge, MA: Harvard University Press, 2009.

Selvon, Sam. *The Housing Lark.* London: MacGibbon and Kee, 1965.

Sen, Satadru. *Colonial Childhoods: The Juvenile Periphery of India, 1850–1945.* London: Anthem, 2005.

Shah, Prakash. "Attitudes to Polygamy in English Law." *International and Comparative Law Quarterly* 52 (2003): 369–400.

———. *Legal Pluralism in Conflict: Coping with Cultural Diversity in Law*. London: Glass House Press, 2005.

Sharp, Lesley. *The Sacrificed Generation: Youth, History, and the Colonized Mind in Madagascar*. Berkeley: University of California Press, 2002.

Shaw, Tony. "Britain and the Cultural Cold War." *Contemporary British History* 19.2 (2005): 109–15.

Shepard, Todd. "Algeria, France, Mexico, UNESCO: A Transnational History of Anti-Racism and Decolonization, 1939-1962." *Journal of Global History* 6 (2011): 273–97.

———. "'History Is Past Politics?' Archives, 'Tainted Evidence,' and the Return of the State." *American Historical Review* 115 (2010): 474–83.

———. *The Invention of Decolonization: The Algerian War and the Remaking of France*. Ithaca: Cornell University Press, 2006.

Shils, Edward. *The Intellectual between Tradition and Modernity: The Indian Situation*. The Hague: Mouton, 1961.

———. *The Intellectuals and the Powers and Other Essays*. Chicago: University of Chicago Press, 1972.

Simey, T. S. "Adjustment Problems of Negro and Immigrant Elites." In *Race Relations in World Perspective*, ed. Andrew Lind. Honolulu: University of Hawai'i Press, 1954, 289–310.

Simpson, Christopher. *Science of Coercion: Communication Research and Psychological Warfare 1945–1960*. New York: Oxford University Press, 1994.

Singh, A. K. *Indian Students in Britain: A Survey of Their Adjustment and Attitudes*. London: Asia Publishing House, 1963.

———. "Indian University Students in Britain," *Planning* 27 (November 13, 1961): 283–313.

Sington, Derrick. "The Policeman and the Immigrant." *New Society* (February 24, 1966): 13–15.

Sivanandan, A. *Communities of Resistance: Writings on Black Struggles for Socialism*. London: Verso, 1990.

———. *A Different Hunger: Writings on Black Resistance*. London: Pluto, 1982.

———. "Race and Resistance: The IRR Story." *Race and Class* 50.2 (2008): 1–30.

Smith, Barbara Fletchman. *Mental Slavery: Psychoanalytic Studies of Caribbean People*. London: Rebus, 2000.

Smith, Cyril. "Networks of Influence: The Social Sciences in Britain since the War." In *Essays on the History of British Sociological Research*, ed. Martin Bulmer. Cambridge: Cambridge University Press, 1985, 61–76.

Smith, James Howard. *Bewitching Development: Witchcraft and the Reinvention of Development in Neoliberal Kenya*. Chicago: University of Chicago Press, 2008.

Smith, Jef. "The Early History of West Indian Immigrant Boys." *British Journal of Social Work* 1.1 (1971): 73–84.

Smith, Vanessa. *Intimate Strangers: Friendship, Exchange and Pacific Encounters*. Cambridge: Cambridge University Press, 2010.

Smythe, Hugh H., and Mabel M. Smythe. *The New Nigerian Elite*. Stanford, CA: Stanford University Press, 1960.

Spencer, Ian R. G. *British Immigration Policy since 1939: The Making of Multi-Racial Britain*. London: Routledge, 1997.

Spinley, B. M. *The Deprived and the Privileged: Personality Development in English Society*. London: Routledge and Kegan Paul, 1953.

Spitzer, Alan B. "The Historical Problem of Generations." *American Historical Review* 78.5 (December 1973): 1353–85.

Springhall, John. *Youth, Empire and Society: British Youth Movements, 1883–1940*. London: Croom Helm, 1977.

Stadulis, Elizabeth. "The Resettlement of Displaced Persons in the United Kingdom." *Population Studies* 5.3 (1952): 207–37.

Stapleton, Pat. "Children of Commonwealth Students—The Parents' Dilemma." *Institute of Race Relations Newsletter* (January 1969): 20–24.

——. "Living in Britain." In *West African Families in Britain: A Meeting of Two Cultures*, ed. June Ellis et al. London: Routledge and Kegan Paul, 1978, 56–73.

Starkey, Pat. "The Feckless Mother: Women, Poverty and Social Workers in Wartime and Post-War England." *Women's History Review* 9 (2000): 539–57.

——. "The Medical Officer of Health, the Social Worker, and the Problem Family." *Social History of Medicine* 11.3 (1998): 421–41.

Stevenson, Olive. *Someone Else's Child: A Book for Foster Parents of Young Children*. London: Routledge and K. Paul, 1965.

Stewart, Marjorie. "Courses for Overseas Women in London, *African Women* 1 (1955): 32–33.

Still, R. J. "Mental Health in Overseas Students." *Proceedings of the British Student Health Association* 13 (1961): 59–73.

St. John, John. *A Trick of the Sun: A Tragi-Comedy*. London: Heinemann, 1956.

Stockwell, A. J. "Leaders, Dissidents and the Disappointed: Colonial Students in Britain as Empire Ended." In *Ambiguities of Empire: Essays in Honour of Andrew Porter*, ed. Robert Holland and Sarah Stockwell. London: Routledge, 2009, 144–64.

Stoler, Ann Laura. *Along the Archival Grain: Epistemic Anxieties and Colonial Common Sense*. Princeton, NJ: Princeton University Press, 2008.

——. *Carnal Knowledge and Imperial Power: Race and the Intimate in Colonial Rule*. Berkeley: University of California Press, 2002.

——, ed. *Haunted by Empire: Geographies of Intimacy in North American History*. Durham, NC: Duke University Press, 2006.

Stoller, Alan. "Migration and Mental Health in Australia." *British Journal of Social Psychiatry* 1 (1966): 70–77.

Stone, O. M. "Ninth Report of the Law Reform Committee (Liability in Tort between Husband and Wife)." *Modern Law Review* 24.4 (1961): 481–86.

——. "Sowa v. Sowa: Maintenance of Family Dependents." *Modern Law Review* 24.4 (1961): 500–502.

Street, Harry. *Freedom, the Individual, and the Law.* Harmondsworth: Penguin, 1963.

Stuart, Andrew. *Of Cargoes Colonies and Kings: Diplomatic and Administrative Service from Africa to the Pacific.* London: Radcliffe, 2001.

"Students from the Colonies." *Planning* 20 (November 29, 1954): 281–300.

Sudarkasa, Niara. *Where Women Work: A Study of Yoruba Women in the Marketplace and in the Homes.* Ann Arbor: University of Michigan Press, 1973.

Summers, Carol. "Youth, Elders, and Metaphors of Political Change in Late Colonial Buganda." In *Generations Past: Youth in East African History,* ed. Andrew Burton and Hélène Charton-Bigot. Athens, OH: Ohio University Press, 2010, 175–95.

Sword, Keith. "Their Prospects Will Not Be Bright: British Responses to the Problem of the Polish Recalcitrants, 1946–1949." *Journal of Contemporary History* 21.3 (1986): 367–90.

Sword, Keith, with Norman Davies and Jan Ciehchanowski. *The Formation of the Polish Community in Great Britain 1939–50.* London: School of Slavonic and East European Studies, University of London, 1989.

Sykes, John. *The Newcomer.* London: Hurst, 1956.

Symonds, Richard. *Oxford and Empire: The Last Lost Cause?* Houndmills: Macmillan, 1986.

Tabili, Laura. "Empire Is the Enemy of Love: Edith Noor's Progress and Other Stories." *Gender and History* 17 (2005): 5–28.

———. "A Homogenous Society? Britain's Internal 'Others,' 1800–present." In *At Home with the Empire: Metropolitan Culture and the Imperial World,* ed. Catherine Hall and Sonya O. Rose. Cambridge: Cambridge University Press, 2006, 53–76.

———. "Outsiders in the Land of Their Birth: Exogamy, Citizenship and Identity in War and Peace." *Journal of British Studies* 44 (October 2005): 796–815.

Taft, Ronald. "The Assimilation of Dutch Male Immigrants in a Western Australian Community: A Replication of Richardson's Study of British Immigrants." *Human Relations* 14 (1961): 265–81.

———. "Discussion." In *The Study of Immigrants in Australia,* ed. C.A. Price. Canberra: Department of Demography, Australian National University, 1960, 207.

———. *From Stranger to Citizen: A Survey of Studies of Immigrant Assimilation in Western Australia.* Perth: University of Western Australia Press, 1965.

———. "The Shared Frame of Reference Concept Applied to the Assimilation of Immigrants." *Human Relations* 6 (1953): 45–55.

Tajfel, Henri, and John L. Dawson. *Disappointed Guests: Essays by African, Asian and West Indian Students.* London: Oxford University Press, 1965.

Tannahill, J.A. *European Volunteer Workers in Britain.* Manchester: Manchester University Press, 1958.

Tewfik, G. I., and A. Okasha. "Psychosis and Immigration." *Postgraduate Medical Journal* 41 (1965): 603–12.

Thane, Pat. "Happy Families? Varieties of Family Life in Twentieth-Century Britain." Plenary address delivered at the North American Conference on British Studies, Denver, 2011.

———. "Population Politics in Post-War British Culture." In *Moments of Modernity: Reconstructing Britain 1945–1964*, ed. Becky Conekin, Frank Mort, and Chris Waters. London: Rivers Oram Press, 1999, 114-34.

Thomas, Christopher S., et al. "Psychiatric Morbidity and Compulsory Admission among UK-Born Europeans, Afro-Caribbeans, and Asians in Central Manchester." *British Journal of Psychiatry* 163 (1993): 91–99.

Thomas, Graham. "The Integration of Immigrants: A Note on the Views of Some Local Government Officials." *Race* 9 (1967): 239–48.

Thomas, Leslie. *The Virgin Soldiers*. Boston: Little, Brown, 1966.

Thomas, Lynn M. *Politics of the Womb: Women, Reproduction and the State in Kenya*. Berkeley: University of California Press, 2003.

Thomas, Nick. "Will the Real 1950s Please Stand Up? Views of a Contradictory Decade." *Cultural and Social History* 5.2 (June 2008): 227–35.

Thomson, Mathew. "'Savage Civilisation': Race, Culture and Mind in Britain, 1898–1939." In *Race, Science and Medicine, 1700–1960*, ed. Waltraud Ernst and Bernard Harris. London: Routledge, 1999, 235–58.

Thornberry, Cedric. "Law, Opinion and the Immigrant." *Modern Law Review* (1962): 654–71.

———. "A Note on the Legal Position of Commonwealth Immigrants and the White Paper Proposals." *Race* 7 (October 1965): 177–84.

Timmins, Nicholas. *The Five Giants: A Biography of the Welfare State*. London: HarperCollins, 1995.

Titmuss, Richard. *Essays on the Welfare State*. London: Allen and Unwin, 1958.

———. *The Gift Relationship: From Human Blood to Social Policy*. New York: Pantheon, 1971.

———. *Social Policy: An Introduction*, ed. Brian Abel-Smith and Kay Titmuss. New York: Pantheon, 1974.

Titmuss, Richard, and Brian Abel-Smith (with Tony Lynes). *Social Policies and Population Growth in Mauritius*. London: Methuen, 1961.

Titmuss, Richard, et al. *The Health Services of Tanganyika*. London: Pitman Medical Pub. Co., 1964.

Tolstoy, Dimitry. "The Conversion of a Polygamous Union into a Monogamous Marriage." *International and Comparative Law Quarterly* 17.3 (July 1968): 721–29.

Torrey, E. Fuller, et al. "Endemic Psychosis in Western Ireland." *American Journal of Psychiatry* 141 (August 1984): 966–70.

"Tough Deportation Regime for Immigrants Angers Lawyers." *New Law Journal* 139 (May 12, 1989): 634–35.

Townshend, Charles. *Making the Peace: Public Order and Public Security in Modern Britain.* Oxford: Oxford University Press, 1993.

Trevelyan, Mary. "Welfare Services for Overseas Students." *Proceedings of the British Student Health Association* (1961): 51–55.

Tuke, D. Hack. "Increase of Insanity in Ireland." *Journal of Mental Science* 40 (October 1894): 549–61.

Twine, France Winddance. *A White Side of Black Britain: Interracial Intimacy and Racial Literacy.* Durham, NC: Duke University Press, 2010.

Useem, John, and Ruth Hill Useem. *The Western-Educated Man in India: A Study of His Social Roles and Influence.* New York: Dryden, 1955.

Uwemedimo, Rosemary. *Mammy-Wagon Marriage.* London: Hurst and Blackett, 1961.

Van Beusekom, Monica, and Dorothy L. Hodgson. "Lessons Learned? Development Experiences in the Late Colonial Period." *Journal of African History* 41.1 (2000): 29–33.

Van Beusekom, Monica. *Negotiating Development: African Farmers and Colonial Experts at the Office du Niger, 1920–1960.* Portsmouth, NH: Heinemann, 2002.

Van Gennep, Arnold. *The Rites of Passage.* Chicago: University of Chicago Press, 1960.

Vaughan, Megan. *Curing Their Ills; Colonial Power and African Illness.* Cambridge: Polity Press, 1991.

Vellenga, Dorothy Dee. "Attempts to Change the Marriage Laws in Ghana and the Ivory Coast." In *Ghana and the Ivory Coast: Perspectives on Modernization,* ed. Philip Foster and Aristide R. Zolberg. Chicago: University of Chicago Press, 1971, 125–50.

Vernant, Jacques. *The Refugee in the Post-War World.* London: Allen and Unwin, 1953.

Vernon, James. *Hunger: A Modern History.* Cambridge, MA: Harvard University Press, 2007.

Vincent, David. *The Culture of Secrecy: Britain, 1832–1998.* Oxford: Oxford University Press, 1998.

——. "Government and the Modern Management of Information 1844–2009." In *The Peculiarities of Liberal Modernity in Imperial Britain,* ed. Simon Gunn and James Vernon. Berkeley: Global, Area, and International Archive / University of California Press, 2011.

Viswanathan, Gauri. *Masks of Conquest: Literary Study and British Rule in India.* New York: Columbia University Press, 1989.

Wainwright, A. Martin. *'The Better Class' of Indians: Social Rank, Imperial Identity, and South Asians in Britain, 1858–1914.* Manchester: Manchester University Press, 2008.

Wainwright, David. *The Volunteers: The Story of Overseas Voluntary Service.* London: Macdonald, 1965.

Walcott, Rex. "The West Indian in the British Casework Setting." *Probation Journal* 14.2 (1968): 45–47.

Walker, Anneliese. "Social Influences on Disturbed Immigrant Children." *Case Conference* 15 (1968): 231–38.

Waller, Richard. "Rebellious Youth in Colonial Africa." *Journal of African History* 47.1 (2006): 77–92.

Ward, Stuart, ed. *British Culture and the End of Empire*. Manchester: Manchester University Press, 2005.

Watt, D. C. "Rethinking the Cold War: A Letter to a British Historian." *Political Quarterly* 49.4 (1978): 446–56.

Waters, Chris. "'Dark Strangers' in our Midst: The Discourse of Race Relations." *Journal of British Studies* 36.2 (April 1997): 207–38.

———. "Havelock Ellis, Sigmund Freud and the State: Discourses of Homosexual Identity in Interwar Britain." In *Sexology in Culture: Labelling Bodies and Desires*, ed. Lucy Bland and Laura Doan. Cambridge: Polity, 1998, 165–79.

Webb, P. R. H. "Ohochuku v. Ohochuku. A Variation of Thynne v. Thynne." *Modern Law Review* 23.3 (1960): 327–31.

———. "Polygamous Marriages Again." *Modern Law Review* 24.1 (1961): 183–85.

———. "Polygamy and the Eddying Winds," *International and Comparative Law Quarterly* 14 (1965): 273.

Webster, Wendy. "Britain and the Refugees of Europe, 1939–50." In *Gendering Migration: Masculinity, Femininity and Ethnicity in Post-War Britain*, ed. Louise Ryan and Wendy Webster. Aldershot: Ashgate, 2008, 35–51.

———. "Elspeth Huxley: Gender, Empire, and Narratives of Nation, 1935–64." *Women's History Review* 8.3 (1999): 527–45.

———. "The Empire Comes Home: Commonwealth Migration to Britain." In *Britain's Experience of Empire in the Twentieth Century*, ed. Andrew Thompson. Oxford: Oxford University Press, 2012, 122–60.

———. *Englishness and Empire, 1939–1965*. Oxford: Oxford University Press, 2005.

———. *Imagining Home: Gender, 'Race' and National Identity, 1945–64*. London: UCL Press, 1998.

———. "Transnational Journeys and Domestic Histories." *Journal of Social History* 39.3 (2006): 651–66.

Weiler, Peter. *British Labour and the Cold War*. Stanford, CA: Stanford University Press, 1988.

Weinberg, Abraham A. "Mental Health Aspects of Voluntary Migration." *Mental Hygiene* 39 (1955): 450–64.

———. *Migration and Belonging: A Study of Mental Health and Personal Adjustment in Israel*. The Hague: M. Nijhoff, 1961.

Wessely, S., et al. "Schizophrenia and Afro-Caribbeans: A Case-Control Study." *British Journal of Psychiatry* 159 (1991): 795–801.

Whitfield, James. *Unhappy Dialogue: The Metropolitan Police and Black Londoners*. Cullompton: Willan, 2004.

Whitney, Susan B. *Mobilizing Youth: Communists and Catholics in Interwar France.* Durham, NC: Duke University Press, 2009.

Wiener, Martin J. "Homicide and 'Englishness': Criminal Justice and National Identity in Victorian England." *National Identities* 6.3 (2004): 203–13.

Williams, Precious. *Color Blind: A Memoir.* New York: Bloomsbury, 2010.

Williams, Susan. *Colour Bar: Seretse Khama and His Nation.* London: Allen Lane, 2006.

Wills, Abigail. "Delinquency, Masculinity and Citizenship in England, 1950–1970." *Past and Present* 187 (2005): 157–85.

Wilson, Kathleen, ed. *A New Imperial History: Culture, Identity, and Modernity, 1660–1840.* Cambridge: Cambridge University Press, 2004.

Winslow, Michelle. "Oral History and Polish Émigrés in Britain." In *The Poles in Britain 1940–2000: From Betrayal to Assimilation,* ed. Peter D. Stachura. London: Frank Cass, 2004, 85–97.

Woollard, Carol. "Private Fostering: Racial and Health Implications." *Health Visitor* 64 (October 1991): 343–44.

Woods, Oscar. "Discussion." *Journal of Mental Science* 40 (October 1894): 559.

Worby, Eric. "Discipline without Oppression: Sequence, Timing and Marginality in Southern Rhodesia's Post-War Development Regime." *Journal of African History* 41.1 (2000): 101–25.

Wunderly, Sir Harry. "A Survey of Immigration and Mental Health in Australia." In *The Study of Immigrants in Australia,* ed. C. A. Price. Canberra: Department of Demography, Australian National University, 1960, 183–91.

Yeo, Eileen Janes. *The Contest for Social Science: Relations and Representations of Gender and Class.* London: Rivers Oram Press, 1996.

Zachernuk, Philip Z. *Colonial Subjects: An African Intelligentsia and Atlantic Ideas.* Charlottesville: University Press of Virginia, 2000.

Zahra, Tara. "'Each Nation Only Cares for Its Own': Empire, Nation, and Child Welfare Activism in the Bohemian Lands, 1900–1918." *American Historical Review* 111.5 (December 2006): 1378–1402.

Zalinser, P. *African Student Opinion.* New Haven, CT: s.n., 1957.

Zimmerman, Andrew. *Alabama in Africa: Booker T. Washington, the German Empire, and the Globalization of the New South.* Princeton, NJ: Princeton University Press, 2010.

Zimmerman, Jonathan. *Innocents Abroad: American Teachers in the American Century.* Cambridge, MA: Harvard University Press, 2006.

Zubrzycki, Jerzy. *Polish Immigrants in Britain: A Study of Adjustment.* The Hague: M. Nijhoff, 1956.

———. *Settlers of the Latrobe Valley: A Sociological Study of Immigrants in the Brown Coal Industry in Australia.* Canberra: Australian National University, 1964.

Zweig, Ferdynand. *The Student in the Age of Anxiety: A Survey of Oxford and Manchester Student.* New York: Free Press, 1963.

Index

Page numbers in italics refer to figures.

Webster, Wendy, 184
welfare: archives of, 11–12, 14–15; changing nature of, 243n7, 267n61; Cold War and, 34; critics of, 23, 45, 57, 63, 69–70; decolonization and, 1–8, 14–15, 21, 24, 38, 237–38, 241, 246n30, 253n4; deportation and, 214, 223; empire and, 2, 243n9; expertise and, 8, 10; illegitimacy and, 194, 286n62; life cycle and, 15–18, 63; migration and, 30–31; overseas students and, 99–100, 106–9, 124, 128; polygamy and, 133–34, 145–53, 160–63; private fostering and, 172, 174, 180–81, 183, 186, 196, 198; uneven effects of, 5–6, 45, 237–39; VSO and, 19, 57, 61, 68–70, 74, 77, 92–94
West Africa/West African: 5, 19–20; child care and, 164–65; 174–201; independence in, 111, 121, 163; Kenneth Little and, 28–30; Man O'War Bay and, 67; marriage customs and, 152–53; 164; students from, 96–97, 102, 113–15, 121, 123, 126–27, 167–68; VSO and, 74, 83. *See also* Ghana, Nigeria, Sierra Leone
West African Pilot, 102, 103, 105, 109, 121, 196, 197
West African Review, 101–2, 110, 111, 112, 128, 166-70, 171, 172–73
West African Students' Union (WASU), 117
West Indies/West Indian: deportation to, 21, 203–8, 210–11, 214. 217, 221, 224–25, 229–32, 234; development in, 193, 243n9; family structures in, and Britain, 20, 153, 164–65, 182–83, 186, 188–95, 200; federation and independence in, 5, 38, 41, 50, 193–94; marriage in,

152–53; mental health and, 37–44, 127; migrants from, 5, 19, 25, 30–33, 37–44, 48, 52, 96, 177, 188, 214; nationalists from, 26; repatriation to, 13, 37–43; students from, 53, 96, 117, 123–24, 167; VSO in, 74. *See also* Caribbean, Jamaica, *and other individual countries by name*
West Midlands Anti-Deportation Campaign, 307n153
Westminster, 6, 12, 24, 113
West Salford, 221
Wheeler, Ada, 171, 172, 291n25
Whitehall, 6, 12
Whiting, Douglas, 86
Whyte, William, 29; *Street Corner Society*, 29
Wilde, James Plaisted. *See* Penzance, first baron of
Williams, Bodi, 173
Williams, Ruth (Mrs. Seretse Khama), 275n43
Wilson, Harold, 8
Wolverhampton, 23, 43
Worcester, 216
World Assembly of Youth (WAY), 80–82, 94; British National Committee (BNC) of, 81–82
World Health Organization, 108
World War Two. *See* Second World War
Wrangham, Geoffrey, 149

Yoruba, 28, 66, 89, 185
Young, James, 77
Young, Michael, 88, 273n7

Zambia, 76
Zoro, Mallam Abba, 105
Zubrzycki, Jerzy, 36, 47
Zwieg, Ferdynand, 280n122